OKANAGAN COLLEGE LIBRARY

03931375

K

D1617547

BRANDING CANADA

OKANAGAN COLLEGE
LIBRARY
BRITISH COLUMBIA

Branding Canada

Projecting Canada's Soft Power through Public Diplomacy

EVAN H. POTTER

McGill-Queen's University Press
Montreal & Kingston • London • Ithaca

© McGill-Queen's University Press 2009

ISBN 978-0-7735-3435-3 (cloth)
ISBN 978-0-7735-3452-0 (paper)

Legal deposit first quarter 2009
Bibliothèque nationale du Québec

Printed in Canada on acid-free paper that is 100% ancient forest free
(100% post-consumer recycled), processed chlorine free

McGill-Queen's University Press acknowledges the support of the Canada
Council for the Arts for our publishing program. We also acknowledge
the financial support of the Government of Canada through the Book
Publishing Industry Development Program (BPIDP) for our publishing
activities.

Library and Archives Canada Cataloguing in Publication

Potter, Evan H. (Evan Harold), 1964–
    Branding Canada : projecting Canada's soft power through public
diplomacy / Evan H. Potter.

Includes bibliographical references and index.
ISBN 978-0-7735-3435-3 (bnd)
ISBN 978-0-7735-3452-0 (pbk)

    1. Canada – Foreign relations – 1945-. 2. Diplomacy. 3. Canada –
Relations – Foreign countries. 4. Public relations and politics – Canada –
History. I. Title.

FC242.P678 2008   327.71009'045   C2008-905527-6

This book was typeset by Jay Tee Graphics Ltd. in 10/13 New Baskerville

To the memory of my parents,
Harold H. Potter and Theresia Hebein

Contents

TABLES

FIGURES

Preface

This book is about how Canada projects itself to the world through its "soft power," a term coined by the American scholar Joseph S. Nye, Jr., to refer to the ability of a country to persuade and attract followers through the attractiveness of its culture, political ideals, and policies.[1] Nye pronounced that Canada, as a middle power, was well positioned to project such soft power and thus to increase its global influence.[2] In the Canadian context, the idea of soft power is most firmly associated with Lloyd Axworthy's tenure as foreign minister (1996–2000), when it became the guiding concept for the Liberal government's human security agenda and led to notable achievements such as the Ottawa Convention on the banning of anti-personnel land mines.[3]

Throughout history, the use (and abuse) of hard power – the ability to coerce through military and economic might – has been the primary organizing principle of the international system. However, beginning in the second half of the twentieth century, with growing levels of interdependence resulting from an expanded multilateral system and advances in communications technologies, not to mention the blurring of lines separating international and domestic policy, countries began to pay increasing attention to how their images and policies played out in the international public domain. There is now a global consensus that the array of interrelated international challenges – running the gamut from increasingly unequal levels of development to environmental degradation and the threat of global terrorism – cannot be resolved by military intervention or development assistance alone. For most countries, exercising soft power has become a necessary complement to hard power (or a substitute for hard power in the case of less affluent nations) to ensure economic prosperity and greater security.

The premise of this book is that Canada, a wealthy, advanced industrial nation with an educated and diverse population, should have considerable soft-power capacity to help it increase its prosperity and address critical global issues that require public support and understanding. The ambitions of this study are necessarily limited. It does not seek to examine all the actors (government, business, or civil society) and institutions that help to define or brand Canada to the world. Rather, it represents the first comprehensive examination of how the federal government projects Canada's national brand to the world by exercising Canada's soft power through the instruments of public diplomacy – international cultural relations, international education, international broadcasting, and international business promotion and tourism. Because Foreign Affairs and International Trade Canada (DFAIT) has been the department with primary responsibilty for cohering Canada's international interests and, thus, for managing its international image, this book will be devoted in large part to how Canada's foreign ministry engages in public diplomacy.

How a nation is seen and heard – how it is perceived and understood –, matters a great deal as we begin a new century in which we can expect to see an ever-increasing number of state and non-state actors (citizens' movements, multinational corporations, even terrorist organizations) exercising their soft power capabilities to achieve their objectives. In this highly competitive environment, the federal government in Ottawa will be challenged to present a coherent, accurate, and compelling image of Canada to the world. If a country fails to tell its own story, its image will be shaped exclusively by the perceptions of others. Understanding how Canadian public diplomacy works and the challenges of portraying Canada abroad will go a long way toward explaining the effectiveness of Canada's international policy in the years ahead. In the future, a measure of a nation's international weight will be its ability to combine its soft and hard power resources to project what Nye calls "smart power."

This book began in October 1998, when I joined the Communications Bureau of DFAIT and was given the responsibility of reporting on Canadian public opinion on international issues, as well as on foreign attitudes towards Canada. Readers will recall that 1998 belonged to a period of significant global citizen activism. The resistance to the proposed Multilateral Agreement on Investment, an ultimately unsuccessful attempt by members of the Organization for Economic Cooperation and Development to negotiate a new system of governance for investment between states, and the success of the Ottawa Convention on anti-personnel land mines ushered in a period of optimism regarding the power of citizens' movements to influence governments. The anti-globalization protests in Seattle in 1999 demonstrated that ordinary citizens, using both traditional and new information technologies, were developing new competencies and confidence for global engagement. A sense was emerging among politicians that few foreign policy objectives could now be achieved without an enabling environment sustained by innovative public diplomacy initiatives to inform and persuade people, as well as their governments.

In light of these developments, the focus of my own academic research shifted from an analysis of broad directions in Canadian foreign policy to the more neglected area of the role of strategic communications in Canada's international relations. My interest had also been inspired by the launch of a Canadian International Information Strategy in 1997. Although stillborn and overtaken by the effort to create the Ottawa Convention on land mines, it nevertheless represented a recognition by the federal government that Canada needed to have a much higher level of information presence abroad. In 2000, I began to teach in the Department of Communications at the University of Ottawa, where courses on communication planning, political communications, and international communications allowed me to marry my professional experience in the field of communications from a foreign ministry's perspective with my research interest in political marketing. It forced me to consider how public diplomacy could be thought of, in its simplest form, as international public relations practised by government. It became clear to me that the only difference between public relations as practised by a private company and a governmental entity is (usually) scale, since each actor has the same basic choice of communication objectives: to create awareness, to reinforce or change attitudes, or to reinforce or change behaviour. The techniques and tools to achieve these objectives are usually the same. Indeed, the term "nation branding" was in vogue during this period to describe how some countries used techniques normally associated with consumer marketing to adjust their images, with varying levels of success.

In 2001, I became a special communications advisor in the Policy Planning Secretariat at DFAIT. Over the next four years, I examined the role of information technology and diplomacy in greater detail, including editing *Cyber-Diplomacy: Managing Foreign Policy in the Twenty-First Century* (2002). It was during this period that I participated in a significant rethinking of the role of public diplomacy in Canada's foreign policy, starting with work on an internal foreign policy review at DFAIT, the *Foreign Policy Update*, between 2001 and 2002, and then a national consultation, *A Dialogue on Foreign Policy*, in 2003.[4] The latter highlighted that Canadians wanted their country to have a strengthened voice on the world stage. These exercises would inform *Canada's International Policy Statement* (IPS), published by the federal government in 2005.

While I freely admit that the internal bureaucratic politics of producing foreign policy reviews is usually of interest only to diehard analysts and retired members of DFAIT, what was significant was the IPS's call for the transformation of Canada's diplomacy, including a "whole-of-Canada" and a "whole-of-government" approach to projecting Canada's voice abroad. After the terrorist attacks on the United States on 11 September 2001, soft power was no longer dismissed as a concept born of a naïve and unrealistic understanding of international relations. The public diplomacy instruments to transmit soft power were now seen – particularly by the American administration of George W. Bush – as deserving of a substantial reinvestment of resources, since it was recognized that a global war on terror could not be won without a parallel, permanent international information strategy to win "hearts and minds" across the Islamic world.

What became evident to me in the course of my professional experience inside DFAIT and through my exchanges with scholars and practitioners at workshops and conferences is that the long-term success of Canada's international communications strategy correlates with the level of investment by Canada in its cultural industries to preserve a distinct national identity (e.g., through the Canadian Broadcasting Corporation (CBC), the Canada Council for the Arts (CCA), the National Film Board (NFB), and the other major federal cultural agencies) and in its innovative science and technology (e.g., through the work of granting councils and the Canadian Institute for Advanced Research). Additionally, the success of this strategy correlates with the level of investment in domestic outreach and consultation programs on foreign policy, as well as international scholarships and youth exchanges, investment made in the hope that a body of Canadian citizens will be created who will have both international experience and a fuller understanding of Canada's global role. While Canadians' perceptions of Canada's primary international role – usually cited in surveys as that of a peacekeeper – have been a source of social cohesion, I am in no way suggesting that the pride Canadians have in their country has been manufactured solely through government programs. Rather, our level of national pride, ranked third in the world after the United States and Austria, is an organic outgrowth of the type of society we have created north of the forty-ninth parallel. To be sure, government has played an instrumental role in creating this society, for example, by helping to explain Canadians to themselves and to explain the world to Canada. What writing this book has shown me is that a nation's public diplomacy is Janus-faced – facing inwards and outwards at the same time. The sense of national identity or the level of pride shown by citizens in their country influences the level of success that a country will have in projecting its national identity abroad.

However, while a national level of government cannot be held completely responsible for the success or failure of a national brand, national governments can be catalytic in harnessing the energy of a society – civil society (including citizens abroad), educational institutions, corporations, other levels of government – in support of the national brand. This should seem obvious but has often been overlooked by generations of Canadian policy-makers, who have tended to view public diplomacy largely in instrumental terms (e.g., trying to develop better evaluation methods for grants programs), while sometimes forgetting that we also need to nurture and invest in the "things" that we are projecting as part of our national identity, whether in the arts to convey that we are an avant-garde nation, in science to demonstrate that we are a high-tech nation, or through innovative policies to show that solutions have been found to vexing public policy problems. Explaining Canada to others forces us to explain Canada to ourselves. It helps us understand who we are as a nation. I thus discovered in the course of writing this book that public diplomacy is not a foreign policy challenge – it is a national challenge.

It is important to state that without the cooperation of my colleagues at DFAIT, both current and former members of the department, this book would not have been possible. They were generous with their insights and recollections; many went further and provided access to documents and answered questions I had not thought of asking. I interviewed a number of government officials involved in the practice of Canada's public diplomacy, and the great majority spent anywhere between one and two hours answering my questions. Still others gamely answered my emails as they were uprooting themselves from their postings abroad. It was my view that attributing particular quotations to particular officials, while no doubt entertaining for some readers, would also have been inappropriate.

I cannot possibly thank everyone who assisted me in my research, but I do want to single out a few. Three colleagues have read this manuscript. Joan McCoy acted as a gracious sounding board. I am indebted to them. I would like to thank Michael Brock, Alan Bowker, and Robin Higham for their insights drawn from their professional experiences on the sharp end of practising public diplomacy. I owe a special debt of gratitude to Daryl Copeland and Paul Chapin, both of whose advice and counsel I value greatly. Although Janet Corden thought this project might have been a mirage, she provided the initial inspiration when I was a graduate student. Sean Rushton and Jason Bouzanis, my graduate students at the Department of Communication at the University of Ottawa, assisted me in the overall research and contributed their own chapters to this book. I would also like to thank Connie Munro, Michael Vladars, and Emilie Brown for diligently working on the manuscript day in and day out over the summer of 2006, and to thank Lynn-Marie Holland for her editorial help with the final manuscript. Louise Crosby was unfailingly cheerful and managed to put up with the aggravation of having the house turned upside down.

As always, I am grateful for the high-quality editorial and publishing expertise of Roger Martin, Joan McGilvray, Ron Curtis, and their colleagues at McGill-Queen's University Press. Support is gratefully acknowledged from Lori A. Burns, vice dean (research), and Lesley Strutt, research facilitator, at the Faculty of Arts at the University of Ottawa, and from the Social Sciences and Humanities Research Council of Canada. Two external peer reviewers offered valuable suggestions for improving the manuscript. Finally, the opinions expressed in this book are mine alone, and they do not necessarily represent the views or positions of DFAIT or of the Government of Canada.

Abbreviations

ACSUS	Association of Canadian Studies in the United States
AEI	Australian Education International
BBC	British Broadcasting Corporation
BSE	Bovine Spongiform Encephalopathy (mad cow disease)
CBC	Canadian Broadcasting Corporation
CCA	Canada Council for the Arts
CEC	Canadian Educational Centre
CIC	Coalition Information Centre
CIDA	Canadian International Development Agency
CNN	Cable News Network
CPR	Canadian Pacific Railway
CRTC	Canadian Radio-television and Telecommunications Commission
CSFP	Commonwealth Scholarship and Fellowship Plan
CTC	Canadian Tourism Commission
DART	Disaster Assistance Response Team
DFAIT	Foreign Affairs and International Trade Canada
DFID	Department for International Development (UK)
ERI	Enhanced Representation Initiative
EU	European Union
G8	Group of Eight
HRSDC	Human Resources and Social Development Canada
MFA	Ministry of Foreign Affairs
NACO	National Arts Centre Orchestra
NAFTA	North American Free Trade Agreement
NATO	North Atlantic Treaty Organization
NFB	National Film Board

NGO	Non-governmental organization
NORAD	North American Aerospace Defence Command
NRC	National Research Council Canada
NWI	Newsworld International
NSERC	Natural Sciences and Engineering Research Council of Canada
OECD	Organization for Economic Co-operation and Development
PERPA	Political, Economic Relations and Public Affairs
RCI	Radio Canada International
SARS	severe acute respiratory syndrome
SSHRC	Social Sciences and Humanities Research Council of Canada
TCS	Trade Commissioner Service
TIFF	Toronto International Film Festival
UK	United Kingdom
UN	United Nations
UNESCO	United Nations Educational, Scientific and Cultural Organization
US	United States of America
VOA	Voice of America
WIB	Wartime Information Board

BRANDING CANADA

1

Introduction: Canada's Warm but Fuzzy International Image

Over the last three decades, the globalization and the communications revolution have created the most striking transformation of society since the Industrial Revolution. This *informational* revolution, to borrow from Manuel Castells, has meant that knowledge and learning (including intercultural communication) are the keys not only to technological progress and economic prosperity but also to social cohesion and global security.[1] Values and ideas are common currency, and the free movement of people – especially the young – is both necessary and inexorable.[2] These transformational trends have made every country more aware of its image, identity, and reputation. Whether a country needs to build international coalitions against terrorism, cooperate to protect the environment, or attract investment, foreign students, and skilled immigrants, influencing global public opinion is critical to national success, because in the absence of substantial military or economic weight, most countries in the world are the image and the ideas they project abroad. In a global system in which this soft power is growing in importance, the competitive advantage should go to countries that are able to present distinct national voices, or "information edges."[3] Countries cannot afford to be anonymous in today's world because, as John Ralston Saul has written, "not being a player in international communications today implies disappearing from the planet."[4] A country that fails to develop an information edge risks losing cultural and financial opportunities and, as Ralston Saul warns, using the dominant American "information empire" as an example, creates a foreign policy problem in that "[c]ountries dependent on American structures to present themselves will be visible only as much and in a way that that structure wishes."[5] In other words, disappearing from international communications is tantamount to relinquishing sovereignty and, therefore, national security.[6] For this reason, the process of one government informing, understanding and persuading citizens in other countries – public diplomacy – is now at least as important as the classic diplomacy of communication between governments.

Classic, or quiet, diplomacy is not being devalued; privileged government-to-government communications have always existed and always will. The revolution in diplomatic affairs,[7] of which the rise of public diplomacy is the most visible manifestation, is not merely a function of advances in communications technology (since advances have happened before, ranging from the telegraph to the Internet) but of the intensity of the global information flow associated with accelerating globalization and the blurring of domestic and international public policy spheres. This blurring of the policy spheres has led to a re-imagining of the craft of diplomacy in its classic and public dimensions. What has changed in the last thirty years is not that classic diplomacy has disappeared but that public forms of diplomacy have become increasingly recognized as vital for addressing the many pressing international challenges, such as the spread of infectious diseases or the need for sustainable development, that require public input and cooperation. It is in this knowledge sphere, or what John Arquilla and David Ronfeldt have termed this "noosphere," that public diplomacy finds its new privileged space.[8]

More than in any previous period of world politics, the international stage is now a mirror of a country's identity. What happens on this stage can have profound effects on domestic identity and vice versa.[9] When a country's citizens see themselves reflected in the mirror of others' perceptions, that reflection can either strengthen or weaken national identity and citizenship; it can reinforce or challenge prevailing values by providing new perspectives on them. This is especially true for Canada, a country that for most of the second half of the twentieth century defined its national identity according to its global role as a "peacekeeper," its inclusiveness as a society, and its sense of being distinct from its giant neighbour to the south. As the world lauded Canada for its non-threatening, "helpful fixer" role, Canadians – aided and abetted by two generations of federal politicians – began to imagine and then believe themselves to be the world's foremost peacekeepers.[10] The United Nations' (UN's) blue berets became synonymous with Canada's international role and thus its national identity.[11] By the late 1990s, Canada had significantly reduced its contributions to UN peacekeeping missions but had nevertheless sustained the peacekeeping myth, intertwined as it was with the inherent benefits of Canadian participation in anything multilateral (particularly within the UN). In the corridors of official Ottawa, the myth also served as a powerful means of reinforcing national unity, since pride in Canada's blue berets was one of the few components of Canadians' self-identity that cut across all linguistic and regional divides.[12] And from a domestic perspective, Canada's official policy of multiculturalism projected an image to the world of a tolerant nation that would welcome newcomers. This perception of Canadian openness served to strengthen Canadian citizenship and national unity at home by emphasizing (and some would say exaggerating) the difference between a Canadian society that celebrates diversity and an American one that celebrates a "melting pot."

The premise of this book is that in a twenty-first-century foreign policy environment characterized by the blurring of the domestic and the international, more non-state actors, and a ubiquitous, converging mass media, the management of Canada's international image has become a key determinant of national success both domestically and internationally. This book argues that Canada, described by some as the first postmodern nation, has a unique contribution to make in this new world of ideas and knowledge. It is not an exaggeration to say that in this informational world, Canada's greatest comparative advantage is not its rich endowment of natural resources but Canadian citizens themselves – who they are, what they have accomplished, and what they stand for.[13] As other countries adapt to the emergence of multicultural, multilingual societies with multiple levels of governance, Canada is in many respects a "model nation"[14] because of how it manages its diversity and what it can teach the world about living with ambiguity and constant evolutionary change.[15] Although it is by no means a perfect model, with its history of inclusion, pragmatism, and the rule of law, Canada has defined itself as a workable federation.

However, just being a model nation is not enough. The world must *see* Canada as a model nation, and this will occur only if Canada has a distinctive brand. As senior Canadian official Alan Bowker has written, such a brand should not be an advertising creation "but one that reflects and symbolizes the complex country that we are ... There is nothing we could dig from the ground, draw from the oceans, harvest from our fields and forests, or make with our hands and our machines, that will in the coming generation equal the value of what we will create with our minds."[16] Many countries are richly endowed with natural resources. However, the leading nations of this century will be those that harness their citizens' knowledge and ideas to provide innovative solutions to the world's challenges. It is, therefore, essential that an accurate image of Canada be projected to the world, one that reflects Canada as a modern, sophisticated, creative, diverse, tolerant, caring, and technologically advanced society based on a largely peaceful compact among its three founding peoples – the Aboriginal population and the French and English settlers. This image is essential for Canada (as the most trade-dependent of all Group of Eight (G8) countries) to export its products and services; to attract portfolio and direct investment, to attract talent in the form of students and skilled workers in order to maintain its economic growth, and to gain international respect that will, in turn, allow Canada to play an important role in maintaining international peace and security. After all, Canadians can build a caring, just society only in a world that nurtures such values.

The overarching argument in this book is that refining and managing Canada's international brand should be central to the agenda of the Canadian government in the twenty-first century. This brand is much more than the sum total of Canada's cultural expression, however. As Simon Anholt, the creator of the Anholt Nation Brand Index, has shown, culture is but one component of the total brand that includes a nation's attractiveness as a tourist destination, its economic power, its openness to immigration, and how it governs itself.[17] Branding a nation means projecting a unique national identity and, as Ralston Saul has argued, this identity goes "far beyond the world of dance and music."[18] Canada's identity, therefore, includes how Canadians understand federalism, the way civil liberties are dealt with by law enforcement and intelligence agencies, how Aboriginal governments manage their affairs, and the Canadian military's rules of engagement in peace enforcement operations. The classical forms of culture – literature, film, music, theatre, dance, and the visual arts – represent but one track for projecting a country's identity, albeit an important one, since artistic expression can reach the broadest global audience. Public diplomacy is the management of this national brand, or identity, by government, and the challenge for the Canadian government is how to present Canada fully by projecting, to use Ralston Saul's phrasing, "how we imagine ourselves, how we think of our country, our civilization; and so how we wish others to imagine us."[19]

Projecting national identity implies inviting a world that is increasingly receptive to Canada to see it multi-dimensionally: as a country whose natural endowments and technological achievements have allowed it to provide its citizens with an enviable standard of living; as a country whose history and public policy have created a society that values diversity; as a country that has used its intellectual leadership to address global problems (e.g., through the Ottawa Convention on anti-personnel landmines); and as a country that is trying to bridge growing regional cleavages and stem shamefully high levels of child poverty and that must redress the regrettable treatment of its Aboriginal peoples. In terms of public diplomacy, as this study will show, it means providing accurate, in-depth information about Canada abroad; understanding the implications of technological convergence for telling the Canadian story; marketing Canadian culture and education; promoting research so that Canada is a player in the global marketplace of ideas; and encouraging Canadians to open up to the world and the world to encounter Canada through the exchange of people (especially through youth and student mobility), information, knowledge, and ideas.[20] Projecting a compelling international image starts at home with Canadians "discovering their own voices and being prepared to listen and to understand the voices of others, and thus seeing themselves as citizens of the world."[21]

How, then, does this projection of national identity support Canada's broader foreign policy objectives? As Ralston Saul writes, "[t]o the extent that foreign policy is dependent on foreign public recognition – an identifiable image and a sense at all levels of what we stand for, what kind of society we are, what we sell – that policy is dependent on our projection of our culture. What is more, we are more dependent on that cultural projection than the handful of larger countries who are our allies and our competitors and who have other ways of projecting their image."[22] While it is being argued that culture is but one element of a national brand, for Canada, it is clear that expressions of national identity through the arts, transmitted by the mass media, are still essential for capturing global mind space, that is, the attention and awareness of a global public.[23]

As Canada seeks to define a new role for itself in a post post–Cold War world characterized by a partially paralyzed multilateral system that has spawned new forms of alliances to deal with new types of threats (globalized terrorism, failing states), a southern neighbour for whom security now trumps trade, and emerging (Brazil, India, China) and re-emerging (Russia) powers, it is an opportune time to examine how Canada has exercised its soft power through the conduct of its public diplomacy campaigns to support its national interests. The purpose of this book is to provide a historical backdrop to the conduct of Canada's public diplomacy and examine the challenges that Canada has faced in promoting itself. It will describe the key instruments of public diplomacy and their records of achievement, show how public diplomacy is organized as a process within the Canadian government, particularly within Foreign Affairs and International Trade Canada, demonstrate the application of public diplomacy through three case studies, and finally, distill the lessons that have been learned in order to present some modest suggestions for improving Canada's future public diplomacy.

This book will argue that Canada has the very national qualities that fuel
soft power: support for mediation and multilateralism, a recognized intellectual leadership in addressing global problems, and expertise in the use
of communications technologies. But as the record of US public diplomacy
since 2001 (and particularly after the invasion of Iraq in 2003) shows, an
abundance of soft-power assets (including Hollywood) does not automatically translate into successful diplomacy. It is also sobering to acknowledge
that, although Canadian policy-makers have long recognized the importance of projecting Canada's national identity abroad as a key instrument
for strengthening its international policy and using these efforts to reinforce national unity at home, relative to other forms of public investment
in Canada's international instruments (e.g., international assistance),
there has been only modest – some would say very limited – investment of
resources and strategic thinking since the end of the Second World War on
how best to project Canada's identity to the world. As the Royal Commission
on National Development in the Arts, Letters and Sciences, also referred to
as the Massey Commission, wrote in 1951:

> Ignorance of Canada in other countries is very widespread. People in
> many countries are aware of our material resources, it is true; but our
> rapid growth as a world state, and our assumption of world responsibili-
> ties, have naturally outstripped the knowledge among other nations of
> Canadian institutions, habits, people, geography ... It is not unnatural
> that Canada has been frequently called "the unknown country" ... It is
> obvious that the Canadian voice is listened to most attentively when the
> hearer has some familiarity with the Canadian scene and with Canadian
> achievements. The promotion abroad of a knowledge of Canada is not
> a luxury but an obligation, and a more generous policy in this field
> would have important results, both concrete and intangible.[24]

With slight alteration, these words could be an apt reflection of reality
today. The two decades that followed this call for the promotion abroad of
Canada witnessed a concerted effort to develop homegrown cultural industries through regulatory intervention (e.g., Canadian content rules for television and radio) and the creation of new cultural institutions such as the
Canada Council for the Arts and the Canadian Film Development Corporation (now Telefilm Canada). Paradoxically, this substantial investment
in developing a Canadian identity at home did not translate into a commensurate level of investment in international promotional tools such as
Radio Canada International (RCI) and the information and cultural affairs

divisions of the Department of External Affairs. By 1995, lip service was being paid to the projection of Canadian values, and the government's white paper *Canada in the World* had concluded that "in the medium- and long-term, a country that does not project a clearly defined image of who it is and what it represents, is doomed to anonymity on the international scene."[25] However, the fiscal reality of the time ensured that no new investment would be possible. A decade later, *Canada's International Policy Statement* would again reaffirm the importance of projecting Canada's identity, but now it was referred to as public diplomacy, and it assumed a mobilization of Canadian society as a whole to increase Canada's international influence:

> Modern diplomacy is increasingly public diplomacy. Public diplomacy is about projecting a coherent and influential voice to all those who have influence within a society – not just within its government. Canada's credibility and influence abroad will be built not only by Government action but by Canadians themselves – artists, teachers, students, travelers, researchers, experts and young people – interacting with people abroad. Public diplomacy includes cultural events, conferences, trade shows, youth travel, foreign students in Canada, Canadian studies abroad and visits of opinion leaders. All this cultivates long-term relationships, dialogue and understanding abroad, underpins our advocacy and increases our influence. Public diplomacy is also crucial to achieving our foreign policy goals. By persuading others as to the value of our proposals and strategies, or by engaging in cross-cultural dialogue, we can take important steps in furthering shared objectives of importance to Canadians.[26]

As this book will show, over the past half century, initiatives to project Canada abroad have fallen victim to the particular Canadian disease of doing the right thing but underfunding it. As Canada sits on the cusp of a transformation of the international system in an informational world, the rationale for projecting the national brand identity is stronger than ever before and critical for Canada's future social cohesion and prosperity. Robert Greenhill, in his seminal 2005 study of international perceptions of Canada's international role, sums up Canada's predicament most succinctly:

> Canada's performance since 1989 is nothing for a country of our wealth and history of international engagement to be proud of. Our

performance appears to have been well below our exaggerated rhetoric, well below our historical performance, and well below global expectations ... [T]here was absolutely nothing necessary or inevitable about the decline in Canada's international impact over the past [fifteen] years. True, the international scene has become more crowded. Yet Canada's relative economic position has strengthened over the past [fifteen] years ... [I]n the meantime ... smaller countries – Australia, Norway – have carved out distinct value-added roles. We have a size and a position that should allow us to do much more. As one Australian said: "we belong to practically nothing, you belong to practically everything" ... The world believes that we can make a difference, and the world needs us to make a difference. "The world needs more Canada" is a nice slogan. Our interviews suggest that what the world really needs is more from Canada. More commitment, more focus, more impact.[27]

The world does indeed need more Canada, but as the Massey Commission surmised more than half a century ago, the world still knows very little about Canada, and despite Canada's extensive international commitments, Canada is neither seen nor heard to the degree that it should be.

The remainder of this chapter will provide the reader with some context for understanding Canada's challenges in managing its international image. Although this book provides a history of Canada's public diplomacy, for the purposes of this introduction, the reader will be provided with a synopsis of the challenges and opportunities for Canadian public diplomacy. The period 1993–2005, covering the Liberal governments of Jean Chrétien and Paul Martin, has been selected to illustrate the unique constraints and opportunities for managing Canada's global image, because this period puts in stark relief the changing international landscape facing Canadian policy-makers, including the post–Cold War promise of a global wave of democratization (the so-called "end of history" thesis),[28] accelerating globalization, and domestic fiscal and political uncertainty (e.g., Quebec's 1995 referendum).

CANADA'S IMAGE PROBLEM

Following the end of the Cold War until at least 2003, the Canadian media, conflating Canada's international image and role, mainly lamented the decline of Canada's international stature.[29] Typical of the "Canadian image in decline" school was a May 2001 article in which journalist Miro Cernetig decried Canada's unsophisticated image and claimed that "Brand

Figure 1.1   The global community responds to Canadian influence.

Source: Dale Cummings, "Global Community Flicks Finger at Canadian Influence," *Winnipeg Free Press*, 4 February 2005

Canada" was in crisis.[30] In 2003, the publication of Andrew Cohen's book *While Canada Slept,* chronicling the decline of Canada's international leadership, received extensive media coverage and contributed to fervid national introspection on what it meant for Canada to no longer be singled out for its diplomatic acumen and ability to furnish peacekeepers.[31] Soon after, *Time* magazine (Canadian edition) weighed in with a provocatively titled cover story, "Would Anyone Notice If Canada Disappeared?"[32]

Then a few months later, in September 2003, the influential British weekly newsmagazine the *Economist,* pointing to Canada's tolerant society and pioneering stances on same-sex marriage and the decriminalization of marijuana, declared the country the epitome of cool by putting a moose with sunglasses on its cover.[33] Such is the influence of this newsmagazine within both media and policy circles in Canada that its largely positive article was reported on effusively by the domestic media. Not surprisingly, references to the *Economist*'s assessment of Canada soon appeared in government speeches. After a decade of negative media coverage of Canada's international image and scholarly work questioning Canada's international commitment,[34] the *Economist*'s report seemed heaven-sent for the Liberal government's domestic public-communications strategy, since it was a validation of the government's policy direction by a highly credible foreign source and it served – presumably – to reinforce pride among Canadian opinion leaders (e.g., the Canadian readership of the *Economist* and elite Canadian newspapers such as the *Globe and Mail* and the *National Post*). It became a textbook example of how the international media can play an important part in allowing Canadians to see themselves through the mirror of foreign eyes.[35]

However, this positive portrait of Canada's image appears to have been the exception rather than the rule. Most of the discussion and coverage of Canada's international image within Canada's media and academic communities was highly unflattering to Ottawa (see figure 1.1). In many parts of the world, it was noted, Canada was viewed as little more than a minor North American adjunct to the United States. The Canadian contribution to global security was often ignored by the international community, even by its close allies such as the United States, the United Kingdom, and other G8 partners. Awareness of Canada was very weak in the United States, where focus group findings indicated that participants could not identify Ottawa as Canada's capital, nor did they know that Canada was a member of the G8 or a partner with the United States in the North American Aerospace Defense Command.[36] For years, the Chicago Council on Foreign Relations' regular surveys had shown that Canada had the distinction of being perceived by the American public as their closest friend (with the United Kingdom a very close second).[37] However, according to a March 2004 survey, a majority of Americans (62 percent) believed that the United Kingdom was their best friend.[38] While these survey findings in a post–Iraq war environment should not be overstated, the symbolism was nevertheless stark and was noted in both Ottawa and Washington. The self-flagellation over Canada's international image continued.

How real is this image problem? Is it overblown? There are, of course, the oft-recounted successes of the Ottawa Convention on anti-personnel land mines and Canada's victory over Spain during the "fish war" in 1995, when Canada seized the *Estai*, a Spanish trawler,[39] not to mention the much ballyhooed Team Canada Trade Missions inaugurated during Prime Minister Jean Chrétien's tenure, although these success stories began to appear dated by the turn of the century. Country-specific initiatives that are profiled in this book, such as the Canadian Consulate General's innovative campaign in New York City (the Upper North Side campaign) starting in 1998 and the Think Canada Festival campaign in Japan in 2001, are also held up as public diplomacy success stories. To be sure, these high-profile campaigns succeeded in giving Canada an increased presence in

Figure 1.2 Jean Chrétien flexes Canada's soft power at the UN.
Source: Michael de Adder, *Halifax Daily News*, 27 February 2003

Manhattan and Japan, two of the toughest markets in the world in which to get attention. However, they also raised questions about whether it was feasible to sustain such high-visibility and expensive efforts over time, given the tendency for Canada's regional and country priorities to change every few years.

Although traditional cultural and international education programs (including some new media) were used only selectively in the 1990s as a "force multiplier" for Canadian foreign policy, as the examples cited above show, public diplomacy was becoming more and more central to the success of Canadian diplomacy overall. In specific cases, Canada's strategic use of its public diplomacy assets has enabled it to act as a knowledge broker, to influence others, and to ensure that its political and economic objectives are taken more seriously. However, it should be acknowledged that not everyone views this as a halcyon period for Canadian public diplomacy. Lloyd Axworthy, Canada's then foreign minister, pushed a soft-power agenda, which irritated Washington and raised questions about whether Canada was not really using a feel-good agenda to do foreign policy on the cheap (see figure 1.2), a form of "pinchpenny diplomacy."[40] And for every success in the order of the land mines convention, there has been a seal hunt or clear-cut logging public relations black eye.

More fundamentally, however, by the end of the 1990s it was apparent that there was a large gap between how Canadians viewed themselves and how broad swathes of foreign audiences perceived them. In the eyes of the world, Canada remained largely what it was a century ago, namely, a resource economy. And according to a study of Canada's international brand undertaken in 2000, contemporary elements – dynamism, innovation, technology, tolerance, competitiveness, and multiculturalism – were conspicuously absent.[41] Although Canada had a high "likeability" factor around the world and positive values were attributed to the Canadian brand ("best place to live," "tolerant," "welcoming"), it had little presence, and few foreign audiences had any up-to-date knowledge about the country.[42] A federal government review of all public opinion research on how Canada was perceived abroad concluded that Canada suffered from a chronic lack of profile, was regarded as a past player in world affairs, had solid though unspectacular products, had boring tourist attractions, and was not a top-of-mind destination for foreign investment. The *Globe and Mail*'s Geoffrey York, writing in 2005 about Canada's image in China (a key investment and commercial partner), reported on a poll that found Canada was

> [O]ne of the three favourite foreign destinations for the Chinese people, along with the United States and Australia. But that's only half the story. Many Chinese believe that Canada is also a little too sleepy and dull – a good place to live in retirement, but not a vibrant place to build wealth ... despite the warm feelings generated by the Bethune saga, the vast majority of Chinese know very little about Canada ... Certainly, Canada has a high level of brand recognition in China ... However, despite the high likability factor and the fact that most Chinese agree that Canada is friendlier than the US, this has not translated into high levels of Chinese investment in Canada.[43]

There was a sense that Canada was being routinely passed over when foreign governments and businesses were contemplating direct investments or partnerships. The evidence was clear: Canada's share of inward foreign direct investment within North America alone dropped precipitously, from

21.3 percent in 1990 to 12.8 percent in 2002.[44] An international poll conducted in 1997 by the Angus Reid research organization found that less than 1 percent of Germans and Japanese associated Canada with telecommunications or other technologically based products, while more than 50 percent associated Canada with lumber, pulp and paper, and food.[45] In the words of Daryl Copeland, a foreign service officer with a keen eye for the vicissitudes of Canada's influence, "there was a sense that Canada was coasting on an international reputation – liberal internationalism, honest brokerage, environmental activism, generous aid giving – that was increasingly difficult to sustain and that the growing gaps between reputation, rhetoric and reality would become an unbridgeable chasm."[46] In short, Canada had an image problem, with "image" being defined as one part presence and one part promotion.[47] However, a world characterized by "connectivity" thus presented multiple avenues through which to gradually provide foreign audiences with a more balanced and accurate view of Canada through both increased presence and promotion.

SOURCES OF THE IMAGE PROBLEM

As discussed, this image problem was directly related to Canada's lack of investment in promoting itself. One factor contributing to Canada's image problem has been its lack of an official presence in global broadcasting. Although Canada is the second-largest exporter of English-language television in the world after the United States and a leading producer of computer software and although it has among the highest per capita producers and users of information on the Internet (especially in the French language), such activity remains largely invisible to the rest of the world.[48] This is because Canadian television programming is often absorbed into local broadcasters or, increasingly, into the program schedules of US-based specialty channels. With the partial exception of TV5, the Paris-based international French-language network that is partially funded by Canada, most Canadian programs are, in fact, deliberately not branded as Canadian.

Canada remains largely invisible with regard to government-financed international broadcasting. Canada's main G8 competitors far outspend it on public diplomacy, as shown in table 1.1, and Canada's disproportionately small investment in public diplomacy is most evident in international broadcasting. The very modest Can$21 million (2004–5) annual federal appropriation for RCI and Canada's contribution to TV5 are together a small fraction of the amount spent by the first tier of international broadcasters (mostly Canada's G8 counterparts). As table 1.1 shows, the Ameri-

Table 1.1
International Expenditure on Public Diplomacy, 2004–5 (Can$million)

	Total	Audiovisual and broadcasting	Cultural programs	Academic; scholarships and research	Educational Institutions	Official development assistance	Other
United States	1,652	707	367	483			362
United Kingdom	1,308	477	394				
Germany	848	424		201			
France	2,876	503	503	525	791	503	
Canada	108.8	21 (Radio Canada International; TV5)	4.7	12.7 (DFAIT); 6 (CIDA)		18 (Canada Fund for Local Initiatives)	12 (International exhibitions); 10 (Trade routes); 3 (US advocacy programs); 4.6 (Young Professionals International); 5.8 (Post Initiative Funds); 8 (Public Diplomacy Program); 3 (Team Canada Inc.'s Brand Canada Program)

Sources: Budgets for the United States, the United Kingdom, France, and Germany are drawn from Lord Carter of Coles review of the UK's public diplomacy: Lord Carter of Coles, *Public Diplomacy Review* (December 2005), 72–3.

Note: The public diplomacy budgets cited in the review were denominated in American dollars for the US, British pounds for the UK, and Euros for France and Germany. In order to provide some comparative context, the author converted the budgets to Canadian dollars at the prevailing exchange rates in May 2006. All statistics converted to Canadian public diplomacy budgets are rounded to the nearest million dollars. Some countries provide total public diplomacy budgets along with the budgets of specific public diplomacy activities and programs. As the reader can see, for some countries the sum of the budgets for the individual public diplomacy activities do not necessarily add up to the total public diplomacy budgets that these countries made available to the Carter review team. It can, therefore, be assumed that some types of public diplomacy activities fall into the "Other" category. As well, France considers its official development assistance budget to be part of its public diplomacy. The Canadian budgets are drawn from internal and public government sources.

can, British, French, and German governments spend up to twenty or thirty times more on their international broadcasting operations than the government of Canada does. The United Kingdom's BBC World Service, which is converting rapidly into a multimedia broadcaster, has a budget of close to Can$500 million (the BBC World television network is self-financing); Germany's Deutsche Welle has had a budget of some Can$400 million. The Canadian federal government's investment is also small when compared to smaller players such as Radio Netherlands or Vatican Radio.[49]

Canada's investment in promoting its identity abroad is modest in other forms of public diplomacy. The United States, for instance, funds five thousand VIP Visitor Exchanges; Canada, through its Foreign Visitors Program, invites fewer than one hundred foreign opinion leaders to Canada each year. Australia, often compared to Canada as a middle power, has been punching well above its weight, particularly after the success of the 2000 Sydney Olympics, to brand itself globally as a business and tourism destination of choice. It has made strategic use of its institutions of higher learning, marketing them intensely to attract future leaders with a view to increasing its influence in Southeast Asia. As a result, Canada's influence in the international arena is diminishing, especially as it relates to emerging markets in India and China. Clearly, Canada is not in danger of overspending on the export of its image, particularly when compared to its closest friends and allies.

A second factor contributing to Canada's image problem may be less a problem than a reality that now needs to be turned to Canada's advantage. Globalization has driven other levels of government (provincial, regional, and municipal), as well as other federal departments and agencies previously considered to have only a domestic mandate, to launch or further develop their international relationships. On the federal front, with instant electronic access to counterparts abroad and combined funding for foreign operations that equals more than 50 percent of DFAIT's budget of approximately Can$1.8 billion,[50] other federal government departments must now be managed as major components of Canada's overall capacity for projecting international influence.

Among the most active departments are the following: Canadian Heritage, which manages Canada's participation in international expositions (also known as world fairs) and its international cultural-diversity efforts, and which supports Canada's limited international broadcasting capacity through its ministerial oversight of CBC/Radio-Canada, which in turn provides the budget for RCI; Agriculture and Agri-Food Canada, which has an international promotional budget for trade fairs that dwarfs the funding available to DFAIT to promote Canada abroad; Indian and Northern Affairs Canada, which is active internationally on Aboriginal issues (in activities that would not necessarily fit into traditional conceptions of public diplomacy programming); and Industry Canada, which promotes innovation and investment into Canada and is also responsible for the Canadian Tourism Commission (a federal Crown corporation), the National Research Council Canada (NRC), and Canada's academic granting councils. In response to the need to equip young people for a globalized world, there are programs to facilitate the work and travel of young Canadians overseas, which are coordinated primarily by the Canadian International Development Agency (e.g., through International Youth Internships) and DFAIT (e.g., through working holiday programs).

DFAIT does not play a major role in the areas of science and research cooperation (the domain of the NRC and the Natural Sciences and Engineering Research Council of Canada (NSERC)) and international academic mobility (the domain of Human Resources and Social Development Canada (HRSDC)). DFAIT shares the funding of education marketing with Industry Canada and HRSDC, and the Canadian Education Centre network is partially funded by DFAIT and CIDA. DFAIT also shares postgraduate scholarships with CIDA, the NRC, the Social Sciences and Humanities Research Council of Canada (SSHRC), and NSERC. In fact, the only areas in which DFAIT has sole authority are the international network of Canadian Studies programs and the management of the government's Internet portal, CanadaInternational.gc.ca.

As mentioned in the preface, the major arts organizations such as the Canada Council for the Arts and the National Film Board of Canada are active internationally. In addition to marketing culture and lifestyle, the Canadian Tourism Commission promotes Canada's natural geographic endowments as a destination for outdoor vacations, a promotion that may make it more difficult to project an image of Canada as a sophisticated high-tech nation.

As the above discussion illustrates, a major challenge has been that most of Canada's public diplomacy resources available at the federal level of government – the largest concentration of dedicated resources – have been scattered across several departments and agencies (see table 1.2). According to a DFAIT official, Canada's public diplomacy programs have in the past often operated "in isolation and competition, driven by divergent agendas, riding on domestic programs with very different mandates to which they are often marginal, vulnerable to changing priorities, and lacking resources."[51] It is reported that program delivery at missions

Table 1.2
Canadian Public Diplomacy: A Shared Responsibility at the Federal Level (2005)

Public diplomacy activity	CIDA	DFAIT	HRSDC	Canadian Heritage	Canada Council for the Arts (Canadian Heritage)	Industry Canada	Canadian Tourism Commission (Industry Canada)	Industry Canada, Granting Councils (SSHRC, NSERC, CIHR)	Industry Canada, NRC
Arts promotion		*			*				
Cultural export	*	*		*					
International academic research and postgraduate scholarships		*						*	*
International academic mobility			*						
Canadian Studies abroad		*				*			
Education marketing		*	*	*					
Working Holiday Program		*							
Young Professionals International		*							
International Youth Internship Program	*								
International exhibitions				*					
International broadcasting (RCI, TV5)				*					
General promotion of Canada's image abroad		*							
Government On-Line		*	*			*			
Investment promotion		*				*			
Science and technology cooperation									*
Tourism promotion							*		

Source: Evan Potter

abroad is often equally fragmented. Resource cutbacks starting in the 1990s were particularly severe in cultural and public affairs programs, and a number of Canadian heads of mission (ambassadors and consuls general) expressed frustration at the lack of resources to enable embassies to play the central role required to deliver these essential programs.

A third factor contributing to Canada's image problem is its federal structure, which is, at the same time, often hailed outside Canada as a model of governance. Generally, the relations between the federal and provincial governments abroad are cooperative. Given the growing levels of interdependence, both levels of government must increasingly work together not only in trade negotiations but also in international negotiations on health and the environment. The Team Canada trade missions around the world during the years when Jean Chrétien was prime minister were a manifestation of this attempt to mine the synergies of federal and provincial activities abroad and to promote a single, unified image of Canada. Of course, provincial governments – primarily Quebec, Ontario, British Columbia, and Alberta – also have their own specific international agendas to promote trade and investment and cultural relations.

Historically, Quebec has been the most active province outside Canada. Quebec has a network of twenty-five offices and three business agents abroad located in North America, Central and South America, Europe, and Asia.[52] Quebec's international activities focus on its areas of jurisdiction, such as business development, education, research, health, and cultural relations, all of which are used to promote a distinct identity.[53] Uniquely, for a Canadian province, Quebec is responsible for selecting its own immigrants, which means that it has an added incentive to convey an attractive portrait of itself to specific regions of the world.

Starting in the early 1960s, Quebec's existing international presence developed rapidly as a result of the Quiet Revolution and, not surprisingly, the province's international ambitions would become intertwined with federal-provincial relations, at times resulting in friction between Ottawa and Quebec City.[54] Luc Bernier notes that three events launched Quebec's "foreign policy": the establishment of a provincial "délégation générale" in Paris in 1961; the signing of the first two ententes on education with the French government; and the articulation of a "doctrine" in 1965 by Paul Gérin-Lajoie, the provincial minister of education, to justify the province's international activities.[55]

The Gérin-Lajoie doctrine sought to extend Quebec's jurisdiction over its domestic affairs as enshrined in the British North America Act into international affairs. As Jeffrey Simpson has noted, invoking this doctrine has created tension on the Ottawa–Quebec City axis, whether a secessionist provincial government has been in power or not, because "Quebec governments tend to have expansionist interpretations of what those domestic jurisdictions are," making it possible for the doctrine to be expanded very widely.[56] Ottawa has had concerns that Quebec's independent projection onto the world stage of its jurisdictional responsibilities in, for example, culture, education, health, and economic development may at times weaken the federal government's ability to project a national interest by speaking with one voice.

In a 2005 open letter, Benoît Pelletier, the provincial Liberal intergovernmental affairs minister, succinctly summarized the long-standing provincial position: "Since the federal government cannot guarantee the implementation of the treaties it signs in matters of provincial jurisdiction, and since Canada sits as the accredited member on most international bodies responsible for drawing up these agreements, it seems obvious that Québec, and all the other provinces, should be more implicated in the process surrounding the negotiation of these agreements."[57]

While it is beyond the purview of this study to examine Quebec's international activities in depth (the province has a minister of international affairs), two events put into stark relief the sensitivities of having provinces pursue their provincial interests abroad. In November 2004, Liberal premier Jean Charest joined French prime minister Jean-Pierre Raffarin in a joint trade mission to Mexico, making Charest the first premier to go abroad on a trade mission with a foreign leader. Though the federal government did not publicly criticize the trip, there was an outpouring of criticism in the English Canadian media: many editorialists and columnists questioned the propriety of a province allying itself with a foreign power and thereby making Canada look "weak" internationally, not to mention the perception that Quebec was using its experience in the Mexican market to give France a competitive edge and was thereby undermining the trade and investment prospects for other Canadian provinces in Mexico.[58] Of course, this was not just any province; the undertone of the coverage was that France was somehow meddling in the internal affairs of Canada and that Quebec City was cozying up to Paris in an effort to generate more diplomatic space for itself outside Canada's borders. More than a few commentators went so far as to remind their readers and listeners of French president Charles de Gaulle's famous pronouncement "Vive le Québec libre!" during his 1967 official visit to Canada. Less than a year later, in 2005, the same provincial Liberal government, in the tradition of its secessionist predecessor, the Parti Québécois, called on Ottawa to allow it to have membership status inside Canadian delegations to international organizations and international negotiations so that it could speak freely at such bodies as UNESCO, the World Health Organization, and the International Labour Organization.

Since the 1960s, Quebec provincial governments, whether the Parti Québécois or the Quebec Liberal Party (Parti Libéral du Québec), have thus forcefully asserted the province's right to strengthen its relations with international organizations in areas pertaining to provincial responsibilities, which has often put the province at odds with Ottawa on how to present a unified national position to the world.[59] Furthermore, while the federal government has the exclusive responsibility for managing Canada's international security, the Quebec government stated in its 2006 policy statement on international relations that it has an interest in promoting greater security of the North American continent, especially since it is becoming more difficult to draw a distinction between internal and external security.[60] There has also always been the risk that Ottawa will leave the image-playing field in the United States to Quebec, which is determined and able to promote itself as a modern, attractive society by pushing a soft agenda related to fashion, design, and the arts. Quebec's Can$100 million annual expenditure in support of its international objectives,[61] which would, simply by virtue of the division of powers under the Canadian Constitution, be focused directly on highlighting the province's image through public diplomacy, demonstrates the ongoing challenge in presenting Quebec's distinct identity as part of the Canadian mosaic. There is no sign that Quebec intends to restrict its growing international role.

In short, while the Ottawa–Quebec City axis on international affairs is for the most part cooperative, the province's distinctive history and development within Confederation has, at times, created nettlesome diplomatic situations in Canada's multilateral and bilateral relations (particularly with regard to Canada-France relations) and highlights the difficulty and, at times, fragility of Canada's public diplomacy as a shared responsibility among the federal government and the provinces.

Through the Ontario Ministry of Economic Development and Trade, Ontario maintains a number of international marketing centres to promote trade and investment. These are located within Canadian consulates, embassies, and high commission offices in Los Angeles, New York, London, Munich, New Delhi, Shanghai, and Tokyo. British Columbia, using a sectoral (energy, life sciences, advanced manufacturing) rather than a country approach, has four representatives covering the European Union. The province also has a representative in San José, California, to cover the high technology sector and one representative each in Shanghai and Tokyo. The province's view is that since Canada already has members of the federal Trade Commissioners Service (part of DFAIT) assigned to the EU, China, and Japan, it does not seek to duplicate their business development work, which includes working to enlarge business opportunities in individual provinces through the federal government's network of International Trade Centres across Canada.[62] Alberta also has a number of offices to promote economic development, similarly located within Canadian consulates, embassies, and high commission offices, albeit with a greater presence in Asia. Alberta is visible in Mexico City, Washington, London, Munich, Taipei, Seoul, Tokyo, Hong Kong, and Beijing; the province also operates a separate Alberta Petroleum Centre in Beijing.

The "paradiplomacy" of Canada's provinces, led by Quebec, has become more complex to reflect the internationalization of domestic policy. It is worth noting that apart from Quebec with its highly developed cultural diplomacy, most provinces confine their international efforts to the economic domain. In general, some confusion can occur among foreign audiences if the provinces engage in high-visibility events abroad that project only a partial image of Canada's identity. That said, the existing international activities of other federal government departments and those of other levels of government, when pooled and coordinated, provide an extraordinary resource to increase Canada's international voice.

POSITIONING CANADA'S INTERNATIONAL IMAGE

Based on the discussion, how can Canada's image be conceptualized? J.B. Mannheim and R.B. Albritton classify national images in media in terms of two dimensions: visibility and valence. Visibility refers to the amount of media coverage that a country receives, and valence refers to whether this coverage is either favourable or unfavourable. The relationship between the two dimensions is reflected in an adaptation of Mannheim and Albritton's four-quadrant model of national image (see figure 1.3). The model is useful because the level of visibility (high or low) and the valence (positive or negative) of a nation in the global media will be an important factor in determining the degree of difficulty a country will face in using its public diplomacy instruments to project its soft power to achieve its international goals.

Mannheim and Albritton's model can be adapted to illustrate Canada's national image relative to that of its closest G8 allies, Australia, and four countries that have been identified as Canadian foreign policy priorities –

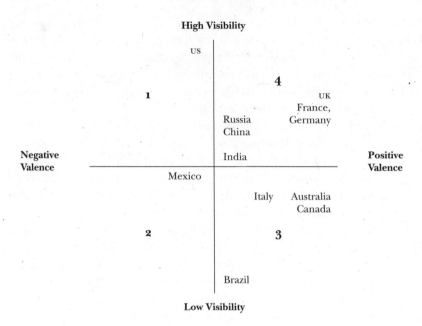

Figure 1.3   Dimensions of national image.

Source: Author's adaptation of figure by Mannheim and Albritton, *Changing National Images*, 646

Brazil, Russia, India, and China. The placement of Canada in the third quadrant next to Australia, indicating that these countries have low visibility but very positive valence, is not based on a detailed content analysis of international media coverage, but rather is suggestive and based on what little empirical evidence exists (e.g., a search of the New York Times database would reveal very few stories on Canada's politics or economics, but those that exist would be more positive than negative). Positioning Australia, a country with two-thirds of Canada's gross domestic product, next to Canada suggests that Australia (especially after having hosted the Olympic Games) receives at least as much positive international media coverage as Canada (in other words, there are probably as many positive mentions of Australia in the *New York Times* as there are of Canada). In contrast, it would not be incorrect to suggest that Mexico belongs in quadrant two. Mexico's image within the English-language elite media (e.g., the *New York Times*, the *Financial Times of London, The Economist*) is that of a country that exports its impoverished citizens to the United States and is home to violent drug cartels, an image that is difficult for the Mexican government to shake at the same time that it is billing itself as a trade and investment partner in the

North American Free Trade Agreement. Countries such as the United Kingdom, France, and Germany garner significantly more sustained international media coverage than Canada; China and Russia receive considerable international media coverage, but with a mixture of negative and positive stories, given the attention that is paid to both their economic development as well as their military build-ups and human rights records. The United States, by far the most visible country in the international media, is a magnet for both negative and positive coverage. Judging by the Pew Research Center's global surveys, since the invasion of Iraq, the United States' national image as constructed by the global mass media is probably more negative than positive.

What can one conclude from figure 1.3? As Michael Kunczik points out, communications research has shown that "the protective shield of selective perception works asymmetrically, that is, that in contrast to positive information, negative information is not filtered out."[63] This finding has important implications for national image maintenance because it is much easier for a country to gain (and keep) a negative image "even among supporters of one's own position than to build a positive image among opponents of that position." Since images, once created, over the long term tend to remain stable, a country that has developed a negative image (e.g., Mexico) will find it much harder to reverse this image in global public opinion. However, for most countries, negative media coverage on a particular issue will not do long-term damage if they have had a positive image. Therefore, countries will likely move very slowly within each of the four quadrants and rarely between them (the "Irish Miracle" is likely the exception that proves the rule).[64] But this is not to suggest that countries such as Canada, with relatively sparse but positive international media coverage, should be complacent. Countries that do not invest adequately in managing their international images are in effect throwing themselves at the mercy of international media, who play a predominant role in framing national images either negatively or positively. Countries such as Canada that are highly dependent on global markets for their economic prosperity need to be the most concerned about their international images.

THE APPROACH OF THIS STUDY

Overall, *Branding Canada* is about the challenge of promoting a medium-sized country in the world today. Yet, even though it is one of the most respected nations in the world, as this chapter has shown, it remains very difficult to get Canada into the imaginations of people around the world.

This study traces the challenges of immersing Canada in a global conversation, so that, as Ralston Saul has written, the world "will think about our way of doing things, our approach towards world governance or peace or economics or trade. Our desires in international negotiations of every sort. Our desire to convince people to sign treaties, which we have initiated or which we support."[65]

This study also explores how the Canadian government organizes itself to get the attention of people around the world. The problem, according to Ralston Saul, is

> Not simply [getting] their attention for a short moment on a specific issue or product. How can we get [foreign audiences] to understand Canada; to fix in their minds an idea of what Canada is, so that when specific issues and needs and the desire to sell specific products come up, they are able to respond with a sense – a general and continuing sense – of what Canada is? If they have that general sense, their whole approach towards our specific interventions changes radically. This is something which countries such as the United States, France and Britain have always understood for themselves and have worked very hard to accomplish.[66]

As a foreign service officer once remarked regarding the role of diplomats in this national branding effort: "Reputations are earned, not bought, and diplomats can't be more effective than the policies they seek to advance – although they can be more entertaining, engaging and well-liked!"[67]

The purpose of this study is to examine a number of questions:

• Why is public diplomacy such a contested term?
• Why has public diplomacy moved increasingly to the centre of the craft of diplomacy?
• What are the major debates concerning the public diplomacy process?
• What is the historical evolution of Canada's public diplomacy?
• How is Canada's public diplomacy organized and what instruments are being used to project Canada's international image?
• What can be done at home and abroad to create a more effective public diplomacy for Canada?

This study also raises more general questions about the practice of public diplomacy:

- What are the attributes and conditions of an effective public diplomacy campaign?
- How do a country's soft-power resources contribute to the effectiveness of its public diplomacy?
- How can the shift to branding and advocacy be reconciled with the recognition that dialogue and collaboration will be the hallmarks of the future practice of public diplomacy?

Organization of the Study

This study consists of 10 chapters that are grouped into three parts:

- Part One: "Definitions, Debates, and History." Chapters 2 and 3 outline the definitions and debates regarding the term "public diplomacy" and the history of public diplomacy in Canada.
- Part Two: "The Instruments." Chapters 4 through 7 deal with the primary instruments of public diplomacy that Canada utilizes to project itself abroad: media relations and international cultural relations, international education, international broadcasting and the new media, and the economic face of public diplomacy – international business promotion and tourism.
- Part Three: "The Process." Chapter 8 discusses who carries out public diplomacy and how it works on the ground and is followed by three examples (chapter 9) of Canadian public diplomacy campaigns in action. The concluding chapter, chapter 10, seeks to provide some observations on creating a more effective Canadian public diplomacy for the future.

This study presents an overview of Canada's public diplomacy efforts in a number of areas, ranging from the traditional public diplomacy instruments, such as cultural relations and international broadcasting, to nontraditional activities such as international business promotion and tourism. The author invites the reader to consider all these elements as fundamental and important aspects of Canada's public diplomacy

CONCLUSION

This book explores how Canadian public diplomacy has evolved and why it is so important. In an age of instantaneous information, power is becoming distributed more evenly and, as a consequence, has altered the craft of diplomacy. Canadian policy-makers have been more concerned with the "how" of Canada's public diplomacy and less with the "why." For Canada, a country whose relative power has been declining since the end of the Second World War, public diplomacy is a means of slowing the loss of power. The fundamental challenge for government is using the techniques of public diplomacy in direct service of its international policy goals. This book argues that Canada needs to adopt a more strategic, whole-of-government and whole-of-Canada approach to its public diplomacy, one that will take into account a multitude of interests such as culture, tourism, the attraction of investment, and the promotion of international peace and security.

PART ONE

Definitions, Debates, History

2

What Is Public Diplomacy?

This chapter seeks to examine public diplomacy as an essentially contested concept. While the intent is not to theorize public diplomacy, there is merit in noting the profound disciplinary silos that exist – ranging from international relations to communications – when analyzing how countries manage their international images and attempt to persuade foreign audiences. Is it propaganda? Is it branding? Is it public relations? Is it a communication process that incorporates different forms of persuasion, using different techniques depending on the communications objectives that are being sought? The confusion is not confined to academe, however. There is also frequent misunderstanding among practitioners (diplomats, aid workers, soldiers) about exactly what they have been doing when they interact with foreign publics.

This chapter will show why public diplomacy has been moving rapidly to the forefront of diplomatic practice. It will suggest that it is not the techniques of public diplomacy that have changed; rather, it is the environment in which diplomacy takes place that has changed radically.

Following the definition of the term "public diplomacy," a review of the scholarly literature across a number of fields (international relations, communications, business studies, public relations), and an analysis of the changing international conditions contributing to its ascendancy, the chapter will suggest three ways of thinking of public diplomacy: as a process of statecraft in three time frames (the short, medium, and long term); as an instrument of statecraft with multiple tools; and as a form of statecraft whose effectiveness will depend on the domestic dimension – on a country's sense of itself in terms of its citizens' sense of pride and identity, as well as on the domestic architecture that is available to build social cohesion (e.g., the level of support that exists for culture and the nature of the education system). The chapter then reviews some common debates about the labels attributed to public diplomacy, including whether it is a process or value, whether propaganda and psychological operations are forms of public diplomacy, and whether public diplomacy is the same as nation branding. This discussion is followed by a review of some of the debates over public diplomacy's functions, including whether it should be seen through the metaphor of a "rifle" or a "shotgun," whether governments can execute public diplomacy objectives through the filter of an agenda-setting mass media, whether public diplomacy can contribute to intercultural learning, and whether public diplomacy as a function is inherently restricted in an age of heightened concerns over public security. The chapter ends with an examination of whether public diplomacy in the twenty-first century constitutes a new form of diplomacy.

DEFINING A CONTESTED CONCEPT

Public diplomacy is the effort by the official institutions of one nation to influence the elite or mass public opinion of another nation for the purpose of turning the policies or views of that target nation to advantage.[1] In the words of Hans Tuch, it is "a government's process of communicating with foreign publics in an attempt to bring about understanding for its nation's ideas and ideals, its institutions and culture, as well as its national goals and current policies."[2] Michael Kunczik agrees, stating that "[f]or the nation-state, [public relations] means the planned and continuous distribution of interest-bound information by a state aimed (mostly) at improving the country's image abroad."[3] It is not a one-way street, however. Gifford Malone expands the definition by pointing out that the requirement to understand others – through dialogue – is indispensable to success: "If we strive to be successful in our efforts to create understanding for our society and for our policies, we must first understand the motives, culture, history, and psychology of the people with whom we wish to communicate, and certainly their language."[4]

Recognition or presence is a necessary but not a sufficient condition for successful public diplomacy. For instance, the Nazis had a high-recognition factor when their propaganda machine was at its height, and the Americans, by virtue of their vast influence and economic power, are the most visible nation in the world. But if public diplomacy is to be successful, such high recognition must be coupled with a certain amount of positive feelings and a great deal of relevance to prospective partners.[5] In the American formulation set out by Edward R. Murrow when he was director of the

United States Information Agency during the Kennedy administration, public diplomacy contributes to a nation's international standing by understanding, informing, and influencing foreign audiences.[6] At its core, public diplomacy is an instrument of statecraft in which one government is trying to influence the public and, therefore, the political environment in a foreign jurisdiction. More broadly, public diplomacy is action initiated by a government to influence foreign public opinion for a diplomatic purpose, or for wider national interests. Public diplomacy activities, less and less the exclusive purview of foreign ministries and national cultural agencies, help develop a three-dimensional image of a country, leading to a more complete and balanced perception of the country's economic, political, and social development. Finally, what distinguishes public diplomacy from classic diplomacy is that, although the former's programs may include government officials as direct targets, the programs are not designed to be privileged government-to-government interactions.

Fundamentally, public diplomacy requires an official purpose. Contacts between citizens from different countries constitute public diplomacy only if they are supported by a government – either directly or indirectly – for a strategic purpose. A non-governmental actor, such as a firm or a non-governmental organization (NGO), engaging in cross-border public relations is not engaged in public diplomacy, since it is not being supported by an official government institution. This is a form of intercultural communication only. Public and private interests in projecting a nation's image – for example, in tourism or investment promotion – can be compatible, but this does not imply that the coincident promotion of a country or region abroad will necessarily contribute to an effective form of image management, especially if the private and public campaigns show radically different national images or, in the case of investment, if private business associations launch marketing campaigns that compete with official national tourism marketing campaigns. Of course, the international public relations activities of private actors can become a form of public diplomacy if governments either become involved actively and visibly as co-sponsors or in a more low-key but nevertheless supportive fashion, such as when embassies provide behind-the-scenes advice on local conditions and audiences. This complements the definition of international public relations proposed by D.L. Wilcox et al., who state that it is "the planned and organised effort of a company, institution or government to establish mutually beneficial relations with the publics of other nations."[7]

As more public-private partnerships evolve to promote countries or regions internationally, the line dividing public diplomacy from the more generic international public relations will become less stark. Ultimately, it will be the degree of government involvement that will continue to allow the continuum of communication objectives (informing audiences, reinforcing or changing attitudes, and reinforcing or changing behaviour) to be labelled as public diplomacy. If a government provides general direction (it does not necessarily have to try to control communication content), resources, or strategic advice, then public relations events and programs in other countries become part of a country's public diplomacy.

Two Canadians have made significant contributions to the understanding of public diplomacy. Allan Gotlieb, who pioneered the art of Canadian public diplomacy as Canada's ambassador to Washington from 1981 to 1989, has written that "[t]he new diplomacy is, to a large extent, public diplomacy and requires different skills, techniques and attitudes than those found in traditional diplomacy as it is practised in most countries, including Canada."[8] Bruce Gregory, director of the Public Diplomacy Institute at the George Washington University, has written that Gotlieb recognized that public diplomacy "is not only the work of press and cultural attachés or of public affairs officers. It is central to the daily activities of ambassadors and political counsellors and presidents and foreign ministers – if they are to be successful."[9] Gotlieb was talking about "mainstreaming" public diplomacy long before it was fashionable to do so. Echoing Gotlieb's sentiment, in 2003 Ashton Calvert, permanent secretary in Australia's Department of Foreign Affairs and Trade, writing in a departmental handbook on Australian public diplomacy, sent out a clear message about the new mainstreamed status of public diplomacy. He said that all Australia's foreign service officers in its embassies abroad were to consider themselves to be practitioners of public diplomacy.[10]

John Ralston Saul, one of Canada's best-known public intellectuals, has a long-standing interest in cultural relations and was at the forefront of Canadian public diplomacy as the vice regal consort of Canada's former governor general, Adrienne Clarkson (1999–2005). In an incisive report for the 1994 parliamentary review of Canadian foreign policy, he wrote something that is fairly obvious yet often overlooked: "[c]ulture is ... the face of Canada abroad. To the extent that foreign policy is dependent on foreign public recognition – an identifiable image and a sense at all levels of what we stand for, what kind of society we are, what we sell – that policy is dependent on our projection of our culture."[11] Ralston Saul understood that most countries in the world – and Canada is no exception – are the images that they project. In other words, as in politics or business, perception is reality. National image is not who *you* say you are but who *others* say you are. Naturally, this is why most images of countries are stereotypes that often leave an inaccurate national portrait. But all countries must live with, or at least attempt to manage, inaccurate national images. Canada has plenty of such images to be sure. Canadians always wince at the thought of being identified only by the three Ms – Moose, Mounties (Royal Canadian Mounted Police in bright red tunics), and Mountains. Large, complex countries such as Canada, of course, should not be reduced to outdated generalizations. However, governments must be realistic and cannot expect the world's attentive publics and opinion leaders to make the extra effort to become more knowledgeable about their countries. Despite the existence of the Internet, there are still only twenty-four hours in a day. The reality is that most people's first contact with another nation is second-hand through the impressions of friends and family and, much more likely, through exposure to that nation's culture, most often through the mass media. This is how the world will continue to come into contact with Canada.

A MULTIDISCIPLINARY PERSPECTIVE

Since the late 1990s, there has been an upsurge of interest among policy-makers and scholars in the function and role of public diplomacy,[12] particularly in the aftermath of the terrorist attacks of 11 September 2001 on the United States. At that time, there was considerable consternation among American politicians about why they had lost the "hearts and minds" of the Islamic world.[13] Indeed, the most comprehensive analysis of public diplomacy can be found in American congressional reports and studies (a summary of which can be found in the Department of State's *Cultural Diplomacy: The Linchpin of Public Diplomacy*), as well as reports produced by the Foreign Policy Centre in the United Kingdom.[14]

Public diplomacy falls within a number of disciplinary silos. It straddles four areas of scholarly inquiry – international relations, communications, international marketing and public relations. Until Joseph Nye's book *Bound to Lead* (1990), in which he first developed the concept of soft power, the international relations literature makes little explicit mention of public diplomacy as defined in this study, although there are references to national "prestige" and, of course, frequent references to the role of propaganda (usually associated with international broadcasting efforts).[15] The communications function is linked closely to the theory of complex interdependence.[16] The idea is that, as nations become ever more interdependent and their peoples increasingly aware of common interests, solutions to global problems depend on broad communication networks and the

interchange of ideas. This view of a changed world calls for increased dialogue – a two-way public diplomacy. Indeed, in the pluralistic perspective,
governments are competing with many more states and non-state actors for
a share of the global conversation. As the number and variety of players
increase in a highly interconnected system, communications become more
complex. Two-way communication becomes the norm, challenging traditional concepts of public diplomacy as consisting of largely one-way flows of
information and cultural programming.

Public diplomacy is but one of the components within the broad sub-
field of international communications.[17] This field can be further subdi-
vided into an additional seven principal areas, each of which has received
scholarly attention.[18] These areas include propaganda,[19] military-media
relations,[20] information warfare and information operations,[21] international broadcasting,[22] international telecommunications policy,[23] global
news and information flows,[24] and communication and culture.[25] For the
most part, scholarly discussions of public diplomacy focus on international broadcasting, telecommunications policy, and historical treat-
ments of the New International Information Order. Another of the most
popular strands of what can loosely be termed international communications is that of media diplomacy, with works examining the "CNN effect"
and the role of the media in conflicts.[26] A comprehensive treatment of
public diplomacy, albeit from a historical perspective, has been docu-
mented by Philip M. Taylor in his book *Global Communications, International Affairs and the Media since 1945*.[27]

Two other bodies of scholarly literature directly relevant to the study of
public diplomacy – one long standing and the other emerging – are often
overlooked by researchers in political science. The international marketing literature has for some years provided the most detailed empirical work
on country branding and country-of-origin effects.[28] In general, it is quite
evident that country image matters and has an important effect on tourism
flows, investment, and exports.[29] British author, Simon Anholt, in his book
Competitive Identity: The New Brand Management for Nations, Cities and Regions,
has developed a comprehensive model of branding that reaches beyond its
economic dimension.[30]

Public relations literature, which has usually focused on multinational
corporations' communications behaviours in the global arena, has made
only some sporadic attempts over the last decade to recognize that nations
can and do engage in public relations. This is odd, as Jacquie L'Etang and
Magda Pieczka note, since diplomats and public relations practitioners
share boundary-spanning roles as representatives (advocates), dialogue

participants (collaborators), and advisors (counsellors).[31] Benno H. Signitzer and Timothy Coombs' 1992 article "Public Relations and Public Diplomacy: Conceptual Convergences" has likely been the best-known attempt to theoretically bridge the spheres of public diplomacy and public relations to show how both spheres share the same models; as a result, it has acted as a springboard for further studies on the topic.[32] Signitzer and Coombs compared James Grunig and Todd Hunt's four models of public relations[33] with H. Peisert's four models of cultural communication,[34] since cultural programs are often the anchors of national public diplomacy campaigns. They found considerable conceptual convergences between the typologies of communication set out by Grunig and Hunt (e.g., one-way versus two-way communication; asymmetrical versus symmetrical communication) and Peisert (e.g., one-way transfer of culture abroad versus the nurturing of broad understanding and sympathy), as well as the descriptions of actual public diplomacy programs and initiatives. Signitzer and Coombs state that public diplomacy and public relations are "two areas which could benefit from a union [but] remain divorced from one another,"[35] and they credit German public diplomacy theorist Hansjürgen Koschwitz as the only one to have used the term "public relations" in reference to public diplomacy activities.

Another important concept in the public relations literature is the measurement of interpersonal power or influence as explicated by Geert Hofstede,[36] which can easily be imported into an examination of interstate relations. It seems logical that when a country assumes its position in the international system, it assumes a power position relative to other countries and adopts a corresponding communication style that is indexed to its "power-distance" in relation to the country with which it wishes to communicate. In other words, in those diplomatic relationships where the power inequalities are very high (high power-distance), one should expect communications to be very asymmetrical – not the most effective form of public diplomacy. Conversely, the smaller the power-distance, the more likely it is that symmetrical communication, or what Grunig terms "excellent" communication, will take place.

It is suggested that countries situating themselves in the middle range of nations may have smaller power-distances both with other advanced industrialized nations and with the developing world, thereby enabling them to practise two-way symmetrical communication with both and to earning a reputation for superior and more effective public diplomacy. Indeed, Mark Leonard states that for just this reason, excellence in public diplomacy might be strongly associated with middle-ranking countries such as Sweden under Olof Palme, Norway in the Middle East peace process, and Canada on land mines.[37] To add yet another layer would be to describe the impact of culture and the political system on how countries (notably foreign ministries) conduct their public diplomacies: just as culture and the political system determine public relations domestically, so too will they affect a government's external public relations. This has led to the proposition that countries with a low power-distance, a highly collectivist culture, and a more corporatist political system are more likely to practise a strategic, symmetrical, and, by definition, more effective public diplomacy. According to this hypothesis, middle-ranking states such the Scandinavian countries and Canada have an advantage over some of the greater-power states in their ability to exert influence.

Based on this close conceptual fit between the models of public relations and public diplomacy, Signitzer and Coombs called for public relations theory-based empirical research in the areas of public diplomacy.[38] The exact ideas and concepts, which have been transferred from one sphere to the other, have yet to be fully delineated and tested, however. As well, the focus on national image from the business literature and the role of soft power from the international relations literature have not been adequately considered in the existing public relations literature. Only a series of theory-based empirical studies will facilitate the convergence of models from all these traditions, leading to the development of a theory of public diplomacy. However, this is not the purpose of the present study.

Scholarly literature on public diplomacy from a Canadian perspective has been relatively sparse.[39] The role of culture in Canadian foreign policy has generated just a handful of book chapters and a few academic articles.[40] There has, however, been no attempt to approach the topic of Canadian public diplomacy holistically and to explore its constituent time spans, ranging from medium-term strategic communications programs supporting specific initiatives to longer-term efforts to produce lasting relationships through cultural and academic programs.

THE CHANGING CONTEXT OF PUBLIC DIPLOMACY

The management of a global image, or brand, was not always uppermost in the minds of diplomats and government leaders. In an earlier era, when nation-states had fewer competitors, foreign ministries were usually too conservative and too accustomed to managing the high politics of international security, or, later, even the low politics of trade and economic relations, to pay much attention to what would have been called cultural diplomacy. It is not that cultural or educational programs – often the "safe" high culture of classical art, music, and dance – were not deemed necessary; rather, for the most part, they were seen as a much lower priority. Simply put, public diplomacy in the form of networking with foreign publics, whether through culture or academic relations, was not perceived to be crucial to achieving national interests.

The Changes

What has changed? The art of public diplomacy has not changed radically, although the introduction of the Internet and new media has certainly had an important impact. Instead, it is the environment in which public diplomacy takes place that has changed radically. A number of overarching developments have increased the importance of both public affairs and public diplomacy in contemporary diplomacy and will affect any re-thinking of Canadian approaches. These developments, discussed below, include

- the increased importance of public opinion;
- the spread of democracy throughout the world;
- the rise of a more intrusive and global media;
- more diaspora communities;
- a broadened definition of security;
- increased global transparency brought about by advances in communications and the related phenomenon of a more activist civil society;
- the rise of a global culture leading to a reflexive desire to protect cultural diversity; and
- an alteration to the definition of state power.

Public Opinion and Democracy. First, in an increasingly interconnected world, public opinion matters more than ever. The progress of democratic movements around the world (including in the developed world itself) has meant that understanding and managing public opinion is now crucial to achieving policy objectives. With publics more distrustful of government and demanding greater transparency and input into policy-making, governments can no longer count on "spin" to overcome communications challenges.[41] And with so many players and a 24/7 news cycle, foreign ministries, like domestic departments, are under pressure to provide substance on demand, be aware of and responsive to the public mood, and, in some cases, aggressively refute misinformation and untruths in the public domain.

We are witnessing a qualitative change in the relationship between the state and its citizens that is spreading across the globe. However imperfect in design, the sweep of democracy through Eastern Europe, Russia, and Latin America since the late 1980s has led to a greater need to understand and manage the opinions of at least another half-billion people. From a time when contact with local civil societies was strictly circumscribed, we have moved to the point where the rise of pluralism in previously closed societies has led to an abundance of interest groups that have to be taken into account when engaging in public diplomacy. In fact, more public diplomacy and greater advocacy skills are now required, since there are more points of access in the policy-making process.

Global Media. Second, as noted, we are in what Manuel Castells has defined as the *informational* revolution, running ever smaller, cheaper, and faster circuitry that has facilitated overlapping and cross-cutting policy networks peppered with non-governmental actors, running the gamut from large NGOs, such as the International Federation of the Red Cross and Crescent Societies, to someone with a computer who can self-publish his or her views to a global audience.[42] The ever-expanding array of global satellite news networks combined with the ability of citizens to access, use, and disseminate information poses a fundamental challenge to diplomacy. The explosion of information technology and communications infrastructures provides the public with the ability to research, engage, and advocate positions on a wide range of issues. This trend has led to the presence of "wired diasporas" – worldwide communities based on common ethnicity, homeland, or faith. Families can emerge with nodes in several nations, defying conventional notions of nationality.[43] However, as David Bollier illustrates, the Internet also has the effect of "decontextualizing" information from the social frames that give it meaning, making it more complicated than ever to align the intended meanings of the sender with the interpretations of the receiver, offering a rationale for keeping embassies.[44]

Security. Third, as the concept of security has been broadened, the gap between domestic and international policy has rapidly closed, making citizens' everyday concerns the concerns of foreign policy-makers. The domestic and the international agendas increasingly overlap. Diplomats must take notice, because resolving the non-traditional security issues lying high on the public's agenda often requires much closer links with NGOs and the mobilization of public opinion at home and abroad.

The foreign policy agenda of the twenty-first century is full of interlinked issues – the spread of infectious diseases, competition for natural resources, migration, poverty – that cannot be resolved by governments alone. A good example is the place of infectious diseases on the international agenda. A decade ago it would have been very difficult to have a serious discussion about health issues in a foreign ministry. The outbreak of severe acute respiratory syndrome (SARS) in Toronto in 2003 is a perfect Canadian example of how a "local" health problem quickly evolved into a serious international image problem for Canada, which eventually cost Toronto, Canada's largest city and economic hub, Can$2 billion in revenue and the rest of the Canadian economy a further Can$1–$1.5 billion. People simply refused to fly to Canada for business or for pleasure.

In a global "infosphere" of satellite television, this disease outbreak soon turned into a national crisis and caused Canada's global brand as a safe country to be tarnished. Canadians were surprised at how quickly their international image suffered and how quickly inaccuracies filled the global airwaves and bandwidths. This case also perfectly illustrates how one government department – be it a foreign ministry or a health ministry – cannot be expected to manage such a crisis alone. Public policy is increasingly "intermestic" – international and domestic at the same time – and this means that public diplomacy must be managed by the entire government, not just the foreign ministry.

Transparency, Activism and Global Culture. Fourth, the expansion of trade liberalization, the emergence of global media giants (e.g., Time Warner, Disney, Bertelsmann), and the increasing mobility of people and changing demographic patterns (exploding youth populations) are creating not only global markets but also global societies. These trends have raised concerns that cultural homogenization (often interpreted as Americanization) will limit the ability of countries to maintain their cultural distinctiveness. On the other hand, greater mobility and citizen activism on a global scale have also created new, non-territorially based social movements and, importantly, have amplified the ideological power and cohesion of diaspora communities.[45] Cultural diversity, rather than being a barrier, is now a strategic resource that, in a global knowledge-based society, drives innovation, creativity, and reconciliation. According to Richard Florida, this new economy is a creative economy; the arts not only drive cultural industries but also drive global communities.[46] It could even be conjectured that, in the same way that the environment was heralded in the 1970s and 1980s as essential to quality of life, by the 1990s cultural diversity was increasingly recognized as a focus of global strategies towards economic development.[47]

Soft Power. Fifth, we are living in an age when the nature of power has clearly changed. To use Joseph Nye's term, it is much more fungible[48] – that is to say, power can shift from one plane of international relations, say, the military level, to the economic or cultural levels, and vice versa. The traditional hard-power resources, both military and economic, that for centuries have been used to coerce and induce fellow nations to accept the foreign policy decisions of structurally powerful countries are no longer sufficient in a world where global public opinion matters and the competition for global "mind space" – the attention of the world – is as aggressive as the arms race once was. To achieve their objectives, countries now have to think about soft power – the ability to create willing followers by the compelling power of a country's ideas and reputation. Soft power has been derided by some observers as an excuse for countries not to do the heavy lifting of international affairs, such as sending ships to support relief efforts or sending soldiers into crisis zones. This is a misunderstanding of the concept. In the past, when diplomats talked about the intangibles of international power relations, they would often refer to a country's "prestige." The inference was that this conferred some form of attraction and respect.

Not surprisingly, business people have always been very concerned about how their communications and marketing will persuade clients and customers to buy their goods and services. Business people call it "goodwill" and "brand loyalty," and it can be quantified. According to Simon Anholt, when we talk about a nation's brand, we are talking about the sum total of a person's perception of a country – its governance, its people, its cultural heritage, its immigration policies, and the quality of its exports.[49] The sum total of other people's perceptions of these qualities is the nation's reputation, or its ability to attract support. In other words, the brand is the nation's soft power.

This does not mean that traditional sources of power have disappeared. It just means that public forms of diplomacy will increasingly have to complement the traditional hard power of military and economic inducements and sanctions. Public diplomacy is the process by which soft power is applied.[50] Nye, in his book *Soft Power*, has described the careful calibration of soft- and hard-power assets on a given policy issue as an exercise in "smart power."[51] Nye also reminds us that information is no longer a scarce resource. In a world of information overload, attention is the scarce resource. Nye calls this the "paradox of plenty." He writes: "Plenty of information leads to scarcity – of attention ... Attention rather than information becomes the scarce resource, and those who can distinguish valuable information from background clutter gain power ... credibility is the crucial resource, and an important source of soft power ... political struggles occur over the creation and destruction of credibility."[52] As Bruce Gregory pithily summarized it in a speech delivered in 2005 to Canadian public diplomacy practitioners, "[t]oday, power flows to the credible. Reputations matter more than ever before. Nation-brands matter. Sources of information matter. What's around information matters."[53] There are now fewer issues that can be readily resolved through military or economic power.

CONCEPTUALIZING PUBLIC DIPLOMACY

Three ways of thinking about public diplomacy may bring some clarity to what has become a contested concept. Public diplomacy should be seen as a process across several time frames; it should be understood with respect to the instruments employed; and there should be some appreciation of the role played by a country's own citizens with respect to the promotion of the national identity abroad.

Public Diplomacy as a Process

For the world's major industrialized countries, comprising most members of the Organisation for Economic Co-operation and Development (OECD), the public diplomacy process generally has seven objectives:

1   to increase exports and attract investment and mutually beneficial science and technology collaboration,
2   to encourage beneficial immigration,
3   to increase tourism,
4   to attract international students and promote scholarly exchanges,
5   to project and promote good governance (e.g., through the rule of law, respect for diversity, accountable and transparent government),
6   to create support for a country's international trade and security policy, and
7   to reflect back international success to domestic audiences in order to validate and promote national identity.

The intensity of public diplomacy efforts in each category will vary from country to country.

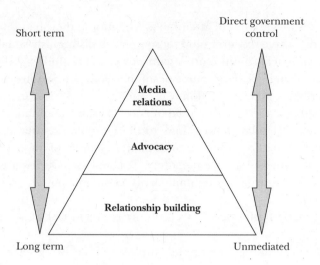

Figure 2.1   The public diplomacy pyramid. *Source:* Author's version of a public diplomacy schema originally designed by Michael Brock and Alan Bowker of Foreign Affairs and International Trade Canada

As Bruce Gregory has stated, "[w]hen Canada's Prime Minister or a Canadian ambassador gives a newsmaker an interview on satellite television, we have little trouble identifying their actions as public diplomacy. When a Canadian Minister of Defense or military commander appears on camera, however, the optic shifts."[54] Whether an initiative is referred to as a public affairs or a military information operation, Gregory is of the opinion that it is all public diplomacy, since there are political actors trying to understand, engage, and influence public opinion at home and abroad.

This public diplomacy process can be conceptualized as being carried out across three time frames that reflect short-, medium-, and long-term goals. Mark Leonard sees these time frames as consistent with three additional dimensions of public diplomacy – reactive, proactive and relationship-building dimensions.[55] Part of the confusion in defining public diplomacy is that there are many labels attached to its practice in each of the three time frames. The public diplomacy pyramid in figure 2.1, which was developed by Canadian officials at DFAIT, provides a useful visual representation of the three temporal dimensions. The first, reactive dimension is media relations and other information activity, consisting largely of targeted messages directly managed by the government, often through its central communication apparatus (e.g., the office of the political leader) and through the media relations office at the foreign ministry's headquarters and at missions (see chapter 8). It occurs over hours or days and involves the management of day-to-day communications issues. For Gregory, the "24/7" news cycle and media relations define short-term public diplomacy: "If political leaders and diplomats do not get inside the news cycles, others will, usually to the disadvantage of diplomacy."[56] A diplomatic mission's media relations office will either proactively (e.g., in advance of a known public relations problem such as the annual cull of harp seals on Canada's East Coast) or responsively (e.g., in response to a crisis or routine inquiry) defend and explain specific policy positions to target publics in order to ensure, if not support, at least an accurate understanding of issues. For Leonard, short-term public diplomacy reflects the need to align foreign and domestic public opinion with a country's international priorities as it engages in traditional, state-to-state diplomacy.

The second dimension is proactive public diplomacy, or strategic communications. This dimension is characterized by strategic, mostly government-controlled messages over the medium term (usually months and sometimes years) and is often labelled issues management, advocacy campaigning, political marketing, or "special pleading,"[57] whereby a variety of communications channels are used to achieve specific policy objectives. Simply put, advocacy campaigns are planned series of activities or events designed to plead or argue in favour of a cause, idea, or policy.[58] They are multi-dimensional, involving strategic planning, the development of key messages, audience research, and a variety of public diplomacy activities and vehicles using more than one communication medium. An example of an advocacy campaign occurred when Canada built an international coalition to ban land mines, which eventually led to the Ottawa Convention in December 1997. For Leonard, strategic communications differ from longer-term relationship-building, because the government directly authors the messages and employs public diplomacy activities to reinforce them. The key objective in this dimension is a shift in perception, which can be related to an important key policy area or to efforts to change how the country is viewed by foreign audiences in general. However, not everyone believes that advocacy as special pleading, or lobbying, is the same as public diplomacy. Allan Gotlieb adopts a narrower definition of public diplomacy when he writes: "public diplomacy is creating understanding about one's country. Advocacy, like lobbying, is no substitute for good relations."[59] Of course, not all of a country's international policies require advocacy or strategic communications campaigns.[60] Just as in the case of a public relations campaign, Gregory notes that "[t]he foreign ministry will have to decide what themes, messages, messengers, symbols, and communication tools are best suited to persuade, to tap favourably into emotions, and to serve political objectives."[61] Given the expense of launching advocacy campaigns in foreign environments, hard choices have to be made, since there are always certain issues, particularly where national security and national pride are involved (e.g., Pakistan's view that it has a right to defend its interests through nuclear deterrence) that are virtually immune from foreign advocacy campaigns.

The third and final dimension of the pyramid concerns long-term, unmediated (by government) relationship-building and maintenance designed to create a wider and deeper understanding of a country. This dimension focuses on developing relationships over years and even generations through traditional public diplomacy instruments such as international academic relations (e.g., overseas studies programs, scholarships, student exchanges, youth internships, education marketing) and cultural relations (e.g., arts, international exhibitions, youth travel, translation). Leonard is unique in defining the core objective of the long-term dimension as relationship-building between peers, be they politicians, business people, academics, or those involved in the cultural industries. These activities, which are less and less the exclusive purview of foreign ministries and national cultural agencies, help to develop a three-dimensional image of a country, leading to a more complete and balanced perception of the country's economic, political, and social development.[62] International, cultural, and academic relations are not linked to one particular foreign policy objective but, rather, support general themes. Such low-risk general constituency building is valuable because it can communicate universal messages that aim to generate a profile of excellence internationally.[63]

Unlike strategic communications, the third dimension allows for the development of a more nuanced perspective in the foreign audience that can be positively leveraged in times of crises or that can underpin advocacy campaigns. The guiding philosophy is the development of a "mutuality" of interests between countries; the government acts as a catalyst to allow an exchange of ideas and perspectives.[64] It is accepted that foreign audiences will occasionally disapprove of particular policies of a country or see the negative attributes of a national culture (prevalent corruption, poor treatment of minorities or women), but it is hoped that through the goodwill generated by sustained relationship-building, they will be more sympathetic to the country in general and may at least understand the rationale behind a given policy or practice. Risks are clearly associated with having foreigners see both a country's positive and its negative attributes, but greater international credibility will accrue to a state that is willing to

embrace its struggles as well as its triumphs. The better the long-term relationship-building has been – in other words, the more familiar a national
identity and national aspirations have become through less confrontational
and more positive contacts in cultural and academic settings – the higher
the likelihood that advocacy efforts, even unpopular ones, will receive a
more sympathetic hearing by the receiving audience. In the words of Hugh
Stephens, a former senior Canadian official responsible for DFAIT's public
diplomacy, "[a] relationship with a solid foundation ... will be more reliable
when the chips are down. And one of the best ways to foster a relationship
in a non-threatening way is to engage in public diplomacy."[65]

In summary, longer-term strategies to build mutual understanding help
to mitigate short-term fluctuations in a country's relations with other countries. Although short- and medium-term public diplomacy work is sometimes labelled government propaganda because it is largely one-way and
intended to create an immediate effect in its intended audience, the longer-term activities constitute an investment in image management in which
the payoff is not immediately visible or measurable. However, given political pressures – domestic and international – to respond to particular problems and irritants, governments (perhaps with the exception of the French
government's approach to public diplomacy) tend to invest proportion-
ately less in understanding other cultures (through long-term programs
and public opinion research on local elites and general populations) than
in influencing those other cultures through advocacy programs. Finally,
the cultural and academic forms of public diplomacy must be differenti-
ated from, first, the international activities undertaken by artists and scholars who have neither direct nor indirect support from governments and,
second, the international activities of national arts organizations, such as
the Canada Council for the Arts, that seek to develop and maintain robust
cultural industries by encouraging artists to gain international experience.
Certainly, these longer-term cultural and academic links contribute to a
nation's image, but they do not properly constitute public diplomacy, as
this book seeks to define the term, if they are not directed by governments.

DFAIT considers the continuum of short- to long-term public diplomacy
to be critical to Canada's international relationships. Also, it is acknowledged that all levels of public diplomacy rely on the interpersonal dimension, or what Edward R. Murrow famously described as "the last three feet"
– whether it is the diplomatic mission's public affairs officer or the press
attaché making a personal connection with a foreign interlocutor or the
invited Canadian academic (whose trip has been paid for by the Canadian
government) having the chance, after a formal presentation on some

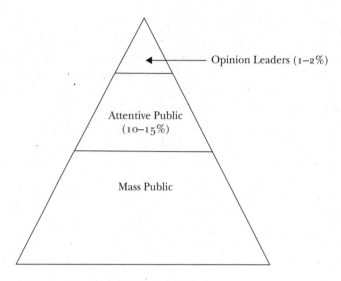

Figure 2.2   The target audiences for public diplomacy.
Source: Director General, Communications, Israeli Ministry of Foreign Affairs

aspect of Canada, to make a point about his or her country in a social, face-to-face meeting with local scholars. As figure 2.1 illustrates, most governments consider the three dimensions of public diplomacy to be interlinked. The media relations and information work, often the day-to-day firefighting, is the sharp end of the public diplomacy pyramid. The success of advocacy strategies will, in turn, depend both on good information work and on how well perceptions have been nurtured over the longer term. Long-term cultural and educational programs are certainly not a guarantee for achieving every policy objective, but, over time, their absence would be felt in a negative way in the management of a country's international relations.

As figure 2.2 indicates, most public diplomacy, but especially advocacy, will target opinion leaders (1 to 2 percent of the population) and attentive publics (10 to 15 percent of the population). Some public diplomacy, however, will be directed at the mass public, such as in the case of crises (e.g., the spread of infectious disease, natural disasters) or when a government must justify its decisions or dispel misinformation propagated in the media (e.g., information about Canada's annual seal hunt). Greater global transparency means that tactical problems – for example, a Danish newspaper's publication in 2005 of a series of cartoons depicting the Prophet Mohammed, which led to an outcry in the Islamic world – can quickly become larger strategic problems for countries (in this case, Denmark). Through the ease of communication and the advent of twenty-four-hour satellite television news, an isolated incident can incite worldwide tensions, as the debate moves quickly from one between attentive and relatively sophisticated publics who would understand the necessary context to mass publics.

It goes without saying that the tools of communication need to be tailored to different countries and regions. From a diplomatic perspective, a decision needs to be made on when the ambassador is the best messenger and when third-party validators would be more appropriate. The big difference between a domestic public relations strategy and a public diplomacy strategy abroad lies in the repercussions, should something go awry: public diplomacy is more sensitive since it may deal with interstate matters of life and death. A private actor engaged in public relations in another country can leave and soon be forgotten; a public affairs failure associated with a nation-state is unlikely to be forgotten as quickly.

As an alternative to the temporal conceptualizations discussed above, one may consider the process and practice of public diplomacy as occurring along a power continuum similar to that proposed in Nye's power schema of hard versus soft power.[66] The continuum based on two time frames, short- to medium-term and medium- to long-term. Traditionally, nation-states have invested in soft power as an alternative to hard power. The goal has been to achieve foreign policy objectives over the medium to long term by co-opting other nations to one's own country's preferences, as opposed to resorting to the threat of hard power. Through academic and cultural relations, countries attempt to set the international agenda or win a general international following through what Nye calls the "power of attraction."[67] The idea is that one country becomes more favourably disposed towards another country's international policies and perspectives when it has been exposed to the country's language, culture, and people. This still is true. However, countries have come to realize that public diplomacy is not just about the number of foreign students attending its universities or a tour of the national ballet; it is increasingly about responding to international coverage of a local epidemic and about attracting international investment (see table 2.1).

Overlaying public diplomacy as conceived in terms of time frames with Nye's typology of hard and soft power, one would logically conclude that there are hard and soft forms of public diplomacy. Hard public diplomacy is not an oxymoron. Practised over the short to medium term, activities in this time frame are considered to be hard public diplomacy because they share similarities with the exercise of hard power. Governments generally

Table 2.1
Continuum of Hard and Soft Public Diplomacy

	Hard	Soft
Time frame	Short term to medium term	Medium term to long term
Spectrum of behaviours	Command/control coercion – inducement	Co-opt/validate/follow agenda-setting – attraction
	• White propaganda • Grey propaganda • Black propaganda • Media relations • Advocacy campaigns • Government relations (diplomats as lobbyists); e.g., Canada's Congressional relations personnel in its Washington, DC embassy • Personal diplomacy (profile builders/personalities of influence); e.g., consul general's speeches to Wall Street executives; see chapter 9, Upper North Side campaign • Symbolic events: Canadian fisheries minister Brian Tobin holding up a turbot and an illegal fishing net confiscated from the Spanish trawler *Estai*, to the international media during the 1995 Canada- Spain "fish war"	• Cultural and academic relations • International sport (government-supported participation in, or hosting of, international athletic competitions – Olympic, Commonwealth, and Francophone Games) • Investment and trade promotion • Tourism
Resources	Embassies and consulates, Canadian military, Canadian International Development Agency	Students, academics, ecumenical workers, artists, authors, scientists/ researchers, athletes and teams, Canada Corps, Canadian tourists (including backpackers), Canadian businesspeople and entrepreneurs, volunteers (Executive Volunteer Overseas Canada, NetCorps Canada International), participants in DFAIT and the Canadian International Development Agency's international youth programs

Source: Evan Potter

employ short- to medium-term public diplomacy to attain foreign policy objectives through the management of international public opinion. For example, the foreign media can be leveraged by the government in country

A to pressure the government of country B into decisions that are favourable to country A's national interests. In this way, if country A uses implicit or explicit threats in its media releases or public pronouncements, then it is using public diplomacy for coercion or inducement (e.g., as President George W. Bush did when he used the Voice of America to deliver the message that Iran is a member of the Axis of Evil and, therefore, that states associating themselves with Iran through economic or political links will elicit the United States' disapproval). Hard public diplomacy campaigns are usually *directly* controlled by governments. The hard public diplomacy activities (e.g., press releases, communications strategies, official editorials on Voice of America) are closely managed, and they support key objectives that are in line with current foreign policy priorities. Key government messages are carefully crafted, and in the case of advocacy, most campaigns serve a policy-related function. In this author's view, hard public diplomacy includes all forms of propaganda (white, i.e., standard public relations strategies; grey, i.e., information without an identified source or author; and black, i.e., information reportedly from one source but actually from another), foreign-assistance announcements after a natural disaster (if the announcement is designed to remind the recipient government that at some future date, there will be a quid pro quo, such as first consideration for future government contracts), and military information programs in pre- and post-conflict stages. As we have seen, in the short and medium terms, most public diplomacy activities involve media relations conducted by officials of the diplomatic mission (in person, by telephone, or on the Web). The diplomat is often cast in the role of lobbyist, tasked with obtaining immediate objectives, such as lifting a ban on imported meat after a "mad cow" scare.

Soft public diplomacy occupies the end of the continuum that Nye correlates with soft power; that is, it consists of those activities performed over the medium to long term to create a favourable impression and increase understanding among foreign audiences. These activities can be likened to the public diplomacy that occurs in the relationship-building tier in figure 2.1. Like soft power, soft public diplomacy helps set the international agenda and relies on the power of attraction as opposed to coercion or inducement. Activities typically include, but are not limited to, academic and cultural relations. Country branding activities for the purpose of investment (e.g., Team Canada trade promotion trips or presentations by business leaders in one country to business leaders of another country in the context of a government-driven initiative) and tourism promotion advertisements are also forms of soft public diplomacy. The government has the capacity to set the agenda for many of these activities, but the longer the time frame over which these activities take place (months and years in the case of tourism campaigns and decades in the case of a student exchange agreement), the less control the government has over the message. As figure 2.1 shows, communication over time becomes increasingly unmediated. Foreign audiences interpret messages from their world view. Though there is less control at the soft end of the spectrum, the messages, whether delivered by visiting academics or through media coverage of athletes at an international competition, are associated by foreign publics with greater legitimacy because of their arm's-length relationship with the government. Soft public diplomacy calls upon participants in international youth exchanges, touring academics, artists, entrepreneurs, and volunteers to become "ambassadors" in government-sponsored medium- to long-term public diplomacy programs and activities.

Public Diplomacy as a Multi-purpose Instrument of Statecraft

A second way to think about public diplomacy is not only as an instrument of statecraft with three time frames and dimensions but also as a multi-purpose instrument cutting across all of a country's international security, economic, and military objectives and as essential to their implementation and success. According to Gregory, "[a]lthough we can define and think about public diplomacy as a single instrument, it has multiple components, each with their own organizations, budgets, tribal cultures, and rules for applying principles to behavior."[68] The public diplomacy instruments include political communication by one government directed at another government through, as already noted, the mass media, cultural diplomacy, educational exchanges and scholarships, speakers' programs, international broadcasting, and new media, but also through democracy-building (e.g., through foundations that receive public funding) and the military's psychological and open-information operations. In each case, one state is seeking to engage, understand, and influence another state. The great change today is that governments are seeing the synergy that can develop by giving their public diplomacy greater direction.

Canada's mission to Afghanistan, particularly its Provincial Reconstruction Team in Kandahar, is a good example of the effort to coordinate the public diplomacy activities of its military, aid agency, and foreign ministry. Another example of adopting a synergistic approach to public diplomacy is integrating long-term and shorter-term public diplomacy instruments to protect Canada's public image abroad, particularly in Europe, with respect to managing foreign publics' reactions to the seal hunt in Newfoundland and Labrador. It is foreseeable that a coherent, long-term academic-relations strategy focusing on exchanges between Canadian and British biologists and naturalists could lessen the negative public perception of Canada that regularly surrounds the cull each spring. A media relations strategy flowing from longer-term contact between Canadian and British experts could be premised on the exchange participants being able to speak to the British public about the rationale for the cull; hopefully, their contact would foster a more sympathetic position towards Canada on this issue.

Frequently overlooked in a discussion of public diplomacy instruments is the role played by international sport. We need not look further than the Olympic Games or any number of international sport rivalries, such as the Russians versus the Canadians in hockey, to understand the importance of sport on the international stage. El Salvador and Honduras even exchanged real bullets in the infamous "soccer war" of 1969. International sport offers insight into the powerful intertwining of sport and national image.[69] For Canada, sports play an essential part in defining the national image. Canada is associated with hockey: the image of a rugged, scrappy, northern people – a frontier image that can be compared to the American Marlboro icon. Indeed, international sports as an instrument of public diplomacy probably has the most powerful domestic feedback loop because of its ability to engender pride at home. In addition, sport can send a powerful message to the world: for example, Canada's willingness to allow Quebec and New Brunswick athletes to compete under their own flags in the Jeux de la Francophonie (the Francophone Games, a combination of artistic and sporting events for French nations) offers the world a vivid demonstration of Canada's commitment to its core values of tolerance and diversity. Sport diplomacy showcases a country's athletes and is a manifestation of the excellence of the country itself, because athletes literally represent the country's society: they are a country's ambassadors. Every country uses international sport for diplomatic advance. In fact, there is no difference between using sport and using culture as diplomatic tools. Both are means of gaining positive attention for one's country; through the efforts of their athletes, nations garner international prestige.

International business (trade and investment), tourism, and immigration, too, are often overlooked in conceptualizing public diplomacy instruments, yet they are often the most critical elements of international image management. The huge sums spent by governments and their agencies on destination branding and the efforts of countries to attract skilled immigrants (especially in the face of declining population growth in the industrialized world) cannot be ignored when seeking to understand public diplomacy. The Canadian Tourism Commission's annual budget of Can\$80 million is enviable when compared to the budgets of other Canadian public diplomacy programs. As with the Canadian Trade Commissioner Service and investment promotion, the Canadian Tourism Commission's ability to successfully brand Canada as a destination of choice, for tourism as opposed to investment, is central to the success of the Canadian economy. The goal of advertising in tourism is to create an image of Canada as a place people want to visit, that is, to associate Canada with positive images. The unintended benefit of advertising in tourism is the goodwill and positive images that it instills in the audience, even in those who never actually visit. For example, the Australian tourism campaigns of the 1980s employed images of koalas, crocodile hunters, Foster's Lager, beaches, and "shrimp on the barbie"; though now quaint and somewhat outdated, these images are nevertheless positive in that they continue to evoke favourable perceptions in foreign audiences.

Although governments have an array of public diplomacy instruments and institutions at their disposal to shape international perception, this multi-purpose form of public statecraft is not a panacea. Robin Higham, the former director general of international cultural relations at DFAIT, writes that public diplomacy is "who we say we are," but also recognizes that "what you do trumps what you say," and, therefore, what you do abroad with your foreign policy will go a long way to determining the effectiveness of your public diplomacy efforts.[70]

The Domestic Face of Public Diplomacy

A third way to think about public diplomacy is to recognize its domestic face. A country's national brand or reputation – soft power – is embedded within its society. If the values and image of a society are viewed as a national soft-power asset that will attract foreign audiences, then it is the role of the foreign ministry to harness and develop the potential of its society – its universities, business communities, and not-for-profit sectors – in support of its public diplomacy goals, which in turn support the national interest abroad. In this respect, the foreign ministry becomes a domestic department as well. The successful diplomats in today's world become what Brian Hocking calls "boundary spanners,"[71] as opposed to playing their traditional role as "gatekeepers" between governments. This is a significant change and one that highlights a major transformation of the role of foreign ministries around the world. Although public diplomacy is about

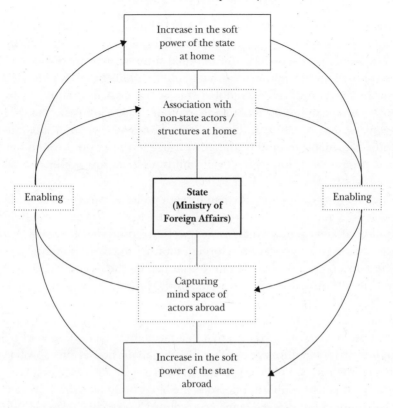

Figure 2.3   The relationship between public affairs and public diplomacy.
Source: Bátora, "Public Diplomacy between Home and Abroad," 80

engaging people outside a country's borders, an essential pre-condition for successful public diplomacy is, in the words Jozef Bátora, the "attractiveness of the ideas and values that state represents to the actors inside the state." The state needs to be attractive not only to foreigners but also – and perhaps most importantly – to its citizens, "who will then gladly associate their actions abroad with their state and hence promote its soft power."[72] This points to the need for a new networking model of diplomacy. It is now in the foreign ministry's strategic interest to enable domestic publics – students, artists, journalists – to be more informed about the country's international role. Foreign ministries need to be in the domestic game in order, for example, to understand the implications of the growing internationalization of higher education for public diplomacy activities.

To be sure, a complex picture of the future of foreign ministries and, by extension, public diplomacy is being painted. As figure 2.3 illustrates, a country cannot engage in successful public diplomacy or have a powerful national brand if its own citizens do not share, or at least understand, the government's perception of the national interest. It is in this domestic dimension of public diplomacy – that is, public affairs programs directed at its own citizens on Canada's global role – that Canada stands out from many countries in the world. More than other foreign ministries, DFAIT has recognized that domestic and international outreach are interdependent: helping Canadians to understand and engage in the world through public affairs programs at home effectively builds national soft power, as well as individual capacity.

That being said, not all Canadian foreign policy experts believe that it is necessarily a good thing for a foreign ministry to develop an active domestic public affairs agenda. Analysts such as Kim Nossal view this as undemocratic and essentially a way for a foreign ministry to co-opt domestic public opinion in support of political interests, usurping the role of Parliament.[73] The United States, through the 1948 Smith-Mundt Act, prevented the former United States Information Agency from using its substantial public diplomacy assets for domestic purposes.

It is my contention, however, that in a more interdependent world, foreign ministries need to inform their citizens about how events abroad are affecting their lives. Public diplomacy is the international face of a foreign ministry's domestic public affairs role: the latter often uses similar activities and techniques but directs them at the country's own citizens to help them interpret the outside world from a national perspective. In an increasingly "connected" world, it is difficult and, indeed, counterproductive for foreign ministries to attempt to adopt completely separate public diplomacy and public affairs tracks in their external communications activities. Domestic outreach supports public diplomacy. Domestic outreach expands a country's reach with key foreign publics by, for example, developing policy capacity on international issues of interest to the government (e.g., inviting foreign experts to Canada for seminars), and it responds to a growing desire among key segments of the population (e.g., youth, minorities, Aboriginal peoples) for greater opportunities to engage with foreign publics on international issues of shared concern by promoting informed dialogue. In addition, it reflects government priorities.

This is especially so for Canada, which, given its "liberal internationalist" foreign policy heritage, uses its role in the world, whether in peacekeeping/peace enforcement or aid-giving, to forge a national identity domestically. Considering Canada's close proximity to the United States and the spasms of national self-doubt this periodically engenders, the reflection back to Canadians of foreigners' perceptions of them is an important element of Canadian nation building.[74] Indeed, Canada's relationship with the United States is such a powerful frame of reference that it permeates virtually all expressions of national identity and pride. Canada's actions and image abroad have an impact not only on the country's international standing but also on its citizens' sense of a distinct Canadian identity and their national pride in, and attachment to, their country. In a presentation on Canadian pride, the firm Bensimon-Byrne D'Arcy defined national pride as "both the sense of self-esteem a person has for one's nation, and the pride or self-esteem a person derives from one's national identity."[75] Given the increasing number of state and non-state actors now active on the world stage, the trend towards regionalization in Canada and the diverse histories and cultures that characterize the new Canadian identity, national outreach on international policy provides one way for the federal government to speak with a national voice on behalf of all Canadians. Promoting the understanding of Canada's global role can, therefore, be a powerful source of social cohesion.

Over the last thirty years, Ottawa has been strongly of the view that promoting greater consensus at home on Canada's global role will allow Canada to make a greater contribution internationally. The 1991 Speech from the Throne stated, "to reduce Canada's vulnerability in an age of rapid, even turbulent change and of growing interdependence, it is more important than ever that we speak to the world with one clear and united voice."[76] Canada's foreign policy, especially the nostalgic attachment to peacekeeping and international assistance, reflects the values and beliefs Canadians have in common. And to the extent that Canada's contribution to world affairs is recognized, these values and beliefs are strengthened. Canada's success and reputation abroad, especially in sports, are a source of pride for all Canadians and provide them with an interpretation of the world from a Canadian perspective. Public diplomacy derives its strength from successful national public affairs programs: a country must believe in its own brand before it can expect others to do the same. Indeed, it could be argued that reaffirming Canadians' own sense of self by regularly publicizing Canada's international achievements is just as important as projecting the nation's self-image to outsiders. Therefore, Canada's international messages must resonate with and engage Canadians as much as they do the foreign audiences they are intended for, because domestic support is crucial to the success of public diplomacy.

A further perspective on the domestic face of public diplomacy concerns a country's citizens who study and work abroad and who could potentially

be a great asset to public diplomacy as "citizen diplomats." As will be elaborated in chapter 4, some countries, notably India, France, and Israel, have
given their expatriate citizens special attention (e.g., as Non-Resident
Indians) and occasionally mobilize these communities, often in times of
elections. These citizens, because they are not government spokespersons
and because they volunteer their own pride, can have greater credibility in
the eyes of local hosts. Diaspora communities can potentially play a huge
role in favourably promoting a nation's image. Conversely, because public
diplomacy tries to influence "mind space" abroad and is conditioned by a
society's belief in itself, a society that has self-doubts and does not have confidence in its government (e.g., Colombia) has citizens and diaspora communities that will not be allies in a government's public diplomacy efforts.
Indeed, they can be vehemently against the home government and may live
abroad because they cannot tolerate living in the nation of their birth.
However, enabled citizens, aware and knowledgeable of their government's policies and proudly supportive of their country, will enhance a government's public diplomacy efforts because of their credibility as
representatives abroad as students, expatriates, business people, or NGO
workers. These groups are an unexploited resource in public diplomacy.

   In sum, accelerating globalization, coupled with growing democratization, more enabled citizens, an expanding and, at times, intrusive global
media, and less reliance on hard-power assets, has meant that what governments do and say abroad rapidly translates into public debates at home. As
a result, diplomats are increasingly being called upon to become good
public communicators at home, and not just when they are assigned to
foreign postings.

   At the same time, expatriate communities, if they are positively pre-
disposed to their home countries' governments and if they have sufficient
knowledge of their home countries' national priorities, can be powerful
public diplomacy assets, since they have the potential to add credibility to
a country's public diplomacy efforts. They can also become a huge public
diplomacy challenge if they actively oppose their home countries'
regimes and lobby their host governments against their home countries'
policies. For instance, in the 1980s elements of the Sikh community in
Canada violently opposed the Indian government of Indira Gandhi and
actively resisted the efforts of India's public diplomacy efforts in Canada.
The blurring of foreign and domestic policy in tandem with a more activist civil society is thus making public affairs with domestic audiences and
public diplomacy with expatriate communities a central element of contemporary diplomacy.

THE DEBATES ABOUT PUBLIC DIPLOMACY

The Boundary Problem

Part of the confusion in defining public diplomacy, both as a concept and as a process with multiple instruments, results from competing ideas of its boundaries and scope. Some see public diplomacy as limited to long-term, government-supported educational and cultural programs (e.g., the programs of the British Council, the Goethe Institute, the Japan Foundation) and thus, presumably, as free of advocacy, since there is less control of scholars and students. Others, however, view public diplomacy as an all-encompassing term, reflecting a variety of government-supported communication activities.

Another boundary problem concerns the degree of government involvement. For instance, when Coca-Cola or the Disney corporations, as exemplars of American capitalism, engage in international public relations (e.g., when Coca Cola provides scholarships to underprivileged Mexican students), they are projecting – presumably – positive values and seeking to establish themselves as positive brands. Since these companies are so strongly identified with the United States, are they engaging in a form of public diplomacy? Certainly, they would be trying to create a positive image in Mexicans' minds about an iconic American brand, much like the successful efforts to market the Marlboro brand abroad by linking it to the American values of independence and self-sufficiency. Or, is public diplomacy being engaged in only when the lead organizing body, both directly and indirectly, for an event or initiative is government, as when the Canadian government supports Canadian Studies programs abroad? What happens if the United States organizes cultural programs around the world with the sponsorship of American corporations such as Coca Cola or Disney? Or what happens if a diplomatic mission uses its network of local contacts to showcase artists who would be in the country anyway? Can any government support directed at foreign audiences – tacit or explicit, long- or short-term, direct or indirect support – be considered public diplomacy? As noted earlier in this chapter, the line between international public relations and public diplomacy is becoming less distinct.

Delivering Public Diplomacy. Another area of confusion surrounding public diplomacy concerns whether it should be treated primarily as a medium of delivery (e.g., printed communications such as pamphlets; interpersonal communications between government officials and foreign citizens;

conventional broadcast media such as film, radio, and television; or new media), or as a value in itself, since a major component seeks to be long-term and focused on building intercultural understanding. Public diplomacy is both. The content conveyed through public diplomacy programs can be commodities if a government is promoting, for example, a cultural product (books, music, multimedia expositions, performing arts) and, at the same time, such a promotion could express the values of the country. Taking Canada as an example, foreign audiences who are exposed to the books of Rohinton Mistry or Douglas Coupland or who listen to the rock group Nickelback form a particular idea of Canada.[77] The Canadian government, by providing an opportunity for such authors or musicians to participate in foreign tours is also projecting the idea of Canada around the world.

To properly define the subject, one must consider the paradox of public diplomacy. This paradox is most evident in cultural and academic relations, where, for example, touring academics may criticize the very government that is sponsoring their international lecture series. However, as Biljana Scott writes, there is no paradox if "diversity of perspective is an essential part of the values message [that a country] wishes to export. If diversity is a key message that [a country] wishes to project abroad, then [a country] will not want [its] cultural and academic programming to be rigorously on message, as this would be perceived as a propaganda exercise." It is therefore helpful to demonstrate that there are "cleavages in [a country's] society and different points of view, including those that are highly critical" of the government that is funding the cultural and academic activities.[78]

Is It Propaganda and Psychological Operations? If "propaganda" refers to persuasive, one-way communication designed to reinforce or change opinion in the interest of the sender, then all advocacy campaigns are a form of propaganda, and by definition, some public diplomacy efforts are also propaganda.[79] The real question is whether grey and black forms of propaganda (see table 2.1), representing a continuum of deception and misinformation, can also be considered public diplomacy. There is, in fact, nothing in the generic description of public diplomacy that would exclude information campaigns or psychological operations directed by one country at the general population of another before, during, and/or after a military conflict, except that propaganda notoriously represents a one-way flow of information that is often characterized by inaccuracy and bias.[80] However, dropping leaflets over towns and cities, occupying radio bandwidth to

direct programming at civilian and enemy combatants, setting up specialized websites, sending foreign military-civilian liaison teams into conflict
zones after hostilities have ceased in order to re-establish and, in some
cases, reconstruct damaged mass media infrastructure, and creating new
programming or censoring existing content are all facets of public diplomacy, since they are communications campaigns designed by one government (or a multilateral organization representing many governments, such
as the North Atlantic Treaty Organization or the United Nations) to influence foreign publics. The only difference is that the environment in which
these information campaigns take place is one of conflict and not peace.
Public diplomacy turns into propaganda when the rhetoric far outstrips
the reality.

The United States government's use of propaganda to counter the threat
of global terrorism is particularly insightful. As reported by Jeff Gerth in
the *New York Times* in 2005, a US military psychological-operations unit
based at Fort Bragg, North Carolina, produced messages for Muslim audiences in support of the US government's objectives. The stories and news
articles, however, were admittedly one-sided and hid American author-
ship.[81] The article also noted that a Pentagon contractor, the Lincoln
Group, paid Iraqi newspapers to print positive articles written by American
soldiers at Fort Bragg – a practice decried by the US Congress and others in
Washington for its potential impact on US credibility. To underscore this
point, Gerth wrote that Iraqis claimed that no amount of money spent on
placing articles in the news or paying off journalists for positive press would
have had an impact, given the difficult and chaotic conditions being experienced under US occupation. However, the US government, according to
Gerth, sees its radio stations and newspapers in Iraq and Afghanistan as
part of "influence campaigns" that are essential to the success of its missions in these countries.

Is It Nation Branding? The discussions above raise an important question:
What is the connection between public diplomacy and nation-branding?
We are only now beginning to map the intersection of international public
relations, public diplomacy, and nation branding. International culture
and education programs, for example, assume a more dialogical and,
therefore, to use Grunig's term, a more "symmetrical" two-way approach to
public relations, one that improves mutual understanding.[82] The purpose
of these programs is to increase, over time, the degree of esteem in which a
country is held by foreign audiences; they serve to attach positive values to a
country's image. According to Kotler and Gertner, a country's "brand

equity" refers to the different reactions by different audiences to the words, actions, and products provided by that country (e.g., whether they display high or low levels of trust, confidence, and support).[83] Accordingly, a country's brand equity will permeate not only all facets of its public diplomacy strategy but, indeed, all of its diplomacy.

Scholarship in the business studies literature points to the essential contribution culture makes in national branding and diplomacy. As Simon Anholt notes, "culture, like geography, is an incontrovertible [unique selling proposition]"; however, it is the direct reflection of a country's "one-ness" that product-style marketing often erases.[84] Culture provides that all-important quality of dignity to a country's image. Anholt writes that the challenge for all countries (and this is particularly true for Canada as it attempts to modernize its image) is "to find ways of continually presenting and re-presenting their past cultural achievements alongside their modern equivalents in ways that are fresh, relevant and appealing to younger audiences."[85]

As chapter 7 will show, Canada also employs public diplomacy to help it attract foreign investment in today's increasingly competitive international marketplace; it is used as an exercise in "profile building." The goal of investment promotion is to portray Canada as an advanced trading nation through its products and services, such as those in the biotechnology industry. Its objective is to inform and influence non-government audiences, such as American chambers of commerce, public regulators, and economic lobby groups, given the major role that American firms play in the Canadian economy.

Investment promotion aims at positioning Canada as an attractive investment destination. This kind of promotion is qualitatively different from trade promotion, which involves promoting specific (Canadian) products and services in foreign markets. To further elaborate, developing Canada's image as a reliable business partner, post 9/11, is different from focused activity by trade commissioners to match their country's companies with those of their strategic partners, or from business trade shows that focus on specific sectoral business development. For example, when the Canadian Consulate General in Atlanta encourages a Canadian business person to speak to the Atlanta Chamber of Commerce about the virtues of doing business in Canada, this is a form of public diplomacy. When the trade commissioner at the consulate then subsequently tries to develop direct links between Canadian and local firms, this is business development taking place out of the public eye. The local business people have, however, been sensitized to the general Canadian business climate through the public event.

The Canadian trade commissioners' role is to use public communications to advocate for action on policies or regulations in local jurisdictions and, thereby, to create favourable conditions for Canadian business. Canada's advocacy campaigns in the United States on bovine spongiform encephalopathy (BSE, or "mad cow disease") and softwood lumber provide good examples of public information campaigns designed to sensitize both US consumers and US producers to the belief that Canadian beef is safe and that the imposition of American duties on softwood lumber is not in the interests of furthering economic ties. As discussed in chapter 7, perhaps the best example of branding Canada as a trade destination involves the Team Canada missions between 1993 and 2003.[86] Their raison d'être was long-term relationship-building, which included a strong academic-relations initiative, to bolster Canada's relationship with the host countries. It is essential for a country to have a comprehensive brand model: potential foreign investors not only want to know about marginal tax rates and the capacities of local employees; they also want to know whether this is a country in which they and their families would want to live. Thus, branding must take into account all of the associations with a country.

DEBATING THE FUNCTION OF PUBLIC DIPLOMACY

In addition to the debates around the definitions (the "what") of public diplomacy, this book also raises a multiplicity of debates around the functions (the "hows" and "whys") of public diplomacy. Some of the major ones are summarized below.

The Rifle and Shotgun Approaches to Public Diplomacy

Perhaps the longest-standing debate about the functions of public diplomacy, which started with the rise of modern public diplomacy during the Cold War, has been framed as that between the "rifle" and "shotgun" approaches, apt metaphors for short- or medium-term public diplomacy and longer-term public diplomacy. The debate pits those who view the primary purpose of public diplomacy as advancing more narrowly defined national interests against those who see public diplomacy as a self-justifying activity with an underlying "rationale of utility to the Canadian Government and its people."[87]

A variant of this debate deals with the question of whether it is ethical to have education and cultural programs housed within the same organization that is responsible for information programs and advocacy work. The reasoning is that shorter-term programs with clear objectives are somehow antithetical to developing a longer-term intercultural understanding. In short, the propagation of specific national points of view will, by definition, contaminate longer-term programs that are intended to be a country's safety net in the absence of other diplomatic relations. For example, when the United Kingdom severed official ties with Myanmar, the British Council's office in Yangon (formerly Rangoon) was allowed to remain open. Some observers have suggested that if the British Council had been associated with the United Kingdom government's official diplomacy, as it would have been had it been an organic part of the Foreign and Commonwealth Office, then the British Council would not have been allowed to maintain its cultural programs and the United Kingdom would have been without an unofficial channel with which to continue British-Myanmar relations.

While educational and cultural programming should be insulated from day-to-day advocacy and diplomatic firefighting, this does not mean that these government-sponsored programs cannot be used *strategically* to support governmental priorities. There is nothing wrong or illegitimate about matching cultural programs with Canada's diplomatic or economic policy objectives. However, the goals for longer-term programs should not be compromised for shorter-term expediency. The issue is one of balance and should be decided case-by-case.

There will always be some disparity between a government's shorter-term advocacy goals and its longer-term relationship-building goals. This disparity is normal and not necessarily a contradiction. Short-term and long-term public diplomacy can co-exist without harming the objectives of either. Presenting Canada's approaches to managing public health care, federalism, or Aboriginal governance in a foreign university is a form of Canadian public diplomacy. So, too, is convincing foreign lawmakers to change a specific piece of legislation that undermines Canadian interests if the Canadian lobbying is being conducted in a public way or more indirectly by convincing local NGOs that Canada's position has merit. Obviously, the long-term form of public diplomacy activity (the "shotgun" form) will likely pursue broader goals by trying to create a general impression of Canada, and it is likely to be directed at multiple audiences.

In contrast, short-term public diplomacy will have specific, measurable objectives – for example, did Canada succeed in changing potentially harmful legislation? However, the presentation of an aspect of Canadian public policy in an academic setting, where all points of view could be given a full airing, may also serve to sensitize local decision makers to Canada's particular positions, as long as public diplomatic efforts are well coordinated and the Canadian contingent has targeted the right audience to receive its message. Under these circumstances, short- and long-term public diplomacy complement each other. In other circumstances, when the needs of shorter-term political cycles require "hard conversations" between countries on issues where little mutual compromise is possible and where one country will eventually gain advantage or the perception of advantage (either by economic or military coercion), it may be more prudent to detach relationship-building and listening (which assumes humility, openness, and global citizenship) from the need to achieve specific short-term goals that may be attained only on the basis of a *raison d'état* and that may involve less laudable public diplomacy strategies (e.g., no-holds-barred, hard-edged public relations campaigns that may raise questions about the ethics of the source).

Such calibration of short-, medium- and long-term public diplomacy is what we should expect from political communication at the international level when national interests are at stake. It is a fact that governments must now give much greater attention to information management as fundamental to controlling "battle space." As a consequence, governments will continue to use all available means to create both a positive information space and, when deemed necessary, to engage in more directed forms of public diplomacy, such as issue advocacy and one-way forms of information campaigns that were once called propaganda (in all its variations – white, grey, and black).

This study contends that all countries engage in both "rifle" and "shotgun" approaches, from the smallest Pacific island states that may use their colourful postage stamps or rely on natural endowments such as pristine beaches to get on the global radar screen to the Great Powers with billion-dollar public diplomacy budgets. The only differences in the public diplomacy of large-, medium-, and small-sized countries lie in the organization of the structures and the budgets that can be devoted to each type of public diplomacy.

Mass Media: Agenda-Setter or Indexer?

The rise of the information age has put the role of the mass media as a framer of public opinion into stark relief. The debate revolves around whether the mass media sets the public policy agenda or whether it functions more as an "indexer" of policy positions. Politicians and government officials often assume that the mass media's role should be to reflect the world back to its audiences rather than to interpret it. They are particularly concerned that the ubiquity of the commercial mass media (e.g., twenty-four-hour satellite news channels) has made it into a powerful global agenda-setter, albeit one with a limited attention span that skips from one topic to the next as it reduces the most complex issues to sound bites. This leads to a distortion of government messages as they pass through the filter of the mass media. The challenge for governments is, therefore, to reach audiences with an unfiltered message through alternative channels such as websites, publications, personal visits to communities, and state-supported international broadcasters. However, none of these alternative channels can possibly have the reach of the commercial mass media, and it is for this reason that government seeks to manage the news. This battle to control the media agenda displays a misunderstanding about the appropriate role of the media in a democratic society. It is unrealistic in a free society to expect media to do anything at government request. In fact, the ability of a free and independent media to offer a platform for dissenting perspectives is essential to democracy. It is thus inevitable that governments will try to use "friendly media" to place stories. This is entirely legitimate, since the public has a right to know about worthy stories that are not getting the coverage they deserve.

In reality, the media is both an agenda-setter *and* an indexer. The media's power to influence decision makers will depend on the issue. A comprehensive analysis of the literature on the so-called CNN effect by Eytan Gilboa has shown that media agenda-setting is most powerful when there is a leadership vacuum and the issues are not well understood: "[t]he critical factor in all of these conclusions is leadership. If leaders don't have a clear policy on a significant issue, the media may step in and replace them."[88] Furthermore, media agenda-setting appears to be most powerful on issues that are high on the public's agenda. Since domestic issues, particularly economic growth, health care, and education, dominate the top tier of Canadians' concerns, the media's impact will tend to be highest in these areas. It would be fair to conclude that day-to-day foreign policy-making, since it is often a more elite-driven facet of public policy decision making, is far less susceptible to media pressure (especially if there are clear goals). Foreign policy decision makers thus have considerable latitude to conduct their planning and operations, though this does not mean they can ignore the media or that the media has no effect. Rather, the challenge is to manage the media, as the United States and the United Kingdom governments did by skilfully embedding journalists in combat units during the invasion of Iraq and the subsequent occupation, thus showing the increasing sophistication of government communications machines. The Canadian government adopted a similar practice by embedding Canadian and international journalists in its military mission in Afghanistan.

The debate over the degree to which the mass media can influence foreign policy decisions has profound implications for the implementation of public diplomacy programs. We cannot assume, for example, that generating local media coverage in liberal-democratic states on an issue of Canadian concern will automatically put any pressure on foreign government decision makers, especially if the issue is perceived to be a lower-rung priority in the minds of local citizens. Why would local legislators feel compelled to respond? This is not to say that Canadian embassies should cease to try to influence local media coverage in those countries where the mass media can have agenda-setting power. After all, a media strategy could attempt to develop increased awareness of an issue of interest to Canada in the local media as a way of moving an issue up the hierarchy of local priorities. This would, however, likely require a long-term strategy and sustained contact with local media organizations.

Cultural Interpenetration versus "Culture Collapse"

Globalization has led to cultural collapse with both negative and positive consequences. On one hand, governments have sought to protect cultural identity and prevent cultural loss through a variety of policies and instruments, including the UNESCO Convention on the Protection and Promotion of the Diversity of Cultural Expressions.[89] Diversity, when understood as a strategic resource instead of a barrier, can drive national innovation, creativity, and reconciliation, prompting some states to be more protectionist than others. On the other hand, the reality is that the free flow of information means that loss of diversity is inevitable. As Thomas L. Friedman, *New York Times* columnist and author, notes, a flatter world implies a convergence of norms, highlighting universal values such as the desire for freedom.[90] Educating foreign elites as part of public diplomacy programs can provide a "forceful impetus" for increasing intercultural understanding. However, it is not the case that all these foreign elites will necessarily be "converted." As the case of the Western-educated Islamic extremists responsible for the attacks of 9/11 shows, Western governments must respond directly and sensitively to the very real fear of cultural assimilation (which can turn violent) by helping local communities see the common ground between their cultures and ours. This development can be encouraged by helping to preserve local languages, creating outreach mechanisms to promote free media, and encouraging business to adapt to local cultures.

This book does not suggest that having enhanced programs to expand mutual understanding means accepting the values of another society. Cultural interpenetration does not imply diluting the fundamental values of societies. Do we, for example, accept uncritically the status of women in Saudi Arabia, the proposal for Sharia law in Ontario, or the fact that over forty-five million Americans have no health insurance? However, there is a difference between, on the one hand, seeking to understand another society better and, in so doing, coming to disagree on fundamental issues with it (and not engaging in moral relativism in public statements) and, on the other, being disagreeable or patronizing. Canadian leaders have often been guilty of the latter in their public statements on bilateral relations with the United States.

Openness versus Security

Although the current American preoccupation with public security is real and understandable, there is a debate on whether governments must choose between openness and security in a post-9/11 environment, since the two are not mutually exclusive. In public diplomacy terms, openness *is* security, since it conveys a less threatening view of a country to the rest of the world. Openness is thus a sustained value that is critical to effective public diplomacy. Some of the domestic efforts to increase security have alienated domestic multicultural communities in the United States, Canada, Australia, and the United Kingdom, making it more difficult to launch effective public diplomacy programs abroad. Especially troublesome in the eyes of some have been the restrictive visa policies that have caused a downturn in the number of foreigners choosing to study in the United States. While these policies will surely have deleterious consequences for US foreign policy in the decades ahead, since future generations of foreign elites will not be able to draw on their personal experiences of living and studying in the United States, in theory they should benefit Canada. However, statistics show that Canada has been losing its global market share of foreign students. As chapter 5 (on international education) will show, with industrialized countries competing heavily for foreign students as sources of revenue and future skilled labour, recruiters say "a country's image is everything."[91] Canadian universities are being passed over by foreign students, who wish instead to study in the United Kingdom or Australia. Canada, it seems, is perceived as bland.

THE NEW DIPLOMACY: PUBLIC DIPLOMACY

Do the above trends and debates mean that public diplomacy constitutes a "new diplomacy"? In Brian Hocking's view, "whilst newness is predicated on the argument that public diplomacy transcends an intergovernmental model of public diplomacy, in fact it relies in part on a traditional image of diplomacy. In short, is it the re-working of an old idea in response to a changing environment?"[92] The means of exercising public diplomacy are for the most part not new (with the exception of the use of new media), but the contexts in which power is being projected and the broader reformulation of where diplomacy (including its public dimension) fits into an emerging pattern of global politics are new. The wider array of governmental (central-government departments other than foreign ministries, including states, provinces, and municipalities) and non-governmental players has highlighted the relevance of a network model of diplomacy. This model recognizes the importance of public diplomacy, but in the new context of a more complex international security agenda in which the diplomat's role is increasingly to act as a coordinator and facilitator to a wide array of societal actors to address global issues. As previously stated, the major foreign policy problems of the twenty-first century – infectious disease, failed and fragile states, environmental degradation, the sustainable development of natural resources – cannot be solved by governments alone and will require the assistance of non-governmental actors and broad public support.

The diplomat in the new diplomacy adds value to the process. The diplomat lends an element of the big picture to public diplomacy by being able to sense what French historian Fernand Braudel called "the thin wisps of tomorrow that can be just picked up today."[93] According to Peter Hennessey, diplomats can recognize "those *longue-durée*, slow-pulse questions beneath the rush of events and daily reporting that shift a country, its people, its economy, its thinking, its scholarship and its identity."[94] It is the responsibility of the effective diplomat who understands public diplomacy to pick up on the significance of these slow-pulse questions because today's diplomacy is practised on a much larger playing field with many more actors vying for the public's attention.

The defining issue in Canada and elsewhere is the increasing number of government actors that are becoming involved in the process of public diplomacy. Despite the fact that the Canadian International Development Agency (CIDA) funds most Canadian scholarly visits abroad, other federal and provincial government departments and agencies are becoming actively involved as well. The same holds true in the cultural arena. Canadian Heritage plays a prominent role on most fronts, including in its responsibility for Canada's participation in such events as Expo 2005 in Aichi, Japan; government agencies such as Telefilm Canada have equally important roles in promoting Canadian culture abroad. Likewise, Canadian youth on international internships that have been facilitated by government are important public diplomacy instruments. But perhaps the most compelling public diplomacy is performed by Canada's military in some of the most unsettled regions in the world, such as Afghanistan and Haiti. In terms of the structure of public diplomacy, it is worth noting that almost every Canadian government department now has some form of public diplomacy program simply by virtue of the fact that every department now has an international relations division to allow it to deal directly with foreign interlocutors (both governmental and non-governmental).

This network of actors extends well beyond government. Much of what public diplomacy needs to be successful actually occurs outside of government. A government could never have enough resources to have a significant impact on image management and country branding. Public diplomacy, therefore, must be seen as a catalyst. While a government plays a relatively small role in overall image management, it must be able to do the following:

- articulate a cohesive national position, taking into account the history of an issue, all the facts, players, and local sensitivities;
- intervene to address misinformation or a lack of information; and
- leverage resources in support of particular policy interests (whether from the private or not-for-profit sectors or simply by mobilizing expatriate Canadians).

The most successful public diplomacy programs will use local events as "platforms" to project a favourable image of Canada to a foreign audience (e.g., by featuring a Canadian artist on a tour with a well-known local artist, rather than trying to promote a solo tour by a Canadian artist). For this reason, the most efficient public diplomacy either leverages the efforts of the private sector's international public relations activities or works with other countries' public diplomacy efforts (what Mark Leonard has called "cooperative public diplomacy").[95] So, what is a government's niche? It can connect the dots and identify the synergies, such as when a number of Canadian artists converge on a particular country. And since the diplomatic mission has the overall picture of a bilateral or regional relationship, government is best positioned to identify the timing of strategic investments (e.g., to identify when to invite a Canadian scholar to give a particular speech). The foreign ministry's unique boundary-spanning role within global networks justifies its leadership role in leveraging more dispersed public diplomacy resources from different levels of government, civil society, the private sector, and other countries in order to address common global problems.

Evaluating Public Diplomacy

In the face of globalization, governments across the world, especially those in OECD countries, have been consumed with measuring the results of their programs and policy development. The combination of the need to demonstrate value for money and the perceived failure of the United States's public diplomacy efforts in the Islamic world prior to 9/11 has prompted all members of the G8, most prominently the United States and the United Kingdom, to become much more preoccupied with trying to create an "evidence-based foundation" to justify their substantial increases in investment in public diplomacy programs and activities (e.g., through the establishment of new international broadcasting services to reach the Islamic world). The pressure for investment has occurred against a backdrop of severe criticism of past public diplomacy efforts because of what Copeland describes as their lack of transparency; blatant misallocation resources; unwillingness to terminate programs that had outlived their usefulness; lack of coordination among actors, notably between military and aid organizations; lack of alignment between public diplomacy objectives and international policy objectives; and lack of credible metrics for measuring effectiveness and, most importantly, outcomes.[96]

A report by the Advisory Group on Public Diplomacy for the Arab and Muslim World (known as the Djerejian Report, after the committee's chairman) perhaps best summarized the frustration of policy-makers with the traditional approach to measuring the effectiveness of public diplomacy: "The proper unit of measurement is not the number of publications distributed by embassies, the number of households reached by radio, or the number of speeches made by advocates of US policies. Those are all important inputs, but the key measurement is ... influencing people's views and attitudes." [97] The "cultures of measurement" are also evident in Canadian government debates on the future of public diplomacy, with the major difference being one of scale: the public diplomacy function is considered, by historical accounts (see chapter 3) and by more current and past practitioners, to be chronically underfunded, which has meant that efficiencies have been sought in programs for which there was never a critical mass of resources or objectives to begin with, making measurements of effectiveness less meaningful.

As will be elaborated in chapter 8, public diplomacy is notoriously difficult to measure (and to defend politically) because the outcomes often provide fewer tangible benefits than traditional diplomacy, and, as a result, the effectiveness of public diplomacy spending on longer-term initiatives is less likely to be measured. How do you measure the outcomes of international academic relations? What is the optimal number of foreign student scholarships that would ensure that your country has an acceptable or high level of influence – one hundred? five hundred? one thousand? Does the amount or duration of each scholarship make a difference to your country's current and future influence? Most of the evaluation is done by means of public opinion research, which is conducted following advocacy campaigns. While evaluation is necessary for both shorter- and longer-term programs to determine if public diplomacy has been successful in influencing public perception, the absence of baseline surveys hinders the interpretation of evaluation results. It is therefore impossible to calculate the impact of Canadian public diplomacy over the past thirty to forty years, because Canada does not have a public evaluation program to serve as a baseline measure of the effects of its activities abroad.

It has been an article of faith for decades among the public diplomacy cognoscenti in Canada that more funding for more Canadian Studies centres, more translated works, and more international exposure of Canadian artists is inherently positive (how could it not be?) and that the benefits to Canada, economically and diplomatically, far outweigh the government's actual investment. While the economic cost-benefit ratio is indeed good, questions have persisted about the extent to which longer-term cultural and academic programs have assisted Canada in achieving its international policy goals.

CONCLUSION

Public diplomacy has been defined as "the sum of efforts by government to promote policies and interests abroad by influencing international public opinion."[98] In the "infosphere" of ubiquitous communication, where the twin forces of global culture and cultural diversity are vying for ascendancy, the diplomatic advantage goes to countries that are able to present distinct voices and attract support based on their credibility. Globalization and the communications and media revolution have, according to van Ham, "made each state more aware of itself, its image, its reputation, and its attitude – in short, its brand."[99] For Canada, attention to developing this global brand or image is an essential part of its strategic equity.[100]

Public diplomacy, employing various time frames, instruments, and actors, continues to have many labels and represents a broad array of public relations strategies and techniques of persuasion, running the gamut from one-way information flows associated with propaganda to intercultural dialogues to build mutual understanding, and, increasingly, to military information campaigns. For the most part, the public diplomacy efforts of liberal-democratic governments rely on the powers of attraction rather than on coercion or inducement. At its core, then, public diplomacy represents a form of soft power, a commitment to the benefits of dialogue with foreign audiences. The most effective public diplomacy is not one that is supported only by government; rather, it is one whose underlying support comes from a knowledgeable and supportive domestic audience. A foreign affairs ministry's domestic public affairs strategy to generate support from its own citizens for its international goals is, therefore, the foundation for a successful public diplomacy strategy (although, surprisingly, it is one that is often overlooked). Just as globalization has led to a blurring of domestic and international policy, so too has it forced a greater connection between a nation's public diplomacy efforts and its domestic public affairs activities in support of its international interests, thereby making them mutually reinforcing.

It goes without saying that public diplomacy (directed by government) has much in common with nation branding (which can be done by government or by the private sector): they both seek to develop a long-term, positive relationship with external target audiences (albeit different audiences) in support of national interests, be they political, commercial, or security-related. Successful public diplomacy and country branding seek to "evoke a smile rather than a scowl."[101] Nation branding and public diplomacy involve positioning and, therefore, differentiating one country from another – highlighting, in a communications sense, the competitive advantage of nations. A coherent, long-term public diplomacy strategy will project a unique national identity and promote a country's values; in short, it will support and promote the national brand. It will be a way of "telling a country's story in an open, transparent and inclusive way."[102] As this book will describe, a middle-sized power such as Canada, which must navigate a more fluid twenty-first-century international system characterized by shifting alliances and emerging powers, will have to pay much more attention to its image and thus to the government-supported instruments of its soft power – its public diplomacy – if it is to fully realize its national and international objectives.

3

The Origins and Development
of Canada's Public
Diplomacy

SEAN RUSHTON

The modern context in which discourse on public diplomacy takes place is characterized by differences of opinion – sometimes subtle, sometimes overt. The debate frequently focuses on three concerns: what is public diplomacy, why is it important, and what can Canada hope to accomplish in applying it appropriately? The long road to the present concepts and practices of public diplomacy, through a landscape of Canadian governments, private industry, and war, has been fraught with ambiguity and confusion, brilliant leaps and frustrating doldrums. Yet if one thing can be said with confidence, it is certainly that the development of public diplomacy in Canada is one for which no single entity, public or private, can take credit. Competing agendas have abounded, and an overall strategy has been, on the whole, non-existent. The history of public diplomacy in Canada can be seen by some as one of controversy and improvisation.

This chapter will examine the historical development of policies, structures, and programs for Canada's information efforts abroad. It will not focus solely on the history of public diplomacy in the context of Ottawa and Foreign Affairs and International Trade Canada (known as the Department of External Affairs until 1982); to do justice to a history of Canadian public diplomacy, a wide net must be cast. And to capture the most prominent actors and organizations that have helped shape what is now known as public diplomacy, one must reach back to the time when great efforts were being made to populate Canada's vast and untamed territories and to develop its economy.

THE EARLY YEARS: IMMIGRATION AND PRETTY PICTURES

After Confederation in 1867, the Canadian government's attempts to influence foreign audiences' perceptions and attitudes toward Canada were focused on using print media to raise awareness of Canada abroad, with the view to attracting new immigrants, especially to Western Canada. Posters, pamphlets, and flyers directly related to the process of immigration were used to foster a positive image of Canada, and they had the decided effect of presenting a lifestyle based on opportunity and initiative. The idyllic prairie life depicted by government publications such as *Canada West* in the early twentieth century, targeted at skilled British and American farmers, was helpful in attracting an estimated two million prairie settlers between 1896 and 1914.[1] Although some, like scholar Laura Detre, question the success of the print campaign in attracting immigrants to Canada,[2] there are no arguments about the interest created by the wide diffusion of Canadian government-sponsored print media, a clear use of early public diplomacy by Canada to create a positive impression of the country. Even for those who did not leave their homes for a new life in Canada, a "sense of Canada" began to emerge in the international consciousness.

However effective print media may have been in influencing the global audience, new technology had emerged at the end of the nineteenth century, and the use of the motion picture projector and the rising popularity of motion picture exhibitions around the world provided a new medium for Canadian public diplomacy efforts. According to historian Gary Evans, at a time when most governments did not seem to be very impressed with the new medium as a means of communicating their educational or political agendas (they relied instead on traditional print media sources), Canada was a pioneer in recognizing the potential of film to achieve specific political ends.[3] As with print-based public diplomacy, the promotion of immigration to Western Canada was a primary objective.

As part of the effort to entice new immigrants to Canada, the Canadian Pacific Railway (CPR) was encouraged by the Canadian government in 1900 to produce the *Living Canada* series of film shorts to promote the agricultural potential and pristine beauty of the Canadian landscape. If the *Living Canada* films were in any way responsible for attracting Britons to Canada, their success was as much a result of what they did *not* show of Canada as what they did show. According to Evans, the CPR made sure that any winter scenes captured by the filmmakers ended up on the cutting-room floor, because the sponsors at the time did not want to contribute to the stereotype held by the majority of British that Canada was a land under a permanent cover of ice and snow. In any case, while it would be next to impossible to establish the impact that these films had at their premieres in England, Ireland, Scotland, and Wales in 1903, it remains a matter of record that 440,419 British immigrants came to Canada between 1900 and 1908.[4]

In addition to the CPR's charge to promote British immigration, the government also had a vested interest in attracting settlers and investors in Canadian agriculture from south of the border.[5] Many early government promotional films were sent to the United States for this purpose on a quid pro quo basis: the Canadian government arranged to have US theatres show Canadian shorts with the promise that Canada would not place any quotas on the number of US films distributed to major theatres in Canada. Canada did not place any restrictions on how US theatres would play these shorts, as long as they were played.

By 1918, the government was regularly producing commercial films to support its trade and tourism initiatives and continued to do so until World War II commenced. Canada possessed the first government film production unit in the world, and the travel films it produced between 1918 and 1927 under the direction of the Canadian Government Motion Picture Bureau were well regarded internationally for their high quality and the new perspectives they offered on Canada's wilderness.[6] Yet for all the acclaim, these early government productions were truly no more than pictures of pretty landscapes – they said nothing about the cultural or political climate of Canada. According to Evans, they were more remarkable for what they lacked than for what they portrayed: "Neither political nor propaganda, they did not appeal to basic human emotions, nor did they try to define the national purpose or seek to elicit or provoke collective action. It would be during the national crisis of war that Canada, closely allied with Britain in the struggle, would discover the capacity for mass suggestion in film propaganda's verbal and visual message."[7]

If the early films were highly apolitical, devoid of any perceptible ideological underpinnings, then Canada's participation in the two world wars certainly awakened the Canadian government to the power of film as a persuasive communication tool able to serve political ends. It should come as no surprise that Canadian public diplomacy and related information activities truly blossomed during World War I and were rekindled with great passion during World War II.

Just as the US government under President Woodrow Wilson during World War I, created the Committee on Public Information (otherwise known as the Creel Committee) to make its wartime intentions known to the world, Canada was similarly occupied, sponsoring film propaganda to support its wartime goals. These propaganda activities primarily concerned recruitment efforts and domestic concerns, such as national savings, but were prominent nonetheless. However, the real battle for the attention of foreign audiences would come some twenty years later, in World War II, as Canada sought to define its independent national identity to its allies. Following World War II, the Ministry of Information was abolished in the United Kingdom; its short tenure was marked by a perpetually strained relationship with the British Foreign Office, a tension that foreshadowed the interdepartmental strains and abrasions that would later come to characterize public diplomacy efforts in Canada.

While Canada's Government Motion Picture Bureau went back to making and distributing picturesque scenery films after World War I, the "magic" these films had once held over international audiences had been lost as audiences became accustomed to the medium. According to Evans, the films had become so mediocre and predictable in content and style that by 1935 their poor reputation preceded them around the world. In order to revive the ailing bureau, John Grierson, a renowned Scottish documentary filmmaker, was invited to "advise" the bureau on how it could revamp its work to meet the demands of global (although the emphasis was on British) audiences once again. Providing more than simple administrative advice, Grierson presented a vision of Canada's film potential that suggested government film propaganda could serve four objectives – general information, departmental information, trade publicity, and national prestige. Grierson so impressed Prime Minister Mackenzie King and his advisors that a bill was quickly drafted and passed in Parliament to enable a single body to give final approval of the film activities of all the various government departments.[8]

In 1939, the National Film Act was passed, and shortly thereafter the National Film Board (NFB) was created. With Grierson at the helm, this body became one of the primary vehicles of Canadian public diplomacy well into the late 1970s. The NFB would quickly rival the film propaganda efforts of other nations in terms of calibre and sophistication, and, according to Evans, it was successful in both "formulating a national image in the minds of Canadians and translating the national programme of communication into an international programme."[9]

Catalysts for Information Abroad: John Grierson and World War II

As World War II began, Canada realized that any semblance of control over its part in the global conflict required an unprecedented control over the

flow of information in and out of the country. German cultural imperial-
ism and aggressive Nazi propaganda efforts (especially in Latin America)
demanded a strong and coordinated counter-response, something that
Prime Minister King believed would be very difficult to achieve without a
separate information bureau. Canada had to make its war plans and efforts
better known, both domestically and abroad, and an information oversight
body would help achieve those ends.[10]

Thus, in December 1939 the Bureau of Public Information was formed
in order to fulfil a fairly simple mandate: "collect, coordinate, and disseminate to the public information concerning all phases of the Canadian war
effort."[11] The sequestering of Canadian radio and film services was executed with similar goals, but also in order to explain Canada's involvement
in World War II to foreign audiences. The subsequent production and dissemination of documentaries to Britain and the United States to portray
Canada's role in the conflict (for example, escorting Allied merchant ships
across the Atlantic with the Canadian Merchant Marines) is thought to
have marked the beginning of Canada's coordinated cultural relations
efforts with foreign countries.

During the initial phases of Canada's transition from peace to war,
Grierson recognized the need to draw film, information, and radio services
into a more cohesive and coordinated relationship, envisioning a bureau
of information similar in function to Britain's Ministry of Information.
Grierson surmised that this new bureau "should follow a considered and
single policy with respect to the problems of national unity, presentation of
Canada to the United States and [in] advising the British on Canadian realities."[12] Fortunately, Prime Minister King was of the same view. In 1941,
King reached the conclusion that if Canadians thought they were now
embroiled in a "total war," significant problems related to the delivery of
timely and accurate information about that war were widespread in the
Canadian media. As a result, King's displeasure with the media's uncoordi-
nated approach to the war effort and the failure of the Bureau of Public
Information, the "agency he had envisioned as a kind of helping hand to
speakers like himself," was clear, as the Canadian effort was criticized for
being highly unfocused and irrelevant, often sending out materials that the
press was never likely to use.[13]

Based on a report emphasizing the importance of seeing the war as a
struggle for mind and spirit, not just soldiers and weapons, the Bureau of
Public Information was temporarily replaced by the Wartime Information
Board (WIB) in September 1942, as the importance of disseminating effective and entertaining propaganda to American audiences was deemed

critical. Shortly thereafter, it was recommended that Grierson become the general manager of the WIB. Prime Minister King had concluded that "nothing was so important as the war information" and that "the government and country [were] suffering from not having proper publicity."[14] When it came to generating favourable publicity for Canada, Grierson had established on previous occasions that he was the best candidate for the job. The WIB provided him with unprecedented power to combine information policy under one roof. Already with an eye to the future, Grierson attempted "to develop the idea of Canadian nationhood looking toward a postwar and international context ... [where] there was no room any longer for the luxury of insularity and isolationism."[15] According to Evans, the result was "the establishment of a central coordinating agency which would articulate the new world the war had created. Information would be 'total' in the sense that total war had created a need to direct aims and goals externally and internally toward a larger prospect than victory for its own sake."[16]

The creation of the WIB was a direct acknowledgement of the growing importance that external audiences were beginning to play in the formation of government policy. While the WIB was allocated the responsibility of informing domestic audiences about Canada's progress in the war, it was specifically "enjoined to carry out programs beyond the borders of Canada."[17] The board was thus authorized to set up offices outside the country, which it did with some expediency, as they were quickly established in New York, Washington, London, Canberra, and Paris, as well as at various locations in Latin America.

According to Evans, in its first few months of operation, "the Wartime Information Board acted primarily as a facilitating agency, rather than itself engaging in media activities."[18] As early as spring 1943, the WIB came under attack in the Canadian press, although in a characteristically modest "Canadian tone." The criticism was levelled at "Canada's Publicity Jamboree" – an indictment of the WIB's policies and actions that few could justify as damning or even openly sceptical.[19] Yet the WIB and the NFB conducted their propaganda with minimal, if any, hate-mongering, a fact that gave Canada "a new and respected international stature."[20] Indeed, by spring 1943, the NFB reported that its film distribution in the United States alone had reached more than five thousand theatres. It appeared as though the NFB's attempt to "influence and direct the political attitudes of international audiences toward an internationally oriented post-war ethic" had struck a chord, at least with Canada's neighbour to the south.[21] In the words of Gary Evans, "One of the new attitudes which the war had fostered was the acknowledgment of the interdependency of nations on a scale never before realized. It was this new reality which ... Grierson ... hoped would replace the old nationalism which had been partly responsible for both world wars. If people and governments could be convinced that an era of international brotherhood was to follow the war, there would indeed be a brave new world."[22]

While the end of the war necessitated the demise of the WIB, along with other wartime agencies, "the patterns of production and distribution abroad of information materials initiated by the Wartime Information Board were to be maintained fairly intact." This was achieved through the creation of the Canadian Information Service and, later, the Information Division of External Affairs.[23]

When Grierson left the NFB in August 1945, he was Canada's undisputed "propaganda maestro," with a global audience for NFB newsreels estimated at a whopping forty to fifty million each week because of his efforts.[24] Since his entire film propaganda crusade had been created in the cauldron of war, would there be a place for inspirational film propaganda in the postwar world? While Grierson had grand visions of the NFB becoming the vehicle to promote what he thought should be External Affairs' postwar policies and programs of "internationalism," by 1948 the NFB had, for the most part, returned to strictly promoting tourism. Evans questions whether the NFB had come "full circle," destined to produce simple travelogues as the Canadian Government Motion Picture Bureau had done previously.[25] Arguably, there was more positive news available on Canada at the end of World War II for a global audience to consume than at any other time before or since, owing to the aggressive efforts of the Canadian government to promote itself to a receptive global public.

PEACETIME INTERLUDES AND THE COLD WAR

Like the WIB, Radio Canada International (RCI), originally named the Information Service of the Canadian Broadcasting Corporation, was also spawned by World War II. The most notable Canadian voice in international broadcasting during the Cold War, the utility of RCI has always been questioned. From its inauspicious beginnings, housed in a former brothel in Montreal, to being responsible to equally demanding masters in the Canadian government and in the CBC, RCI's challenges often appeared rather Sisyphean. Nonetheless, RCI was arguably Canada's strongest voice in Europe and its most powerful instrument for propaganda during the final months of the "hot war" against Nazi Germany and, later, during the Cold War against communism.[26]

According to historian Arthur Siegel, the relationship between the Department of External Affairs and RCI "began smoothly; it was wartime and everyone pulled together to get the service launched."[27] External Affairs insisted that it be consulted on all broadcasts, not only on the basis of being the prime organizer and financier of the young organization but also on a more legal basis, as it had positioned itself as the final authority on all policy matters during the war, exercising peerless influence and control of the International Service and the WIB. However, while the postwar expansion of RCI between 1946 and 1947 was characterized by a smooth and cordial relationship between Ottawa and the CBC, this relationship would change significantly with the onset of the Cold War.

Because it was responsible to two masters, it was not always easy to identify the voice of Radio Canada International. At times, RCI spoke as an instrument of foreign policy for the foreign minister and at others, as the more politically independent voice of the CBC. According to Siegel, these voices became most discordant during the Cold War, when a tension often developed between the degrees of truth as RCI "sought to find a working balance between its journalistic fonctions [sic] of information and communication and the interests of External Affairs in disinformation and propaganda."[28] By 1948, External Affairs' influence over RCI appeared heavy-handed. Ottawa acknowledged that RCI was the only practical vehicle for disseminating information in communist countries (where film and print distribution was not viable) and, as such, that it should at all times broadcast information that accurately represented Canadian policy objectives. The early Cold War era would witness External Affairs questioning certain loyalties within the CBC and the CBC growing resentful of its accusations and of perpetually being told "what to do and how to do it."[29]

If RCI's direction was commandeered by External Affairs during the first two decades of the Cold War, it could at least take comfort that it was headed in a single direction. The 1970s began with a renewed sense of optimism within RCI, the result of unprecedented growth and a lessening of government involvement. However, the subsequent decades would see RCI struggle not only financially but in finding its relevance in the post–Cold War era. Given that RCI served Ottawa's political aims faithfully – if reluctantly – and with a high degree of success during the Cold War, one would have thought that the international broadcaster's future was secure. However, governments of every stripe in Canada have failed to protect it, and its budget has consistently been on the chopping block. The history of RCI in promoting what would come to be called public diplomacy is highly chequered.

A Cultural Subtext

The Department of External Affairs was never content to put all its eggs in RCI's basket of information dissemination. Even before World War II had officially ended, the department had laboured to create a small information division that could act in parallel with the efforts of RCI in conducting "diplomacy" abroad. There were two broad areas of activity for the newly created division: press and information and cultural relations. According to former senior Canadian foreign service officer L.A.D. Stephens, press and information was to include "press relations in Canada, distribution of Canadian news abroad and distribution of general information material about Canada," while the latter was to cover "distribution and exchange of books, distribution abroad of films and photographs, both short-wave and recorded radio programs, supply of Canadian music art exchanges, exchange of lecturers, exchange of scholarships and arrangements of visits."[30] John Hilliker and Donald Barry write in their volume on the history of the department that the Information Division also "shared responsibility with the Department of Trade and Commerce for the distribution of noncommercial government films abroad."[31]

This was the first mention of the need for a separate External Affairs Information Division to handle cultural relations work abroad, a division that could assume the responsibility for coordinating the information services efforts of the NFB, the CBC, and the Department of Trade and Commerce.[32] The intention, as noted above, was for RCI and External Affairs to coordinate their efforts in good faith; in practice, however, this often proved impractical, as different approaches to writing material on foreign policy questions led to inter-agency squabbles and confusion.[33] It was not until 1948, with the circulation of a memorandum to Canadian diplomatic missions, that the government officially acknowledged that little attention had been paid to the philosophy of information abroad. The introduction to this memorandum is worth quoting at length, as it revealed for the first time the outlook and steps that the Department of External Affairs and the Canadian government in general were taking towards what would eventually be called public diplomacy:

> All responsible governments sincerely committed to international cooperation firmly believe that the provision of authentic public information to other countries is an integral and essential aspect of the conduct of foreign affairs. There is also growing realization that there is a similar responsibility on governments to provide fuller information within

each country on foreign policy and international affairs. Fundamentally, the reasons are straightforward enough. The speed of modern communications and of technological developments has created the physical conditions whereby the world has become a neighbourhood. Foreign affairs today are not the exclusive province of government, but are of direct, immediate and vital concern to the man and woman in the street. In the democratic states the influence of public opinion on policy is continuous and ultimately decisive. To act wisely public opinion must be in possession of the facts. In the last resort international relationships depend upon mutual understanding and comprehension not merely at the official level – but at the grass-roots.[34]

According to Stephens, Canadian intellectuals and artists had been sent abroad to Canadian missions, while CBC recordings were being sent to foreign media outlets such as radio stations and libraries: "From 1946 to 1947, diplomatic posts reported regularly or spasmodically on their information activities and it is apparent that quite a number of missions were carrying on some level of what would now be regarded as cultural relations."[35] In 1945, the Canadian mission to France installed its first cultural counsellor position, influencing this trend.[36] However, the cultural accomplishments of these various missions were sporadic and unfocused, as were half-hearted attempts in 1947 and 1948 to determine what value Canada was getting for its investment in these efforts.[37]

This situation changed dramatically during the early 1950s, when cultural relations work underwent a considerable period of growth, mainly as the result of a key initiative set into motion by the recommendations of the Massey Commission. In 1949, Prime Minister Louis St Laurent asked, *inter alia*, for the Massey Commission's advice on "methods for the purpose of making available to the people of foreign countries adequate information concerning Canada."[38] The Massey Commission was especially fervent in its belief that Canada should get behind more cultural exchanges, and it concluded that at that time, in 1950, they were virtually non-existent. The commission envisioned a central body with expert capabilities "in the fields [of] education, the arts, humanities and social sciences which would be supportive of the external dimension of Canadian cultural life."[39] The body that the Massey Commission had in mind eventually received royal assent, and in March 1957, the Canada Council for the Arts came into existence, thus paving the way for "a significant program of international cultural relations" to begin the next decade that was just on the horizon.[40]

THE BIRTH AND GROWING PAINS
OF CULTURAL RELATIONS
ABROAD

While the Massey Commission underscored the importance of culture in international relations as early as 1951, recognizing it as a component of effective foreign policy, it said very little regarding the specific ways in which culture might be put to use in serving Canada's foreign policy agendas, although it did emphasize the use of "highbrow" culture.[41] This is not to say that the government and its affiliated agencies had been lax in creating and distributing cultural materials to the United States, Europe. or South America from 1951 to 1968.[42] Indeed, the NFB, the CBC, and the Canadian Government Exhibition Commission were quite active during this time.

Yet opinions continued to differ on the need for a central information-coordinating body. While it was the view of many that information activities – whether from the CBC or the NFB, for immigration, trade, or tourism – had seemed to do just fine on their own, operations at diplomatic missions continued to be "random, *ad hoc* affairs, often no more than the chance product of pressure from an interested official or senior officer, subsequently shaped by whomever the Department [of External Affairs] could throw into the slot."[43] What was missing was a guiding strategy to provide cohesiveness for all the cultural activity. Without a clear and unified directive, departments and agencies duplicated efforts at the best of times and contradicted each other on a more frequent basis.

One problem identified by the Royal Commission on Government Organization (otherwise known as the Glassco Commission), launched in 1960, was the rotational nature of staffing in the Information Division of External Affairs. In the commission's view, this produced a considerable challenge to the continuity of functions within the division. According to Stephens, this problem was most likely twofold: on one hand, the senior staff placed little importance on the information officer function, while on the other, the post itself was not considered profitable for the careers of those holding the positions.[44]

In November 1962, Marcel Cadieux, then the deputy undersecretary in the Department of External Affairs and a strong supporter of cultural diplomacy, was asked to speak at the Sixteenth Annual Conference on Canadian Information Abroad at Montebello, Quebec, to discuss the coordination of all federal agencies involved in international cultural activities.

It was hoped that Cadieux's belief that "information and cultural work is not a matter for a few specialists but ... is the responsibility of all our officers at all our missions"[45] would spur a renewed interest in staffing positions at missions for the conduct of information and cultural programs. But it did not. Interdepartmental coordination would continue to be marked by frustration and an unwillingness of departmental members to diminish their role within their own departments. In response, Cadieux attempted to draft an interdepartmental formula to increase cooperation, but he would soon confess that his efforts were hampered by the fact that there were "few common threads running through the diverse programmes of the twenty departments and agencies."[46]

While cultural affairs activities moved ahead with an awkward yet undeniable momentum, it was not until 1966 that a separate Cultural Affairs Division was created from the strictly information stream of External Affairs. According to Stephens, the reason for the sudden need of a separate cultural body was essentially threefold:

- requests from other countries for cultural exchange arrangements had grown louder and demanded an immediate response;
- the creation of the Canada Council for the Arts had provided a resource base of cultural expertise and operational capacity for application abroad that needed to be deployed; and
- the Quiet Revolution in Quebec and the province's particular interest in its own international relations had spurred the government into a rather urgent demonstration of its leadership in foreign relations and its sympathetic views toward Quebec's aspirations within Canada.[47]

When Quebec asserted itself more strongly in the international arena with plans to negotiate academic exchanges with France, the government, under the charge of Prime Minister Lester B. Pearson, responded in kind with cultural and academic arrangements with the governments of France, Belgium, and Switzerland.[48] Fuelled by competitive pressures, the formation of Canada's "biculturalism" as a cultural export was well under way. Artistic exchanges in French-speaking countries were particularly popular, and bursaries and scholarships for these were plentiful. In 1965, the Accord Cadre, a formal cultural agreement, had been signed with France, and financial resources for cultural programs with French-speaking countries were increased by Can$750,000, a seemingly small sum by today's standards but quite a treasure chest in the mid-1960s.

With the establishment of the Cultural Affairs Division, the Department of External Affairs was for the first time treating cultural activities as distinctly different from information activities. In the words of historian Mary Halloran, "Ottawa had moved, however tentatively, into the arena of international cultural relations."[49] Ironically, as the government was taking its first steps toward an official program of Canadian diplomacy abroad, a large number of Canadians were beginning to take an interest in other countries and were becoming more vocal about the scarcity of information about Canada abroad.[50] With criticism of this perceived laxity on the part of the federal government on the rise, a full departmental review of public information activities abroad was conducted by External Affairs in 1966, a review that, according to Stephens, was to be a harbinger for how information activities would be perceived in the 1970s.[51] The review detailed the raison d'être of Canadian public diplomacy (still called public information activities abroad) in the following way:

Since the Second World War ... the Department of External Affairs and other Government Departments have made an effort to make Canada, its people, their life and aspirations better known to the world ... From many quarters the impulse to share knowledge of our country has been spontaneous, born of pride in our national resources, institutions and achievements and the determination to gain wide recognition for these ... Under rational examination, simply to impart information to the rest of the world about Canada is not a self-evident national objective; information work abroad must aim to and, in a broad sense, must be shown to support and advance Canadian interests. The ultimate objectives of such information work are those of external policy; to guarantee the security of the nation, to attain the highest possible degree of national prosperity and, in this pursuit, to fulfil those specific obligations to the rest of the world which enlightened self-interest or the humanitarian desires of the Canadian people may demand.

The central work of a Foreign Office and a Foreign Service is the conduct of government-to-government relations and in this work an information service has no direct role to play ... In the modern world of fast communication and of vastly expanding literacy and general education, it is not enough to talk to governments and to persuade them; the people – at least an informed cross-section of them – must be aware of the nature, intentions and the country with which their government is talking and, in the long haul, the people must be persuaded that

certain features make that country a valid and worthy interlocutor. To
present such a picture and to persuade public opinion ... is the underlying job of an information service.[52]

Despite this lucid articulation of purpose and intent for projecting Canada's image and values abroad, a period of austerity clouded the department in 1969, and any momentum gathered was abruptly halted or even
reversed. External Affairs was called upon to curtail most of its expenditures and activities, and plans in the making for ambitious extensions of
domestic influence abroad had to be deferred – jobs were lost and missions
were closed.[53] Yet, as will be shown, whatever momentum was lost during
this period of fiscal restraint was recovered during the tenure of Prime Minister Pierre Trudeau (1968–84, with a brief Conservative interlude from
1979 to 1980). Some consider it no coincidence that it was during the Trudeau years that foreign cultural relations returned to prominence, particularly because of the importance placed by the government on projecting a
united image of Canada – especially after the 1980 Quebec referendum –
around the world. The reinvigorated effort to share Canada's values and
culture was personally championed by Prime Minister Trudeau. Over
twenty years later, following the 1994 parliamentary review of Canada's foreign policy, cultural diplomacy would be referred to as the "third pillar" of
Canada's international relations.

THE TRUDEAU YEARS: RENEWAL AND INVIGORATION

The importance of international cultural relations was recognized by the
Trudeau government early on. According to Mary Halloran, Trudeau had
shown "a willingness to challenge some of the underlying assumptions gov-
erning the conduct of Canadian foreign relations" even before he had
taken office, and it was not long after doing so in 1968 that he initiated a
Department of External Affairs–led review of Canada's foreign policy.[54] It
had become clear to the Trudeau government that the preceding years of
austerity had led to a "dispersion and Balkanization" of government information endeavours abroad and that a "new and different machinery" was
urgently needed.[55] A series of six booklets setting out the general principles by which foreign policy was to be governed, *Foreign Policy for Canadians*,
was subsequently published in June 1970.

The foreign policy papers emphasized that a single entity that would be
responsible for implementing the extension abroad of national policies
was needed and that cultural activities would be the vehicle for those poli-

cies. When the review considered whether External Affairs or a relatively independent information service should be set up, it recommended that, to be effective, "information policy must be closely related to other aspects of Canadian international policy. The logical organization to plan and carry out the information programme would, therefore, be the Department of External Affairs."[56] The study reaffirmed that cultural exchanges should seek to underline Canada's commitment to a bilingual, if not a multilingual, society. With that end in mind, Canada reached out once again to strengthen ties not only with France but with other French-speaking countries in Africa, Asia, and the Caribbean. The report also reiterated the importance of academic exchanges, recommending that "new and desirable links" be initiated with universities, also emphasizing that the department had already "provided financial assistance to university professors to assist in research projects ... [and] summer employment to university professors to work on specific projects of interest."[57] The main goal of this push for renewed and vigorous university relations was straightforward – to obtain "understanding for and, as far as possible, support for Government external policy ... as indirectly, assistance in recruitment, training and research from the universities can bolster the Department's capability to do its job of carrying out established policy and recommending the development of policy."[58]

Out of all the "think tanking" going on, a set of conclusions and recommendations was made, most notably,

1 That an advisory panel of scholars be appointed to assist the Department in conducting the various aspects of its relations with the academic community; and
2 That the Department undertake a systematic programme of commissioning scholars to work in the department to undertake research for Departmental purposes which cannot be performed within the present personnel limitations by our own officers.[59]

In addition to recognizing the importance of systematic links with domestic actors, another critical feature of the Trudeau government's foreign policy was the so-called "third option," a proposal in 1972 to lessen American cultural and economic influence on Canada.[60] In addition to the stated objective of strengthening national unity, the Trudeau government made no secret of its desire to build and export a Canadian cultural identity that was distinct from that of the United States, in order to reduce the country's "excessive reliance" on its American neighbour, chiefly by exposing

Canadians to the benefits of trade diversification.[61] The department's Cultural Affairs Division was a leading player in furthering these goals, and, following the lead taken by Prime Minister Pearson to extend cultural exchanges beyond France to other countries that were substantially represented in the Canadian population, agreements were reached with Italy, West Germany, the Netherlands, and Switzerland. Relations with the Soviet Union and China were also pursued, and scholarship programs and academic exchanges with these two countries were established.

As Halloran notes, new cultural centres were also opened in London, Brussels, and New York, in addition to the original location in Paris, and cultural affairs officers continued to administer the department's programs in important locations such as Bonn, Mexico City, Moscow, New York, Rome, Tokyo, and Washington.[62] The work of cultural promotion celebrating performing artists, Canadian art and film festivals continued, often through bilateral relations with the NFB, the CBC, the Canadian Government Exhibition Commission, and Information Canada. The latter came into being in April 1970 and was based on Trudeau's foreign policy review recommendation to create centres abroad to inform foreign publics about the actions and policies of the Canadian government; the first of these centres were opened in London and Paris the same year. While the Trudeau government did not successfully implement a *long-term* strategy for the continuation of cultural relations programs and activities abroad (although it did adopt one), Halloran notes that the Trudeau era was "undeniably one of enormous growth in the range and sophistication of Canada's activity in international cultural relations."[63]

THE POWER OF THE PODIUM: SPORT IN PUBLIC DIPLOMACY

A fair sketch of Canada's chequered public diplomacy legacy would not be complete without mention of the historical importance of sport in Canada's foreign relations policies and related activities. Indeed, it is through sport that the more general progress of public diplomacy in Canada can be seen. While the 1980s generally ushered in an era of severe budgetary reductions that have disproportionately affected cultural programs to this day, the decade was also briefly witness to a renewed interest in a unique vehicle of Canadian public diplomacy: sports. In 1987, the Secretary of State for External Affairs, Joe Clark, very publicly confirmed the government's intention to harness the power of sport to promote Canada's image abroad and to become more involved in the international sport scene in general.[64] Yet international sport had played a significant, if less formal and politically self-aware, role in Canada's "branding" and other foreign relations activities as early as 1883, when Canadian lacrosse teams – in a fashion very similar to what happened with the *Living Canada* film shorts – toured the United Kingdom acting as, according to Macintosh and Hawes, "both athletes and emigration agents to attract settlers to the Canadian West."[65]

This informal and relatively unconscious form of diplomacy through sport was typical of the era preceding World War II. Although Prime Minister Mackenzie King even expressed public disdain for the 1936 Olympic Games, which were hosted by Nazi Germany, ironically, this public expression was evidence that sport was beginning to play a role in international politics.

It was once again the spectre of war, this time the Cold War, that catalyzed the Canadian government into action. Influenced by the Soviet Union's decision to use sport as a tool to promote its communist ideology abroad, sport began to take on an increasingly important role in Canadian society, both domestically and internationally. In 1949, Lester Pearson, then Secretary of State for External Affairs, simply stated that international sporting contests "had grown into events of some political importance." In the 1950s, the exponential growth of television viewership and its influence on society made it all the more important for Canada to perform well in front of an ever-increasing viewing audience around the world. In addition, Canadian ambassadors abroad "were quick to inform the secretary of state for external affairs about the extent to which international sports events were used for political purposes in Europe, particularly in the Soviet Union."[66] By the 1970s, most developed nations were already recognizing the power of athletes and sport to promote prestige and recognition abroad and were investing in state-sponsored athletes and programs accordingly.

However, as was the case with rallying support for World War II, domestic concerns were also a key reason for Canada to develop an international-calibre sporting capability. Seeking to bridge a growing gap between Quebec and Canadian society at large, the Canadian and Quebec governments saw sport as a way to strengthen national unity. One outcome of this concern was the creation of the Canada Games in 1966. The first games were held in Quebec City the following year, during Canada's centennial celebration. Similarly, the decision to establish Hockey Canada in 1969, along with a multitude of other government-supported sport organizations, was motivated by the desire to promote national unity. Yet, as was the case with the early war propaganda efforts, these sports organizations, and indeed the athletes themselves, would soon be used as tools of foreign policy and image building abroad.

Macintosh and Hawes identify the emergence of "hockey diplomacy" in Canada's international relations as a product of the Cold War. It was during this time, when Canada endeavoured to use sport, and hockey in particular, in its position as a "middle power" and "peacekeeper" to mediate the tensions between the East and West, that it had some success.[67] Interestingly, it was not until the 1972 Canada-Soviet hockey "summit series" that the impetus was provided for the creation of the International Sports Relations Desk in the Public Affairs Bureau in the Department of External Affairs. This bureaucratic development symbolized the dynamic between international sport and foreign affairs as expressed through Canada's ongoing commitment to multilateralism and peacekeeping.[68]

The Ben Johnson doping scandal of the 1988 summer Olympics in Seoul, the Canadian decision to boycott the 1980 Olympic Games in Moscow, and the poor performance of Canadian athletes at the 1976 summer Olympics in Montreal revealed a less favourable national image, just as a world hockey championship or the composed performance of Jamie Salé and David Pelletier at the 2002 Salt Lake Olympics reinforced a positive national image. In an era of instantaneous twenty-four-hour news coverage, the power of the podium had become increasingly influential. The positive impact of a country's athletes winning gold medals or the shame incurred during a national doping scandal, played out in front of billions of people around the world, highlighting the tremendous influence that sport exerted over a country's image and prestige.

CONCLUSION

As noted at the beginning of the chapter, no one entity, public or private, can take credit for the development of Canada's public diplomacy. Competing agendas flourished, but a comprehensive national strategy did not exist. The history of public diplomacy in Canada is, therefore, essentially one of improvisation. While some efforts – ultimately stillborn – were made to coordinate public diplomacy by establishing a cross-government governance structure, considerably less attention was paid to designing and executing a whole-of-country approach (one including the private sector) to the management of Canada's international brand.

This chapter has also shown that Canadian public diplomacy came into real focus in the 1970s, especially in the arena of international sporting events. Starting in the late 1980s and continuing into the 1990s, Canada's public diplomacy would become seriously out of focus owing to major government-wide budget cuts in response to the federal deficit and confusion over departmental mandates. Within DFAIT, the resources for international culture and education shrank and the profile of cultural affairs work declined. Following a re-organization in 1992, the department transferred its responsibilities for international exhibitions and international sport to other federal departments. DFAIT's cultural relations programs would have been transferred to the Canada Council for the Arts had the Senate of Canada not intervened to block this action. The federal government's 1995 foreign policy statement would offer a respite to this downward trajectory of the role of cultural diplomacy by validating the importance of the promotion of culture and values as the "third pillar" of Canada's foreign policy. As this study will show, in the subsequent decade, Canada's public diplomacy would begin to recover some ground but would also continue to be the subject of debate over adequate levels of funding, organizational mandates, the evaluation of results, and the best means of using traditional and new media tools.

PART TWO

The Instruments

4

Public Affairs and International Cultural Relations

Cultural relations represent the "linchpin of public diplomacy."[1] Canadian visual arts, music, dance, film, and literature have influenced many within Canada and inspired countless others throughout the world. Together, they represent an intellectual dimension of Canadian public diplomacy. The unique character of Canada has been expressed in myriad ways, including through the art of Emily Carr and the Group of Seven and Tom Thomson, and through native Canadian artists such as Norval Morrisseau; the music of Glenn Gould, Neil Young, Diana Krall, Leonard Cohen, Oscar Peterson, and Shania Twain; the choreography and skill of Cirque du Soleil and the National Ballet of Canada; the acting of Mary Pickford, Christopher Plummer, and Roy Dupuis; the directing of Norman McLaren, Claude Jutras, Denys Arcand, and Norman Jewison; and the inspired writing of Robertson Davies, William Gibson, Alice Munro, Margaret Atwood, Michel Tremblay, Rohinton Mistry, and Yann Martel. Indeed, as John Ralston Saul has written: "Canada's profile abroad is, for the most part, its culture. That is our image. That is what Canada becomes in people's imaginations around the world. When the time comes for non-Canadians to buy, to negotiate, to travel, Canada's chance or the attitude towards Canada will already have been determined to a surprising extent by the projection of our culture abroad."[2]

The work of Canada's "cultural diplomats" thus helps to create a "foundation of trust" with people around the world, which in turn contributes positively to the environment in which Canada practises its international relations.[3] There are also Canadians who have garnered name recognition among the attentive international audience and who are known for their achievements and contributions to public life. They include, but are certainly not limited to, Norman Bethune, Lester B. Pearson, Marshall

McLuhan, Stephen Lewis, and Michael Ignatieff. They, too, contribute to creating a more sympathetic international audience and thus a more receptive environment in which to project the national interest.

Cultural relations and public affairs or information activities (e.g., media relations, official publications, websites, public policy seminars, and speech management) at missions abroad are what most informed observers associate with a country's public diplomacy. The purpose of this chapter is thus to describe the various instruments and programs, the objectives they are designed to fulfill, the audiences that are to be reached, the channels that will be used, and how the effects will be measured. The discussion will begin with what is the bread and butter of foreign policy communications, namely, the shorter-term information programs anchored by the media relations conducted by diplomatic missions, and it will then move to the longer-term platforms of cultural diplomacy and international sports events for projecting influence. International education, which is frequently perceived as part of cultural diplomacy, warrants a separate examination (see chapter 5).

PUBLIC AFFAIRS: EXPLAINING AND ADVOCATING

The strategic use of the media is elemental to the craft of diplomacy for Canadian officials overseas. Given the media's primary agenda-setting role in modern society, media relations are one of the most powerful forms of public diplomacy. The media, or "fourth estate," has become, in certain political environments and to the chagrin of many observers who lament the decline of civic democracy, more important than the elected members of legislative assemblies. The assumption is that in liberal democracies the media is an independent actor, scanning the public domain, choosing certain topics and not others, and putting particular "frames" on the stories that are covered. Although the relative independence of the mass media is the subject of intense debate by scholars and practitioners alike, outlining this debate is beyond the purview of the present study. What is not debated, however, is that the mass media can be a powerful actor and agenda-setter: it can reach broad swaths of the general public, the attentive public, and opinion formers.[4] In this way, it can either assist or hinder the efforts of nation states to achieve their international objectives.

For foreign ministries, there are actually two media relations operations under way at any given time: operations by the media relations office at headquarters, which is responsible for managing relations with domestic media and foreign correspondents, and the media relations operations by

individual missions abroad. (In many foreign services the size of the mission will dictate whether the press attaché's function is separate from the
public affairs function.) The operating style of the media office will depend
on the level of openness of the society and the local media cultures. As in
Canada, the global media can be divided into various categories based on
the medium (print, broadcast, Web-based), the ideological perspective,
and specialized or mass circulation. It is the mission spokesperson's job to
match the right message with the right media outlet, depending on the
policy objective. The foreign press attaché (an individual working in the
media relations office of a diplomatic mission) in a country with an open
media culture such as the United States will have different challenges and
opportunities from those of his or her counterpart in Tehran or Beijing.
Local media cultures and, in particular, the type of relations between the
domestic media and local governments will dictate the style of foreign press
attachés. For instance, in some countries (e.g., Japan), there are foreign
media clubs that function as networking hubs for local press attachés; in
other countries, press attachés have to establish more independent working relationships with local journalists and institutions.

The primary responsibility for the media relations officers at Foreign
Affairs and International Trade Canada, whether at headquarters or
abroad, is to ensure that the department's and the federal government's
messages and initiatives receive media coverage and that the coverage is
fair and accurate. Media relations officers are trained to *explain* rather than
advocate government policy, although sometimes it is hard to differentiate
between the two activities. At times there is confusion on this point, since
advocating the government's position is perfectly acceptable for a Canadian official abroad. However, the standard caveat for public servants working in these information service roles for the federal government in
Canada is that their work should not become politicized; their job is to
explain government policy, programs and, services.[5] Ministers' political
staffs, such as a director of communications or communications assistants,
advocate in the political party sense. The line between the two types of
activities can obviously become a grey one, and most experienced government media relations officers, when they are operating in Canada, have an
intuitive sense of the difference between explaining/informing and advocating in their day-to-day interactions with the media.

Canadian media officers abroad have the more general objective of
informing local audiences about Canada and ensuring, if not positive coverage of Canada and its priorities, then at least accurate coverage. Unlike
media relations officers at headquarters, media officers at missions have

more latitude to operate, since they do not have to coordinate their activities with a minister's communications team. As the local media are often
the most informed members of a society, it is important for mission media
relations staffs to cultivate relationships with members of the local media
and also with Canadian foreign correspondents (e.g., with correspondents
of the CBC/Radio-Canada, the *Globe and Mail*) in London, Paris, New York,
Washington, or Beijing. However, a quid pro quo is involved here. Local
journalists must be provided with a story that does not reflect a sense of
Canadian self-importance, or, to put it laconically, have "yet-another-
important-Canadian-initiative" feel about it. It should not be forgotten that
while both the foreign official abroad and the journalist (foreign and Canadian) want to know what is going on, they want that information for very
different reasons. The journalist's responsibility is to get as close to the
truth as possible through dogged but fair and balanced reporting; the diplomat's responsibility is to represent his or her country's interests to a foreign audience or to reflect them back to a domestic audience. Sometimes
the respective loyalties overlap, but not always. At the same time, each pro-
fession needs the other: the journalist needs access to decision makers; the
public diplomat needs the platform of the media to reach broad and
narrow audience segments.

Canadian public diplomacy officials have an opportunity to make a political impact in a wide range of countries. However, interviews with Canadian
heads of mission (past and present) suggest that in smaller- or medium-
sized countries, a modest investment in public diplomacy resources can
result in a greater media impact than if a more sizeable investment is made
in large Canadian missions. Often, in larger countries, the competition for
attention is much fiercer, and, historically, Canada's competitors have concentrated their public diplomacy resources at a level that is several times
greater than Canada has been able to realize. The job of a Canadian media
attaché abroad in the G8 countries, where Canada would have significant
interests, can therefore be frustrating. The reality is that, with a few exceptions, references to Canada are virtually nonexistent in the world's major
print and broadcasting outlets. A regular reader of the higher-quality newspapers in the United Kingdom would most likely have his or her stereotypes of Canada confirmed (e.g., in recent years, stories of bear attacks on
unsuspecting joggers in Canada have been popular) or receive only the
most rudimentary information about Canada's political and social landscape.[6] This means that either Canada is not interesting enough for local
audiences to be covered on a regular basis or that Canadian media relations officers are not doing enough to get local editors to pay attention to

Canadian stories, much less to Canada's international policy priorities. Significantly, a content analysis of quality British newspapers by Canada's High Commission in London found that 60 per cent of the news coverage of Canada dealt with culture, suggesting that culture is an effective means of keeping Canada top-of-mind for foreign audiences.

Canada's agenda-setting challenge (that is, its attempts to "earn" media coverage in major international media centres such as London and New York) can be perceived either as being an impossible battle for attention, because there is simply too much competition, or as offering a multiplicity of opportunities to get noticed, given the wide range of media outlets. A front-page story in the *New York Times* on Canada or on a policy proposed by Canada, if positive in tone, can provide a degree of publicity that would be impossible to afford through paid advertising. On the other hand, foreign media coverage of Canada, particularly in the United Kingdom, the United States, and France, receives instant playback in the Canadian media, particularly if it is negative. The Canadian media, for example, reported with glee that the *Economist* had labelled Prime Minister Paul Martin as "Mr Dithers." The label stuck and was soon used by domestic commentators. Similarly, repetitive and extensive coverage of Canada's record on border security since September 2001, notably by the pundits and commentators of Fox News, is less helpful to Canada, since it is often only a partial rendering of the facts (see chapter 9).

John Ralston Saul makes the apt observation that one reason Canada is largely off the global radar screen is that it is often absent in the international media's coverage of trends, for instance, when a journalist compares national performances in education or industrial production or health care. The American media tends to include statistics from the United States, some European Union (EU) member states (typically the United Kingdom, France, and Germany), and Japan. The European media's coverage, meanwhile, would typically include more EU member states and the United States.[7] The cumulative effect of being left off a graphic representation of a trend is that Canada is absent from the "imagination of the reader."[8]

As described in the history of Canadian public diplomacy in chapter 3, the introduction of cultural relations into the arsenal of Canada's public diplomacy during the Cold War meant that media relations, or information programming as it was then called, was no longer the primary means of communicating with foreign audiences. Although media relations lies at the heart of a mission's information programming, it is by no means the only means of getting key messages out to influential, or potentially influential, audiences. Ambassadors spend large portions of their working days giving speeches to local business audiences, universities, and service clubs, in support of strategic communication objectives. There are also other information programs, such as sponsoring and hosting seminars (e.g., creating a program of dialogue to encourage the peaceful resolution of local conflicts), as well as publishing mission newsletters and managing the mission website. In addition, all G8 foreign ministries have some form of foreign visitors program, which they use to invite targeted foreign opinion leaders (e.g., journalists, academics, business leaders, military officers) to their countries. The purpose is to cultivate beneficial current and future relationships. Although information programming is part of the routine of public diplomacy, it could be argued that cultural programs have the power to reinforce a Canadian presence, especially given the absence of Canada from international media coverage.

INTERNATIONAL CULTURAL RELATIONS

Governments exercise very little direct control over the total volume of international cultural exchanges, which invites the question: why is cultural diplomacy important?[9] Culture has always been used for diplomatic advantage, for several reasons. One of its great advantages as an instrument of influence is that it is a lower-risk form of international relations. Moreover, it can represent excellence (most of the time) and universal values, such as the right to freedom.[10] Also, audiences regard cultural diplomacy as a more legitimate form of public diplomacy than information programming (e.g., government-supported radio and television programming and publications) because it is perceived to be less mediated. In short, governments have less control over the messages conveyed through culture. This can create a fundamental dilemma: the government uses its international communications tools to counter misinformation, carry out international "damage control," and attract global attention for its initiatives, yet the greatest foreign credibility accrues to those activities and symbols of national identity that are perceived to be at arm's length from government and that the government supports but does not control. (See also the discussion on international broadcasting in chapter 6.)

There will, however, be times when the messages emanating from cultural programming (e.g., promotional tours for books, television, and film programming) will not be flattering to the country that is promoting them. This seems paradoxical, yet it is probably a more powerful form of public diplomacy for just this reason. For example, if the Canadian government sends groups of Aboriginal leaders to foreign countries to discuss the history of Canada's treatment of its First Peoples, this will surely cover some uncomfortable ground. However, it will also send a message that Canada is an open nation, willing to discuss the darker parts of its past. Germany has adopted a similar, more open approach to dealing with the period of Nazi dictatorship, and this is reflected in its cultural diplomacy with some success.

Although Canada, unlike France, has not used culture as a main pillar of its foreign policy, it is nonetheless true that Canada is one of the few countries that can both defend the inherent benefits of cultural diversity to a global community and also be a significant exporter of culture. The federal department of Canadian Heritage has six cultural trade commissioners engaged in some of Canada's major international posts (London, Paris, Berlin, Beijing, Shanghai, and Tokyo) as part of a wider global network to promote Canadian culture. As Canadian senator Serge Joyal wrote in his seminal 1994 report, "[i]nternational cultural affairs is one instrument which is capable of enhancing public perception of our diplomatic initiatives, strengthening networks at home and abroad, and providing a basis for a wide range of Canadian and foreign partnerships."[11] For Canada, cultural diplomacy should, in theory, have prime importance, since some observers have claimed that Canadians are often so preoccupied with telling the world that they are not the United States that they have little time to define who they are. Because of geography and given that Canada's 32 million citizens live next to more than 300 million Americans (with 75 percent of Canadians living within 150 kilometres of the border with the United States),[12] Canada's position, especially on foreign policy matters, is frequently assumed by those outside of North America to be that of a follower. Ralston Saul indicates that, as with certain East European nations such as Poland, Bulgaria, and Ukraine, it is difficult for Canada to project a distinct image abroad. Public diplomacy through cultural relations thus represents a primary means of informing the world that Canada does not share the same perspective as the United States on every issue and that it should not, as a result, be confused with its southern neighbour.

As chapter 3, on the history of Canada's public diplomacy, demonstrates, Canada's international cultural relations are really a product of the Massey Commission, the Cold War, and Quebec's growing desire to present itself on the international stage. As a result, Ottawa made a significant investment in international cultural and educational programs between the late 1960s and the early 1980s. However, by the 1990s, the confluence of budget cuts and post–Cold War euphoria (and triumphalism) meant that there

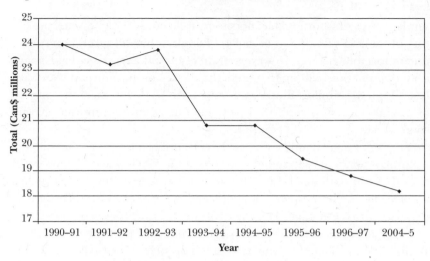

Figure 4.1   International cultural affairs and academic relations budget, DFAIT.

Sources: Joyal, *Refocussing Canada's International Cultural Policy in the Nineties*, table 12; and DFAIT budget, 2004–5. The budgets are in current dollars.

were fewer incentives and needs in Canada and other Western countries to continue to invest aggressively in building intercultural understanding.

As a result of the 1995 foreign policy review, the promotion of culture and values was recognized as a "third pillar" of Canada's foreign policy;[13] in theory, it was equal to the first two pillars of promoting economic growth and international peace and security. However, just when it seemed that public diplomacy would receive some well-deserved attention, the federal government was forced to engage in a major budget-cutting exercise to reduce the federal deficit. Instead of investing in the instruments of Canada's foreign policy, it called for across-the-board budgetary cutbacks, which sliced disproportionately into the communications and, therefore, the public diplomacy functions. There was soon a gap between the rhetoric of enhancing the third pillar of Canada's foreign policy and the reality of budget cuts under the government's Program Review.[14] Rather than being one of expanding public diplomacy programs, the issue became one of survival. As figure 4.1 illustrates, DFAIT's total budget for cultural and academic relations was lower in 2004–5 than in 1990–91.

Canada's public diplomacy budgets have never fully recovered, because the role of culture is frequently misunderstood in the context of Canada's foreign policy. As an expression of Canadian identity representing the values of Canadians, can culture be an instrument of foreign policy whose

efforts can be measured? Is it primarily a commodity that contributes billions to the national economy and supports some fifty thousand Canadian
jobs from exports alone?[15] Over the years, some Canadian artists and cultural groups have been under the impression that the purpose of DFAIT's
Can$4.7-million Arts and Cultural Industries Promotion Program, created
to assist both established and emerging artists and cultural groups to perform and display abroad, was to support Canadian culture as an end in
itself. However, the purpose of the cultural grants of the program is not to
subsidize Canadian culture per se, as there are other programs for this purpose; rather, it is to select specific cultural activities that will reinforce foreign policy objectives.[16] Cultural programming, in the public diplomacy
context, as opposed to the more generic process of intercultural relations
(which could involve any form of intercultural exchange and need not
involve government), is about achieving international policy goals *through*
creative expression.

As described in the first chapter, another defining characteristic of the
management of Canada's international cultural and educational relations
is that programs are scattered across a number of federal departments and
agencies; cultural diplomacy is also shared with a number of provinces,
notably Quebec. At its most general level, DFAIT is responsible for promoting Canada abroad; however, the tools at its disposal are somewhat limited
because, as table 1.1 (chapter 1) shows, it controls only a fraction of the
federal government's estimated Can$109-million annual public diplomacy
budget (based on traditional culture, education, and information programs
and not including the public affairs expenditures of either the military or
CIDA). While many other government and non-government players are
engaged in promoting Canada's identity abroad, only Canadian Heritage,
through its management of Canada's international expositions, its promotion of cultural industries through the Trade Routes program, and its lead
role in managing Canada's international cultural diversity agenda, can be
said to be a natural and significant partner with DFAIT in such activity.[17]

Cultural diversity has become increasingly important for the strength
of Canada's soft power. Since culture is often the first point of contact
between nations, Canada's cultural diversity is thus a valuable foreign policy asset. Promoting and nurturing this respect for diversity allows other
cultures to identify themselves within Canada's cultural mosaic, thereby
providing Canada with both a distinctive identity abroad and greater
international credibilty. It is for these reasons that Canada was instrumental in the creation of the UNESCO Convention on the Protection and Promotion of the Diversity of Cultural Expressions. Without such protection

for Canada's cultural industries, Canada's identity would be at risk of becoming subsumed within a greater global culture. Sustaining the value of cultural diversity means that there will be a greater likelihood that Canada's creative communities will continue to be able to showcase their talents to the world and, as a result, that the world will continue to be able to encounter Canada.

Cultural Centres

The idea of cultural centres as the focus of Canada's public diplomacy has been given expression through the designated free-standing centres in London (Canada House) and Paris (Le Centre culturel canadien). There is often a clash between how diplomats view such centres ("prestige and dignity") and how the cultural performers and their audiences view such national platforms.[18] Ralston Saul believes that for these centres to succeed they must have an "open, free and easy atmosphere," in addition to allowing the promotion of "shocking or outrageous" cultural works.[19] In his view, the requirement for the preservation of national dignity is anathema to successful cultural diplomacy. In short, a country must be prepared to threaten its national dignity to make a true mark in cultural diplomacy.

The requirement for security has also always been a key factor affecting the status of cultural centres, in particular Canada House, which sits on one of the most visible pieces of real estate in London – Trafalgar Square. From the public diplomacy perspective, it is hard to imagine a more prestigious and central location; it is impossible not to notice Canada House, as it takes up a full block of the square. Given its prominence and location, Canada House requires more security considerations than it would if it were located elsewhere in London, thus driving up the cost of maintaining its accessibility to the public. That being said, observers can be forgiven for wondering whether Ottawa has not been engaging in false economies in the past several decades, when on any given weekend, tens of thousands of tourists have milled about Trafalgar Square and Canada House has sat closed. Banners announcing Canadian artists could occasionally be seen hanging limply from the building, but tourists and locals alike have had no opportunity to visit the exhibitions during peak periods because the cost of maintaining weekend access has been deemed too high. Ralston Saul observes that the requirement for security has created an atmosphere of exclusivity and prestige, "both of which are death to culture."[20]

The debate on whether to invest in cultural centres is premised on whether it is wiser to invest in programs or in "bricks and mortar." Some practitioners feel that prestige locations are less important than the actual ground campaign of getting more Canadian art and artists into foreign countries, while others see the benefit of having a nucleus for Canada's cultural programming and public events. Clearly, a cultural centre is seen as an institution that openly and visibly represents Canada to the local community. It is a place where local citizens can find information about Canada, and, in addition to presenting lectures, concerts, exhibits, and films, it provides an opportunity for face-to-face encounters between Canadian personalities and their local target audiences. Not to be overlooked is the utility of such centres as focal points for attracting Canadian expatriates. While the electronic culture centre provided through a dedicated CanadaInternational web portal (see chapter 6) is certainly useful, it in no way replaces the interpersonal dimension of public diplomacy – captured in Edward R. Murrow's famous dictum of "the last three feet."

Cultural centres, however, can also represent liabilities. They are expensive to run and can have large overheads, such as expenditures on print libraries that may not see much public traffic. Concerns have been raised that these centres are no longer even cultural centres anymore and are now simply visual arts spaces.[21] For this reason, some practitioners working in public affairs have advised against using them and, instead, have emphasized the benefits of using local platforms to highlight Canadian talent. The investment spent in organizing a one-off exhibit of Canadian Aboriginal art at a Canadian cultural centre, so the thinking goes, would yield better results if it could be tied to local events and creative talent. It is rarely a good idea for Canada to organize solitary events.[22]

Although it is unlikely that Canada's cultural centres in London and Paris will be closed in the coming years, the possibility of creating new centres will ultimately be weighed on a country-by-country basis.[23] For instance, while it may make sense to establish such cultural centres in cities of the future, such as Beijing or Mumbai, it would probably be less attractive to build a centre separate from the Canadian mission in countries that are not in the first tier of Canada's geographic priorities. A number of fundamental questions would need to be asked before going the bricks-and-mortar route: Would there be a sufficient audience for such a centre? Is such a centre necessary, given the existence of local platforms? Would security considerations require that the centre be located far away from its natural constituencies?[24] What would be the diplomatic impact of a separate centre and how would it fit in with Canada's longer-term public diplomacy strategy for the country? Would a centre allow for contact with local audiences who would find it politically difficult to be seen in a Canadian embassy? In

the end, if a government is unwilling to put its best foot forward internationally with high-profile and expensive cultural centres, then there is little
reason to keep them. Countries as different in size as Austria, with its Cultural Forums (integrated within Austrian embassies), and China, with its
twenty-seven new Confucius Institutes (including one located on the cam-
pus of the British Columbia Institute of Technology), have concluded that
bricks-and-mortar does matter.

The Governor General

The role of the governor general as an instrument of cultural diplomacy is
frequently overlooked. Most Canadian governors general, with a few exceptions, have tended to focus on building a sense of national pride at home
and have not made it their mission to travel beyond Canada's borders to
highlight Canada's accomplishments to the world. In his John W. Holmes
Memorial Lecture, "Projecting a Middle Power into an Imperial World,"
delivered at York University's Glendon College in February 2004, John
Ralston Saul showed how state visits by the governor general have changed
over the years, from short, ceremonial affairs to travelling road shows of
leading Canadians who participate in a complex strategy designed to
explain what Canada is really all about.[25] These new-style visits may be more
costly than the earlier ones, but they are an extremely effective way of
explaining Canada to the world. They are made at the request of the Canadian government largely because the countries in question are of particular interest to Canada for political, economic, or other reasons, and
Canada's profile can be raised during a visit led by the governor general.

In Canada, the governor general is supposed to be above politics and is,
therefore, the perfect institutional embodiment of Canada's soul. As a
result, for most of the past century (and increasingly over the past decades),
governors general have played an important role in the regular conduct of
Canada's relations with other countries by travelling abroad on state visits.
Such visits began in 1927, when Lord Willingdon was invited to the United
States by President Calvin Coolidge. Ten years later, John Buchan (Lord
Tweedsmuir) was received at the White House by President Franklin D.
Roosevelt. Later, Jules Léger, Edward Schreyer, Jeanne Sauvé, and Ramon
Hnatyshyn would travel to Europe, Asia, and Latin America.[26] But not until
1998, when Governor General Romeo LeBlanc visited India and Pakistan,
did the Canadian government make a conscious decision to use the state
visit as a more active tool for branding Canada. Today, state visits by governors general are vastly different from those of their predecessors. They are

driven more by content than ceremony, and they feature an entourage of skilled and talented Canadians from various disciplines who attempt to show what Canada is all about by establishing links and building relationships with their counterparts in other countries.

If Romeo LeBlanc's visit to South Asia launched the democratization of the state visit, then his successor, Adrienne Clarkson, who served as governor general from 1999 to 2005, gave it full expression. In 2001, she was asked by the government to lead a state visit to Chile and Argentina. This time thirty-nine Canadians, including members of parliament and senators, were invited along to take part in public debates, roundtables, and working sessions regarding topics such as communications, writing and the visual arts, peacekeeping, and Aboriginal issues. As Ralston Saul writes, "[t]he inclusion of an important First Nations component was a first in Canadian foreign policy ... By bringing an impressive delegation led by Joe Gosnell, President of the Nisga'a Nation, and Cree leader Marilyn Buffalo,"[27] Canada started an ongoing dialogue between the First Peoples of Chile, Argentina, and Canada. Historically, there has been a strong bond between Canada's Aboriginal peoples and the governor general, and, given the global interest in the culture and status of Canada's Aboriginal population, their inclusion in governor general–led state visits helps to present Canada's diversity, which is a compelling dimension of the Canadian brand.[28] As the *Ottawa Citizen* stated in its editorial of 5 February 2001, "[b]eyond the formal dinners and military honour guards, Madame Clarkson wants to use her current tour of Chile and Argentina to spotlight some of the best things that Canada has to offer the world. From peacekeepers to authors, artists to wines, the Governor General has taken along some of this country's unofficial ambassadors to demonstrate Canada's incredible diversity."[29]

Clarkson followed up her 2001 trip to Chile and Argentina with a groundbreaking visit to Germany, accompanied by thirty-seven Canadians and organized around the themes of modern Canadian music, theatre, high-tech communications, immigration, citizenship, and federalism. The Can$1.2 million cost of the visit was more than double the cost of previous ones. What was accomplished? Canadian-German bilateral cooperation was improved. The work of the Forum of Federations, a Canadian-led nongovernmental organization designed to promote cooperation among countries that have federal systems of government, was strengthened. The existence of the Canadian Universities Centre in Berlin, now promoting permanent relationships between professors and students in both countries, was solidified. Canadian filmmaker and delegation member Atom

Egoyan was made president of the jury at the Berlin Film Festival the following year.[30] Despite the high price tag and the fact that little effort had been
made to explain the strategy behind these new-style visits, public reaction
was positive. "Well done, Madame," said the *National Post*. "The Crown is
meant to be situated above politics, and Madame Clarkson, as the institution's representative, correctly understands this is not a limitation, but an
opportunity. The manner in which she has chosen to undertake her overseas duties serves to strengthen Canada's ties with Germany, and also
achieves the stated goal of her travels: to enhance Canada's reputation as a
complex, contemporary – dare we say hip – society."[31]

The gradual evolution of the governor general's international activities
since 1998 has provided an important boost to the local public diplomacy
activities of Canada's missions abroad. A senior Canadian official with considerable experience in organizing international trips observed that for
diplomats, "[i]t is a constant battle to get attention and to infiltrate the
local society and local government, and try to ensure that your phone calls
are returned. [Canada] is important in some circles, less in others, so anything you can do to get some attention, like a state visit ... is very important
... After that, you are on the map."[32] Ralston Saul concurs, reporting that

[T]hese state visits give a remarkable momentum to the embassy's day
to day work. We have high-quality diplomats and effective embassies.
However, they are ... struggling on a daily basis to attract the attention
of the local government, local organizations, and local citizens ... Normally, our diplomats must do this through a series of one-off events – a
high-tech fair, a cultural event, a food fair, a conference on immigration. The new Canadian approach to state visits provides them with an
opportunity to present their country as *the* cutting-edge society and to
do so thanks to the use of an integrated critical mass of leading Canadian citizens willing to volunteer their talents through intense, carefully
thought-out programmes ... This is a brilliant approach towards the
branding of Canada, but more than that, to projecting both a sense of
the country and an understanding of Canada, which has a good chance
of remaining long after the state visit is over.[33]

As argued in this book, Canada's great struggle for global mind share is a
function, in part, of being overshadowed by its neighbour to the south and
likely also a function of Canadians' inherent sense of modesty and reluctance to market themselves aggressively.[34] The pomp and ceremony surrounding the longer visits of Canadian heads of state since 1998 have had

the effect of thrusting Canada into the local limelight and creating platforms and focal points for Canada's existing public diplomacy activities in the countries and regions that are being visited.

Following the release in 2000 of a foreign policy statement that focused on Canada's North (the aptly named "The Northern Dimension of Canada's Foreign Policy"), the Canadian government asked Governor General Clarkson to undertake a series of visits to northern countries. Three themes guided her subsequent visit to Russia, Finland, and Iceland in 2003: environmental and economic development, circumpolar cooperation, and culture. The environmental spotlight in Russia was on the clean-up of decommissioned nuclear submarines, which supported a major international foreign policy initiative to which Canada had committed Can$100 million per year for ten years.[35] In Finland and Iceland, it centred on alternative (geothermal) energy. The presence of Canadian Inuit on this trip was vital to the success of this theme, given the overarching importance of the environment to their traditional lifestyle and general well-being.

In Russia, the theme of circumpolar cooperation focused on democratic development and federalism.[36] It is noteworthy that the cultural program was carefully matched to each country. As a senior Canadian official described it, "[i]n Iceland we focused very much on writers and music because that is what they responded to, and Finland was very much about music and visual arts, as we tried to tailor it to a certain extent. In Russia, we had writers, but we also had dance and theatre, more so than in the other two places." Because of this blend, the same official stressed that "Governor General Adrienne Clarkson's track record in utilizing culture as a tool of foreign policy is unparalleled, and the fact is [Canada] did receive significant and highly positive media attention there."[37]

Despite the apparent foreign policy benefits of Madame Clarkson's trips, one of the perennial concerns in managing public diplomacy is the difficulty in evaluating the effectiveness of its longer-term activities and programs (see the discussion in chapter 8). Madame Clarkson's state visit to the northern countries offers a glimpse into how public diplomacy may be evaluated: the trip resulted in more than three hundred print, radio, and television reports of "real importance" in Russia, thirty-eight in Finland, and sixty in Iceland.[38] According to Ralston Saul, by the standard industry calculation, the total earned media exposure was equivalent to nearly Can$9 million in advertising costs.[39]

This northern trip was criticized in certain quarters of the media, notably the *National Post*, for being extravagant in style and excessive in the size of the entourage. The reported cost of Can$5.3 million was judged by some Opposition parliamentarians to be excessive, even though the Governor General had been asked by the Canadian government itself to conduct the trip. The level of public vilification of the office of the governor general was unusual, even by the falling standards of Canadian public life. The problem was that the public had not been sensitized to the benefits and accompanying costs of such trips. No one had a benchmark on what was a "reasonable" amount to spend to promote Canada's image abroad. Indeed, what should international diplomacy cost? As Ralston Saul notes, it is almost impossible to do a basic cost/benefit analysis of different missions, since "they are going to be successful according to their own particular purposes."[40] As with other forms of longer-term public diplomacy, state trips are long-term investments in making Canada known on the world stage and turning Canada into an international player.[41]

While a state visit may have multiple purposes, one of the ever-present and overarching goals is to insert Canada into a particular country's mainstream thinking about the world beyond its borders. As a result, these new-style governor general's visits are less formal and less traditional than their precursors and are driven more by content and the projection or branding of Canada. Next to Canada's participation in world fairs, these trips are probably the most complex branding projects undertaken by Canada, and they involve a great amount of planning and concentrated effort by officials at Rideau Hall, DFAIT headquarters, and Canadian missions. As Ralston Saul opines, "Rather than thinking of this as an increase in the cost of state visits, the more accurate way of thinking would be that this was and is a conscious investment in the third pillar of our foreign policy which, up until 1998, had not received the investment required in order to make it an effective third pillar."[42] The state visits have thus become "the concrete manifestation" of the third pillar and the embodiment of what it takes to project Canada abroad in a more effective and coordinated way.

Translation

Another often-overlooked instrument of cultural diplomacy is the role played by translation. Translation is often ignored as a tool in public diplomacy, even though it is probably one of the most effective ways of conveying one's culture to another society. Promoting Canada through the translation of its literature creates an impression on foreign audiences and contributes directly to Canada's visibility in an increasingly competitive world. Translating Canadian literary works into local languages is an accessible way to increase foreign audiences' knowledge of Canada, even though the process of translation may create a portrait of Canada that is not entirely intended by the original Canadian author. Maria Sierra Cordoba Serrano, for example, observes that since the 1990s, there has been a growing interest in Quebecois Studies among students in Spain.[43] According to Cordoba Serrano, one factor explaining this interest is that many Spaniards have a positive perception of Canada. Canada is perceived as outgoing and open, but Quebec is seen as particularly progressive and avantgarde, and its literature innovative. Not surprisingly, Quebecois Studies is most popular in Catalonia, where the quest for independence and autonomy is a unifying link between the two sub-federal entities; it would explain the interest in Catalonia in Quebecois literary works. These growing cultural links led Catalonia and Quebec to ratify a bilateral cooperation agreement in 1996, the only such agreement between a Spanish regional government and a province of Canada.[44]

In a similar vein, according to Luise von Flotow, translation of Canadian literary fiction has also led to Canada becoming "somewhat of a cultural success in Germany and Austria."[45] Von Flotow provides the example of the launching of anthologies of Canadian literature overseas, with the support of government translation initiatives that "render Canada attractive or interesting to ... any country where neither French nor English are major languages."[46] Perhaps a more curious public diplomacy effect through translation has been created by the iconic Canadian poet and singer Leonard Cohen. In his foreword to the Chinese edition of his book *Beautiful Losers,* Cohen builds an intercultural bridge from Canada to China:

> It is an honour, and a surprise, to have the frenzied thoughts of my youth expressed in Chinese characters ... When I was young, my friends and I read and admired the old Chinese poets. Our ideas of love and friendship, of wine and distance, of poetry itself, were much affected by those ancient songs ... So you can understand, Dear Reader, how privileged I feel to be able to graze, even for a moment, and with such meagre credentials, on the outskirts of your tradition ... May I suggest that you skip over the parts [of the book] you don't like? Dip into it here and there ... After a while, if you are sufficiently bored or unemployed, you may want to read it from cover to cover.[47]

Ralston Saul's 1994 study refers to translation as a primary vehicle for the export of Canadian culture abroad. Although translation is an effective and integral component of the telling of Canadian stories across cultures, as von Flotow notes, "the amount of control on image-making that government agencies can ever hope to exert in such a variegated environment where the interest of authors, translators, publishers, and readers crisscross seems questionable."[48] Yet as von Flotow argues, the translation of Canadian writing and its success abroad can motivate writers at home, enabling them to reach new audiences, and although there is little control over how translations are consumed and interpreted by foreign audiences, this lack of control legitimizes the success and quality (and hence the global diffusion) of these Canadian narratives.

By the mid-1990s, two translation grants programs existed in Canada, both funded by the Canada Council for the Arts. The Translation Grants Program finances translations of Canadian books from English to French and French to English. The program not only enables a cultural exchange between the two founding nations but makes Canadian literature accessible to a larger global audience, since as Ralston Saul observes, "English and French remain the two most important languages in literature."[49] The program has since been expanded, allowing for translations into several Aboriginal languages as well. The second program, the International Translation Grants program, assists in the translation of both English and French literary works by Canadian authors into foreign languages for publication abroad.

International Exhibitions

International exhibitions constitute a major public diplomacy medium for countries, and Canada has participated in virtually every world fair since the first international exhibition was held in London, England, in 1851. Throughout much of the twentieth century, the focus was on Canada's natural resources; however, the goal of Canada's participation in recent decades has been to use these exhibitions to project images of cultural diversity, the environment, and technology and innovation.[50] In 1967, Canada hosted the World's Fair in Montreal (Expo 67), which drew more than fifty million visitors and representation from sixty-two countries and which made a deep impression on the national consciousness at a time when Canada was celebrating the centenary of its Confederation. Since then, Canada has been a regular participant at all world fairs, attracting tens of millions of visitors to the Canadian pavilions. In 1986, Canada welcomed twenty-two million people to Expo 86 in Vancouver, with the exposition theme of transportation and communication. The British Columbia government sent invitations to five thousand of the top business leaders in the world; about one thousand of them visited Canada.[51] As with Expo 67, this world fair introduced another Canadian city to the world. It highlighted the Asian face of Canada's multi-ethnic makeup. Beyond the nation-branding effects of the fair and the domestic economic benefits for the province, according to journalist Gary Mason, it also "changed the way people felt about themselves and about the place where they lived. It instilled a sense of pride in us."[52] For Mason, Vancouver would never be the same. Expo 86 gave British Columbia and Vancouver worldwide exposure, which became the catalyst for a tourism explosion in the subsequent decade (see chapter 7).

Canada's participation at the 2005 World Exposition in Aichi, Japan, illustrates the power of such international exhibitions to project positive national images. Canada's theme was the Wisdom of Diversity, and within this context Canada sought to promote greater understanding of its geosphere (earth, water, climate), biosphere (micro-organisms, plants, animals and humans), and ethnosphere (human-to-human and human-to-nature relations). The overarching goal, through communication and public affairs programming, cultural performances, and student exchanges over three years, was to make Canada better known to people in Japan and Asia and to reinforce existing diplomatic, commercial and cultural ties with Japan.

The Canada Pavilion received over three million visitors and significant positive media coverage in the Japanese press. But were the Canadians hitting the target market and playing to the target audiences? It is difficult to measure the longer-term impact – in public diplomacy terms – of an effort that cost approximately Can$12 million over three years and that represented about 3 percent of the federal government's total annual public diplomacy budget.[53] On balance, Canada probably did get Can$12 million worth of publicity, although it would be almost impossible to measure the broader impact. Canadian officials noted that there was good cooperation between the Canadian embassy in Tokyo and the representatives of the Canadian pavilion, even though the organization of Canada's participation at Aichi cannot be described as a whole-of-government approach.

World fairs, along with major international sports competitions such as the Olympics, with their long lead times are the ultimate national prestige events, and it is highly unlikely that Canada would not be a regular participant. Certainly, there would be little public outcry if Canada were not present at a world fair, but it is hard to imagine the government consciously deciding to absent itself when the countries that Canada compares itself to, such as Australia and the members of the G8, are participants. At the official, state-to-state level, this would be a case of Canada's absence being noticed more than its presence. More positively, the public diplomacy benefits of world fairs for Canada have been most pronounced when they were hosted by Canada: not only did they provide an extraordinary opportunity for branding Canada to the world, but they also contributed to domestic social cohesion. In the words of a senior Canadian official, these exhibitions reflected for Canadians, "not just who they were, but what they wanted to be."[54]

Touring and Arts Promotion

The bread and butter of Canada's cultural diplomacy is arts promotion, and touring is perhaps the classic example of this activity. Certainly one of the great successes of government support, both federal and provincial, has been Cirque du Soleil. It is reported that when group founder Guy Laliberté launched the idea for Cirque during the 1980s, he "pestered the Quebec government for grants to support his troupe."[55] Since then, the show has expanded tremendously into venues around the world, earning praise for its unconventional style and performances. As one journalist phrased it, the uncompromising "Quebecoisity" of the show has delivered this element of Canadian identity to all corners of the world, from permanent shows on the Las Vegas Strip to touring shows.[56] However, despite the success, the question remains whether the existence of the Cirque "buys" sympathy for Canadians and/or Quebecois or whether this investment in a cultural commodity has paid off handsomely simply in terms of the economic return to Canada.

Ralston Saul has argued that the lasting effect of cultural touring may be felt only if the performers are able to maintain a presence; merely touring with a large symphony orchestra or dance company is expensive and likely to involve single performances in the cities that are visited, while audiences react best to continuity. The initial feelings of prestige are quickly lost, and the carefully scripted acts may not engender the emphasis on creativity that Canadian arts thrive on.[57] Many major cultural attractions (such as those of the theatre district in Toronto) have endured in one primary location, where they become a destination attraction. To accomplish this success through touring, Ralston Saul has advocated a different approach, one that relies on smaller dance companies and musical groups (to reduce cost) with original material, performing in festival-like atmospheres. This strategy would place Canadian talent before a wide variety of audiences – ones that would be highly engaged by the act of attending the event itself and that would perhaps be more open to experiencing new cultures – thus building upon "Canada's reputation as an energetic place of creation."[58]

A senior Canadian official takes a slightly different perspective on the use of large touring groups, arguing that "large companies do make an interesting impact, and often get a higher profile."[59] This official argues that bringing a large group, such as the National Ballet of Canada, into familiar places can be beneficial. In the case of dance, he states, "England is known for ... its classical ballet ... for a reason – there is a market there. So why not [take] the National Ballet [to England] if there is a market there, and show some of these people what we can do."[60] This use of touring emphasizes the ongoing value of traditional cultural tools that raise general awareness of Canada, something that should not be discounted even during a period in the evolution of the practice of public diplomacy in which governments are seeking to target cultural programming in support of more specific foreign policy goals.

Individual Canadian missions throughout the world currently play an integral role in determining which Canadian artists receive DFAIT's arts promotion subsidies for their international tours. The embassies and consulates are able to decide what is needed, whether it be a high-culture performance by the National Ballet of Canada or classical musicians, or something associated more with mainstream culture, such as a rock band or hip-hop artist, to help deliver the Canadian messages or to increase Canada's profile in a given country. Gauging the market receptivity for potential acts is critical; for countries such as Pakistan or Iran, where a significant portion of the country's population is below the age of twenty, there is little reason to expect high culture to have much effect. There are countries that are diverse enough to provide a captive audience for any Canadian performer, but these countries are often not high foreign policy priorities (for example, smaller European countries), and therefore it would not make strategic sense to concentrate Canada's limited cultural grants funding on them. The ability of the diplomatic missions to exercise a high level of control over which Canadian artists will be promoting Canada in their territories is critical to ensuring that the mission's messages are conveyed clearly and effectively in support of both wide-ranging and local Canadian concerns. In the view of a former senior Canadian official, Canadian missions must be given the lead in selecting artists; the tail (DFAIT headquarters) should not be wagging the dog.

However, there are still other experienced observers of Canada's cultural diplomacy who believe that touring needs a significant overhaul. They note that in future years, the Canada Council for the Arts will be much better resourced for cultural promotion, including international touring, and should assume that role, thus freeing DFAIT's cultural grants funding for other priorities.[61] Some have suggested that DFAIT should take the nearly Can$5 million earmarked for its cultural grants program and follow the Australian example.[62] That is, in the words of a senior Canadian official, "[p]ick a place, pick a Canadian artist, pick the exact plan that needs to be followed, and pick the appropriate partners, largely private sector, and execute."[63] According to this view, Canada's approach to cultural diplomacy through touring has been too reactive and needs to be more strategic to justify the expenditure of a relatively small budget.[64]

Yet, despite the pressures to make traditional forms of public diplomacy such as touring conform to a results-based public management framework, the fact remains that they can pay large dividends. One of the success stories of Canadian international touring is that of the Ottawa-based National Arts Centre Orchestra (NACO), which has expanded its international cultural impact around the world on behalf of Canada by adding an educational component to many of its tour destinations. During its tours in the 1990s, orchestra musicians began to lend their time and professional services to lead local workshops for aspiring student musicians. While these workshops earned a large degree of positive publicity from the local media in foreign markets, they also served to foster fond memories of Canadian generosity and skill with the young musicians and further reinforced the Canadian brand.[65] As a result, this practice has continued. The workshops are also bundled with other public affairs events on the NACO's tour, such as receptions at Canada's embassies and consulates with the opinion leaders in the countries visited. In the words of a Canadian cultural affairs official, "[t]hese events are a type of conversation starter or lubricant for when you meet next time ... it's almost the personal aspects that let you make deals."[66]

Successful touring does not restrict itself to the performing arts. Canadian authors have also enjoyed the benefits of cultural promotion. Such was the case when Canada was made the guest of honour at the 2003 Turin International Book Fair in Italy. It became apparent to both Canada's mission in Rome and the International Cultural Relations bureau at DFAIT in Ottawa that Canada could use the book fair as a platform through which to project its identity more broadly in Italy. Although the primary objective of the book fair was to help Canadian publishers sell their books and the rights to their books in a foreign country, the Turin International Book Fair allowed Canada to adopt a whole-of-government approach by coordinating the efforts of DFAIT, Canadian Heritage, and the Canada Council for the Arts. Canada was thus able to amplify a number of key messages and images: Canada as a bona fide trade and investment partner, Canada as a cultural player, and, not to be overlooked, Canada as a worthy host of the 2010 winter Olympic Games (at that time, Turin was preparing for the 2006 winter Olympic Games). Although the Turin International Book Fair was ostensibly about selling more Canadian books, it was used successfully to brand Canada in its entirety.

INTERNATIONAL FILM AND TELEVISION

The domain of film and television production is one area in which the intersection of public diplomacy and trade interests is highly apparent. Canadian Heritage, DFAIT, and Telefilm Canada are part of a federal-provincial partnership that guides and directs the international activities of Canadian film through an International Initiatives Advisory Committee. Furthermore, in countries where major international film and television trade shows or film festivals take place, cultural trade commissioners and cultural attachés in the Canadian embassies and consulates play an important role in assisting Telefilm Canada with industry and networking events, thus leveraging Canadian public diplomacy by promoting the country's arts and culture.[67]

Nonetheless, the English-language Canadian feature film industry, in stark contrast to the much more vibrant Quebec film and television industry, has not blossomed internationally, as many had hoped and expected. Some long-time observers of the cultural scene in Canada have advocated for direct Canadian government intervention in the film distribution market. Effectively, this would constitute screen quotas for Canadian films as a way of creating a healthier Canadian film industry and ensuring that there would be a constant supply of Canadian film for domestic and international consumption. Existing Canadian production funds, such as those of Telefilm Canada, with annual budgets less than the cost of one medium-budget Hollywood film, are fighting a very difficult (some would say losing) battle in getting Canadian stories on domestic screens, much less on the world's screens.

On a more positive note, a senior DFAIT official suggests that the Canadian experience in supporting Canadian film and television production is highly pertinent to other states, creating an inroad for the Canadian regulatory model in the field of communications. Indeed, informing other countries of Canada's experience in this area (e.g., numerous royal com-

missions, a regulatory body in the form of the Canadian Radio-Television
and Telecommunications Commission (CRTC)) is one of the most under-
recognized instruments of Canada's public diplomacy abroad. Many public
broadcasters around the world look to Canada's own television regulatory
standards and experience as an inspiration for their own efforts to ensure
cultural diversity in response to the volume of American programming. As
a consequence, over time Canada's image in terms of its ability (however
flawed) to protect and carve out a separate identity in North American cultural production is seen in a very positive light by, for example, German
decision makers. This is a subtle and long-term means of presenting Canada's values of tolerance and respect abroad.[68]

It is to be noted that Canada, through the myriad co-production agreements signed by Canadian companies, has become the world's second-
largest exporter of children's programming. Indeed, as a result of these
agreements, there is virtually no German television network without links
to Canadian production companies. However, since television programming with high production values is expensive to produce, Canadian co-
productions pre-sold for pre-financing to foreign markets are seldom very
Canadian in content. On the other hand, a primary goal of these joint productions is not necessarily to get Canadian content onto the screen but
rather to make the appropriate business contacts off-screen. One of the
best routes for promoting Canadian content abroad may be to sell locally
the idea of television screenings of "best Canadian films," as the CBC has
done in promoting the "Best of Britain" in its own television schedule.[69]

Lastly, while the Canadian commercial film industry has at times stum-
bled, some of its success can be attributed to film festivals – in Toronto,
Montreal, Vancouver – which have helped put Canada on the global cultural map. The Toronto International Film Festival (TIFF), started in 1976,
has been identified by film critics as one of the premier annual global film
festivals. Roger Ebert has stated that "although Cannes is still larger,
Toronto is more useful and more important."[70] Over the years, the TIFF has
been the venue of choice for major film premieres. In addition to presenting the "star quality" inherent in premiering major motion pictures, the
TIFF supports Canadian film in several ways. It showcases up-and-coming
Canadian filmmakers with its *Canada First!* program and its short-film program *Short Cuts Canada,* while also promoting older Canadian films
through programs such as *Canadian Retrospective* and *Canadian Open Vault.*
Promoting Canadian talent on this major world stage is critical, and TIFF
takes advantage of a captive audience (both at the festival and through
worldwide publicity) to provide a forum within which Canadian film-

makers can present their work to the world. Using Canadian film festivals to brand Canada to the world by providing Canadian talent with access to an international audience may have a bigger impact than the combined efforts of all Canada's trade commissioners at Canada's missions, who promote the film and television industries.

INTERNATIONAL SPORT

Sport may be one of the best platforms for public diplomacy, as the discussions in chapters 2 and 3 have shown. Branding a country positively through sport packs considerable punch and provides a foundation of goodwill that assists public affairs officers at missions. Australia received a huge boost in its international image following the success of its athletes at the 2000 summer Olympics in Sydney in front of a worldwide audience of over 3.7 billion. A country that was off most people's radar screens suddenly saw its nation brand "advance by 10 years" – meaning that what the world knew about Australia in 2000, it would not have known for another decade without the games.[71]

Hosting an international sporting event or having a country's team among the top contenders in the arenas of international competition captures massive global mind share and provides enormous economic benefits to host and participating countries. For example, the 2006 World Cup of soccer captured an estimated cumulative thirty billion viewers worldwide, seven times that of the Olympics. Moreover, it was estimated that the thirty-two participating countries received a £13-billion (about Can$27.8 billion) boost to their economies.[72]

One of soccer's traditional powerhouses, Brazil, provides the quintessential example of the role sport can play as a form of public diplomacy. Brazil exports its soccer players (footballers) to countries around the world, including Saudi Arabia, New Zealand, and other Latin American countries, and to regional soccer hotspots such as Europe. According to Alex Bellos, author of *Futebol*, Brazilian soccer players can earn much more even in remote outposts than they would at home, and they also play an important cross-cultural role.[73] As Bellos writes: "The number of soccer players who leave Brazil is four times the number of diplomats sent to work in Brazilian missions abroad, and their effect is often similar. There are so many Brazilian footballers around the world, spread across so many countries, that they function like a parallel diplomatic service. They are cultural ambassadors as well as sporting ones, since Brazilian lifestyle is so closely linked to how they play football."[74]

International sport plays a vital role in helping to promote Canada abroad, too. Canadian participation in the Olympics, world championships, the Commonwealth Games, and the Jeux de la Francophonie promotes an image of Canada that is arguably more far-reaching and pervasive than that generated through some traditional long-term public diplomacy activities. Canada has defined itself internationally by high-level performances in a range of sports: hockey, in which both the men's and women's teams have competed successfully at international competitions including the Olympics, the world championships, and the 1972 Summit Series between Canada and the Soviet Union, and through individual players such as Wayne Gretzky, Bobby Orr, and Gordie Howe; figure skating, where Canada's stars have included Elizabeth Manley, Kurt Browning, and Elvis Stojko; skiing, notably the Crazy Canucks skiing team of the 1980s; swimming, including the 1984 Olympic team, represented by Alex Baumann and Victor Davis; and by other individual performances, such as those of Mike Weir in golf and Donovan Bailey in the hundred-metre dash. The measured and "classy" way Jamie Salé and David Pelletier handled the figure skating controversy at the 2002 Salt Lake Olympics probably did more for Canada's image internationally than a year's worth of official public diplomacy.[75]

Likewise, Dick Pound, as head of the World Anti-Doping Agency, was among the most-quoted Canadians in the foreign media. Not a high-profile, drug-related international athletics scandal went by without some comment from this Canadian denouncing the use of drugs in sport. The anti-doping agenda has generally been accepted as necessary and has been assigned a high priority in international sport. It represents an effort to ensure fairness, equality, and transparency in athletics. The fact that the International Olympic Committee's anti-doping agency is based in Montreal means that other countries may view Canada as a nation that values ethics. Dick Pound enhanced this message whenever he was interviewed, and the global association of fair play, made in connection to the cause of eradicating doping from sport, invariably extended to Canada.

The close association of Canada with hockey internationally plays a significant role in defining the Canadian national image – northern, rugged, and determined. As such, the athletic dimension of public diplomacy gains further importance because of its ability to provide a domestic feedback loop to Canada's public diplomacy, increasing the pride that Canadians feel as the result of national accomplishments. Furthermore, as noted, Canadian values of tolerance and diversity are well represented by international sport, as demonstrated by athletes from New Brunswick and Quebec competing at the Jeux de la Francophonie under their provincial, rather than Canadian, flags. It is unlikely that many other national governments would allow such a potential dilution of the national image, and it suggests why Canada has been referred to as the first post-modern nation.

CANADIAN EXPATRIATES: A HIDDEN PUBLIC DIPLOMACY RESOURCE

With an estimated 2.7 million Canadians living as expatriates outside of Canada, an opportunity exists for using this pool of citizens to help reinforce key Canadian messages and to increase global awareness of Canadian identity. Expatriates present a unique challenge in that while they may be a tremendous asset for promoting Canada and its values abroad, harnessing that potential for purposes of public diplomacy may not be so easy.

Currently, the registry of Canadians living abroad covers less than 10 percent of the Canadian expatriate community.[76] For Ottawa to utilize this segment of the population, recognition of Canadians abroad by the government must increase substantially. Canada's expatriate community is approximately the same size as the French expatriate population, and while it is unlikely that Canada will be able to replicate the success of French expatriate institutions such as the Alliance Française or India's Non-Resident Indian program, Canadian citizens are adequately represented in many countries. Perhaps the best place to start registering Canadian citizens abroad is the United States, where one-half of all Canadian expatriates live. The online Connect2Canada network, begun in 2005, has proven successful in identifying Canadians living in that country, operating as a platform to launch messages about Canadian initiatives and policy decisions.

Another significant challenge facing the potential utilization of Canadian expatriates is the degree to which these citizens, a portion of whom have spent most of their lives outside Canada, are willing to embrace their Canadian identity. Do these expatriates hold Canada in high regard, or are they wont to dismiss it given their new surroundings and experiences? Since little data exist on the perspectives held by Canadian expatriates, Canadian missions cannot be sure of their reactions should they attempt to promote Canadian culture and key messages through them.

Creating pools of "citizen ambassadors" around the world could create a new public diplomacy tool. It could, in the opinion of a senior Canadian official, be as simple as engaging with the leading cadre of Canadians in a given country and offering a few media lines on major issues affecting

Canada. In this official's words, "I don't see how that could hurt. I think it's
a good thing, and I think that we need to do it more – it's a public diplomacy tool we don't use ... if you give them lines, and not tell them to use
them but at least educate them, it's normal that people will bring things
up."[77] However, attempting to harness all expatriate citizens may not be the
best option. Another official has noted that with so many expatriates with
few, if any, long-standing ties to Canada, there are better resources to utilize – such as Canadian university alumni who have returned to their home
country and assumed positions of relative significance across society. That
being said, for Canada's image to achieve greater visibility in foreign countries, properly managed outreach programs such as Connect2Canada can
make a significant difference, given expatriates' knowledge of local languages and culture and the familiarity of a proportion of them with local
political and business decision-making networks.

CONCLUSION

While the context may have changed for public diplomacy in recent years,
the process – representation, advocacy, image-building, delivering messages, interpreting, and explaining – remains part and parcel of the daily
routines of diplomacy. What, then, has been learned about the components and instruments of Canada's cultural diplomacy?

The challenge in the media-saturated capitals of the major global powers, such as London and Washington, is for Canada simply to be noticed.
Canadian media relations officers must be entrepreneurial, proactive,
and aggressive. It goes without saying that if Canadians are to be exposed
to the local media, they should be, as Ralston Saul says, "*completely* fluent
in the local language *before* arriving."[78] They cannot be passive monitors of
local views; rather, they need to go out and nurture relations with local
journalists and media personalities. They, along with their public affairs
and cultural-relations colleagues, must ensure that Canada's initiatives
present compelling media angles and that there is a "story" to address
local interests, as well as one for relevant segments of the expatriate Canadian community. Given the transnational nature of most global threats
(e.g., threats to the environment, of disease, of illegal migration), linking
Canada's interests to local concerns should not be an impossible task. In
fact, the public or civic journalism movement, started in the United States
in the early 1990s to bridge the growing gap between media coverage and
the actual concerns of citizens, could provide some guidance to media
relations officers on the benefits of publicizing Canadian initiatives that

are indexed to local priorities. Clearly, media relations by press release is not sufficient.

Ralston Saul's analysis of touring in relation to exporting Canadian culture is highly instructive. The "one-off" appearance of individual performances may not be effective in promoting Canadian culture, and there is much to learn from private firms and their marketing strategies. The cumulative effect of Canadians performing internationally still helps to raise Canada's visibility abroad, offering a wide spectrum of Canadian talent to meet the interests of all age brackets. Because of this, Canada must avoid making a Hobson's choice regarding its cultural diplomacy, that is, between grants designed to raise the visibility of Canadian artists abroad (i.e., grants provided by the Canada Council for the Arts through its international programming) and cultural grants from DFAIT that are strategically designed to support specific foreign policy interests. It may be that the Canada Council for the Arts will do more to raise Canada's visibility abroad with its increased funding. However, there should not be a forced choice: Canadian cultural centres abroad, such as those in London and Paris, cannot be abandoned in favour of government-sponsored touring groups and official expositions. Former senior Canadian cultural affairs official Michael Brock has added that public diplomacy is more about "building a consensus around fundamental values that can be expressed in different ways" than simply focusing on one solitary task, and his assertion is correct.[79] Canadian public diplomacy assets must all be employed and utilized effectively to promote the reality of Canada to the rest of the world.

As popular culture pervades the globe, cultural diplomacy will have to move from its traditional highbrow form (symphony orchestras, ballet, theatre) to middle-brow or popular forms of entertainment in a process of mainstreaming public diplomacy, including entertainment forms that involve youth and young adults (e.g., sports and global online gaming). As popular culture increases in relevance, so will mainstreamed cultural diplomacy. While many people around the world have heard of Wayne Gretzky, comparatively few have heard of the Group of Seven. This does not mean that traditional cultural diplomacy (in the form of museums, visual arts, classical music, and dance) needs to be abandoned, but as the importance of foreign popular public opinion escalates, so will the need to use popular culture to open doors. Modern cultural diplomacy will mean reaching beyond elites to youth and sports.

DFAIT, as a result of having its own cultural grants program, has a valuable role to play in promoting Canada's foreign policy interests through cultural diplomacy, and it can collaborate with other departments and agencies such as Canadian Heritage, the Canada Council for the Arts, the National Film Board, and Telefilm Canada. John Ralston Saul has stated bluntly that Canada's "[i]nternational cultural policy is dependent on a healthy home market."[80] The value that Ralston Saul sees in Canadian culture cannot be lost, and it should form the basis for increased public diplomacy in countries around the world. Canada is distinct, because it is a "massive, cooperative, decentralized country with its strong aboriginal presence and bicultural population ... [with] an astonishing variety of cultural influences."[81] Canadian public diplomacy must be shaped by these cultural factors, but to do so, Canada must avoid being subsumed in a North American culture (i.e., an American culture). In short, the world should be able to learn more about Canada without assuming that all Canadian performers are actually American. Nations also need to achieve a balance between the promotion of their national and their subnational cultures, in order to project "a more realistic (and at times less flattering) national image," which, as suggested by Louis Bélanger, will be more effective in exercising Canada's international influence.[82]

It is important to clarify that in this context the promotion of culture is to be viewed not as an end in itself but as a valuable tool in promoting the aims of Canadian foreign policy. A senior Canadian official offered a sharp rebuke of the Canadian mentality: "We have to realize that the Canadian ambassador doesn't have access to much – we have to realize that Canada is not that important on the world stage. Therefore, these tools are actually essential ... where you can, you use what you've got to bring in an artist, and have your Ambassador chat with the Governor [of the central bank] during the performance – they're too important to stay a minute later."[83] According to this line of thinking, instead of DFAIT relying on a grants-based approach to its cultural programs, the department could use cultural tools selectively to achieve specific foreign policy goals.

That being said, a senior Canadian official emphasizes that "foreign policy is no longer the exclusive purview of Foreign Affairs," and consequently, there are new realities concerning how DFAIT is able to support Canada's intermediate priorities. Finding a way to meld the different objectives and instruments of the principal departments involved with Canadian culture is difficult. While organizations such as the Canada Council for the Arts are heavily focused on developing the careers of Canadian artists by providing them with international exposure and Canadian Heritage has wide-ranging arts and culture trade promotion objectives, it has been DFAIT's role to "promote Canada through the arts, and Canadian interests through the arts" – within a foreign policy context.[84] To be sure, this has been an unen-

2

7

viable task for a department that has been chronically under-resourced for such a broad mandate. Echoing the conclusion of earlier chapters, one of the great challenged for Canada is to reach a political consensus on how to best realize the synergies that exist across multiple levels of government to strengthen Canada's international "information edge" through the domain of culture.

5

International Education

If it is assumed that one of the most effective forms of building long-term intercultural understanding is through personal persuasion, then the role and impact of international education should not be underestimated or overlooked as an instrument of public diplomacy. International education enhances Canada's international presence by encouraging student mobility, fostering international cooperation in higher education and research, providing Canadians with international experience, creating forums for the exchange of ideas, and contributing to international development. The domestic impact of hosting foreign students is substantial in terms of both the economic benefits to the Canadian economy and the culturally enriching effect on Canadian society.

International education programs are obviously not instruments of Canadian foreign policy in the way an official communiqué would be, but they nevertheless play an important role in creating goodwill between Canada and the world. Traditional diplomacy, focused as it is on contacts between foreign ministries and government officials, is not the best way to foster intercultural ties and create mutual understanding between societies. Some of the most enduring relationships are those forged between Canadians and students who come to Canada and subsequently return to their homelands. Canadian universities themselves have become more internationalized, and they see the long-term and sustainable benefits that globalization has conferred upon higher education. The Association of Universities and Colleges of Canada has stated that if Foreign Affairs and International Trade Canada (DFAIT) were to rebalance its interests, it could put "greater emphasis on projecting Canadian values and culture abroad," largely by integrating Canadian students and faculty into the public diplomacy process.[1]

The purpose of this chapter is to describe the mechanisms, programs, and resources that are at Canada's disposal to promote its longer-term foreign policy interests through international education. The first part of the chapter focuses on academic relations and describes Canada's global network of Canadian Studies programs, the federal government's scholarship and exchange programs, and the array of initiatives designed to expose young Canadians to the world through work and travel. The second part of the chapter describes Canada's efforts to maintain its market share of international education.

CANADIAN STUDIES PROGRAMS

The crown jewel for many long-time observers of Canada's international academic relations has been the Can$5 million Canadian Studies program, which supports Canadian Studies associations and centres in foreign countries through research and study awards, travel grants, and assistance to university libraries. There are more than 7,000 individuals who specialize in Canadian Studies, appropriately titled "Canadianists," in approximately 45 countries, teaching at least 150,000 students annually.[2] In addition, over 2,000 books, articles and PHD dissertations dealing with Canada are published each year, and 10 periodicals on Canadian Studies are published regularly in countries that maintain close partnerships with Canada.[3] The Canadian Studies network, for a relatively small investment, ensures that knowledge and understanding of Canada reaches present and future decision makers. It, therefore, prepares the ground for Canada's commercial and political interests.

Before 1970, there was no institution responsible for the administration of the Canadian Studies program. As described by Canadian scholar Kim Nossal, specialized programs focused on Canada emerged at the Canadian-American Center at the University of Maine and the School of Advanced International Study at Johns Hopkins University in the late 1960s, with the rapid expansion of universities across North America.[4] With the increased scholarly interest in Canada, it was at a conference of Canadianists at Duke University in 1971 that the first Canadian Studies association, the Association of Canadian Studies in the United States (ACSUS), was formed. At approximately the same time, as Nossal notes, the Canadian government sought to expand Canada's global academic footprint, and the Department of External Affairs began funding Canadian Studies programs internationally in 1975. This allocation of funds spurred the growth of Canadian Studies programs, and five internationally based associations for Canadian

Studies were established by 1979. The creation of the International Council for Canadian Studies in 1981, with funding from External Affairs, again spurred the growth of international Canadian Studies associations; by 2005, twenty-one full-member associations were associated with the council, covering Canadian Studies programs in thirty-eight countries.[5]

Canadian missions are responsible for supporting Canadian Studies programs in their territories. However, few Canadian missions abroad have employees dedicated full-time to managing academic relations, with the exception of the major Canadian missions – in Washington, London, Paris, Berlin, and Tokyo. In all other missions, the management of academic relations is combined with media relations and culture under the broad guise of public affairs, which is usually the responsibility of a locally engaged staff.

Canadian Studies academics are often Canada's most effective, long-term dialogue partners with foreign institutions and audiences, since they typically work some distance from the capitals in which Canadian officials do most of their representation work. However, nurturing academic networks to serve Canada's foreign policy interests can be challenging. Scholars, by their very training and acculturation, take more critical approaches in their research; they also jealously guard their independence and are more concerned about being co-opted by government agendas. As well, many scholars, though perfectly happy to give lectures to hundreds of students or presentations at conferences, view media work in a completely different light, as they are not trained to deliver memorable sound bites.

The size and composition of Canadian Studies programs vary from country to country; the largest program is located in the United States. Although Canadian Studies are largely promoted by the Canadian government, there has been limited support from the US government in the form of grants from the US Department of Education's National Resource Centers Program and the Foreign Language and Areas Studies Fellowship Program.[6] With a total annual budget of Can$1.2 million (2004–5), there are over 50 Canadian Studies programs in the United States. Approximately 500 universities and colleges offer courses related to Canada, and nearly 800 faculty members teach an estimated 25,000 students per year in these courses.[7] Throughout the 1980s and into the early 1990s, Canadian Studies grew steadily in the United States, but then, according to Duncan Edmonds, a long-time observer of the Canadian Studies movement, growth began to level off and membership in ACSUS declined by several hundred.[8] The decline in the program was worrisome and indicative of subtle but important shifts in Canada's place in the American consciousness.

The evolution of the Canadian Studies program in the United States illustrates both the benefits and the challenges of managing such an enterprise. There is an assumption that because most Canadians live within 150 kilometres of the Canada-US border and because there are hundreds of thousands of border crossings each day, the human, cultural, and intellectual dimensions of the Canada-US relationship will take care of themselves. The tendency in Ottawa, for good reason following the terrorist attacks of 9/11, was to focus on the economic, political, and security dimension of Canada's relationship with the United States, rather than the civil society links.

The necessary focus on mutual interests in the global war on terrorism brought into stark relief the gaps in mutual understanding between the two countries – despite the explosion in information outlets. The persistent myths in the United States about Canada as a country soft on terrorism demonstrated the need for greater public diplomacy. Canadian pollster Michael Adams, in his book on how Americans and Canadians view each other, *Fire and Ice*, describes the growing values gap between the two nations.[9] Adams argues that there has been a divergence of values and that while Canadians have followed social liberalism, Americans have taken the path of social conservatism – a trend that has manifested itself in Americans becoming more religious than Canadians, being less receptive toward immigration and same-sex marriage, and holding a less positive view on the role of government in society. Though contested, this growing values gap, along with the shift of American economic, intellectual, and political power to the South and West in the United States, has, to use Edmonds' words, "[brought] about changing viewpoints and preoccupations in both countries and end[ed] the days when cross-border understanding between like-minded intellectuals and political leaders was almost automatic."[10] Consequently, it became apparent that the traditional compact between so-called East Coast liberals in the US Congress and administration and successive Canadian governments of both liberal and conservative ideological bent was coming apart at the seams. Moreover, Canada would have to connect with and explain itself to new, likely more conservative American elites. It was with this change in mind that David Anderson, Canadian minister of the environment (1999–2004), asserted, "Canadian studies at American universities help people in both countries to understand sensitivities and differences."[11] Canadian Studies enhance understanding, helping Canadians see themselves through others' eyes.

The expansion of Canada's diplomatic presence in the United States since 2003, through the US Enhanced Representation Initiative (see chapter 8), signalled the Canadian government's desire to enlarge the scope of its public diplomacy activities, including Canada's academic footprint. Given this program's short-term objective of increasing awareness of Canada-US social differences and Canada-US interdependence in North American security and economic relations, the contact between the new consulates and local educational institutions could only serve to increase Canada's profile.[12] According to Edmonds, "[i]t is crucial that the cultivation of academics as contacts for information, advocacy and long-term commitment through the Canadian Studies Program, be an important element in the activities of these posts, even if the resources are limited."[13]

THE CHALLENGES OF MAINTAINING A GLOBAL ACADEMIC FOOTPRINT

While the benefits of having seven thousand Canadianists around the world may seem obvious, given the need for Canada to be heard and involved with the global conversation, the challenges are nevertheless manifold: the persistent sense among some Canadian diplomats that academic relations are too far removed from the day-to-day work of diplomacy to contribute meaningfully to Canadian interests, the "greying" of the Canadianists (most of whom were hired in the 1970s and early 1980s), the dependence on limited government support; and the general isolation of academic relations from other Canadian government programs.

There is often confusion about the appropriate role of foreign academics who are supported by grants from the Canadian government through Canadian Studies programs. Some ambassadors are under the misapprehension that the value of Canadianists is contingent on them being used as strategic instruments of the embassy, like pieces on a chessboard. This displays a fundamental misunderstanding of the role of Canadianists. The very advantage for Canada in having these Canadianists around the world rests in their academic integrity and objectivity.[14] The credibility of Canada's public diplomacy – in any time frame – is enhanced if Canadianists, who function as high-credibility third-party sources, can be allowed to offer their views (whatever they may be) on their own terms. As Edmonds notes of Canadianists in the United States, "[b]y speaking, teaching, networking, researching, and writing texts and articles, the reach of academics extends deep into all sectors of the US educational system and the general public."[15] This does not mean that Canadianists are in any way subordinate to, or agents of, the Canadian federal government; they are independent entities, not "fifth columnists." As a result, Canadianists create unique public spaces for dialogue because they allow Canada to be seen and understood through local eyes.

Another criticism is that Canadian Studies programs have become embedded in the humanities (literature, cultural studies, history) and are known only to a small coterie of like-minded scholars. Since the late 1990s, Canada has been working to diversify the Canadian Studies disciplines as much as possible, trying to reorient the programs more to public policy and even to the sciences. That being said, it is often more difficult to connect the idea and image of Canada in pure sciences, such as biology and chemistry; in addition, such scholarly work reaches a smaller audience. However, if Canadian Studies programs are being managed by Canadian missions with clear, long-term strategic interests in mind, they will have a visibility that furthers Canada's foreign policy while respecting the independence of the participating scholars. These are not contradictory objectives, as is sometimes asserted.

A distinction must also be drawn between events designed to create awareness of Canadian views among local decision makers (e.g., inviting a Canadianist to testify in a local legislature) and events designed to project Canada's image to a broader public (e.g., Canadianists talking about Canada on local television or radio). Canadian Studies programs can, in fact, do both. For example, the Canadian High Commission in the United Kingdom effectively used its Canadian Studies program between 2000 and 2003 to position Canada as a leading authority on federalism as the British Parliament in London devolved powers to the Scottish Parliament and the National Assembly of Wales.

The greatest challenge, however, is the changing university environment itself. Scholars leaving Canadian Studies positions, often through retirement, are not always being replaced, forcing the dwindling number of new Canadianists to ask what incentives exist for them to remain in the field. Unlike historians or political scientists, those hired into Canadian Studies programs have no guarantees that their departments are likely to remain intact, which creates further disincentives for future Canadianists. To address this situation, in 2003 ACSUS launched an effort in the United States to identify researchers working on Canadian issues – nominally unaware Canadianists. Eventually, 420 people were identified who were not members of academia or other associations but were working on Canada-related subjects. This has re-energized Canadian Studies in the United States and, as a result, the ACSUS model has now been applied to other "greying" Canadian Studies networks in the United Kingdom, Italy, and Germany. David Archibald, executive director of ACSUS, has also identified growth in an "interdepartmental" approach, whereby researchers from different academic disciplines (mostly specialists in public administration, health policy, economics, sociology, and political science) have been encouraged to use Canada as a focal point by comparing and contrasting Canadian policies and social models with those in the United States. He notes that "[b]y establishing a comparative research framework and analyzing alternative approaches, American researchers gain much greater insight not just into the Canadian model, but also the US model, thereby creating a valuable space for policy discourse."[16] This type of interdisciplinary approach emphasizing public policy research should also help to bring in curious analysts and thus broaden the bases of all Canadian Studies programs around the world. It may also begin to dispel the misconception that Canadian Studies programs exist primarily to expand awareness of the novels of Alice Munro and Margaret Atwood.

Canadian Studies programs abroad will never be self-financing enterprises. As Edmonds concludes in his study of three decades of Canadian Studies in the United States, the program "did not emerge organically and cannot and will not survive without the ongoing support and encouragement from the Government of Canada."[17] Canadian Studies also face a particular dilemma with regard to support from charitable foundations and the private sector. If Canadian Studies are not visible and are not seen to be achieving specific objectives related to Canadian or the host country's interests, they will not garner corporate support – Canadian or foreign – thus making ongoing Canadian government support essential. In the case of Canadian Studies in the United States, it is ironic that traditional business support dissipated in the 1990s, just as the bilateral Canada-US relationship became more important in both countries and the level of economic integration increased substantially.[18] A related problem is that Canadian Studies grants are often not large enough to interest major universities and established scholars (where the visibility of such a program would be the highest), making the distribution of grants so diffuse as to never reach a noticeable critical mass.

Arguably, Canadian Studies will have the least impact – relative to the other levers of Canada's public diplomacy – on societies with which Canada already has deep historical, cultural, economic, and political ties, such as the United States, the United Kingdom, France, and many countries in Western Europe. In such media-saturated societies, where fierce competition for nation brands exists, Canada would be perceived as "familiar," and thus highly likely to be overlooked. As a result, increasing Canada's profile through Canadian Studies requires significantly more effort and investment. Given scarce resources and demands for measurable results, a Canadian Studies program could, therefore, have more impact in a middle-tier or emerging country such as Mexico or India, as it does in Brazil.

As Edmonds advocates, efforts should be made to make Canadian Studies part of a broader public diplomacy strategy (see chapter 8, "The Practice of Public Diplomacy") that would exploit the synergy among different elements of academic relations – education marketing, mobility, scholarships, exchanges, cultural programs – in support of well-defined foreign policy goals.[19] If Canadian Studies programs were conceived as operating in concert with other programs, rather than in relative isolation, then the managers of these programs would encourage academic discourse in areas of direct policy relevance. In the North American context, for example, American scholars who are part of Canadian Studies programs have been encouraged (through Canadian government academic grants) to further scholarly exchanges and public dialogue on the sometimes contentious issues of border management, health care, the environment, and water management, as well as on other elements of the bilateral relationship. This does not mean that the Canadian government should promote only scholarship that validates its current policy priorities. Although third-party validation by high-credibility academic sources is obviously helpful, the ultimate objective should be to generate discussion of issues directly relevant to Canada's public policy objectives, which may or may not be on the host country's public policy agenda.

With regard to marketing Canadian Studies to a new generation of students and scholars around the world, the renewal strategy adopted by the Canadian Studies program in the United States is instructive. Taking the study of Canada out of area studies, especially given the reluctance of American universities to invest in permanent chairs in Canadian Studies at a time when Chinese and Middle Eastern studies were more popular, was a necessary first step. Also, there must be sustained funding for faculty research, including exchange programs such as the Canada-US Fulbright Program. In light of the growing integration of the North American economy and the consequent need for professionals who will be able to work comfortably on either side of the border, presenting Canadian Studies (including French courses) as an undergraduate minor may become an attractive option for American students seeking a competitive advantage. As Archibald writes, "[t]he level of economic interdependence, the large volume of cross border trade and investment, the US dependence on Canadian oil and natural gas, and cross border environmental and security cooperation all point to why Canada should and must be studied by all Americans."[20]

Measuring the Impact of Canadian Studies

Despite its challenges, the Canadian Studies program continues to be an important instrument of influence because it gives Canada a level of soft political access abroad that it would not have otherwise, especially in those countries in which it has no official diplomatic relations (e.g., Taiwan). A noteworthy feature of the Canadian Studies program compared to the academic relations programs of some of Canada's largest competitors, such as the United States, is the emphasis it places on preserving academic freedom. Such a high level of academic freedom is not always tolerated in official government-supported academic relations programs.

A few examples will illustrate the impact of Canadian Studies. As Jean Labrie, head of Canadian Studies at DFAIT, explains, "I'd been going to Mexico once every two months to explain to the Mexicans why we excluded the cultural industries from the Canada-US Free Trade Agreement and why we wanted to keep it out of the North American Free Trade Agreement. And they were very polite and said 'yes,' but I was a government agent. Then the founding president of the Asociación Mexicana de Estudios sobre Canadá went in person to explain the same thing I did – and it was done."[21] In 2001, when Canada briefly banned the import of Brazilian beef because of a BSE ("mad cow disease") scare, the decision, not surprisingly, upset the Brazilians. But the Brazilian Canadianists were very good at explaining Canada's agricultural policy to the media – not defending Canada, but explaining Canada's actions – and this proved to be an important step in helping to defuse the situation. Overall, such interventions by third parties give Canada a level of credibility that other countries do not have.[22]

In 2005, the Asociación Española de Estudios Canadienses organized a conference comparing Spanish and Canadian approaches to federalism, a high-profile event that demonstrated the evolution of the use of Canadian Studies. Although organized by the Asociación, the conference was not advertised as a Canadian Studies event. Indeed, of all the participants, there were only two Canadian Studies scholars. The featured participants were Spanish intellectuals and policy-makers, including the Spanish minister of justice, who reportedly had studied in Canada, and King Juan Carlos, who awarded ten scholarships to accomplished Spanish students to study in Canada. Combining the conference with the scholarship awards significantly increased the importance and prestige of the event. Also present was the Canadian minister of the environment at the time, Stéphane Dion, who presented his book *Straight Talk: Speeches and Writings on Canadian Unity* (translated into Spanish) at the event in Spanish.[23] These examples demonstrate how Canadian Studies, in concert with other public affairs programs (e.g., scholarships, high-level visits), can achieve certain foreign policy objectives and influence decision makers in other countries.

If the Canadian Studies program is to prosper abroad in the years ahead, its role will have to be redefined, and the scope of how Canada is to be studied will have to be broadened beyond a focus on teaching and research in the humanities (as valuable as this is) to include greater attention to comparative public policy. By broadening the scope, the program will invite interest from a greater spectrum of scholars and students. The primary purpose of Canadian Studies should not be to increase general knowledge about Canada among foreign audiences; there are more effective ways to have a broad societal impact, and most of these involve the use of the mass media. As Kim Nossal notes, Canada must strive to make a lasting impression on target populations; however, in its current constitution, the success of Canadian Studies is demonstrated "not [by] what actually occurs on the ground, but rather that a maple leaf can be planted on a map."[24]

SCHOLARSHIPS, STUDENT EXCHANGES, AND ACADEMIC MOBILITY

Just as Canadian Studies provide soft access in foreign countries, government scholarships and exchanges offer a balance between enlightened self-interest and a genuine desire to promote international goodwill and development. The motive is certainly to "win friends" in other parts of the world, friends who, if favourably impressed, will in turn maintain a positive disposition and influence policy or public opinion towards their former hosts later in life.[25] Another motivation is to provide policy capacity and key skills to successor generations, particularly in developing countries and fragile states, to help improve global living standards. Scholarship programs, in particular, target individuals who will rise to the highest levels of their professions – academic, government, or business – where they can influence policy and "have catalytic effects on others."[26]

The purpose of Canadian scholarship and exchange programs is to develop a network of Canada-friendly persons of influence around the world. It is hoped that once they return to their homelands they will continue their networking with Canada. The government of Canada offers a variety of scholarship programs to encourage high-calibre foreign students and scholars to come to Canada and to encourage Canadians to study abroad, primarily through DFAIT's Can\$7 million postgraduate scholarship

and academic relations program and the Can\$6 million Canadian Franco-
phone Scholarship Program offered by the Canadian International Development Agency (CIDA). It is not the purpose of the following sections to
provide details on each provincial or federal government program or pri-
vate-foundation scholarship program, since this information is available
elsewhere, but rather to highlight some of the more important programs
offered by the Canadian government as part of its educational public diplomacy. The major DFAIT programs include the Canada-US Fulbright Program, the Commonwealth and Fellowship Plan, and the Government of
Canada Awards program.[27] CIDA's main academic program, not surprisingly, supports students from developing countries, while Human
Resources and Social Development Canada (HRSDC) offers an academic
mobility program, and Canada's engineering and health granting councils
offer a variety of fellowship programs directed at foreign researchers.[28]
The following section will discuss each of these in turn.

The Canada-US Fulbright Program

The Fulbright Program, which started in 1946 and is a well-respected
American public diplomacy initiative, sponsors academic exchanges of students and scholars between the United States and over 150 countries
around the world. In 1990, the Canadian and American governments
jointly created the Foundation for Educational Exchanges, a bi-national
organization with the primary task of administering the Canada-US
Fulbright Program. The Canada-US Fulbright's mandate is to "enhance
mutual understanding between the people of Canada and the people of
the United States by providing support to outstanding graduate students,
faculty, professionals and independent researchers."[29] It is believed that
these academic exchanges, which have supported nearly six hundred excep-
tional Canadian and American graduate students and scholars, contribute
leadership skills to future influential Canadians and Americans. Furthermore, the exchanges encourage "a more nuanced appreciation of each
other," which is essential in view of the vicissitudes of the Canada-US relationship.[30] Reinforcing and promoting good bilateral relations with its
southern neighbour is essential to Canada's prosperity and security.

This program, by deepening academic networks between the two countries, has provided excellent visibility for Canadian experts and institutions
in the United States, especially beyond the academic hubs of Boston and
Washington, DC.[31] Starting in 2004, the Fulbright Program expanded to
include a mobility program for award recipients, so that they would be able

to travel more extensively within the host country. This has resulted in greater visibility for visiting academics and has extended Canada's brand within the United States to a greater degree.[32] Since 2000, the Fulbright Program has negotiated formal partnerships with twenty Canadian and thirteen American academic institutions, in addition to a wide coalition of Canadian and American schools involved in the Pacific Northwest Canadian Studies Consortium, under the auspices of the Visiting Chairs Program. In 2006, there were twenty-nine visiting research chairs for American scholars in Canada (six of which were at the University of Alberta) and seventeen visiting research chairs for Canadian scholars in the United States.[33] Edmonds believes that there is great value in having Canada associate itself with the excellent reputation of the Fulbright Program and that it plays a pivotal role in the enhancement of Canada-US academic relations. Also, it will facilitate the recruitment of more American students and faculty members to Canadian institutions of higher learning.[34]

The Canada-US Fulbright Program, along with the Canada Institute at the Woodrow Wilson Center for Scholars in Washington, DC, represents promising efforts to build bridges of understanding between Canadian and American societies.[35] Such efforts, which deepen the presence of the Canadian brand in new and existing academic communities, are explicitly designed to allow for greater intellectual fermentation beyond the world of academe on issues of mutual concern to Canada and the United States.

Government of Canada Awards and Commonwealth Scholarships

The Government of Canada Awards are used as instruments to reinforce Ottawa's bilateral relations in twelve countries of priority for Canada. The Canadian heads of mission in these countries play a key role in selecting individuals with strong potential for these awards. Except in the case of Brazil, the awards are reciprocal, meaning that Canada covers the tuition fees for the selected foreign graduate students and the other countries do the same for Canadian students. Seventy-five Government of Canada Awards have been distributed annually, and in any given year there are three hundred award holders at Canadian universities.

The Commonwealth Scholarship and Fellowship Plan (CSFP), which is one of Canada's oldest international scholarship programs, was originally proposed by Canada while it was hosting a 1958 Commonwealth Trade Ministers' Conference, after Canadian universities had previously suggested the idea to national authorities.[36] It was formally established at a Commonwealth Education Ministers' Conference in 1959. Since then, some twenty-two thousand individuals have received the award, and there have been approximately five hundred new recipients each year. Canada, along with the United Kingdom, is the most generous sponsor of the CSFP.[37] It was conceived with two objectives in mind. First, the scholarships needed to provide benefits for home countries. Second, they were awarded with significant flexibility so that the plan could evolve in order to reflect different and changing needs over time.[38] The purpose of the CSFP is to create stronger ties within the Commonwealth and to encourage development in developing Commonwealth countries. The foreign policy benefit of these awards is that they provide an opportunity to create a focus on Canada in countries of interest.

Additionally, the Canadian government, through DFAIT, participates in the long-standing Canada-China Scholars Exchange Program. DFAIT has identified 394 Chinese scholars as having participated in the four-to-twelve-month-long program since it began in 1973. As with most exchange programs, the goal of this one is to increase mutual understanding between the two countries' intellectual communities. In 2004, the program was redesigned and enlarged to better reflect the increasing growth within the Canada-China relationship. As a result, Canada has extended the program to include Chinese non-academics (e.g., economists, broadcasters, judges) in exchanges, in the hope that these individuals will return to China with not only a better understanding of Canada but also a better appreciation of Canadian values, such as human rights and respect for democracy.

The Canadian Francophone Scholarship Program

The Canadian Francophone Scholarship Program, managed by CIDA, focuses on Canada's ties with francophone countries.[39] The program combines Canada's altruistic and pragmatic objectives. Each year, CIDA offers scholarships to qualified graduate and undergraduate students from the thirty-seven countries that form *la francophonie*. The goal of the program is to offer highly qualified students from developing countries the opportunity to benefit from the knowledge, resources, and expertise of Canadian universities and colleges, and to strengthen the ties between Canada and these countries. Endowing foreign students from developing countries with professional skills and abilities falls within the parameters of Canada's development objectives. Canada's national interests are served, since many of the candidates go on to become prominent and influential leaders in their home countries. Through such scholarships, Canada can maintain its profile as a leader within the French-speaking world.[40]

Academic Mobility Agreements

Although the vast majority of academic mobility exchanges and international academic projects are funded by CIDA and are designed to find solutions to social, economic, and environmental problems in developing countries, other federal departments have smaller international education initiatives. Canada's research councils offer a variety of research fellowships to foster international scientific collaboration. They include the Natural Sciences and Engineering Research Council of Canada's Industrial Research and Development Fellowships, Japan Society for the Promotion of Science Fellowships, and Visiting Fellowships in Canadian Government Laboratories. Additionally, the Social Sciences and Humanities Research Council of Canada sponsors its own doctoral-fellowship program. Recognizing that mobility – in people and ideas – is essential to making a country competitive, HRSDC's International Academic Mobility initiative provides three to four hundred Canadian students every year with learning opportunities abroad. Canadian universities and colleges are encouraged to jointly develop projects that focus on themes in higher education and training. According to HRSDC, "[t]he central element is student mobility and cooperative activities [that] include the development of joint courses, curricula and teaching materials which take advantage of new education technologies and distance learning."[41] While HRSDC does not have an international mandate per se, its interests lie in creating a population that has the appropriate skills for an increasingly global and high-technology economy.

The purpose of the International Academic Mobility initiative is to enable young Canadians to benefit from globalization by enhancing their skills and providing an opportunity for personal and professional development (including language skills and greater awareness of foreign cultures) through direct international experience. Very modest levels of government funding are available for this initiative, through two main programs: the Program for North American Mobility in Higher Education and the Canadian-European Union Program for Cooperation in Higher Education and Training (all twenty-five EU member states participate).[42] The North American program, drawing together academics from Canada, the United States, and Mexico, has supported fifty projects since its inception in 1995. Each program requires participation from six colleges and universities – two in each of the participating countries. While the funding levels are very modest, the programs provide another means by which Canada increases its visibility abroad. As Senator Serge Joyal wrote in 1994 in a report on Canada's cultural diplomacy: "[t]he involvement of institutions of higher education in exchanges, research and development serves to strengthen Canada's distinctive identity on the international scene."[43]

It comes as no surprise that many of the academic and student exchanges take place between Canada and its traditional partners in the United States and Western Europe. And just as foreigners educated in Canada can become a "long-term arm" of Canadian interests, so too can Canadians educated at foreign universities. Thousands of Canadian students studying abroad support Canada's public diplomacy indirectly, as they project a Canadian presence wherever they may be studying. Furthermore, once these students return to Canada, they will be able to continue to foster their international ties, both in the course of their careers and also in their contributions to making Canadian society more sensitive to foreign cultures. However, the greatest advantage will accrue to Canada if Canadian students begin to choose emerging countries such as China, Mexico, and Brazil as their destinations of choice for post-secondary study, rather than following the well-worn routes of the Anglo-American world or France. For example, while thousands of Chinese students come to Canada every year, only twelve hundred Canadians study in Chinese universities.[44] As Ralston Saul noted in his 1994 report, there is a very good reason for Canada to use exchange programs to increase its visibility in emerging countries, since it is in these countries that Canada's role "can be less limited by the colonial fixation" and thus provide Canada's foreign policy with balance.[45]

YOUTH PROGRAMS: EXCHANGES AND DEVELOPMENT INTERNSHIPS

One dimension of Canada's international education programming that is often unheralded – probably because it does not involve prestigious scholarships and fellowships – is comprised of its international youth exchanges, which allow Canadian and foreign post-secondary students to work temporarily while touring in each other's country. These programs, which started in the 1950s, are perhaps Canada's best-kept public diplomacy secrets. Two characteristics distinguish them from most other youth-oriented international programs:[46] they are reciprocal, in that Canada and partner countries agree to host each other's young people, and they are not subsidized by the federal government (participants must find their own jobs and cover their own expenses). The Canadian government acts as a facilitator and, where necessary, negotiates treaties and ensures that bilateral exchange quotas are met.

Between 1995 and 2005, DFAIT facilitated over 365,000 youth exchanges worldwide, with 54,000 exchanges alone in 2005. Canada brought in 30,000 young people and sent 24,000 young Canadians to work abroad, an almost fivefold increase from the number of young Canadians who benefited from the program in 1995.[47] Canada, which competes with Australia as one of the top four most popular destinations for travel for the world's young people (the United States is the most popular, followed by the United Kingdom), has about forty exchange programs in ninety countries. For example, each year Australia hosts about 8,000 young Canadians, and Canada hosts as many young Australians.[48] The exchange programs have been rated highly by those Canadians who have used them, but because they are not actively marketed, many young Canadians are not even aware that they exist.[49]

For young Canadians possessing a post-secondary degree, DFAIT and CIDA also offer professional internships abroad as part of the Career Focus Program of the government of Canada's Youth Employment Strategy (YES).[50] Young Professionals International (YPI), a program that would be discontinued in 2007, offered paid, non-reciprocal, career-related overseas internships that contributed to the general advancement of Canada's image in foreign countries by helping future Canadian leaders to bridge "the gap between formal education and career."[51] The implementing organizations, which included private and public sector partners, NGOs, and international organizations, were located in Canada and sent interns to their host organizations in other countries for six to twelve months. Between 1997 and 2003, DFAIT offered 3,215 internships to young Canadians, with approximately 400 placements annually.[52] CIDA, through its International Youth Internship Program, offers similar overseas placements in developing countries, and the purpose of the program is to contribute to Canada's international development objectives.[53]

In addition to these international exchange programs, the government of Canada (primarily through CIDA) has supported myriad other programs over the decades to encourage young Canadians to gain international experience in developing countries. These programs include Canada World Youth, Canadian Crossroads International, and the International Rural Exchange. As is the case with all of Canada's public diplomacy assets, historically there has not been a focal point in government for the promotion of the international dimension of Canada's youth policy.

By 2004, following a national public dialogue on Canadian foreign policy in which Canadians stated that they wanted Canada to have a bigger voice internationally and with the new Liberal prime minister, Paul Martin, wishing to put a personal stamp on Canada's international policy, officials in the Prime Minister's Office were signalling to the federal bureaucracy that it was necessary to give some expression to the desire of Canadians – and particularly Canada's young people – to make a difference in the world. Media commentary at the time suggested that this was evidence of the Martin government's nostalgia for a period in the late 1960s when Canadian baby boomers travelled abroad in great numbers to "do good." Canadian officials initially had some difficulty divining exactly what type of new mechanism was needed, given that many Canadian non-governmental organizations, both those involving young people and those involving Canadians with considerable experience, such as the Canadian Executive Service Organization, had already been in the business for many years, if not several decades, of sending Canadians abroad to work in developing countries. It was recognized, however, that government programming related to mobilizing the international aspirations of Canada's citizens needed greater coherence.

To this end, in 2004 the Canada Corps Branch was created in CIDA to act as an umbrella organization for new and existing programs whose mandates were to send Canadian expertise abroad to promote good governance and institution-building in developing countries and fragile states. In the words of Prime Minister Martin, the Canada Corps would "bring new focus and energy to what is already being done, and more effectively match the skills and talents of Canadians – including youth – to help nurture democracy and the rule of law in fragile states in the future."[54] Within two years, the Canada Corps itself would be rebranded as the Office for Democratic Governance, in order to reflect Canada's intention to become a leader in the promotion of democracy.

As previously described, Canada supports numerous scholarship programs, academic mobility agreements, and development-related and student exchange programs. The main purpose of these programs is to endow young Canadians with appropriate skills in the age of globalization and to build a network of potentially influential leaders in other countries that are sympathetic towards Canada. Another motivation is to promote international development by providing policy capacity and key skills to successor generations. While the objectives and motivations behind these programs are laudable, the main challenge comes from underfunding. For instance, DFAIT's and CIDA's combined international scholarship budget is approximately Can$13 million; in contrast, Australia has committed itself to spending Can$1.2 billion on its scholarship program between 2006 and 2010 for the Asian region alone.[55] Considering the gap in the amounts invested, as the next section will show, it is no wonder that Canada is losing important market share in education and, therefore, global influence to Australia and other countries.

EDUCATION MARKETING

Canadian universities, colleges, and training institutes make an important contribution to Canada's competitiveness and knowledge transfer. Although Canadian universities have a long tradition of hosting substantial numbers of foreign students, it was only in the 1990s that the post-secondary education sector emerged as a core trade sector. Until then, the high-quality education offered by Canadian colleges and universities was a hidden nation-branding and commercial resource. By December 2005, there were over 154,000 foreign students in Canada, representing an estimated Can$5 billion[56] infusion into the Canadian economy, as part of an estimated Can$100 billion global education industry.[57]

The international marketing of Canada as a destination for education and training serves a number of domestic and international objectives. Canada benefits from having a growing pool of highly skilled workers who will be able to fill vacancies in the domestic labour market, and the presence of foreign students enhances the experiences of Canadian students by offering different cultural approaches and interpretations to the learning environment. Foreign students' familiarity with Canada can also enhance future business relationships with Canadian firms, since they would be able to promote the quality of Canadian products and industries abroad.

Canadian universities have long been involved in international education programs, and, together, they have positioned Canada as the world's fifth-largest host country to international students, after the United States, France, Germany, and the United Kingdom. Often, these arrangements occur under one of several cooperation agreements that Canadian schools maintain with over eleven hundred foreign partner institutions.[58] According to the Association of Universities and Colleges of Canada, international students represent nearly 5 percent of the total student population at Canadian universities.[59] Canadian universities, not surprisingly, have grown very dependent on foreign students, as they inject a significant amount of money into the Canadian system, largely as a result of increased tuition fees.

However, despite its position as a major destination, Canada has not fully exploited its education assets, and it risks losing more global market share to the aggressive marketing of countries such as Australia. Through Australian Education International (AEI), Australia has advertised itself very aggressively, particularly in the Asia Pacific region, as a source of advanced, high-quality Western degrees.[60] In Canada, one reason education marketing has not been fully exploited as part of a public diplomacy strategy is that the education system is decentralized, since education falls under provincial jurisdiction. As a result, the federal government has only a limited role to play. Senator Joyal has succinctly summarized the inherent difficulties that a scattered federal responsibility for international education presents: "[A] near total lack of investment in international activities, especially in comparison with efforts of other [G8] countries; a much lower level of public funding for initiatives put forward by Canadian institutions in conjunction with counterparts in other industrialized countries ... poorly defined international policies in educational institutions; low mobility among Canadian students and teachers; lack of comprehensive education marketing policy, which should include promotion of education services and language teaching abroad as well as promotion of Canada as a destination of choice for foreign students."[61]

It is certainly challenging to market Canadian education as a national asset when there is no single federal organization to beat the drum on behalf of Canada's education and training sector. This distinguishes Canada's educational diplomacy from that of France, the United Kingdom, Germany, and Australia. As described earlier in this chapter, the federal government has well-respected but very modestly funded programs to encourage academic mobility and international scholarships. The provinces, keen to promote education as a growth industry, pursue their own initiatives individually.[62] The Canadian Education Centre (CEC) Network, the Canadian Bureau for International Education, the Association for Universities and Colleges of Canada, and the Association of Canadian Community Colleges all promote Canada on behalf of their clients or memberships. In addition, the larger Canadian universities, such as the University of Toronto, the University of British Columbia, the Université de Montréal, and McGill University, have the ability to act as global educational players in their own right. Even allowing for the individual success stories of universities and colleges that are able to attract international funding and high proportions of foreign students, this nevertheless creates a limp and somewhat confusing international educational profile for Canada. Canada's provincial ministers travel around the world attending international education conferences (e.g., the Conference of the Commonwealth Education Ministers), but it is hardly surprising that they represent their provincial interests first. As a consequence, Canada's approach to mar-

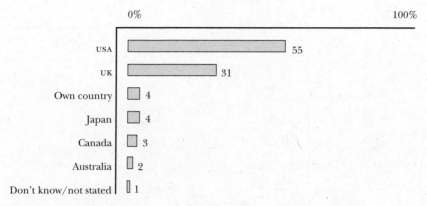

Figure 5.1   Percentage of young people who consider various countries to provide educational qualifications with the most credibility for potential employers.

Source: British Council, *Through Other Eyes* 2, 27

keting education is scattered, and despite being a favoured destination for education, Canada risks losing more global market share in the future.

In a British Council survey in 2000, in which young people (between twenty-four and thirty-five years of age) from twenty-eight countries were asked to rate the quality of education in five countries, including Canada, that are well-known for accepting foreign students, it is not surprising that the educational qualifications from the United States and the United Kingdom were rated most highly (see figure 5.1). What is significant is that Canada ranked behind Japan and was just ahead of Australia. Furthermore, as figure 5.2 shows, Canada was actually behind Australia as a preferred destination.

Despite these challenges in marketing, the absence of a federal education department has enabled DFAIT to take a far more prominent role working with provincial ministers of education to coordinate foreign policy in the area of education and to ensure Canada's active participation in a range of international educational activities abroad, including the Organization of American States, the G8, and the UN Educational, Scientific and Cultural Organization.[63]

Canadian Education Centre Network

There were some predictions that in a post-9/11 environment, with the United States perceived as being unfriendly to foreign students, they would

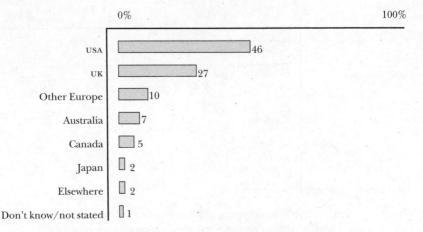

Figure 5.2   Percentage of young people who would prefer to visit various
countries for educational purposes.
Source: British Council, *Through Other Eyes 2, 27*

be diverted away from that country to Canada. It is, however, very difficult
to ascertain the effects of the "war on terror" on international flows of foreign students, given the difficulty in obtaining accurate national statistics.[64]
While Canada's global share of foreign students has declined in relative
terms, especially as countries such as Australia have made huge investments
in marketing themselves, it is true that the number of foreign students in
Canada continues to increase in absolute terms.

The federal government has not stood still in the face of a more globalized market for education. In the early 1990s, Canada's missions in Asia
reported that Australia was beginning to market itself aggressively in the
region as a provider of education and that in the absence of some response,
Canada would lose market share. In 1995, the Canadian government
responded by establishing the CEC Network, financed by DFAIT and CIDA
but wholly owned by the Asia Pacific Foundation of Canada, to help Canadian universities, colleges, primary and secondary schools, language schools,
and training schools to attract foreign students to Canada.[65] Starting with
seven centres in countries from which there was already a continuous flow
of students to Canada (five of them were in the Asia Pacific region) the CEC
Network had expanded to seventeen offices by 2005, with the majority
(thirteen) remaining in the Asia Pacific region.[66]

According to an evaluation of the CEC Network at the end of its first five
years, the existence of this Canadian presence abroad resulted in Canada

receiving about ten percent more students from countries served by CECs than would otherwise have been the case. It was further calculated that the economic benefit of this increased recruitment was seven times more than the cost of operating the CEC Network, leading the DFAIT auditors to conclude that the program had provided an excellent return on the investment. That being said, the CEC Network's own financial reports between 2000 and 2005 show conclusively that any hope that the network would eventually achieve financial self-sufficiency was largely wishful thinking. Although there was a substantial reduction (from Can$3 million down to Can$750,000) in the government's (largely CIDA's) contribution to the network's average Can$7.5 million annual budget between 1999 and 2004, it was obvious that the government's contribution and any in-kind transfers were still critical to the network's viability. Indeed, all of Canada's competitors assume that the longer-term viability of their education marketing efforts rests with public funding.

CONCLUSION

By increasing the resources devoted to international education the government provides more opportunities to Canadian students, opening doors for their future by allowing them to gain relevant international exposure – while exercising Canadian public diplomacy around the world. Increasing the number of foreign students in Canada has much the same effect, because it emphasizes the open character of Canadian society, although the Association of Universities and Colleges of Canada contends that more could be done to facilitate the entry of these students into Canada.[67]

Education initiatives are long-term means of developing and maintaining non-confrontational bilateral links. Where there are barriers to bilateral relations, educational diplomacy can play an important role in, at the very least, creating a forum to discuss differences. Instead of "promoting" Canadian approaches, which may imply that the Canadian way is superior, "presenting" them and inviting comparison of other nations' approaches to Canada's will foster an appreciation of such differences. Frequently thought of as too fluffy and ethereal to have much impact in hard-nosed state-to-state relations, international educational programs should not be underestimated. While government accountants may be looking for metrics to evaluate the impact of student and faculty exchanges, scholarships, and working-abroad programs, they largely miss the effectiveness of longer-term public diplomacy, since the impact of these types of programs will not be seen for some ten to fifteen years, if not longer.

However, this is not to say that individual programs should not be evaluated to ensure that they are fulfilling their mandates. The entire federal system of international education programming should be evaluated periodically to eliminate overlap and duplication. Canada, for example, needs to do a better job of tracking the recipients of its scholarships and establishing networks of scholarship alumni. Only in recent years has Canada begun to trace its scholarship recipients.[68] Doing so has proven problematic, as the lack of a systematic follow-up by Canadian missions abroad with recipients of Canadian government scholarships has not maximized the potential value to be gained from these academic contacts. While other G8 countries, along with Australia, devote entire departmental divisions to managing scholarship and exchange programs, in Canada the number of officials responsible for such programs at the federal level can be counted on the fingers of one hand, although it should be stated that the actual management of the DFAIT-funded scholarships is provided by a non-governmental organization, the Canadian Bureau for International Education. This decentralized system helps to explain why it is difficult for Canada to mobilize a global network of scholarship recipients, although there is now a global alumni association.[69]

John Ralston Saul included a stinging rebuke of Canada's international-education policy in his 2004 speech at York University's Glendon College, noting the main elements that have plagued Canada in this critical area of public diplomacy. Ralston Saul makes four key observations. First, Canada lacks a coherent overarching strategy for pursuing academic exchanges. The lack of a critical mass of academic exchange programs and their limited budgets prevent Canada from receiving long-term benefits of such exchanges. Second, there is no strategy in place to encourage students to study in countries that may be useful to Canada's strategic priorities in the long run. Ralston Saul believes that Canada should encourage students to study in like-minded countries or middle-power countries that face similar challenges, opportunities, and tensions, such as the Nordic countries or Australia, or other federations such as Germany. Third, Canada needs to recognize the initiatives of young Canadians. The impetus for a Canada Corps was the desire to channel young Canadians' leadership skills and concern for international issues and development. Finally, Ralston Saul maintains that high tuition fees discourage foreign students from studying in Canada. Universities, in his view, consider foreign students exclusively in financial terms, rather than as agents capable of promoting Canada abroad.[70] According to Ralston Saul:

We seem to be approaching foreign students as little more than cash cows, instead of seeing them as the easiest and most obvious agents for building an understanding of Canada over the very long term at the international level. The cash cow approach earns us peanuts through tuition, while losing us uncalculated serious investments over the long term. After all, a foreign student who goes home having been educated in a city in a province in Canada becomes a permanent ambassador for Canada and a permanent potential economic and political ally. Twenty years later they may be the Finance Minister of their country or president of a key corporation or a leading film-maker.[71]

Ralston Saul's last example nicely illustrates the crux of the problem. Canada has had no comprehensive international education strategy that incorporates Canadian Studies programs, academic and youth exchanges, scholarships, and internships. There are, instead, myriad programs and strategies across a number of federal departments. Canada also invests very little in promoting international education: DFAIT's expenditure on academic grants and scholarships of approximately Can$13 million annually has represented a small fraction (less than 1 percent) of its annual budget.[72] As this chapter has demonstrated, one of the major disadvantages for Canada's educational diplomacy and marketing is the lack of resources and a whole-of-Canada approach: the combined budgets of the Canadian Bureau for International Education (Can$4.1 million) and the CEC were approximately Can$11.6 million in 2005. In contrast, Australia's budget for international education marketing, led by the AEI (with a budget of AU$56 million in 2005) was supplemented by an infusion of AU$105 million, or about Can$90.8 million, between 2003 and 2007. In the absence of a comprehensive national strategy, the vacuum will continue to be filled by individual university initiatives and a variety of worthy federal and provincial programs that do not do justice to the full potential of the Canadian education brand.

6

International Broadcasting and New Media

Before the attacks of 11 September 2001, the future of international civilian broadcasting was given relatively sparse attention. There are few comparative studies available, even though international broadcasters encompass a variety of mandates and styles.[1] The renewal of interest in public diplomacy because of the need by the West to win "hearts and minds" across the Muslim world precipitated the greatest expansion of interest and investment in civilian international broadcasting across the Anglo-American world – but surprisingly not in Canada – in a generation or more. It became clear that the debate on the "clash of civilizations" had fixed the attention of American policy-makers on what had been nourishing the minds of young Muslims worldwide. As a result, the United States and the United Kingdom, allies in the war on terror and in the Iraq campaign, became focused on determining how opinion towards the West was being formed and what could be done to create a public opinion environment that was less susceptible to manipulation by extreme voices.

The preceding chapters have described a variety of instruments that, together, comprise the public diplomacy process. This chapter focuses on one of the instruments – international broadcasting – that is most closely associated with traditional concepts of public diplomacy. It seeks to place the history of Canada's international broadcasting record in the context of the overall evolution of international broadcasting, particularly the broadcasting styles and mandates of the United States and the United Kingdom. The purpose is not to provide a detailed history of international broadcasting in Canada, since this history has been summarized elsewhere by this author and in an excellent history of Radio Canada International by Arthur Siegel.[2] Rather, this chapter will demonstrate that Canada's international broadcasting services in radio and television have been distinctly underdeveloped tools of Canada's public diplomacy.[3]

Indeed, in contrast to the debates and substantial changes that surround the American and British international broadcasting strategies, Canada's international broadcasting agenda could hardly be described as transformative. Ironically, what *has* been transformative is the use of new media to consult Canadians on future directions in Canada's international role. The attention paid to the domestic dimension of Canada's public diplomacy among Ottawa's mandarins with respect to managing public on-line consultations and reviews (such as in *A Dialogue on Foreign Policy* of 2003 and *Canada's International Policy Statement* of 2005) far outweighs any attention paid to international broadcasting as a key instrument of Canadian public diplomacy directed toward foreign audiences.[4] This chapter argues that in an age of convergence, Canada's innovative use of new media to inform public opinion on international policy should be expanded to target international audiences. However, it is important to place Canada's efforts in the context of what other states have done, and continue to do, in using international broadcasting to brand their countries to a global audience facing multiple (and often contradictory) streams of information and to address the pressing challenges of failed states and international terrorism.

CHANGING DEFINITIONS AND AUDIENCES

As Monroe E. Price, co-director of Oxford University's Programme in Comparative Media Law and Policy, states, "'International broadcasting' is an elegant term for a complex combination of state-sponsored news, information and entertainment directed at a population outside the sponsoring state's boundaries."[5] Simply put, it is the use of electronic media by one state to influence the population of another state. Price notes that international broadcasting was for most of the twentieth century – particularly during World War II and the Cold War – synonymous with government propaganda. The institutions were well known – the Voice of America, the BBC World Service, Radio Moscow – and were financed directly by national governments. These were "state-sponsored" broadcasting services even when, as is the case with the BBC World Service, they retained their independent journalistic standards. While the BBC World Service may have the editorial independence that, for example, the Voice of America lacks, it is no less associated with one country.[6] Similarly, the rapid expansion of private international news organizations such as the Cable News Network (CNN) since 1980 and the more recent satellite broadcasting entrants in the Arab world – Al-Jazeera and Al-Arabya – as well as the commercially sponsored BBC World international television network and its new media arms (distinct from the publicly funded BBC World Service), can be interpreted either as not being state-sponsored or as appearing to be state-sponsored; but it is a fact that these private broadcasters index their content to their primary audiences and thus take on a regional or national character.[7] Even commercially based BBC World television, when covering international events, will give "face time" to British political leaders, thus providing a British perspective on current events. So, too, will France's twenty-four-hour international television news broadcaster, France 24, a EUR80-million (approximately Can$114.6 million) public-private joint venture, which was inaugurated in 2006 and, in addition to French, provides programming in English and Arabic.

As Price notes, there is a variety of styles of international broadcasting: "a British style, a French style, and one or more American styles (reflecting the division between US-sponsored broadcasters.)"[8] Each style depends on individual broadcasting histories and "deep-seated cultural proclivities."[9] For instance, the British view is that the independence of international broadcasting, and of the BBC World Service in particular, is sacrosanct. The American approach is less concerned about whether the world sees its tools, such as the Voice of America, as independent or not. Indeed, according to Brian T. Conniff, acting director (1999–2002) of the International Broadcasting Bureau,[10] the world wants to hear the official US government view on the issues of the day – especially during a crisis.[11]

The American approach is the antithesis of the United Kingdom's international broadcasting model, which equates independence from government control over its editorial agenda as conferring credibility on the BBC and, thereby, albeit indirectly, on the United Kingdom itself. In this view, the BBC World Service enhances the United Kingdom's image precisely because it is not perceived to be government "propaganda." BBC World Service representatives have been at pains to point out that the service does not broadcast information on *behalf of* the British government and that the global audience tunes in because they feel that the information they receive is better than that offered by the alternatives. Pressed to explain why the BBC World Service does not even implicitly take into consideration Britain's broad national agenda, a senior official has admitted that the rationale for commissioning programming is sometimes "British in nature," but that there is no government input whatsoever.[12] In this way, from the

British perspective international broadcasting dovetails perfectly with the long-term time frame of public diplomacy. In the words of the BBC World Service's John Renner, "You don't become the world's best known and most respected voice in international broadcasting by putting out propaganda or by putting out any particular messages that a government of the day finds convenient to send out to the people it wants to reach. And if we are not trusted to give independent and untainted news information, we won't be respected, we won't be listened to and, therefore, we won't bring any benefit to Britain."[13] This results in the "paradox" of the United Kingdom's international broadcasting – the BBC World Service receives £200 million (about Can$430 million) from the Foreign and Commonwealth Office because of the value of operating independently of it.[14]

The category of international broadcasting is also being redefined as the process of technological convergence continues to deepen and as governments demand value for money for all programs. In previous decades, international broadcasters would have been defined by their use of shortwave radio to distribute their signals. The broadcasting model assumed a one-to-many format of public information flow. Today, however, as Price writes, "many technologies, including FM, Internet, and satellite to home, are also involved."[15] The greatest threat to, or innovation for, international broadcasting is convergence and the rise of tools such as the Internet, which encourages unmediated dialogue.

Accompanying this expanding definition is an ongoing debate about the utility of spending potentially billions of dollars on civilian broadcasting with only anecdotal evidence to suggest that it is informing or influencing target audiences.[16] BBC World Service officials proudly promote the figure of 150 million listeners worldwide each week, along with broadcasts in forty-three languages, plus specifically targeted programs that, for example, respond to the educational needs of people in war-torn countries such as Afghanistan. The contrarians, on the other hand, are not convinced that international broadcasters have paid sufficient attention to evaluating the impact of their programming and have concluded that broadcasters prefer instead to hide behind assumptions that the Cold War was won not by the military and economic superiority of the West but, instead, by the "information bombs" delivered through the Western mass media. They ask, if the billions were invested so effectively by liberal democratic regimes for at least four decades in their international broadcasting outlets to convey universal values shared by all the world's major religions and the vast majority of citizens, then, to quote President George W. Bush, "Why do they hate us?"[17] This thinking, however, conveys a misunderstanding of the role of international broadcasting. As Harold Lasswell wrote in 1927, "[t]he truth is that all governments are engaged to some extent in propaganda as part of their ordinary peacetime functions. They make propaganda on behalf of diplomatic friends or against diplomatic antagonists and this is unavoidable."[18]

With the end of the Cold War, there was no longer the need for the "ethereal penetration of sovereign borders."[19] The so-called "peace dividend" came not only from reduced military spending but also from reducing broadcasting budgets for what was an old technology (e.g., the shortwave in the age of the Web) to influence a global audience that was already onside. How could a government lose? Would millions of listeners in foreign countries, many of them poor, rise up and protest? Price reports that during this period in the early 1990s international broadcasting in the Anglo-American sphere was convulsed by a combination of deficit-cutting governments and the inability of the broadcasting organizations to justify themselves in a post-Cold War world. In short, did Canada, the United Kingdom, France, Germany, and the United States all really need to transmit unjammed programming in multiple languages to a "free" Eastern Europe that could now receive programming from commercial networks? Canada and Australia, according to Price, came close to eliminating external broadcasting, and Germany's Deutsche Welle was required to dismiss staff for the first time since 1949. The head of the BBC called for a rethinking of the BBC World Service's programming to make it less elitist and more "international."[20]

Meanwhile, in the United States the growing influence of CNN, especially during the first Gulf War in 1990, and the fact that there was no longer an "enemy" by the late 1990s made "government and society less supportive [of international broadcasting] than it would be less than a decade later."[21] While there was no global enemy, the focus of American strategy changed, and increasingly, the mandates of various international radio operations such as Radio Free Europe/Radio Liberty (RFE/RL) and Radio Free Asia began to overlap with that of the Voice of America, causing growing friction. At the same time, new "boutique" entities emerged, such as the Persian-language service of the RFE/RL, to "facilitate transitions," whether in Asia, the Middle East, or Africa.[22]

Broadcasting and the Post Post–Cold War: The Rise of a New Existential Threat

International state-assisted broadcasting had clearly gone into neglect in the period immediately following the end of the Cold War. However, there appeared to be a renaissance by the late 1990s as the international broadcasters began to transform their way of operating and move out of their Cold War frames of reference. The attacks of 9/11 created a major political focus on how the West was communicating its policies and values to foreign audiences, particularly those in the Muslim world. The re-thinking and experimentation with new media that had been under way now received major attention through congressional testimony in the United States and parliamentary review in the United Kingdom. In Canada, the focus in the two-year period following the attacks was on strengthening domestic anti-terrorism legislation and making the Canada-US border more secure. Canada's international broadcasting did not merit any sustained attention either from within the bureaucracy or in Parliament.

For the United States, however, as the victim of the attack, opinion polls in the wake of 9/11 showed how poorly the country had been doing in the Middle East with its media strategy – attracting only 1 to 2 percent of the potential audience. Radio Sawa (available on FM, medium-wave, and satellite throughout the Middle East and North Africa) was the centrepiece of the new strategic plan for the US government-funded, non-military broadcast services, which was tailored to meet the needs of individual countries. There would be no more one-size-fits-all strategies. Radio Sawa was launched in March 2002 with US$35 million (Can$36.8 million) for its first year and US$22 million (Can$23.1 million) for the subsequent year. Radio Sawa's format, targeting Muslim youth, had a program profile of Arabic and Western pop music interspersed with five- to ten-minute news bulletins twice an hour (lower news content than VOA). Initial audience-share figures proved promising, although there was criticism, and format changes were made. Other changes were occurring to which the international state-assisted broadcasters had to adapt. In specific markets such as India, radio was tightly regulated and listenership had collapsed. The new "name of the game" was less-regulated satellite television. BBC World television wasted no time in seeking market share, and it was reported by Nik Gowing, a BBC World television presenter, that its audience had increased from 10 million to 250 million in ten years.[23]

Broadcasting and the New Security Agenda

The rise of "vicious little wars" as the defining characteristic of the new security environment created an opportunity for international broadcasters to play a much more direct role in crises. The BBC demonstrated that size has many advantages, one of which is the surge power to respond quickly in a crisis. The 9/11 attacks ensured that providing services to the Middle East and

Southwest Asia remained one of the BBC's major objectives. After the invasion to oust the Taliban in Afghanistan in 2001, the BBC World Service responded immediately with a forty-five-hour, non-stop news broadcast in English, Arabic, Pashtu (Persian), Urdu, and Central Asian languages.

In Afghanistan, in addition to the enhanced programming, the BBC World Service Trust launched an initiative to rebuild the broadcasting capacity of that country. A BBC team took part in a needs-assessment mission in Afghanistan and worked with the UN Department of Public Information. As a result of that mission and in support of the 2002 International Conference on Reconstruction Assistance to Afghanistan, held in Tokyo, the BBC World Service Trust was invited to Afghanistan by the government to advise on a framework for an independent media centre in that country. The BBC helped draw up a key policy-directions document, which determined the agenda for the international media set-up in Kabul. The BBC World Service Trust worked to build the capacity of local and national media, including providing digital radio equipment to Radio and TV Afghanistan. It provided studios from which Radio Afghanistan was able to resume broadcasting, train journalists and technical staff, and continue Afghan Lifeline, an emergency radio service set up to provide assistance for newly displaced Afghans. The World Service Trust intends to operate as an independent, non-profit organization until the Afghan media can sustain themselves. The BBC World Service also developed new educational programs, particularly for Afghan women, as well as health programs.

The World Service was able to respond quickly to the events of 9/11 and the action against the Taliban because it has a long history of broadcasting in Afghanistan. It had been a part of people's lives there for many years, broadcasting to regions in the local languages. It had built up audiences that trust it and thus make it a regular part of their lives in good times and in bad. This is an important consideration for the pubic diplomacy process. International broadcasting is clearly part of the long-term time frame, though it can also be used for short-term emergency broadcasts. It can prepare the groundwork for other public diplomacy activities in support of policy priorities, such as delivering long-term or emergency healthcare services or creating support for the building of democratic institutions. It is a well-established axiom that building trust takes a very long time, but it can be lost in an instant, as the United States and most other countries have learned.

Coalition Information Centres

The example of the BBC World Service Trust in Afghanistan shows a more indirect means of how public broadcasters and, by extension, national governments are managing the international information environment. A more direct means of information management was evident during NATO's military intervention in Kosovo in 1999, although it did not involve public broadcasters directly. The information environments during a crisis are messy, to be sure, and governments of every religious and political stripe now recognize that controlling or managing the information environment is just as important as the on-the-ground military campaign. The Revolution in Military Affairs concept explicitly recognizes control of the battle-field information environment and communications capacity as key to fighting and winning the military conflicts (both conventional and irregu-lar) of the future.[24] It is in this context that Coalition Information Centres were established (with offices in the United Kingdom and the United Sates) during the Kosovo campaign, to allow NATO to manage the informa-tion environment more effectively. The United States and the United King-dom (with the French and Germans largely as onlookers) viewed this as another strategic-communication mechanism to direct messages from the NATO governments (principally the United Kingdom and the United States) to a global audience through the media. Presumably these centres were meant to supplement the existing government-supported informa-tion "machinery," because government messages were not getting out in sufficient number through the filter of the large global media giants such as CNN and the BBC, the latter in both its home and world services. As a mechanism to allow the NATO allies to set the global media agenda, the cen-tres were in fact seeking to shore up domestic support in the United King-dom and the United States for the campaign. Journalists, as would be expected, were not great fans of such overt attempts at news management and tended to deride them, despite their ability to push information out to the press. According to the CBC's foreign correspondent, Don Murray, "I have been a correspondent for twenty-odd years, from the Soviet Union to Kosovo to the Middle East, and I [had] never heard of the Coalition Infor-mation Centres, so I would say the impact is very, very small. This is an indi-cation of the problem that government information is facing. There is a disconnect here. When we go out in the field, myself and others like me from other organizations, we don't need to go to the old doors or press the buttons and do the rounds as it used to be when I ... started in the field. There are so many other non-governmental sources of information which represent, in our view, more valuable sources of information."[25]

In retrospect, the Coalition Information Centres may have created a back-lash among journalists. There was a sense that the centres were attempting to export techniques that had worked in their own countries (primarily the United States and the United Kingdom) and that such methods would be unquestioned by the international audience. In fact, they did work on an international audience and journalists – in the first round. But many journalists eventually turned away from the centres and did not use them unless they had to. Inevitably, there will be a backlash when journalists feel that there is more to a story and they simply have to go with what they are being given, relentlessly, day after day. This is the downside of the intersection between public diplomacy broadcasting and journalism in general.

THE CANADIAN CONTRIBUTION

Canada's International Broadcasting Experience

If Canada's soft power, that is, its influence and credibility internationally, is a direct function of public awareness and respect for its society's values, accomplishments, and creativity, then it is worth examining in greater detail how successful Canada has been in using its electronic broadcasting resources to enhance its interests abroad. The experience of other members of the G8, especially the United States and the United Kingdom, reveals that their broadcasting services' fortunes rose and fell with the international political climate. What is revealing about the Canadian case, however, is that Canada's international broadcasting has been largely neglected and underfunded for decades, during the Cold War, the immediate post–Cold War, and today's post post–Cold War.

As table 1.1 shows, Canada's spending on international broadcasting has been very low, both in absolute terms and relative to what is being spent by its major competitors. While the Canadian investment in broadcasting through Radio Canada International (RCI) and TV5 can be counted in the tens of millions of dollars annually (Can$21 million in 2004–5), Canada's G8 counterparts – the United States, France, Germany, and Japan – each spend in the hundreds of millions. And it is not clear that the content being disseminated through Canada's multiple channels is being adequately directed at emerging regional powers, such as India, Brazil, and Mexico, which are each poised to make a significant impact on the course of the twenty-first century.[26]

The most experienced player in Canada's international broadcasting is RCI. Its mandate is to produce and distribute Canadian programming to increase foreign audiences' awareness, appreciation, and general knowledge of Canada, in addition to exposing such audiences to Canadian culture, society, economy, and values.[27] It also has had the most problematic internal history, lacking adequate domestic government support at crucial periods of its evolution, even during the Cold War. In the words of Keith Spicer, the former chairman of the Canadian Radio-television and Tele-communications Commission, "[t]he history of RCI has been a series of intermittent terrors with reprieves at the last minute for a few years and then it starts all over again with a new breed of politicians who again do not know about it."[28]

The weekly audience for RCI is approximately six million (not includ-ing China, India, and Southeast Asia, for which reliable figures are not available). Its broadcasts are available in nine languages, up from seven at the turn of the twenty-first century. By 2001, approximately one-third of the original weekly programming came from the domestic service of the English-language CBC (twenty-one hours), another one-third from the French-language Radio-Canada (twenty-one hours), and the slightly larger final portion came from RCI programming in foreign languages: seven hours in Russian and Ukrainian, seven hours in Spanish, seven hours in Mandarin, and seven hours in Arabic. Since then, the trend has been for the portion of RCI-produced programming to decrease (notably the foreign-language broadcasts), while the amount contributed by the CBC has increased. There has been a concerted attempt by RCI's manage-ment to reposition itself as a niche player in international broadcasting (even though it is the thirteenth-largest international state broadcaster) and to re-brand itself from a broadcaster to a programmer. It has placed its programs through FM radio and compact-disc distribution in three hundred partner stations in seventy-five countries, in addition to main-taining real-audio access on the Internet to ensure 24/7 availability, all in an effort to distance itself from its antiquated image as a shortwave broadcaster.

Since 2004, RCI has endeavoured to reposition itself internationally with programs that reflect global trends and has attempted to influence distinct segments of the world's population. New Portuguese-language program-ming has been instituted, directed specifically at Brazil. Cantonese pro-gramming has been added, to complement the existing Mandarin-language programming available in China. French-language programming has been aired for listeners in North and sub-Saharan Africa, while other region-specific programming has been directed at English speakers in sub-Saharan Africa and India. In an information universe with over one thousand radio and television stations that have some international man-date and where new media sites are created every day, quality – measured in availability, attractiveness, ease of use, feedback, and reliability – is a key factor in allowing Canada's voice to be heard abroad. Embracing new technology has also enabled RCI to operate effectively. In November 2005, RCI established a partnership with Sirius Satellite Radio to create RCI Plus, thereby exposing a domestic audience in Canada to RCI's original multilingual programming. Sylvain Lafrance, executive vice-president of French Services, CBC/Radio-Canada, explained, "Canadian demographics are evolving, and the public broadcaster must provide radio that reflects such changes. RCI is the ideal service to round out a radio offering that will reach Canadians effectively. Until now, only our foreign listeners had access to RCI. Now RCI will be heard in Canada from coast to coast as well."[29] It was anticipated that large diaspora communities in Canada would be attracted to RCI Plus and that, through word of mouth, there would be an expansion of RCI's international audience shares.

There was a belief that even if RCI struggled to create or provide programming for a multitude of local conditions, listeners would continue to look to Canada as an "expert observer" of international issues and events.[30] As Lafrance said, "[a]t a time when audiences face a proliferation of news and information sources, the Canadian point of view is still valued and appreciated."[31] However, the competition for Canada to be that "expert observer" is intense. Don Murray has observed that the BBC is now such a giant presence in the world of the media that it dwarfs others' public diplomacy broadcast efforts with its reach and impact. For example, Murray said that he could testify that 70 percent of male householders in Afghanistan listened to the BBC in Pashtu: "We would go down to villages, and people would be holding their radios at three o'clock in the afternoon – it was the BBC Pashtu service, I believe. This was before the war broke, and as the front lines broke in the war, in the middle of this people were listening intently. This was regarded as important information, key information."[32] As noted, size confers a considerable national advantage. Murray also recalled a meeting in Kosovo in 1999, at which 326 non-governmental organizations were represented, all vying for network television or radio coverage. The BBC determined who would receive global exposure. For a smaller country such as Canada, there is a tendency for its national broadcaster to look explicitly for the Canadian angles and search out expatriates rather than to be the "expert observer." Australia, for its part, has developed a growing reach throughout the Pacific, through the efforts of the Australian Broadcasting Corporation (ABC), representing a possible middle ground between approaches taken by the BBC World Service and the CBC/Radio-Canada. The ABC seeks not only to brand Australia throughout the region but to get people to "think Australian," while tailoring its regional programming to local conditions, thus making the broadcasts more relevant and ensuring a larger audience.

To survive in this crowded and fragmented universe, RCI for its part will have to decide what level of critical mass audience it will require to remain relevant and what types of programming will attract its target audience of sophisticated listeners. A step in the right direction was taken on 21 March 2003, when, after years of funding uncertainty, RCI was formally placed within the CBC under an Order-in-Council. While reporting to the CBC, RCI is expected to consult regularly with DFAIT on target countries, regions, and languages; it must also present an annual report to Canadian Heritage.

The CBC and RCI have become smaller in a field of international broadcasting that has grown more crowded with many more players, and where the largest, such as the BBC, are now state-assisted broadcasting behemoths. RCI, after a few near-death experiences, continues to play a constructive role, even with its limited budget. As Don Murray says,

When I have been in the field, its impact has always surprised me. I just got back from Iraq and at least three people said to me, "CBC," and then the Iraqis said, "Radio Canada," and I said, "You speak French?" They said, "No, no, no." There is an Arabic service broadcast to Iraq by our Radio Canada International, which these people were listening to, and they knew us because of that. I was completely surprised. I didn't even know the service existed, to tell you the truth. The same thing had happened to me in countries of the ex–Soviet Union, the Baltics, the Ukraine. Obviously, from a Canadian point of view, with 800,000 people of Ukrainian descent in Canada, RCI broadcasts there. It had an enormous impact, much to my surprise. So I think that we, smaller broadcasters, we tend to downplay the impact the media have.[33]

International Television

While Canada's radio efforts have not been perfect, the picture is probably less optimistic with regard to its presence in international television. Canada does not have a dedicated English-language international television presence such as BBC World or the United States' Voice of America. It can channel a limited amount of Canadian-produced French-language programming through TV5, the international French-language broadcaster that reaches sixty-six million households on five continents. TV5 is financed by leading members of La Francophonie (e.g., the Canadian government,

Quebec, France, and La Communauté française de Belgique et Suisse). Although France furnishes the bulk of this broadcaster's budget and programming clout, the government of Canada (through Canadian Heritage) and the government of Quebec, acting as partners, together make the second-highest contribution. TV5 has 15 percent Canadian content in Europe, 13 percent in Asia, 12 percent in Africa, and 28 percent in the United States and Latin America, where it is positioned as a specialty channel for French speakers. Although it is an important international projection of Canada's francophone character and a valuable showcase for Canadian French-language programming, the fact remains that TV5 does not broadcast in languages other than French, and its identity for viewers is influenced by the predominance of programming from France.

The CBC, starting in the late 1980s, tried to establish a satellite television service that could be downlinked internationally. The idea never gained any traction because the government of the day felt that extra money was needed for prime-time dramatic programming.[34] In 1996, the foreign minister at the time, Lloyd Axworthy, announced that Canada would pursue a new international information strategy; however, this was dropped as the government pursued what would eventually become the Ottawa Convention on the banning of anti-personnel landmines, itself a highly successful public diplomacy initiative. Advances in cable television enabled some Canadian programs to reach American audiences for a short time in the second half of the 1990s. From 1994 to 2000, the CBC and Power Broadcasting Inc. jointly owned two US-based cable channels – Newsworld International (NWI) and Trio – that reached approximately 11.7 million US subscribers.[35] Much of the programming on these channels was Canadian. Newsworld International was a twenty-four-hour news channel that ran a considerable amount of content from the CBC, and Trio aired quality Canadian, Australian, and United Kingdom programming. During these six years, this joint venture was the largest exporter to the United States of Canadian programming.[36] In 2000, NWI and Trio were sold for Can$155 million to the USA Network, an American cable broadcaster. Trio was dropped by the network and transferred to an Internet broadband channel in 2005. NWI followed a slightly more interesting trajectory. It was re-sold first to Vivendi Universal and then sold again in 2004 to a group led by former US vice president Al Gore. The group rebranded the channel as Current TV, a start-up media company through which a younger demographic could contribute its own programming and be broadcast on the web and via satellite. In 2005, NWI stopped airing CBC programming, thus ending an eleven-year experiment in exporting English-language television news and information programming from Canada to a foreign audience.

THE NEW MEDIA: CANADA ON-LINE

A more promising story can be told with regard to the role of new media in Canada's public diplomacy. By all accounts, Canada has been a leader among the world's foreign ministries when it comes to information technology and information management. Indeed, if one looked at DFAIT's total budget of approximately Can$1.8 billion in 2005, there was a large share, more than Can$400 million, devoted to information technology and information management. Throughout the 1990s, with its SIGNET and MITnet telecommunications systems, DFAIT had one of the most advanced telecommunications infrastructures of any foreign ministry in the world. The department's public face, through innovative web sites at headquarters and diplomatic missions, was impressive and novel, and for a time, few other foreign ministries could challenge DFAIT's on-line leadership. In an attempt to be the first state to put all its services on-line, the government of Canada launched an initiative in 2000 called Government On-Line, which included a role for using the World Wide Web as a platform to reach non-Canadians.

The single portal, whose World Wide Web address is CanadaInternational.gc.ca, was specifically designed to meet the content and navigational requirements of non-Canadians who wanted to engage with Canada in ways that touched on government of Canada responsibilities (e.g., trade and investment promotion, immigration, international relations, culture and identity). This type of web presence reflected the desire to create a single site for people who are interested in Canada. It is efficient and convenient, and certainly becomes highly effective in terms of Canada's public diplomacy efforts when foreign audiences actually get the information that they need. It was a joint federal initiative that included DFAIT and a host of other federal government departments (Canadian Heritage, Public Works and Government Services Canada, Industry Canada, Citizenship and Immigration Canada, among others). Although branding was not the rationale for the international portal, it has actually performed this role with considerable success.[37]

Such national sites – and by 2005, most national governments had them – are effective public diplomacy tools if the information is relevant, timely, and current, and if it can be placed within the government's overall message framework. Such a framework should not be confused with propaganda, as it simply means that in any given time period – weeks, months, years – the government has particular messages that it would like to promote to the world. In Canada's case, for example, a long-term message would be that Canada is making a large investment in the reconstruction of Afghanistan. That message would then be interwoven throughout the CanadaInternational web site. It would also appear on DFAIT's web site and be placed on the web sites of all of Canada's diplomatic missions around the world.

Projecting a long-term message may seem like a small technical task, but it is actually quite complicated. First, the federal government must decide where it should appear and for how long – months, years? How prominent should it be? What other messages will it bump? Will the same message appear on all Canadian government web sites or only those deemed most relevant? Will it be adapted and edited for local context? Who will do the adapting? So, what initially appears to be an easy task that supports Canada's overall foreign policy interests, such as reminding the world that Canada has a strong commitment to rebuilding Afghanistan, suddenly becomes much more complicated and costly.

Even though there is a substantial cost, the web as a tool or platform of public diplomacy cannot be ignored. If the essence of public diplomacy is credibility, then the goal for any government is to maintain and strengthen it, for if it loses it (as happened to Denmark in certain Islamic countries after the controversy in 2005 over the publication of cartoons of the Prophet Mohammed by a Danish newspaper), the need to determine how to rebuild it becomes paramount. The web provides a powerful way to lay the groundwork for such credibility in all three time frames for public diplomacy: the short-, the medium-, and the long-term.

The primary advantage of the web is that it can deliver content to a worldwide audience instantly, given its wide and ever-increasing scope. For instance, a government is able to reach exponentially more people in the developed world through web publishing than through hard-copy publishing. This trend became clear to Ottawa with the publication of *Canada's International Policy Statement* in April 2005. Within the first two weeks, two hundred thousand copies had been downloaded, but fewer than one hundred hard copies had been ordered. Although hard-copy publishing is still needed to disseminate a message in jurisdictions with low on-line use, this is occurring with far less frequency. Additionally, the web has the advantage of timeliness: the latest policy positions are instantly available to the public. Although the traditional media often provides a valuable interpretative role, it also functions as a filter. With the advent of new media, however, this filter can be bypassed through these new channels, thus allowing the governments to deliver their messages directly to the public.

As in many other organizations, public and private, one of the difficulties posed by having the Internet as a new platform is that its immediacy puts pressure on internal work flows, particularly the approvals process and the challenge of some sort of oversight for all the mission web sites. For instance, what information should be unclassified and posted on the web? What information will be translated into languages other than English and French? Who will verify the quality of third-language translations? To what extent do all mission sites have to be compatible or similar in look and feel? Perhaps most importantly, can the government keep pace with changing circumstances and maintain up-to-date content about policies and events at all times? There is always a danger that the web, with all its promise and convenience, could end up draining all of a ministry's public diplomacy resources.

The Internet is not only a new platform for easier one-way messaging; it is also a tool of strategic communication. It is here that Canada can also be regarded as a pioneer among foreign ministries. Indeed, DFAIT recognized at an early date the importance and capability of the Internet in building a domestic constituency for a government's foreign policy. The mainstream Canadian mass media, private and public, is editorially independent and does a fairly good job of informing Canadians, but Canadian foreign policy priorities usually do not receive much coverage.[38] The old system of press releases, while certainly necessary, cannot be relied on to stimulate broad national or even expert debate. The web has become a critical tool in the Canadian foreign ministry's efforts to institutionalize a public dialogue. In 2003, the government used the web as a consultation tool in a national citizen dialogue on foreign policy (*A Dialogue on Foreign Policy*); nearly two thousand people registered as participants, and there were approximately thirty-five hundred responses to the questions that were issued publicly. Using the World Wide Web meant that there was an opportunity for non-Canadians to participate as well, although no statistics were kept on their involvement.

In 2004, DFAIT introduced the International Policy eDiscussion web site, which features new topics for public discussion every few months. Since November 2004, the topics have included on-line consultations on an array of government foreign policy priorities such as renewing multilateral institutions and Canada-US relations. One particularly successful topic was the e-discussion on failed and fragile states, which attracted a large number of public views. The format is simple: DFAIT posts discussion questions and acts as a moderator for a defined period of time. Members of the general public can then post their opinions on the site, and after the completion of the discussion period, the citizens' on-line opinions are summarized and circulated within the department for review and comment. A summary response from DFAIT is then posted on the site, thus providing a feedback loop for the public. This exercise is an example of citizen engagement, and while there has been some criticism, there is no denying that citizens can make their voices heard. The exercise is offering the public another form of access to the foreign policy-making process beyond writing a letter to the minister. It also provides the outside world with an opportunity to see how public policy is developed in Canada. For the optimists, the World Wide Web is being used in an accountable and transparent way. For the sceptics, it is being used as a means of co-opting the public by having the department's positions validated, although there has been no evidence that the incoming opinions are screened for points of view.

Quite simply, the web allows the department to be more proactive in agenda-setting. It permits both the traditional one-way broadcast and a dialogue, a two-way means of communication, and it allows for extensive archiving of information that is instantly accessible. Moreover, it allows a government, or a government department, to select a priority and build a national discussion around it. In these ways, the web can be used as part of a strategic communications approach to public discussions.

Evaluating International Broadcasting

One theme of this book is how to measure the effectiveness of public diplomacy. It is an inherent feature of international broadcasting that its effects are usually visible only over the long term, especially the ambitious outcome of "helping to create a better world." The long-term cause and effect of international broadcasting is not always obvious and can be difficult to measure, given the other causal factors that must be considered. As noted in this chapter's discussion of how international broadcasters are adapting their programming to the new security environment, it is easier to measure the impact of information programs that are dedicated to specific tasks, such as the rebuilding of failed states. In short, the more specific the objectives and the clearer the expectations, the easier it will be for the broadcaster to measure the effectiveness of its programming, whether the information is being delivered through radio, television, or the Internet.

The BBC World Service and other international broadcasters are developing measures to test more narrowly their effectiveness in terms of reach, reputation, relevance, and impact. Reach is the traditional measure that broadcasters use, often through ratings and surveys. For public broadcasters with small research budgets and a global audience, measuring the audience size is clearly less detailed than the overnight television ratings that commercial mass broadcasters use. International broadcasters cannot afford to do national surveys in each country that they serve. The means of assessing impact in focus groups of opinion formers and earned media, or news coverage (e.g., mentions of the international broadcaster in local media) are limited. That being said, broadcasters can get instant feedback on the Internet. For example, there was a massive increase in Internet traffic following the 2001 terrorist attacks. Some of that response rate has since decreased, but to levels that are significantly higher than they were before 9/11. Reputation, relevance, and impact are all qualitative measures of effect, but they can still be wrapped up with hard numbers wherever possible.

The information environment in which RCI and TV5 now find themselves operating is much more crowded than it used to be. Notably, the expansive NGO community often overwhelms the international information environment during crises. As Don Murray states, the NGOs "simply overwhelm the diplomatic efforts of the UN organization ... They are everywhere. They are competitive. They are trying to put their message out, often clearly a very good message and a message code, but they are in competition with one another to get our ear and our cameras and our microphones to report what they are doing. I would say that they too, at least in my eyes and in the eyes of most journalists, are much more important in public diplomacy terms than the people on the ground from individual embassies."[39] This may be the most important observation, namely, that international audiences are being exposed to more and more sources and outlets of information. In such a crowded "marketplace of ideas," surely the key determinant of effectiveness is whether an outlet is seen as credible and relevant. For Canada, it appears that its international broadcasting services are presently too small to have a global presence – or perhaps even a niche presence – though the services and programs themselves have a high degree of credibility.[40] The Canadian experience in international broadcasting reflects the adage "you have to be seen to be heard." Canada, as in many dimensions of its public diplomacy, is not seen or heard enough.

CONCLUSION

It is instructive to note that international broadcasting has always occupied a somewhat ambiguous role within the public diplomacy and foreign policy

of the US government. It has operated on the premise that simply telling a
global mass audience about the United States and its politics would be
enough to advance American interests. Between the end of the Cold War
and the terrorist attacks of 9/11, decision makers entered a period of indifference with respect to strengthening the US's international information
strategy. In the absence of a global political crisis, they did not see a pressing need for international broadcasting. However, the attacks of 11 September 2001 forced international broadcasters to realize that they had to
change the way they communicated – they had to make themselves more
relevant and more attractive. No longer could they expect the youth of the
world, and particularly the youth of the Arab world, to listen to traditional,
long-form, shortwave programming. No longer could they get away with a
one-size-fits-all approach spread across forty to sixty languages. International broadcasters focused on priority regions and countries and targets
within those countries, trying to become more relevant and more attractive. Broadcasting represents a long-term investment of trust, and, as the
BBC soon realized, getting "out" of a country was difficult because the relationship would be difficult to rebuild in a future crisis.

International broadcasters began to reposition themselves, which meant
devoting far more attention to eliminating outdated formats and programs. The emphasis was creating broadcasts that were easily found and
heard by audiences. Although they realized that they had to be heard in a
medium that people were accustomed to listening to, the problem, as
noted, was that listening to shortwave radio in many parts of the world was
declining, although it had huge advantages for the broadcasters, since they
could broadcast from outside their target markets. International broadcasters responded by seizing the benefits of convergence and renting FM vacancies or entering into partnerships with local broadcasters.

Television is inherently more expensive than radio and cannot provide
the same geographical breadth of coverage. However, it does have the
advantage – particularly in the Arab world, where direct satellite-to-home is
readily available – of bypassing many of the local control issues.[41] That said,
establishing a network – a twenty-four-hour network in Arabic or any other
language – is very expensive, though the BBC and France 24 have added
Arabic channels to their international television services. Adding programs
to existing non-state controlled networks is problematic as well, because
there is no control over what comes before or what comes after, and
national governments may not want to be associated with those programs.
For this reason, it is important to be very selective about where to make the
investment in television.

As discussed, the BBC seeks to project Britain's values of trust and pride throughout the international community, provide a forum for the exchange of ideas across cultures, promote the English language, and operate a show-case for British talent around the world. However, smaller countries and smaller broadcast organizations must take different approaches. The BBC, when it moves into an area, is accustomed to doors opening and people wanting to talk to it. That is not surprising. Because of its reputation, it has an enormous impact and reach, which RCI does not have. RCI has therefore sought to reposition itself both as a domestic and an international pro-grammer, especially for those regions of the world that still rely on conven-tional radio.

There is a consensus that it is now much more difficult for any of the international broadcasters to make their voices heard. For this reason, sup-plementary measures can be taken to ensure that key messages get through, such as creating "information centres." Journalists have con-cluded that in the first wave after a crisis, government information pro-grams and conferences can be highly effective, although there is potential for a backlash. Local people often do not tell the same story after the crisis that they were telling journalists during the crisis. The concern among journalists is that government information efforts will not expose these other stories, some of which may not be convenient for the policy of the day.

By and large, the international state-assisted broadcasters are competing for the same sort of audiences and in the same places and languages. They are also competing against the private broadcasters (e.g., CNN). The global listening audience is very sophisticated, and it samples programs across a host of sources. In the end, the growing number of sources actually helps international state broadcasters in their attempt to inform the public. What distinguishes the state broadcasters from the private broadcasters is that the state broadcasters will provide information on a given society or a set of ideals and common values. They will try to show how their society is different.

Canada can learn from the British, American, and Australian experi-ences. While it has been a pioneer in the use of information technology to create a more efficient foreign ministry and to facilitate dialogues on for-eign policy with Canadians, it has lagged drastically behind other states in the internationalization of its broadcast agenda. What is required is an emphasis on making the Canadian brand in international broadcasting the most relevant to its target audiences. Furthermore, as the world moves further away from information-based public diplomacy to a dialogue-based public diplomacy, questions need to be asked about the continued relevance of international broadcasting. The Cold War mentality of information overload has been replaced with the increasing influence of convergence and the ongoing legacy of small wars and failed states. Canada's broadcasting footprint must step lightly into this new post post–Cold War environment. It must re-brand itself using its expertise in new media to become both an "expert observer" and a service directed at local needs.

The Economic Face of Public Diplomacy: International Business Promotion and Tourism

JASON BOUZANIS

Traditionally, the promotion of a country as a location for international business opportunities and as a tourist destination has not been associated with the concept and process of public diplomacy. Yet in many countries, including Canada, both activities are supported by national and sub-national governments, and targeted advocacy campaigns and broader, often expensive public communication campaigns are used to raise awareness and persuade foreign audiences (whether tourists or business people) to choose one country over another.

Perhaps the best way to distinguish international business and tourism promotion from the cultural and educational diplomacy discussed in earlier chapters is to recognize that, as with education marketing, the primary goal of such promotional efforts is to enhance national or regional economic prosperity. In fact, the traditional activities associated with public diplomacy, such as cultural programs (see chapter 4) and educational exchanges (see chapter 5), are increasingly being used not only to create a positive general image of a country but also to help achieve specific international business development and tourism objectives. That is, public diplomacy is being used to create an environment in which business deals can be closed and, as in the case of the world expositions, to create such a high level of international interest and excitement (or "buzz") that there are significant increases in annual tourism flows. In many ways, international business and tourism promotion campaigns unambiguously represent the economic face of public diplomacy.

This chapter will argue that countries that are more exposed to the world economy tend to be more concerned with their images and are consequently more involved in public diplomacy campaigns.[1] By this measure, Canada, the eleventh most popular tourist destination in the world and, among the G8 members, arguably the most dependent on trade and foreign direct investment for economic growth and stability, should pay more attention than many of its competitors pay to how it is perceived by foreign decision makers and mass publics. Canadian export trade increased from 25 percent of the gross domestic product in 1994 to 43 percent a decade later; additionally, each billion dollars in investment represents an estimated twelve thousand domestic jobs.[2] This chapter will show that trade, investment, and tourism are constituent components of the nation brand and contribute as much, if not more, to foreign public perceptions than traditional forms of public diplomacy. And since public diplomacy represents a government's contribution to managing the nation brand, a complete picture of public diplomacy must include an examination of the role of government in international business promotion (i.e., trade and investment promotion, and science and technology collaboration) and tourism.

The examination of public diplomacy efforts from a predominantly economic perspective points to the fine balance between highlighting Canada's comparative advantage as a resource-based economy and maximizing the benefits of its vast geography in terms of tourism revenues, while at the same time presenting an updated image of Canada as a modern country.

CONCEPTUALIZING INTERNATIONAL BUSINESS PROMOTION AND TOURISM AS PUBLIC DIPLOMACY

Increasing levels of international competition brought about by globalization have meant that countries are becoming increasingly aware of their national brands. A strong national brand provides a competitive advantage on the international stage and facilitates the attainment of economic and political objectives. As Peter van Ham notes, "[i]n today's world of information overload, strong brands are important in attracting foreign direct investment, recruiting the best and brightest, and wielding political influence."[3] How, then, are public diplomacy and nation branding connected as concepts? Both contribute directly to how foreign audiences perceive a nation, but a nation brand encompasses the entirety of audience experiences as consumers of a country's products and messages, not just the activities and messages promoted by the government (public diplomacy).

Simon Anholt's pioneering research identifies investment and immigration, exports, and tourism as three of six defining characteristics of national competence (along with governance, culture and heritage, and people) that, taken together, make up the national brand.[4] In Anholt's view, tourism is the "primary stakeholder in promoting the national brand" because it is the brand's most visible dimension – it is the most internationally advertised and marketed characteristic of the six areas of national competence.[5] It therefore has a disproportionate effect on people's perceptions, even though its actual contribution to national economies is usually lower than, for example, foreign direct investment.

Tourism promotion is one of the most powerful ways to communicate a national identity because, as Anholt notes, it is "often the closest a country gets to 'advertising' itself in a literal sense."[6] The importance and pervasiveness of tourism promotion suggest that destination branding affects more than just foreign visitors. Tourism promotion creates a mental picture of a place, and the perception that it engenders in the minds of foreign audiences (whether or not they actually visit) has the potential to influence decisions on investment, immigration, and international education. As such, tourism promotion provides intangible benefits, although for the Canadian government, it may equally reinforce stereotypes of Canada as a drawer of water and hewer of wood. Greg Klassen, vice-president of marketing for the Canadian Tourism Commission (CTC), suggests that his organization has "a huge opportunity to prop up the idea of Canada and position it as this great place, not only just to visit, but presumably it would trickle down to a great place to invest or a great place to immigrate to."[7] Consequently, tourism promotion has drawn interest from all levels of government.

Tourism and international business promotion conform to the definition of public diplomacy adopted in this study:

- governments inform foreign audiences about Canada as both a tourist destination and an international business partner;
- governments seek to influence international attitudes about Canada as a location for business and travel through marketing; and
- governments help to create a better understanding of Canada and its people by contributing to the personal experience of foreign travellers (e.g., through support to museums, national monuments and infrastructure) and business leaders (e.g., by organizing Team Canada Missions).

The broad goal of international business promotion is to portray Canada as an advanced industrial nation with high-quality products and services, an educated workforce, and a hospitable business climate. The forms of public diplomacy used to support international business promotion include information programming (e.g., media relations activities, trade and investment seminars, and lobbying) and international cultural and academic-relations programs. These activities are "scene setters" and are quite different from marketing specific products and services in foreign markets. These tools can be used in combination as part of advocacy campaigns, which are short- to medium-term strategic communications campaigns with specific objectives. The strategic use of paid advertising, earned media, public opinion research, and personal diplomacy by Canada abroad through its mission staff and incoming Canadian delegations will – it is hoped – affect perceptions and, ultimately, the decisions of foreign policy-makers and business leaders. International cultural and academic relations support Canada's international business goals over the long term by promoting goodwill and positioning foreign perceptions in a positive way. They are the proverbial "door openers."

Tourism promotion, when considered as part of public diplomacy, contributes to a more general understanding of Canada among foreign audiences. And the value of tourism promotion is more than economic: tourism connects Canada to the world and showcases its national identity as much as any international cultural activity. Tourism helps foster relationships between Canada and the people of the world. It is a relationship-building activity that involves a genuine, unmediated exchange between citizens, which helps to nurture a more nuanced perspective of Canada in foreign audiences. Anholt's research suggests that there is a correlation between a positive experience of visiting a country and a positive bias toward that country in general. Tourism promotion and international cultural and academic relations both work in a country's national interest. They promote goodwill and favourable perceptions and can be considered within the context of public diplomacy as cooperative ventures that contribute to relationship-building over the long term. In sum, international business and tourism promotion are part of the public diplomacy process and integral components of the nation brand.

A BRIEF HISTORY OF CANADA'S COMMERCIAL DIPLOMACY

Evan Potter has provided a detailed account of Canada's international business promotion efforts in "Branding Canada: The Renaissance of Canada's Commercial Diplomacy."[8] As he notes, "while there is extensive literature on economic and trade diplomacy ... far less attention has been devoted to commercial diplomacy."[9] Commercial diplomacy, of which investment and trade promotion are integral components, can be defined as "the application of the tools of diplomacy to help bring about specific commercial gains through promoting exports, attracting inward investment and preserving outward investment opportunities."[10] Commercial and public diplomacy are interrelated in that they both employ advocacy and nation branding solutions as part of a larger international policy agenda.

The first Canadian "trade" mission was a delegation dispatched to London in November 1865. Since the mission occurred before Confederation, representatives from Upper and Lower Canada were joined by colleagues from what would become the Eastern provinces – Nova Scotia, New Brunswick, and Prince Edward Island – thus establishing the strong provincial character reflected in subsequent trade missions. Early in 1866, this group travelled from London through many of Britain's Caribbean colonies, including Barbados and Jamaica, to stimulate further trade.[11] The prominence of trade was evident in 1894, when the Trade Commissioner Service was created, fifteen years before the foundation of the Department of External Affairs in 1909. Trade issues further dominated Canada's international policy before World War I and, arguably, in the interwar years.[12] The Cold War period then subsumed economic matters within the broader calculus of East-West strategic confrontation. However, at the end of the Cold War in 1991, missions and ambassadors once again became increasingly engaged in economic and trade-related matters.[13] By 2003, Canada had 164 missions abroad with over 500 trade commissioners (including a select number of foreign investment counsellors).[14]

The Trade Commissioner Service became a part of the Department of External Affairs (now DFAIT) in 1982. It migrated from the Department of Industry, Trade and Commerce after it was recognized that in an increasingly interconnected world, foreign policy should be concerned with broader national interests than just traditional diplomacy – international trade and investment promotion chief among them: "Foreign policy would now include the whole range of Canadian interests overseas – economic, trade, immigration, political, aid, culture – centralized under one department."[15] Despite this initial attempt to centralize Canadian efforts and recognize global interdependence, over the subsequent two decades the responsibility for commercial diplomacy and international business promotion became increasingly decentralized again. Other federal departments were entrusted with active roles in support of Canada's commercial diplomacy, and the provinces (primarily Quebec, Ontario, and Alberta) began developing their own networks of offices to establish themselves as actors promoting their own commercial and investment interests abroad. Investment promotion became a key provincial concern, and provinces competed head-to-head with the federal government for business partners. Despite these international business promotion alternatives, the Trade Commissioner Service remained a central institution in Canada's international business development strategy, in which investment attraction was becoming a key component.

By the mid-1990s, attracting foreign investment, and thus investment promotion, became central to the Chrétien government's prosperity agenda. In 1996, a new entity, Investment Partnerships Canada, was created as a partnership between Industry Canada and DFAIT. The purpose of Investment Partnerships Canada, a successor to the Brian Mulroney–era Investment Canada, was to promote the economic prosperity of Canada through investment – a far cry from the purpose of the Trudeau-era Foreign Investment Review Agency, which was widely perceived as being unfriendly to foreign direct investment.[16] Investment Partnerships Canada, through the Trade Commissioner Service, carried out investment promotion activities and raised awareness of Canada's advantages to foreign audiences. Then in 1997, Team Canada Inc. was established to create a focal point for the national-branding effort. The goal was to integrate trade promotion efforts across various government departments, with regional trade networks bringing the provinces into the fold to build upon the successes of the Team Canada Missions.[17]

By 2003, twenty-one Canadian diplomatic missions had dedicated Canada-based staff as investment officers working with provinces and municipalities, developing investment attraction strategies, and meeting with foreign business leaders to identify business opportunities with Canada. Another twenty missions had staff that spent one-third of their time on investment files. The need to promote and attract foreign investment at many Canadian missions also led to the hiring of locally engaged business development officers, who were assigned specifically to this function because of their established connections. This network became critical to attracting foreign direct investment to Canada.

BRANDING CANADA: THE CHALLENGE

The period under study in this chapter is characterized by accelerating globalization and the emergence of economic blocs in Europe, Asia, and North America. The Cold War competition (the geopolitics of previous generations) was replaced in the 1990s by geo-economic competition, and, as a result, Canada's international policy began to reflect a distinctly economic focus. This increase in global economic competition allowed the most industrialized countries, now freed from the moral glue of the Western "alliance," to begin a more intense struggle for national-brand awareness. These new features of the world system enabled the rethinking of traditional approaches to international trade in general, and of investment promotion specifically.

While Canada's foreign policy following the 1995 *Canada in the World* white paper may have been conceptualized as having three equal "pillars," with the "third pillar" being the promotion of values and culture, the primary concern, naturally, was the "first pillar" – trade. As the white paper put it, "The promotion of prosperity and employment is at the heart of the Government's agenda. International markets present tremendous opportunities for Canadians, given the quality of our products and services. We can compete with the best in the world ... We also wish to see other countries and regions prosper ... Prosperity will also allow others to sustain more mature and mutually beneficial economic partnerships with Canada and to be increasingly open to our values."[18] This should not have come as a surprise. The North American Free Trade Agreement, which came into force in January 1994, only served to highlight Canada's reliance on the global economy. Since the early 1980s, growth rates in the total value of foreign direct-investment stock had increased in concert with those of trade. Foreign direct investment in Canada was the second highest in the G8 as a share of gross domestic product. Flows in bilateral-investment stock between Canada and the United States, which totalled Can$80 billion in 1982, had surpassed Can$400 billion by 2004; bilateral trade between the two countries grew 10 percent annually between 1994 and 2004, and almost 80 percent of Canadian exports went to the United States. Trade and investment with Mexico increased even faster, although the level of pre-existing integration was considerably lower. By 2004, Mexico was Canada's sixth-largest export market, while Canada had become Mexico's second-largest. This is remarkable considering that in 1990, Mexico had ranked sixteenth among Canada's export markets.

Despite the absolute increases in Canada's exports and foreign direct-investment stock, Canada had been losing its relative share in the global market between 1980 and 2002. The Canadian share of global foreign direct-investment stock was 7.8 percent in 1980; by 1990 it was 6 percent, and in 2002 it had declined to 3 percent. As noted in chapter 1, Canada's share of foreign direct investment had also declined by one-half between 1990 and 2002 in North America alone, despite the increasing economic integration of the continent. Certainly, Canada was becoming a less attractive destination for international business, although it is difficult to isolate the precise political and economic factors in this decline. According to the 2005 annual report on Canada's trade and investment performance, a general decline in US outward investment, which began in the early 1980s and included the share destined for Canada, was a likely factor. The report also noted that "[t]he emergence of new global investors for whom Canada was a less significant investment location," combined with Canada's nationalistic economic policies of the late 1970s and early 1980s, also contributed to the decline.[19]

At the core of the government's response to reverse its declining global market share was an emphasis on "forging partnerships with other levels of government ... and undertaking pilot projects to gain a better understanding of foreign investor attitudes toward Canada."[20] This "new approach" was the genesis of Team Canada Inc. and the Team Canada Missions, which meant that investment promotion became an integral component in large-scale advocacy campaigns.

Team Canada Missions: A Retrospective

Team Canada Missions can be considered as quintessential public diplomacy initiatives, since they were designed to create awareness and goodwill for Canada at a broad societal level in target countries, as a precursor to advancing Canada's trade and investment prospects. They were partnership initiatives with the provincial and territorial governments, led by Prime Minister Chrétien and designed to build prestige and credibility for Canada on the international stage. These high-visibility, whole-of-government and whole-of-Canada missions evolved into "a key component of Canada's international business development efforts"[21] during the Chrétien era.

The concept of Team Canada – the brand – was created, in part, as a response to Canada's diminishing proportion of foreign direct investment and as a mechanism to convince foreign business leaders to invest in Canada. With the participation of the provincial premiers and territorial government leaders, the minister of international trade, and Canadian business people, the missions created an avenue for access to foreign political and business leaders and provided visibility for the delegates in key international markets. The presence of the prime minister lent credibility and generated an environment conducive to establishing new business relationships. More precisely, the missions aimed to put Canada in the minds of a wider demographic range of attentive publics and elite foreign audiences.

The first of seven Team Canada Missions visited China in 1994, travelling to Beijing and Shanghai with almost two hundred Canadian business people. Business deals valued at Can$5.1 billion, involving more than fifty Canadian companies, were struck, along with a deal by Atomic Energy Canada Ltd to sell two CANDU reactors to China's nuclear power corporation. This trip was followed by the second Team Canada Mission in 1996, to India, Pakistan, Indonesia, and Malaysia, with three hundred business people in the delegation. The total value of business deals accumulated in that mission was reported to have exceeded Can$4 billion. This mission was also used as a platform to announce the opening of a Canadian Education Centre in Jakarta, Indonesia, by Prime Minister Chrétien, to promote Canadian education and training institutions. The primary reason behind the initiative was to help educate the future business and government leaders of Canada's major trading partners, a further discussion of which can be found in chapter 5. According to a report from the Chicago Council on Foreign Relations and the Ditchley Foundation Conference held in 2005, educating foreign elites is a "forceful impetus" for facilitating intercultural understanding.[22] The Canadian centre thus provided a forum to leverage international academic relations for the purposes of branding Canada and favourably influencing the next generation of Asian decision makers.

In January 1997, the Team Canada Mission platform continued to grow, as over four hundred company representatives, in addition to several educational-institution leaders, travelled to South Korea, the Philippines, and Thailand, and returned with over Can$2 billion in new business. The following year, in 1998, Team Canada visited Latin America – Mexico, Brazil, Argentina, and Chile – with almost five hundred companies participating. Education was the third-largest sector represented on the mission, with seven university presidents in attendance. This contributed to educational institutions in each of the ten provinces signing agreements on the trip, as part of a total of 306 business agreements valued at Can$1.78 billion. This 1998 mission featured the opening of four Canadian Education Centres, located in Buenos Aires, Santiago, Sao Paulo, and Mexico City. Two satellite education centres were also inaugurated at universities in Brazil. The Canadian Education Centre initiative demonstrated the importance placed on international academic relations as a catalyst for future trade and investment opportunities by Team Canada.

Returning to Asia in 1999, the next Team Canada Mission travelled to Japan, accompanied by 216 business participants, including a record number of women and Aboriginal entrepreneurs. Education remained prominent and was the second-largest sector represented. Deals worth Can$409

million were signed, along with an additional six agreements that were estimated to bring Can$3 billion to Canada in the following decade. On
this trip, Prime Minister Chrétien used the occasion of a Team Canada
business dinner in Osaka to address the issue of Japanese perceptions of
Canada. Capitalizing on the opportunity to promote Canada as a nation of
advanced technology, Chrétien spoke about Canada as a world leader in
telecommunications, computer software, and space exploration and cited
examples of Canadian software being used by Japanese car manufacturers
and computer game designers. On the topic of investment, Chrétien highlighted the contributions that Japanese investment had made in Canada in
terms of job creation and through the transfer of leading-edge technologies, which help to keep Canada competitive on a global scale. The mission
also featured Rendez-vous with Youth, a forum that included a group of
young Canadians working in Japan. As noted in chapter 4, expatriates and
Canadians working or studying abroad are an important resource in public
diplomacy and can be utilized to help promote a country and dispel
misconceptions.

A second Team Canada Mission to China took place in 2001, with visits
to Beijing, Shanghai, and Hong Kong. The largest Team Canada venture of
them all, with nearly six hundred business participants, this mission
resulted in over Can$5.7 billion in new business deals for Canadian enter-
prises and reinforced Canada's long-term commitment to these key target
markets. The mission's public diplomacy efforts were highlighted by a children's hockey game, the opening in Shanghai of the Canadian Food Festival by the international trade minister at the time, Pierre Pettigrew, and a
visit to the Canadian International School in Hong Kong by the delegation
and their foreign colleagues.

The seventh and final Team Canada Mission, held in 2002, was also the
first to Europe, with stops in Russia and Germany. The mission's aim was
to open doors for Canadian business in Russia and to promote science
and technology, as well as investment partnerships with Germany. It concluded 133 new business deals in Moscow, Berlin, and Munich worth over
Can$583 million. The delegation of 290 Canadian businesses included
more than 150 small- and medium-sized enterprises.

In Europe, education was again a leading focus, since students with experience in Western culture and with second-language training in English or
French are highly desirable in the Russian workforce. Therefore, while in
Moscow, the participants promoted the value of Canadian educational
institutions. Similarly, in Germany exchange opportunities between the
two countries were actively encouraged. Investment and science and tech-

nology seminars held in Berlin and Munich attracted more than nine hundred senior executives from leading companies across Germany. The interest provided Team Canada Mission organizers with a clear indication that their efforts in promoting Canada's highly skilled workforce and Canada's commitment to innovation were coming to fruition and contributing to a global recognition of Canada as a country with a dynamic knowledge-based economy.

There is no question that Team Canada Missions have been successful in raising awareness about Canada in highly competitive foreign markets, where Canada's image as a knowledge economy (with the world's fifth-largest aerospace industry, for example) has been overshadowed by stereotypical images of land, trees, water, and rich farmlands.[23] The missions, with their associated cultural events, self-consciously tried to expose other societies to Canadian attitudes and values. However, a number of criticisms have been levelled against this form of nation branding. First, there was a perception that when Canada's politicians and business leaders travelled to countries with poor human rights records, such as China, they undermined the Canadian values of respect for the rule of law and tolerance in exchange for increased opportunities for trade and investment. Further criticism has been expressed regarding the economic value of the Team Canada Missions. Derek Burney, former Canadian ambassador to the United States and a senior Canadian business leader, has stated: "Team Canada ... junkets are not the answer. If they were, we would be well ahead of the pack but, despite numerous missions of that kind, we have become a 1 [per cent] partner for China; 1 [percent] of our exports, 1 [percent] of their imports. We are falling steadily behind Australia because, for one thing, we do not have a single, coherent strategy on China. We travel and schmooze, we dabble and pose, but where is the follow through and what have we actually achieved? More posture without purpose."[24]

As a means of branding Canada, the Team Canada Missions were closely identified with the tenure of Jean Chrétien. This type of high-profile mission with a cross-section of Canadian business and political leaders, and led by the prime minister himself, was not adopted by the short-lived successor Liberal government of Paul Martin.

INTEGRATING INTERNATIONAL BUSINESS PROMOTION INTO PUBLIC DIPLOMACY

Today's economic reality is characterized by many interests competing for business at the international level. More than ever before, a nation's knowledge and culture are the key factors for economic prosperity and investment attraction. Nations that are able to brand themselves fully – including through education and tourism – will have a greater capacity to influence foreign decision makers and, therefore, have a better chance of securing more foreign direct investment. For example, promoting "people-to-people links among cultural, research and academic groups" was considered the key to the Canada-Mexico Partnership, which was designed to improve opportunities for economic development and investment between the two countries.[25] Similarly, numerous government documents referred specifically to the importance of international science and technology partnerships between Canadian firms and research institutes and their counterparts in other countries, particularly China and India. Science and technology exchanges provide one example of how international academic relations assist Canada's international business promotion efforts. For instance, when the Indian Institute of Technology and the University of Waterloo established a science and technology exchange, Waterloo's vice president (academic), Amit Chakma, stated that academic relations with world-class institutions of higher education, such as the Indian Institute of Technology, "benefit the private sector and universities in both countries."[26] The government of Canada has pursued these types of partnerships actively in order to help create an environment conducive to relationship-building over the long term and to capitalize on the trickle-down benefit that accrues in the form of increased economic ties, whether in the form of trade, investment, science and technology links, or increased numbers of foreign students in Canada.

It is recognized that in order to excel in the global economy, Canada must overcome the perception among foreign leaders that it remains a resource-based economy. Given the emphasis placed on innovation and information technology in today's globalized economy, this is particularly important to Canada's economic prosperity. However, as noted in the discussion of Canada's image problem in chapter 1, there has been a large gap between how Canadians view themselves and how the world perceives Canada. Canada is still categorized in the eyes of the world as a resource economy. The challenge in branding Canada as a trade destination and investment partner therefore involves raising awareness of Canada as a knowledge economy, while maintaining market share in traditional resource sectors.

Regardless of the market, the perceptions of foreign audiences are important and of direct consequence for Canada's economic prosperity. In

"Beefing Up Brand Canada" (an article based on the research of Nicolas Papadopoulos and Louise Heslop on branding Canada),[27] Joanne Stassen relates the trials encountered by the Canadian Beef Export Federation when it began promoting Canadian beef in Asia and Mexico in the early 1990s. The main challenge for Canadian beef exporters was overcoming negative perceptions based on a lack of information about Canada as a food-producing nation. Ted Haney, the president of the federation, related that in Korea, "early on, the perception was that Canadian beef is tough, because Canada has a very long, hard winter and all these animals are shivering."[28] To counter these and other less laughable, though equally damaging, misconceptions, Canada has had to employ targeted public diplomacy efforts.

The Canadian Beef Export Federation launched an aggressive campaign to brand Canadian beef and overcome consumer ignorance. They chose to connect their product to traditional images of Canada – large, clean, mountains, water, trees, and snow – in their supermarket campaigns in Asia and Mexico, and it was the emotional associations made with foreign buyers that brought success. They perceived Canada as being safe and trustworthy, and the federation was able to leverage this perception to promote Canadian beef. Between 1990 and 2002, sales by the federation to its six customer countries grew from Can$24 million to more than Can$498 million.[29]

Canada must leverage the tools of public diplomacy to correct misconceptions in foreign audiences and promote its image not only as a natural resource powerhouse but also as a thriving, knowledge-based economy with a talented labour pool. Targeted advocacy campaigns in key markets are required to raise awareness of the advantages of doing business with Canada. These branding exercises must be supported with follow-up initiatives to maintain the momentum created and thus reinforce the image of Canada as an attractive business destination. Investment and trade promotion components also need to be incorporated into Canada's international cultural and academic relations strategies to foster environments of broader mutual understanding that will benefit economic prosperity. Expanding partnerships with other government departments, the provinces, and municipalities are also necessary for promoting investment and trade. In addition, the effort that goes into evaluating international business promotion activities is essential to determining their success in influencing perceptions held by foreign audiences in both the short and the long term. This information can then be used to adjust existing efforts and shape future plans.

TOURISM PROMOTION

The economic benefits of a successful Canadian tourism industry are self-evident; however, the unintended benefits of the goodwill that destination branding creates in foreign publics and the positive images it instils about Canada, even in those who never visit, are immense. As discussed by Anholt, tourism is the most powerful determinant of national image, and as a result, it is critical to defining the national brand. Greg Klassen concurs and states that "tourism plays a huge, disproportionately large role in contributing to [Canada's] brand."[30] This section will therefore examine the long-term influence of tourism promotion on foreign perceptions of Canada and provide recommendations on how Canada's tourism promotion can be incorporated into Canada's overall public diplomacy strategy.

Tourism promotion is an important generator of growth and employment, contributing directly to national prosperity. The World Tourism Organization reports that tourism is firmly established as the number one industry in many countries and has become one of the world's most important sources of employment. It stimulates enormous investment in infrastructure and provides governments with substantial revenues. Measured by international tourist arrivals, the 19.2 million visitors to Canada in 2006 represented 2.5 percent of global market share, making Canada one of the most popular tourist destinations in the world, according to the World Tourism Organization.[31] Tourism is Canada's sixteenth-largest industrial sector, accounting for nearly 2 per cent of the country's gross domestic product. It is estimated that the tourism sector generated Can\$55.8 billion in economic activity in 2004, up from Can\$37.7 billion in 1995.[32] The Canadian Tourism Commission's (CTC) 2004 annual report states that tourism supported close to 160,000 businesses in Canada and directly employed more than half a million people (almost 4 percent of Canada's workforce). Canada's relatively high ranking as a tourist destination no doubt contributes to its high "likeability" quotient: it is one of the most-liked countries in the world, ranking third in Anholt's thirty-five-country survey behind the United Kingdom and Switzerland.[33]

In today's increasingly competitive marketplace, global mind space is at a premium and the competition is aggressive. The CTC's annual budget of Can\$78 million is paltry when compared to one of Canada's main competitors, Australia, which has an annual tourism budget of approximately Can\$200 million. Increased international competition for tourist dollars and what Joseph Nye refers to as the "paradox of plenty" has made the need to differentiate Canada from other destinations, and indeed other nations, a priority. According to Klassen, "the tourism perspective really focuses on 'come and visit Canada' as a tourism destination, but that has a huge impact in terms of the perception of what our country stands for and what it's all about."[34] For Canada to increase its visibility internationally, destination branding by the CTC must work in concert with other elements of the federal government's public diplomacy strategy in support of a cohesive and positive national brand.

Canadian Tourism Commission

The CTC formulates and implements Canada's tourism promotion strategy and is, therefore, a key player in marketing Canada to the world. In 1995, the CTC was created to replace Tourism Canada as the primary organization responsible for branding Canada as a tourist destination, both at home and abroad. Originally a special operating agency of Industry Canada, the CTC became a Crown corporation in 2001 and was conceived and organized as a partnership between the federal and provincial/territorial governments and the private sector. The CTC is a destination-management organization, the type of organization that Carmen Blain, Stuart Levy, and J.R. Brent Ritchie define as "a critical component of the tourism industry ... whose major purpose is to market their destination to potential visitors, both individuals and groups, to provide economic benefit."[35]

Since the CTC is based on a cooperative relationship between all levels of government and the private sector, it thus takes a whole-of-government approach to public diplomacy. Its organizational structure includes a twenty-six-member board of directors that, in addition to the chair and the CEO, includes seventeen seats for the private sector, representing all facets of the Canadian tourism industry and all regions of the country, and seven seats for public officials from provincial and territorial tourism administrations.

The CTC has focused its international destination branding efforts on nine countries. These countries have a characteristically high concentration of attentive publics: audiences that have demonstrated an interest in travelling to Canada. It is, therefore, no surprise that the bulk of the CTC's global marketing investment is in the United States, followed, in descending order, by the United Kingdom, Japan, Germany, France, Mexico, South Korea, China, and Australia. The CTC also targets foreign media, specifically travel writers – the opinion leaders of the global tourism industry –

and maintains close relationships with them. For instance, the CTC hosts an annual event at a Canadian destination for international travel writers. According to Klassen, the CTC relies "as much as possible on unpaid media because, of course, it's got much more credibility. They are an important channel to get our information out and to highlight what Canada is all about."[36] In the context of public diplomacy, reports about Canada from returning travellers and stories from travel writers are important. Personal experience with a national brand has a profound and lasting influence on people's perceptions, and unmediated messages are accorded more legitimacy in the eyes of foreign audiences, going a long way toward shaping ideas about Canada.

Although a quintessential whole-of-Canada marketing effort, tourism probably represents the single largest federal investment in national image management. At the federal level, Industry Canada performs a coordinating function as the national tourism administrator, overseeing the involvement of more than twenty departments and agencies. According to an Industry Canada report, the federal government invested approximately Can$900 million in tourism-related initiatives in 2003. This included, but was not limited to, an investment in parks, museums, transportation infrastructure, and rural development.

Collaboration between DFAIT and the CTC

The relationship between DFAIT and the CTC is limited. The CTC was formerly present within Canadian missions in certain strategic locations. Because of the missions' restricted hours of operation and increased security measures following the attacks of 11 September 2001, which prevented the CTC from hosting events on-site and receiving casual visitors, the CTC relocated its international offices to separate premises. However, the two organizations work closely together to help promote Canada in the nine countries where the CTC concentrates its marketing efforts.

One example of cooperation has been DFAIT's efforts on behalf of the CTC to negotiate an agreement with the Chinese government to recognize Canada with Approved Destination Status, a goal since 1999. China has given preliminary approval for Canada to become an approved travel destination. Approved Destination Status would allow the CTC to market Canada officially as a tourist destination in China. The benefits to the Canadian economy would be significant. While only seventy-seven thousand Chinese visitors came to Canada in 2005, estimates indicate that with the approved status, as many as one million Chinese tourists could visit Canada, thus

making the agreement negotiated with the Chinese government worth billions of dollars per year.[37] Approved Destination Status would also carry
strategic importance by raising Canada's profile in China, and it would
help build stronger human and economic ties between the two countries.
Chinese visitors would also be exposed to Canadian values of respect for
the rule of law and tolerance, among others, while travelling in Canada.
The long-term impact of increased contact between the two countries' citizens through tourism thus goes beyond economic considerations. Exposure to Canada as a tourist destination would contribute to China's
understanding of the West and, in so doing, potentially quicken China's
slow march toward becoming a more democratic society.

Rebranding Canada as a Tourist Destination

Historically, Canada was almost exclusively marketed through well-known
Canadian symbols. In his article "More than a Maple Leaf," Nathan Wilson examines the Japanese market, in which images of Anne of Green
Gables and Banff continue to be used to promote Canada. Wilson also
notes that Northern Lights travel experiences are also marketed heavily
because of the perceived interest in nature and open spaces within the
Asian market.[38] Although successful in bringing thousands of Japanese
tourists and millions of dollars each year to places such as Yellowknife,
campaigns based exclusively on traditional images of Canada have been
balanced with campaigns showcasing urban Canada.

Tourism promotion can have adverse effects on international trade and
Canada's investment promotion strategies, which are designed to overcome traditional associations with Canada as only a resource-based economy. The Trade Commissioner Service has endeavoured to create an
image of Canada as a dynamic and innovative country in order to attract
trade and foreign direct investment. International destination marketing
can thus undermine DFAIT's efforts when it promotes Canada through the
traditional images of "moose, Mounties, and mountains."

In 2004, the CTC began a comprehensive rebranding exercise, ostensibly
to do away with these traditional symbols, because they were considered
poor reflections of the Canada brand. However, according to Klassen, the
CTC had to overcome many objections from parties within the tourism
industry who were greatly attached to Canada's traditional symbols. The
CTC focused on presenting a more modern image of Canada that would
project a more coherent and persuasive image abroad and be better
aligned with the priorities of other internationally focused federal depart-

ments and agencies. Completed in May 2005, the new branding initiative
was based on ten years of accumulated tourism research and had involved
twenty workshops and eighteen focus groups in twenty-three cities and six
countries. Additionally, it held consultations with industry associations,
tourism operators, and all levels of government. The result was a refash-
ioned brand aimed at communicating and promoting Canada as a more
compelling tourist destination.

· Before the rebranding, the CTC adopted a shorter-term view of destination branding that primarily relied on tactical advertising.[39] The CTC had
invested in its partners' brands, such as Tourism British Columbia, whose
campaigns encouraged visitors to "come now, come in the next few
weeks."[40] Once the seventh most popular tourist destination in the world,
Canada began to see its general tourism market erode toward the end of
the 1990s – a trend that was exacerbated following the 11 September 2001
attacks. Canada found itself losing market share in all its core international
markets. Klassen suggests that this was a direct result of the CTC not investing properly in the Canada brand: "[if] people don't know what Canada
stands for anymore in terms of our brand ... we need to step back and focus
on ... what is it about Canada that makes me want to go there."[41] The
rebranding campaign was intended to address this issue and refocus the
organization's approach to destination branding.

In the industry parlance, tourism is referred to as "a dream factory." To
establish Canada as a preferred destination, the CTC had to "create the
dream." To this end, one of the first major campaigns to be launched following the CTC's rebranding exercise was "Canada: Keep Exploring," targeted at the European market. The campaign featured print and radio
advertisements, posters in the London subway system, bus "wraps," and
three-dimensional posters in high-traffic locations, as well as innovative
marketing techniques, such as a fleet of custom-painted Smart cars in London bearing the catch phrase, "We are all born explorers." The campaign
played on traditional images with twists that spoke directly to consumers.
One print advertisement showed a country resort pool below a beautiful
evening sky with trees in the background. Dotted lines attached to the
labels "midnight" and "mischief" intersected at a pile of clothes on the
empty pool deck. The image was intended to pique the curiosity of travellers and present Canada as more than just a place of beautiful landscapes.
Launched in Britain, France, and Germany, the campaign ran until late
winter 2006, to coincide with, as Klassen notes, "the specific planning time
that people in Europe choose a longer-haul vacation like Canada."[42]

The rebranded image of Canada sought to overcome traditional associations based on geographical location. The CTC's market research indicated that the images most often associated with Canada are "cold, pristine, and natural." The rebranding exercise was intended to move away from the popular concept of Canada as a vast, northern country to a more modern idea of Canada as "intimate, evocative, and upbeat." It is worth noting that of all the instruments of Canada's public diplomacy, tourism promotion campaigns have the distinction of relying the most on market research.

INTEGRATING TOURIST PROMOTION INTO PUBLIC DIPLOMACY

There is certainly a case to be made for the integration of Canada's tourism promotion strategy into the country's broader foreign policy framework. As noted, tourism promotion is the key driver of the national brand. It shares similar goals with public diplomacy, as they employ similar techniques to influence key foreign audiences by projecting Canada's image abroad using attraction and persuasion. The federal government has committed significant resources to tourism promotion (much more than to international broadcasting), recognizing that national identities are increasingly shaped by the full range of the messages received by foreign audiences.

Public diplomacy instruments help to promote Canadian culture and identity abroad. However, better integration of international priorities between government departments, agencies and Crown corporations would allow Canada to maximize communications opportunities and interdepartmental resources to reinforce rather than dilute the Canada brand. For example, DFAIT's cultural program has made strengthening cultural ties with China a priority. If Canada receives Approved Destination Status in China, tourism promotion will be able to contribute significantly toward achieving this goal. DFAIT has also recognized cultural tourism as a means for promoting Canada. A joint effort by the CTC and DFAIT to target key events and venues, such as the Cultural Olympiad and the 2008 summer Olympic Games in Beijing, would allow tourism promotion to better support a broader range of Canadian public diplomacy goals. Incorporating elements of tourism promotion into DFAIT's public diplomacy strategy will help Canada portray a more coherent image and leverage the disproportionately large role that destination branding plays in projecting Canada to the world.

The 2010 Olympic and Paralympic Winter Games Federal Secretariat provides a forum to connect federal organizations involved in promoting Canada. Managed by Canadian Heritage, the secretariat was founded to coordinate the government of Canada's participation in support of the 2010 Olympic Games in Vancouver and Whistler. According to Klassen, the CTC is helping to lead the efforts in developing a single, cohesive brand for Canada as the host country of the winter Olympics. He suggests that the government stands to "gain huge synergies if we are all singing from the same song sheet."[43] The relationships between the federal partners of the 2010 secretariat may develop into longer-term partnerships, which in turn may open opportunities for further collaboration at the federal level to better showcase Canada's brand to the world.

CONCLUSION

This chapter is not meant to be a definitive investigation of the links between international business and tourism promotion as characteristics of the nation brand, but rather an introductory exploration of the need for a deeper understanding of how tourism contributes to the general image of a country and how it can affect other elements of the nation brand both positively and negatively. It argues for a more diverse consideration of what constitutes public diplomacy and suggests that a broadening of definitions to include international business and tourism promotion in public diplomacy strategies would advance Canada's national and international interests. Although investment, trade, and tourism promotion are usually perceived as being separate from the public diplomacy process, the perspective of this study is that efforts to promote Canada's international economic interests are indeed part and parcel of such a process.

The Chrétien era witnessed a refocusing of Canada's international business promotion efforts, specifically its investment promotion strategies, in response to accelerating globalization and greater competition. Accordingly, the institutions to brand Canada economically were revamped. The role of the Trade Commissioner Service was redefined and Team Canada Missions were launched to help brand Canada internationally as a modern, avant-garde nation. The traditional tools of public diplomacy – culture and education – were employed in more targeted ways to help support trade and investment promotion efforts. Branding Canada as a knowledge economy and an attractive international business destination involves overcoming Canada's traditional image as a resource-based economy. This chapter has also argued that tourism promotion is the key characteristic shaping national image and can play a more significant role in Canada's public diplomacy, especially if there is a greater coordination of tourism campaigns with those of international business promotion, as well as cultural and education programming.

PART THREE

The Process

8

The Practice of Public Diplomacy

Public diplomacy is not a substitute for well-thought-out policy. International policy poorly planned or implemented cannot, in most cases, be saved by communications or public relations. A policy's flaws may in fact become magnified as the government seeks to win over its audience. In diplomacy, where the stakes – war, peace, and economic prospects – are arguably higher than in other domains of government activity, exaggerated expectations by leaders about their ability to sell a policy may cause them to harm national interests. It could be said that on the continuum of persuasive communications, a shift from public diplomacy to propaganda occurs once the inherent benefits of a policy cannot be explained easily and all manner of persuasive techniques must be used to engineer acceptance. That said, as shown in earlier chapters, communications is today, more than ever, a necessary complement to effective international policy-making. As the American diplomat Hans Tuch wrote, having practised public diplomacy for thirty-five years, "public diplomacy, intelligently applied, can enhance the attainment of a foreign policy objective and make foreign policy more comprehensible, even acceptable, by improving knowledge and understanding of our society, our purposes, and our values."[1] The reverse is also true. As this chapter will show, a policy miscalculation (even the lack of a policy) or a diplomatic faux pas can quickly undo years of careful public diplomacy planning and practice.

The questions to be considered in this chapter, then, are, Who does public diplomacy? What is the role of the head of mission and what have been the approaches of some of Canada's savviest practitioners? How is public diplomacy organized and planned? How does public diplomacy work on the ground? This chapter examines Canada's public diplomacy efforts in

the United States, its largest public affairs operation on foreign soil, and in
Brazil, a country that has emerged as a new bilateral priority and one in
which a public diplomacy operation of a different scale is carried out.
Finally, the chapter examines some of the operational issues that affect the
practice of public diplomacy: the training and career development of officers engaged in public affairs work, the search for ways to organize public
events for optimal impact, and the challenges of measuring the effectiveness of public diplomacy.

THE PEOPLE: CANADA'S PUBLIC DIPLOMACY
PRACTITIONERS

The public diplomacy function at Canada's missions abroad consists of
three major programs: information/media relations, academic relations,
and cultural affairs. Depending on the size of the mission, these activities
are sometimes referred to generically as "public affairs," though some
countries – notably the United Kingdom – draw a clear distinction between
public affairs as shorter-term information work that is practised, for example, by the embassy's media relations office in direct support of specific current government priorities and longer-term academic and cultural
diplomacy (e.g., as in the mandate of the British Council) that needs to be
insulated from what would be considered advocacy communication. Without a separate British Council–type international cultural agency, Canada's
public diplomacy programs abroad are carried out under the same roof
(and management) of the Political, Economic Relations and Public Affairs
(PERPA) program. These public diplomacy programs have a mandate to
influence the environment in which Canada is seen and understood by foreign publics and opinion leaders. It is the responsibility of the public affairs
staff at Canadian missions to either reinforce the positive environment or
to attempt to reduce negative perceptions of Canada. Public affairs activities will be either proactive or reactive, depending on the objectives being
sought. As Tuch writes, these public affairs programs also provide important
feedback to the ambassador about local public attitudes and perceptions, in
addition to which "they are not only interrelated but also interactive,
depending on each other for reinforcement and support."[2]

   Some foreign service officers who have ultimate responsibility for Canadian public diplomacy at Canada's 174 missions abroad have not received
enough training for the task and have had a limited range of tools. Unlike
the US State Department or the British Council in the United Kingdom,

the government of Canada does not have a specialized professional career track for public servants who wish to specialize in promoting Canada's cultural and intellectual life abroad. Those responsible for Canada's public diplomacy abroad are, for the most part, generalist foreign service officers who did not join the Canadian Foreign Service to be public affairs officers or cultural attachés.[3] A typical foreign service officer (who would be considered a "Canada-based" public servant and would be posted abroad on a rotational basis) will likely have spent some of his or her early career doing communications and public affairs work in smaller missions as a junior officer (e.g., a third or second secretary) in the PERPA program.[4] In larger missions, such as those in the G8 countries and Brazil, Russia, India, China, and Mexico, most of the public affairs work within the PERPA program is undertaken by specialist, locally engaged staff (foreign nationals or, in some cases, Canadian expatriates). It is not surprising that locally engaged staff are disproportionately represented in public affairs activities: they have built up contacts (sometimes over decades) with the local media and also (in the non-English and French worlds) have the benefit of fluency in the local language. The cultural-relations officer positions, for the same reasons, are often occupied by locally engaged staff who have built up extensive networks of local contacts.

Later in their careers, as they gain seniority, foreign service officers assume overall management responsibility for the PERPA programs either as heads of the political and economic sections of small- and medium-sized missions or as minister counsellors in larger missions.[5] Additionally, in the course of their careers, some foreign service officers rotate through the Media Relations division in the Communications Bureau at Foreign Affairs and International Trade Canada's headquarters in Ottawa, which has historically been seen within the Foreign Service as the principal source of assignments for a foreign service officer in this bureau. Non-rotational Information Services officers (who are not members of the Foreign Service) provide strategic communications advice and write public relations plans as well as act as departmental spokespersons in the Media Relations division.[6]

For their public affairs work, foreign service officers have traditionally been expected either to inherently possess the necessary communication and presentation skills or to learn by doing, while on the job. Since 2000, foreign service officers have been offered public diplomacy courses before going abroad. In those larger, higher-profile missions where there is general recognition that more specialized public affairs experience (including cultural relations) is necessary, a number of the top public affairs jobs have been held by non–foreign service officers on secondment from other federal departments or by senior non-rotational officers from DFAIT headquarters. As mentioned in chapter 4, Canadian Heritage maintains six cultural trade commissioners at some of Canada's largest missions. In general, if public affairs jobs are filled by non-foreign service officers who are members of the federal public service, then certain non-rotational officers have been judged to be suitable for the position and have been given a one-off posting.[7] Unfortunately, there is no formal career track for public affairs officers to gain experience at headquarters and abroad before moving from junior public affairs roles to progressively more senior positions.

Some observers have noted that since the budgetary cutbacks in the mid-1990s and the subsequent reduction in Canada-based officers serving abroad, there has been a growing separation between public affairs activities – conducted in many cases by locally engaged staff – and the political and economic programs (run primarily by Canada-based staff) at Canada's missions.[8] Sometimes silos can develop between and among the many functional operations in a mission – economic and political reporting, international business development, consular and immigration services, and public affairs. For public diplomacy programs and activities to provide the most solid foundation for the pursuit of a country's international policy objectives, it is incumbent upon the head of mission (whether as ambassador or consul general) to ensure that the functional silos are removed. There has to be systematic interaction between a head of mission and his or her entire staff, all of whom should be engaged in public diplomacy activities. This practice has already been recognized by Australia's foreign service.[9] Of course, the top public diplomacy practitioner is the head of mission. As the highest-ranking official representative of one country to another, the head of mission personifies his or her country and, consequently, commands the most respect and credibility.[10] Since the head of mission must connect all the strands of the national interest, he or she is the single most important communicator on behalf of Canada in a foreign jurisdiction. The challenge for the head of mission is to mobilize *all* embassy personnel in support of public diplomacy objectives, which in turn support the policy priorities for Canada in the host country.

Without an integrated and coordinated approach that recognizes that public diplomacy cuts across all functional mandates, Canada's policies will not be implemented and executed to their greatest effect. This holds true even if a proportion of Canada-based staff at Canadian diplomatic missions abroad are not from DFAIT but from other federal government departments. In addition to the traditional political, economic/trade, consular, and immigration sections, a range of other agencies and departments can be represented at a Canadian mission: the Canadian International Development Agency, the Finance, National Defence, and Agriculture departments, Canadian Heritage, the Canadian Security Intelligence Service, and the Royal Canadian Mounted Police. Also, in the case of the Washington embassy, provincial representatives are co-located in the embassy's Washington Advocacy Secretariat. Canadian heads of mission who have made a career in the Foreign Service could easily find themselves heading a diplomatic mission in which a significant number of Canada-based staff are not from DFAIT.[11] However, since the ambassador is Canada's top representative abroad, all Canadian staff at missions, even if they are officials from other government departments, report to him or her.[12] If the ambassador or consul general cannot mobilize all the mission staff to think of themselves as Canada's representatives with common or mutually reinforcing objectives – as opposed to representing their individual departments – then Canada's public diplomacy and, ultimately, its international policy will suffer.

Not all heads of mission had the same conviction about the importance of public diplomacy. It is less a matter of whether public diplomacy should be practised than a matter of the relative importance accorded to it within mission planning. It is the difference between perceiving public diplomacy as a "fenced-off" public affairs activity that exists to raise a general Canadian image or as a strategic tool to advance Canadian interests. There are heads of mission who have had a more difficult time appreciating the benefits of, for example, a Canadian Studies program, viewing such longer-term efforts as tangential to solving immediate bilateral irritants or the pursuit of specific policy objectives. One reason may be the perception that the already small budgets for academic relations are consumed by scholarly work in areas that have little if anything to do with the day-to-day work of diplomacy (e.g., work promoting Canadian poetry or literature). Other heads of mission have concluded that they have already been "doing public diplomacy" and they do not need to talk about doing it. For instance, one former Canadian ambassador to the United States remarked that he spent at least half his time on public diplomacy activities.

THE COMMUNICATION-SAVVY HEADS OF MISSION

A number of Canadian heads of mission have demonstrated an innate understanding of the importance of public diplomacy – even if they did not spend their careers calling it that. One of these is Colin Robertson, whose natural affinity for communications was well honed during his assignments outside DFAIT headquarters as a senior government communications executive. He was the director general of DFAIT's Communications Bureau (1998–2000) before serving as Canada's consul general in Los Angeles (2000–4) and then heading Canada's new Washington Advocacy Secretariat in 2005.

As consul general in California, Canada's sixth-largest trading partner, Robertson was responsible for a number of innovative public diplomacy campaigns. His efforts included what the *National Post* described as a "spirited, five-month campaign of lobbying by the federal government, including a swank cocktail party, private movie screenings, personal letters and phone calls [by Robertson] to influential Canadians in Hollywood" to help secure a nomination, and, ultimately, an Academy Award for Best Foreign Language Film for Quebec director Denys Arcand's *Les invasions barbares* in 2004.[13] According to the *National Post*, in the fall of 2003, when the film had barely been screened in the United States, the promotional campaign became a whole-of-government effort, spearheaded by the consulate under the leadership of Robertson and including representatives of the Quebec government through its mission in Los Angeles and the support of the Société de développement des enterprises culturelles (SODEC) and Telefilm Canada.[14] The branding of this Canadian film culminated with a grand soirée at the consul general's official residence, to which Hollywood's movers and shakers were invited. With a significant contingent of expatriate Canadians in Hollywood's creative community, the consulate's challenge was to use the film as a magnet for these Canadians, to create a media event that would help brand Canada as a country with a deep pool of cinematic talent. While it can never be known to what degree the Canadian government's efforts helped the film garner an Oscar – the first such Oscar by a Canadian production – the film's producer, Denise Robert, likened the government's support on behalf of Arcand and Canada's other nominees to a full-fledged political campaign to get a Canadian film elected.[15] To do this, it was first necessary to make the Academy members, or voters, familiar with the "candidate" – something no individual Canadian filmmaker would have had the resources to do so. However, the combined resources of the federal and provincial governments, as well as government agencies such as Telefilm Canada, were able to successfully raise the profile of the director and the film within Hollywood, where everyone was trying to get noticed. Robertson, who innately understood the power of exploiting the synergy from having so many Canadian organizations and expatriates at his disposal, played the role of artful conductor.

Another Canadian diplomat who has excelled in the practice of public diplomacy is George Haynal, who served as Canada's consul general in New York (1995–98) and whose efforts are described in chapter 9. Haynal was able to assess the sorry state of Canada's reputation in New York, arguably the world's financial and cultural capital, and with his very able colleague, Kevin O'Shea, he developed and implemented a highly visible public diplomacy strategy that used limited mission resources to leverage much greater positive exposure for Canada. Haynal's experience in and out of the Foreign Service (he had spent a year at the Royal Bank of Canada on an interchange assignment) had convinced him that globalization was leading to the "disintermediation" of the state (i.e., the state's role as arbiter of a country's international role was being challenged by other multilateral, regional, and local social and economic actors), which in turn meant that diplomacy had to adapt to the "intermesticity" of international relations (i.e., to the growing overlap between domestic and international issues). In Haynal's view, government has "to be increasingly concerned with the management of what are shared issues within as well as between jurisdictions."[16] Moreover, in addition to the traditional bilateral and multilateral concerns of security and trade policy, modern governments, in managing public policy issues such as health and food safety or telecommunications policy, have to "abandon rigid codes of sovereignty and ... stress coherence and compatibility between domestic and foreign policy in order to manage intermestic issues effectively."[17] Accordingly, the combination of the international agenda intruding on the domestic agenda and the need "for an informed public to help pursue society's interests internationally" leads a foreign ministry to be concerned not only with its public diplomacy but also with how it mobilizes its country's citizens at home.[18] Haynal, who remains optimistic about professional diplomacy's prospects, believes that the key is to view the new sources of power, such as mobilized citizens at home and around the world, not as competitors but rather as potential partners in pursuing the national interest.[19]

A third head of mission who has shown an innate understanding of the value of public diplomacy is Randolph Mank. During his first ambassadorial posting to Indonesia, Mank braved a trial by fire when a tsunami ravaged South Asia on 26 December 2004, severely damaging the Indonesian province of Aceh, in particular. Mank faced multiple, daunting challenges as Canada and the rest of the world began to focus on the disaster: how would he, as ambassador, coordinate all of Canada's emergency relief? How would Canadians in the devastated region be accounted for? All donor nations and aid organizations were well aware that their missteps would be magnified, given the intense global media attention; conversely, the organizations and countries that did respond quickly and effectively would be afforded positive coverage for all the world to see. Although disasters are not often framed as national-branding competitions, that is what in fact happens as a result of continuous global media coverage.

As relief efforts for South and Southeast Asia commenced, criticism began to appear in the Canadian media about the slow mobilization of Canada's Disaster Assistance Response Team (DART), the Canadian Forces' rapid response specialists. The problem, however, was less with Canadian preparation than with the inability of the government to secure access to commercial heavy-airlift capability, given the strong demand for such aircraft worldwide in efforts to assist the tsunami victims. DART was ultimately sent to Sri Lanka, where over the course of late January and February, the team was able to provide medical support and water purification services to the people.

Regardless of the issues that DART was facing in deploying to Sri Lanka, Mank and his embassy team, stationed in Jakarta, worked tirelessly and quickly to open first a forward office in Medan immediately following the disaster and then, when the situation permitted, an on-the-ground presence in the form of "Canada House Aceh" on 30 January 2005. The outpost, a former two-storey house within fifty metres of where the waves deposited the remains of washed-up cars and ruined buildings, served as a focal point for the coordination of Canadian volunteers, personnel, and material support for tsunami victims. It was among the very first such offices opened in what had been for years a closed conflict region. Other foreign governments later followed the Canada House model. CIDA representatives, Indonesian officials, non-governmental organizations, and donors were able to use the building as a contact point for the assistance and reconstruction effort. Always busy, Canada House became a symbol of hope for area residents and tourists, the Canadian flag flying proudly out front. Mank's quick thinking helped establish a highly visible, on-the-ground Canadian presence where it was needed most, and, as a result, Canada was able to coordinate a massive relief effort for the people of Indonesia.

Mank's thinking on the public dimension of diplomacy had been honed in his previous postings as a foreign service officer. While in Japan as a political officer at the Canadian embassy, he had gained an appreciation of the importance of understanding the public environment – the players and the institutions – and planning a public advocacy strategy that would make Canada's interests known to those who mattered on an issue-by-issue basis. Mank's approach to diplomacy was that of strategic advocacy, harnessing the information market in support of Canadian interests, of which the public dimension was a critical component. The use of political influence was central to pushing Canadian messages and, as Mank suggested, "[p]olitical officers cannot possibly hope to compete with journalists for the news. On the other hand, we cannot rely on CNN to advocate Canadian interests either. That is our job. It is real politics."[20] Without knowing, of course, how it would be so desperately needed later in Aceh, Mank had put in place a unique strategic advocacy plan for his embassy upon arriving in Jakarta in 2003. Early successes in advocating political-commercial interests not only encouraged him to continue with this targeted approach but also led Ottawa to require other missions in the region to follow the same model.

Mank's successful application of this theory was critical to the success of his efforts in Indonesia while coordinating Canada's response to the tsunami. Working with both the local government in Aceh and the central government in Jakarta tested Mank's tenacity and determination, but he was ultimately able to oversee the creation of Canada House Aceh – placing Canadian assistance at the centre of the relief effort.

THE COUNTRY STRATEGY

The country plan, or strategy, is the standard way in which Canada's missions establish their priorities. The strategy's broad parameters are established by the government's foreign policy goals as set out in government statements and white papers. These goals are then further broken down into specific priorities for geographic regions. There is a process of negotiation between individual missions and headquarters, with the latter breaking down the more general priorities into specific political/security and economic/trade objectives for individual countries. As Tuch notes, there are relatively fewer public diplomacy objectives, given that they do not lend themselves to the treatment of such issues as intelligence analysis or defence reporting.[21] The country strategy, as a business management tool outlining resources (both existing and desired), thus provides the basis for work plans against which future mission performance will be measured. It provides both the big picture and a view of how resources will be used.

A country strategy is only useful if it is connected to the mandate given to the head of mission. To this end, every new ambassador receives a mandate letter from the foreign minister with specific Canadian objectives for the country to which he or she is accredited. To understand how the instructions in the mandate letter are linked to the country strategy, it is useful to look at the key communication objectives that the head of mission is expected to achieve. For example, in the late 1990s, Canadian heads of mission would have received mandate letters from the foreign minister, Lloyd Axworthy, instructing them to communicate key messages on the government's international agenda, such as the initiative to ban land mines. Heads of mission would have had to show through their personal performance assessments that they had made both public (spoken at conferences, to editorial boards) and private interventions on these topics.

In support of its country strategy, each Canadian mission is expected to produce sub-strategies and work plans reflecting the mission's functional responsibilities, including public affairs. Such strategies show how public diplomacy activities support broader and more specific Canadian priorities for the country. A systematic approach to public diplomacy planning requires an in-depth understanding of the local audiences that matter (what Tuch calls an "institutional analysis").[22] Public diplomacy practitioners will typically seek to identify important institutions and the most influential individuals in a society (e.g., politicians, public servants, journalists, scholars, business leaders, artists, and members of the NGO community). Depending on whether the strategy is designed for an open or a closed society, they will pay particular attention to opinion leaders, that is, to those individuals who would influence the broader "attentive public" – that stratum of local societies with higher socio-economic status and/or political influence. Influencing these local opinion leaders – particularly journalists, business people, academics, and entertainers – and receiving their endorsement is the most efficient way of getting Canadian messages out to a broader audience and of making them more credible. Beyond these established opinion leaders, the mission will also want to target future leaders among local elites through scholarship and exchange programs (see chapter 5).

CANADA'S PUBLIC DIPLOMACY STRATEGIES: THE UNITED STATES AND BRAZIL

While the scale of operations and the specific communication objectives may differ from mission to mission around the world, they all have the same overarching goals: to inform local audiences; to address misconceptions about Canada and the Canadian government's policies, and to create a positive foundation for the pursuit of Canada's objectives. This discussion of Canada's public diplomacy strategies and programs in the United States and Brazil will illustrate the importance of their respective PERPA programs and the challenges of managing the reputation of nation-states.

Public Diplomacy in the United States

Perhaps the most challenging public diplomacy market for Canada in the world is that of the United States. Canada, when it is noticed at all, is frequently viewed as little more than a cold mass of air from the North. When Colin Robertson asked, "[w]hat do [Americans] think about Canada?" he answered himself with, "[t]hey *don't* think about Canada."[23] While the United States is a national obsession for Canadians, Americans have a certain "cerebral hygiene," an unconsciously dispassionate emotional attachment towards Canada.[24] Americans, for the most part, are not attentive to the relationship and, consequently, when asked, they tend to have a favourable view of their neighbours to the North. Canada's role, and particularly that of Canadian ambassador Ken Taylor in protecting several American embassy staff members in Tehran from capture after the Iranian revolution in 1979, was notable in that it elicited a great amount of public recognition and appreciation in the United States for Canada. And for most of the bilateral history, because of the innumerable economic, political, and family ties that bind the two nations, general attitudes in the United States about Canada have been impervious to political vicissitudes. To be sure, some issues, such as Canada's role as a haven for draft dodgers during the Vietnam War, did, for a time, create a negative image of Canada in the minds of a certain portion of the American public. But when compared with other nations, Canada has been typically viewed as America's closest friend. According to the Chicago Council on Foreign Relations' regular polls of Americans' attitudes towards international affairs, Canada received the highest "warmth" rating.[25] Americans' overall perceptions of Canada could be summarized as "decidedly positive," though incomplete, since Canada is often seen as being the same as the United States.[26]

The inauguration of George W. Bush in January 2001 crystallized for Ottawa the new face of America: the ineluctable shifting of the locus of political and economic power from the Northeast to the Southwest. A further message was sent when the new president's first state visit was to Mexico. Ottawa's foreign policy planners concluded that there was an urgent need to reverse Canada's waning profile. This conclusion coincided with a number of other disturbing trends, such as unresolved trade disputes, stagnating exports, and Canada's decreasing share of American foreign direct investment (despite NAFTA's ten-year existence). The consulates in the United States were reporting that American site selectors – professionals who recommend foreign locations for US direct investment – did not list Canada as a favoured location. Urban myths abounded in American business circles about Canada as a socialist country that was unfriendly to business.

There was a perceptible change in the attitudes towards Canada among American opinion leaders (particularly within the US Congress) after September 2001 (see chapter 9). The initial positive image garnered by Canada because of its prompt response in welcoming more than thirty-three thousand stranded American airline passengers was soon overshadowed by the incorrect perception (promulgated by news outlets with considerable reach, such as Fox News) that Canada was a haven for terrorists.[27] The offhand reference to the president of the United States as a "moron" by Jean Chrétien's director of communications at an international NATO conference in 2002 did not go unnoticed by the White House of George W. Bush, nor did the apparent unwillingness of the prime minister to take sufficiently strong action to distance himself from the remark. This further challenged Canada's public diplomacy practitioners and undermined the tone of the Canada-US bilateral relationship, which had not been warm to begin with. More seeds of doubt were sown about Canada's worthiness as "America's best friend" when the Liberal government led by Chrétien refused to join the American government's "coalition of the willing" to remove Saddam Hussein from power in Iraq in 2003.[28] Ironically, British prime minister Tony Blair, closer in political persuasion to Chrétien's Liberal Party than he was to Bush's Republican Party, was being hailed as a hero in the United States, and soon after, the United Kingdom was perceived to be America's "new best friend." The perception of an eroded relationship was manifold.

Adding it all up, it appeared that Canada's stock was falling with its most important neighbour. Over the course of a few years, perceptions of Canada within political, business, and media circles in the United States had gone from a state of benign neglect to a situation in which, for the first time, Canadians detected an open hostility toward their country. Some Canadian consuls general reported that when they made official calls to their local contacts, whether to CEOs to talk about business or to a local politician to talk about legislation, they first had to spend time defending Canada, explaining same-sex marriage and Internet pharmacies and why Canada was not a "haven for terrorists."

A polite but distant relationship between President Bush and Prime Minister Chrétien and growing antipathy toward the US administration's policies by certain members of the Liberal caucus and large segments of the Canadian population (especially French Quebecers), not to mention the long-standing feeling that Canada was not only being taken for granted in the United States but also losing the influence that it did have, prompted many to ask a burning question in Ottawa: how to reverse the growing distance between the two countries? While the number of Canadian missions had been reduced in the United States during the cost-cutting 1990s, there was now a consensus within the Canadian business community and government that the time had come to increase Canada's visibility. As a result, Canada launched the Enhanced Representation Initiative (ERI) in 2003.

Before the launch of the ERI, Canadian public diplomacy was largely fragmented in the United States, as each Canadian consulate ran its own public diplomacy strategy independently of other missions. Curiously, unlike in other countries where Canadian consulates reported to the Canadian embassy, in the United States the consulates were largely independent players who reported directly to DFAIT headquarters. Advocacy was thus conducted by Canada in the United States on many fronts, contributing to some confusion, duplication, and wasted effort.

The purpose of the ERI, a Can$118 million, five-year (2003–8) program, is to stimulate investment and to advocate the full breadth of Canadian interest south of the border. The ERI takes a local-, regional-, and state-level approach, designed to complement Canada's existing efforts at the federal level in Washington. The ERI was designed as a network, representing a whole-of-government approach. It is a partnership of eight departments and agencies, each of which participates in the drafting of diplomatic instructions and maintains direct relations with the missions. The ERI's goals are to inform and influence key American decision makers, focus on strategic geographic areas in the United States, and better identify market opportunities. Although the ERI is sometimes called a business initiative, it is really about expanding Canada's advocacy capabilities outside the Washington Beltway. There was a need to "right-size" the consulate territories so that one consulate, such as the one in Minneapolis, would no longer need to cover eight states – an impossible task. Americans – not only business people – had to become better informed about Canada. It seemed axiom-

atic that a greater familiarity with Canada would translate into more favourable treatment of Canadian interests when it came time to make business
and political decisions.

Put simply, Canada had to rebrand itself to the United States. The program established six new consulates (in Raleigh, San Diego, Houston, Phil-
adelphia, Phoenix, and Anchorage) and one consulate general (in
Denver), upgraded two existing consulates (in Miami and San Francisco)
to consulates general, and added thirteen new honorary consuls and eighty
new positions. These missions would be used to get out the message that
Canada is a good neighbour, an extremely valuable trading partner, and a
solid ally committed to continental security and the global war on terror.
The thinking was that if Canada was successful in getting these messages
across and getting American decision makers to think of Canada in a more
positive way, then there would be "flow down," a cascade of benefits to
investment promotion, border cooperation and defence, and environmental relations. According to John Kneale, the senior Canadian official
responsible for managing the ERI network, "When new consuls general ask,
'What is my job?' I tell them, 'Your job is to get to know the 100 most
important people in your territory: editors, CEOs, governors, members of
Congress, senators, chiefs of staff. Get to know them on a first-name basis so
that when you read the morning paper and see that one of them has said
something erroneous about Canada, you can call them up and say: 'What
you said in your speech is completely wrong. I am coming over to see you in
one hour.'"[29]

The expanded network of representation was badly needed. Canada's
embassy in Washington could only do so much. For example, it is much
easier to get the attention of senators in their home states than it is to
attract their attention in Washington, where at any given time many other
organizations and countries are busy lobbying them. The ERI amounted to
the launch of a sometimes aggressive, proactive, permanent multi-point
public affairs campaign. The approach emphasized building new relationships and being more creative. A good example of such creativity was the
Denver consulate general's "Dueling BBQs" event in June 2005, arranged
to address concern in the United States that Canadian beef was unsafe
owing to bovine spongiform encephalopathy (BSE, or "mad cow disease").
Closing the US border to Canadian beef had caused hundreds of millions
of dollars of damage to the Canadian beef industry in the previous year.
The Canadian consul general in Denver and the governor of Colorado
invited the premiers of Manitoba and Saskatchewan and the minister of

agriculture of Manitoba to Colorado for a cook-off of Canadian and American beef. This manufactured event – a "pseudo-event" designed for positive media coverage – was an opportunity, on the lawn of the Colorado governor's mansion in Denver, to prove that Canadian beef was just as good (if not better) and just as safe as American beef.

A unique feature of the ERI, in the spirit of public diplomacy, is that it represents a true whole-of-government advocacy effort, since DFAIT's partners include six other federal departments and agencies.[30] The partners have full decision-making authority along with DFAIT. Owing to the funding framework, all eight departments (DFAIT counts as two because it has two ministers) act like a board of governors representing Canada in the United States. The partners decide on the strategic priorities for the work of the missions, the allocation of funds, and the selection of candidates for positions. DFAIT, while retaining its authority over the consular function, has, through the ERI, actually given up exclusive authority over two of its traditional mandates abroad – the power of oversight over international business development and advocacy.

In addition to the launch of the ERI, the Canadian government unveiled the Washington Advocacy Secretariat, a new approach to projecting Canada and Canadian interests within the corridors of power in Washington, DC. Because the provinces increasingly recognized that they had their own interests in the United States, they also required a place where they could voice their concerns and push forward their agendas. Hence, the secretariat was also created in response to the premiers' desire to advance their interests in Washington. As Colin Robertson, the minister (advocacy) and head of the secretariat, explained, "[t]he relationships between provinces and states, especially between premiers and governors, are the hidden wiring of the Canadian-American relationship."[31] To underscore this point, there is more trade between states and provinces than between the provinces themselves. Since most trade barriers lie in local regulations, the best place to deal with these barriers and promote trade interests was thought to be in direct state-to-province negotiation. The secretariat is unique, as no other countries have opened specialized secretariats where sub-national levels of government are offered a place for negotiation (Alberta's and Ontario's representatives are located in the secretariat).[32]

Robertson has stated that the purpose of the Secretariat was to brand Canada more effectively, in order to advance Canadian interests within the American Congress.[33] According to him, "[i]t's missionary work in the sense that you are up here preaching to those who are neither converted

nor aware ... We are bringing knowledge of 'Canada.'"[34] This involved outreach programs targeting Capitol Hill, in addition to intensive engagement
with think tanks, media, and US defence studies programs. Given the
American involvement in the war on terror, Canada, through the Advocacy
Secretariat, promoted itself in Washington through programs such as the
CanadianAlly.com media campaign. In this campaign, Canada highlighted
its role as an active supporter in the global war on terror by placing "boots
on the ground" in Afghanistan and by contributing as an active player in
stability operations in fragile states. The campaign also emphasized the
high level of interoperability between the Canadian and the American military. The principle underlying CanadianAlly.com was articulated by John
Holmes in his book *Life with Uncle*: "life is a good deal more comfortable for
Canadians if there is at least a minimum of goodwill across the border. It is
important to our material well being that we be regarded by Congress and
the administration as a good ally."[35] As a result, when inaccuracies about
Canada's role in securing the northern border and its contribution to the
war on terror appeared in the American media, the secretariat had the
capacity to act as a rapid response "war room," to get out Canadian messages to those who have influence and to track coverage of issues affecting
Canada's interests, especially with regard to trade and investment. The use
of expatriate networks, such as Connect2Canada, helps to facilitate the
spread of information regarding Canada's contributions, sensitizing individuals to Canada's role in the war on terror. Thus, the objectives of the
Secretariat can be summarized as (a) making access available through a
network of contacts, (b) acting as an early warning system on emerging
issues and trends, and (c) providing advocacy capacity. The challenges facing Canada's public diplomacy in the United States have been diagnosed,
and action has been taken, but the anticipated results will take years to
materialize in opinion polls and focus groups within the American attentive public. This is in the nature of public diplomacy – a delayed effect that
offers no easy cause-and-effect measurement.

Public Diplomacy in Brazil

Unlike the significant presence of Canadian public affairs representatives in the United States through Canada's consulates and the sophisticated public diplomacy apparatus of the Washington Advocacy
Secretariat that involves members from all levels of government, Canada's
visibility in Brazil, the largest country in South America, falls into the

mid-range of Canadian public diplomacy efforts worldwide. Canada has maintained a presence in Brazil for nearly 145 years, and most of the bilateral relationship has been based on commercial interests such as trade in natural resources and raw materials.

Some of the most significant obstacles to the development of this bilateral relationship occurred in the early 1990s. During the lengthy proceedings to free Canadians Christine Lamont and David Spencer from Brazilian jails, Brazil was characterized by Canadian politicians and media alike as akin to a banana republic. This characterization marred Ottawa's ability to engage the Brazilians on other bilateral files for much of the following decade.[36] What should have been "just another" consular case, albeit one requiring careful management, given the interest of the Canadian media, soon mushroomed into a major bilateral irritant, colouring Brazilians' perceptions of Canada (when they actually thought about Canada at all) as a fair-minded northern neighbour that was *not* the United States. Near the end of the decade, difficulties between national aircraft manufacturers Bombardier of Canada and Embraer of Brazil created new tension in the bilateral relationship. Disputes over government subsidies to the two regional aircraft-producing companies were taken before the World Trade Organization, and rulings were imposed against both countries.[37] This was followed in February 2001 by the public relations challenge of having the Canadian Food Inspection Agency order the removal of Brazilian beef from Canadian grocery store shelves in an apparent reaction to the threat of BSE.[38]

The recent political relationship between Canada and Brazil has thus been framed largely by trade frictions and could be described as lukewarm at best. Canadian political leaders have rarely visited Brazil: a six-year gap separated the visits of Prime Minister Chrétien and his 1998 Team Canada Mission and of Prime Minister Paul Martin in November 2004. Political differences have also emerged over high-profile Canadian-driven initiatives. On the trade front, the two countries held different positions on a proposed Free Trade Area of the Americas, a dominant hemispheric concern over the past decade and more. Canada was a consistent and forceful promoter of the agreement, seeing it as a natural extension of continental free trade and a route to prosperity for all the Americas. Brazil, however, was opposed to the proposal because the plan would have continued American agricultural subsidies without providing the means for Brazil to effectively access foreign markets.[39] The proposal collapsed in 2005 because of differences between the developed and developing countries involved: devel-

oped nations sought an expansion in the services industry and increased
intellectual property rights, while the developing nations followed Brazil's
lead, opposing the government subsidies and restricted (agricultural) market access in the developed world. Another bilateral difference emerged
over the human-security-based agenda of the report of the International
Commission on Intervention and State Sovereignty, *The Responsibility to Protect*, an agenda that had been championed by Canada when it launched the
commission in 2001. Brazil opposed the principle of international intervention in national affairs, and, as a result, it took considerable diplomatic
effort by Canada to clarify the language and intent of the report for the
Brazilians.

Canada's public affairs operation in Brazil has always been of modest
size. In 2005, for example, it had six designated public affairs employees
(four of whom were locally engaged) to serve a country of 180 million
people – a country identified as a twenty-first century foreign policy priority for Canada in Ottawa's *Canada's International Policy Statement* of 2005.[40]
Despite these limited resources, Canada has enjoyed particular success in
reaching Brazilians through the significant presence of sixteen Canadian
Studies programs across the country. Efforts have been made to diversify
the nature of the public affairs programs offered in Brazil, and as a result,
there has been a growing mutual interest in scientific collaboration
between the two countries. Canada has also emerged as a preferred destination for Brazilians hoping to learn a second language. For example, after
11 September 2001, with segments of the world's international student
population choosing to avoid the United States because of tighter visa
restrictions, Canada became (in 2004 and 2005) the primary destination
for Brazilian students studying both French and English.

Canada's public diplomacy priorities in Brazil have long-term objectives:
to project the diversity of Canada and to engage Brazil as a partner in
regional and multilateral forums. The means to achieve these objectives
have included placing a greater emphasis on establishing links with Brazil's
national congress and seeking more access to the Brazilian media. There
are several challenges in furthering Canada's public diplomacy efforts. In
addition to Brazil's language barrier – it is the sole Portuguese-speaking
country in South America – the country remains very much a continent
unto itself. There is limited trade dependence on other nations, there is
no significant enemy or competitor, and there are few clear strategic
interests in the broader world. The long-established immigrant communities (primarily of German, Italian, Japanese, and Syrian/Lebanese

descent) are not outward-looking. According to a Canadian expert on Brazil, it is not surprising that, with no significant outside partner, Brazil evinces a limited interest in what occurs in other nations.[41] This sense of indifference helps to account for Brazilians' low level of knowledge about Canada and helps to explain why it may be more challenging for Canadian public diplomacy ventures – especially if they are short-term in nature – to have a significant impact.

Although access to Brazil's mass media is perceived to provide the best conduit for reaching the wider Brazilian audience with Canadian messages, such action is easier said than done, and Canadian officials have been forced to search out other methods of connecting culturally with Brazilians. Enhancing Canada's profile in Brazil through the print media is somewhat limited, since a great deal of the nation depends on television for its news, and this medium is dominated by entertainment programming. Penetration of the television market is further hampered by the miniscule budgets afforded to Canadian international broadcast efforts, which look especially small when compared to those of the principal Brazilian television empire.[42] That being said, promoting Canadian film has always been a popular option, especially taking advantage of Canada's expertise in animation. As suggested in chapter 4, public affairs staff in Brazil have found that inserting Canada into local events, rather than holding "stand-alone" Canadian events, is a more effective way of projecting Canada. Multifaceted performances, that is, bundling local Brazilian cultural talent with touring Canadian performers to create joint ventures, serve to integrate the Canadian perspective and appear to have a longer impact. In recent years, considerable efforts have been made to project Canada's francophone identity in public affairs programming as a means of carving out a Canadian niche in Brazilians' perceptions of the world.

Canada's public diplomacy goal in Brazil is ultimately about leveraging its position by taking advantage of pre-existing and often local opportunities to insert the Canadian presence into the consciousness of Brazilians. To be sure, Canadian public affairs officials face a difficult task in trying to maintain Canada's visibility. While it has been mildly troubled over the recent past, the relationship has historically suffered more from its lack of depth, given that very little happens in Canada with significant (or any) implications for Brazil, and vice versa. This context makes public diplomacy efforts all the more challenging. Success can come only with a sustained public presence in such a large country, and this presence can exist only with experienced professional public affairs staffs at Canada's embassy in Brasilia and its consulates. Objectives and well-defined target audiences are important, but officials understand that flexibility in planning must remain, or else potential breakthroughs will be missed while officials wait for preconceived "ideal" situations and pre-planned campaigns. While further study is required, Canada's public diplomacy program in Brazil may become the template for other mid-size public affairs operations.[43]

ISSUES IN THE PUBLIC DIPLOMACY PROCESS

Mainstreaming Public Diplomacy

As noted, the attacks of 11 September 2001 caused a significant amount of introspection in the Anglo-American world about the success of its public diplomacy effort in the Islamic world. A recurring theme in numerous academic and government reports was the need to bring public diplomacy out of its public affairs ghetto – in short, to mainstream it. Mainstreaming meant bringing public diplomacy to the policy table, integrating public diplomacy with the foreign policy priorities of the day. Questions of public communication would have to be taken into account in all facets of foreign policy-making. For Canada, mainstreaming public diplomacy was one of six imperatives of change underpinning an administrative transformation of Canada's foreign ministry in 2005.[44] Simply put, if nobody knows what Canada's foreign policy strategy is, then Canada does not have one.[45] The gradual change in perception was already apparent in the 1990s when certain forward-thinking Canadian diplomats, such as Daryl Copeland, called on all members of DFAIT – foreign service officers, non-rotational staff at headquarters, and those locally engaged – to be responsible for projecting Canada's international image. No longer would diplomacy simply be done at the bureaucratic level; mainstreaming public diplomacy meant that local populations would help Canada to advocate its policies to their home governments. Projecting Canada's image and interests could not simply be relegated to public affairs officers. Diplomats were now both gatekeepers and boundary spanners. As Copeland has written about the new breed of diplomat: "These people will be as effective in storefront operations as in boardrooms, and as comfortable in teeming markets as they are in leafy suburbs or downtown office towers. Too many serving ambassadors are more comfortable schmoozing with the diplomats inside the embassy walls than they are mixing it up with the locals in the street. New recruits should be comfortable with assessing risk, prefer cooperation in teams to shovelling in silos and be able to swim like fish in the sea rather than flop around like fish out of water."[46] Under the new approach, a light and flexible public diplomacy was being sought, with a greater focus on aligning and strengthening the links between limited resources and priorities. This approach included moving the Canada Fund for Local Initiatives from CIDA to DFAIT, where it would be redirected to governance-related projects.

As noted in chapter 2, Canada will never be able to maximize its reputation abroad unless it develops a domestic constituency for its international role and initiatives. The foreign ministry must develop a wider role for itself beyond its roles of international representation and negotiation. DFAIT has an opportunity to show its value added at home and abroad when it adds to the public understanding by advocating the Canadian interest on the international dimension of the full array of Canada's priorities. These priorities have included climate change, energy supply, and health, issues for which the primary expertise resides within other government departments, as well as in the private sector and the research community. Integrating domestic feedback loops through public consultations (as opposed to one-way information dissemination) into the development of international policy is thus critical, and it legitimizes the policy-making process. In sum, DFAIT needs to continue to develop its "receptor capacity and ability to advocate privately and publicly on the international dimension of domestic issues" in order to play a meaningful role in the advancement of Canadian interests.[47] This, too, is part of mainstreaming public diplomacy.

A Public Diplomacy Career Stream

Cultural-sector work is about building long-term relationships, a practice not reflected in the rotational diplomatic system. Historically, in the absence of a public diplomacy career stream at DFAIT and with no government-wide public diplomacy strategy, the commendable efforts made by generations of foreign service officers in promoting Canada's image publicly have been most often a matter of coincidence of interest, local-language ability, and good timing. John Ralston Saul suggests that as the old "humanist generalist" profile for the ideal foreign service officer gave way to the managerial technocrat, the likelihood of having officers who were ready to be more sensitive to the importance of understanding local cultures grew even more remote.[48] Ralston Saul recommends having the cultural affairs officers do "postings" at home within the Canadian cultural-affairs community. This will, however, make the posting system even more cumbersome, although it may be possible to send officers on assignment to organizations such as the Canada Council for the Arts.

It should also be noted that there is a certain incompatibility between a cultural-affairs portfolio, which requires officers to be entrepreneurial and assertive in establishing links with the cultural community, and the hierarchical reality of foreign ministries. As Ralston Saul points out, the "representational" culture favoured by, and evident in, traditional diplomacy is damaging to cultural diplomacy.[49] Diplomacy is about control and predictability. The reality is that in the field, the most dedicated and effective cultural affairs officer will make little headway if he or she does not have a supportive head of mission and is unable to take necessary risks to interact with local communities.[50] As well, according to Ralston Saul, cultural affairs officers with inadequate budgets for travel around the country of their posting will be rendered ineffective. They must be able to develop long-term professional contacts, preferably outside the capital cities and, equally vital, at home in Canada.

Some observers of the administration of Canada's foreign policy point out that there is a contradiction in calling for a mainstreaming of public diplomacy, in effect making all diplomats public diplomats, and, at the same time, creating a specialized career track similar to that of the British Council. Besides, they would argue, it would not make operational or financial sense to create a separate classification, since, realistically, only a small pool of public diplomacy officers would be assigned to Canada's largest fifteen missions abroad. While it may not be possible to create a pool of Canadian cultural attachés, it is more likely that there will be more professional development opportunities in the years ahead, so that DFAIT officials – rotational and non-rotational – can conduct public advocacy campaigns in a more sophisticated manner, including making much better use of public opinion research. In the end, the management of those individuals entrusted with Canada's image abroad seems destined to continue to be a case of "if it ain't broke, don't fix it" and a perception that there are other, more urgent human resource challenges.

Developing a Public Diplomacy Strategy

In the past, Canada missions, at times felt under some pressure to continue existing public affairs programming or to deliver programming from headquarters without consultation. Also, an inordinate amount of time was spent connecting domestic groups with international groups, not to mention the ad hoc domestic outreach in Canada which lacked clear performance criteria. Since 2000, there has been a concerted effort towards more rational, longer-term strategic planning. Senior officials are prepared to examine routine public diplomacy activities that have simply outlived their usefulness. The past tendency to adopt an any-press-is-good-press model of public diplomacy is less likely to occur, as there is less of an inclination to expend scarce embassy resources simply because Canadian artists are visiting a particular country. Current practice dictates the need to think strategically, and missions have responded to the challenge.

There has also been an ongoing debate about whether missions should focus on launching big, lavish one-off events that are guaranteed to gain profile or whether they should deliver less ambitious programs throughout the year. In fact, as noted in this chapter's description of Canadian public diplomacy programs and practices, it is not a matter of choosing one approach or the other. The local environment, the levels of awareness of Canada, and the particular priorities of Canada will dictate whether or not its programs should be bundled or held at regular intervals throughout the year. The fact is that a government can never have enough resources (not even the United States or the "cultural superpower," France) to create a significant impact on image management and country branding. Therefore, public diplomacy must be used as a catalyst for achieving desired results. It has been observed that many successful public diplomacy programs, including events held in Canada's showcase embassies (e.g., in Washington, Berlin, and Tokyo) or in the cultural centres in London and Paris, will use local events as "platforms" from which to project Canada.

Evaluation

There is abundant literature on evaluating communications. The purpose here is not to review this literature but to make a number of observations concerning the difficulties of evaluating public diplomacy programs. As noted, the events of 9/11 forced the rapid rethinking of public diplomacy strategies around the world. It also forced a rethinking of how to evaluate public diplomacy effects, given the apparent failure to create a greater understanding of the West and to reduce the influence of militant Islam.

A general difficulty in any evaluation is to distinguish between outputs and outcomes. Measuring outputs (the "things" produced and the number of messages transmitted) is fairly straightforward and uncontroversial, though often ignored by government agencies all the same. Measuring outcomes, or the broader impact of a given public diplomacy program in terms of achieving Canadian economic or security goals, is much harder, given the difficulty of attributing causality (especially in a foreign environment), and is, therefore, politically and bureaucratically unpopular. No matter how much work public affairs staff do to promote a country's image (e.g., by getting extensive earned media coverage), there is no guarantee that their efforts will necessarily lead to decisions being taken in favour of Canadian interests. In the words of a Canadian official, "you cannot draw a straight line between media coverage and legislators casting their votes in favour of Canadian interests." Stéphane Gompertz, a French official speaking at a public diplomacy conference in 2002, conceded that it has been difficult to measure the effectiveness of French public diplomacy because of the inherent problems with quantifying such efforts. Each year, every French embassy selects a number of individuals with prospects of becoming future leaders to participate in a foreign-visitors' program, enabling these individuals to visit Paris for two weeks. Gompertz admitted that it is almost impossible to determine whether participants in such visitors' programs would make future policy decisions in foreign countries more favourable to French interests. Christopher Ross, an American official with extensive experience in public diplomacy, who spoke at the same conference, noted that it is much easier to evaluate the effects of education and cultural exchanges than of information campaigns.[51]

Indeed, what ambassador would admit that a project for which he or she had – in good faith – mobilized the entire embassy over a significant period had little persuasive impact beyond a few flattering newspaper articles? Invariably, failure is not an option, and many public communications campaigns in foreign countries have limited evaluations beyond the anecdotal. The "foreign service disease" of everything having to be a success is all the more apparent on the culture front, where out-and-out failure would actually be almost impossible to quantify unless the artist, say, failed to show up. It has to be said, though, that the risks to careers and Canada's foreign policy interests associated with the failure of a cultural exhibit to garner attention are not the same as the risks associated with failing to negotiate a treaty or rescue Canadians in a war zone. Some would say that two different orders of risk management are involved and that soft diplomacy cannot be evaluated in the same way as other forms of Canada's diplomacy.

It is not surprising, then, that public diplomacy evaluation usually elicits knowing smiles. Yet in the last twenty years, foreign ministries have become more results-oriented. The problem is that evaluation models are either

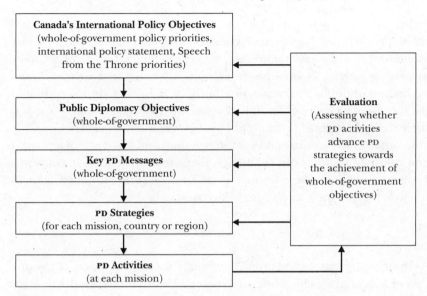

Figure 8.1   Evaluation of public diplomacy.

Source: Author's adaptation of diagram developed by DFAIT officials.

too simple (providing only basic information that does not allow managers to make strategic decisions) or too complex (with so many metrics that they cannot be sustained). This is not to say that government audit departments have not been measuring public diplomacy activities. Traditionally, public diplomacy evaluation has been *output*-oriented: how many events were held and how many people attended? What was the media coverage? Were mission resources used effectively? Evaluations of public diplomacy activities have usually not been *outcome*-oriented, and feedback loops in the form of follow-up surveys or interviews with sample audiences are not done as a matter of course. It is also the case that even when the feedback exists, officials are often at a loss over what to do with the information. It is highly unusual for the cost of comprehensive evaluations to be factored into initial communication plans. Measuring impact is expensive and requires a sustained effort over years of qualitative and quantitative public opinion research.

By 2004, there was a corporate commitment at DFAIT to update the department's approach to auditing public diplomacy. A standard framework was introduced for measuring public diplomacy results. In addition to examining how money was spent and whether the mission had achieved its goals and objectives, audits now also considered local mission priorities, rather than only priorities as set out by headquarters. The appropriately titled *Results-Based Management and Accountability Framework* forced programs to set out the criteria for success over the long term – in effect, demonstrating impact – and this framework formed the basis for future evaluation of public diplomacy programs. As figure 8.1 shows, eventually the success of DFAIT's public diplomacy activities will be evaluated based on their ability to support broader, whole-of-government objectives.

In other words, as intangible as the benefits from longer-term academic and cultural programs can be, there is scope to be systematic in conveying key government messages through them and measuring how they contribute to achieving broader national objectives

CONCLUSION

As this chapter has shown, public diplomacy is part and parcel of the process of statecraft in which one government tries to influence the political environment in another jurisdiction. Public affairs staffs are thus vital guides for Canada's diplomacy; they function as the "eyes and ears" on the ground and are often the best resource for the Canadian government in determining whether it will be able to realize its international policy objectives.

The process of public diplomacy has always been hampered by the comparatively few resources devoted to it and the misunderstanding that exists as to its definition and its role within Canada's foreign policy-making. The difficulty associated with evaluating its results creates further scepticism about its value. As a result, Canada's missions around the world are challenged in their attempts to influence foreign audiences with public diplomacy programs, since they must try to do so with small budgets (often a fraction of their G8 counterparts' budgets) and small public affairs staffs. It is evident that G8 countries, as well as so-called like-minded countries such as Australia, are prepared to expend significant resources to give their countries high visibility in order to promote their cultures and interests. Canada, despite the individual successes outlined in this and later chapters on specific campaigns, cannot yet be a big public diplomacy player. The operative management mantra for modern public diplomacy is not "do more with less," but rather, "go big or go home." Canada's global foreign policy prevents it from going home, and it is therefore content to try, in the words of one former Canadian diplomat, to attempt to manage its way into a stronger global voice by "endless ... reprofiling ... rejigging, reinventing, reprioritizing" of its public diplomacy programs without understanding that, in many instances, what is being sought are actually false economies, because the federal government no longer has a critical mass of public diplomacy resources to allow Canada to be heard and seen by the right foreign audiences.[52] In the fifty years since cultural programs were added to the existing information programs of Canada's foreign ministry, the absence of a government-wide strategy for the management of Canada's public diplomacy resources (people and programs) has prevented Canada from maximizing the potential of its soft power advantage as a rich industrialized nation with an educated population.

Canada is vulnerable in several ways when trying to project itself to the world. For example, if there are difficulties in establishing a continuity of presence within countries, there is little chance that Canadian messages will resonate over the long term. In each of the two countries examined within this chapter, whether it was the Brazilians' perceptions that their country's integrity was being unfairly maligned by the Canadian media and government or the suspicion in the White House that an unflattering word reflected the Chrétien government's assessment of the president, the public affairs staffs in Canada's embassies and consulates in Brazil and the United States suddenly faced highly negative public environments. The high-level political impasses and diplomatic faux pas that characterized Canada's relations with the United States and Brazil between 1993 and 2003 set back the momentum and accumulated goodwill of individual Canadian public diplomacy programs in each country – for several years in the case of the United States and possibly for as long as a decade in Brazil. The public diplomacy experiences in both countries highlight the need for clear public diplomacy strategies, high-level integration by the head of mission, and well-staffed and sufficiently funded professional public affairs teams to help address misunderstandings resulting from changes in the tone of Canada's bilateral relations. Public affairs staffs often have to play leading roles in re-cementing fissures between societies.

As noted, it is difficult to assess and evaluate the effectiveness of public diplomacy campaigns. Will it ever be proved that the existence of the Washington Advocacy Secretariat contributed to a new level of Canadian foreign policy effectiveness in the United States? Methods of public campaign evaluation are time-consuming, expensive, and often times inconclusive. However, this should not stop governments from developing new results-based evaluation systems that will, at the very least, highlight what does not work and why, so that the same errors are not repeated. At present, many of these lessons go unlearned. And without constant communication between missions and with the rotational nature of the diplomatic service, mistakes are bound to reoccur. Well-resourced and well-planned public diplomacy, whether in the form of media relations or longer-term cultural and educational programs, will rarely have the ability to substantially reverse negative public opinion based on issues of identity. But by improving knowledge and understanding, it will make Canada's international policy more comprehensible and, in many cases, more acceptable.

9

How to Brand Canada: Experiences on the Ground

The thesis of this book is that branding and advocacy have become key functions of public diplomacy. As discussed, branding is about creating a positive predisposition in those with whom you interact; advocacy is about achieving specific objectives. The great challenge of diplomacy for smaller and medium-sized countries – historically and today – is making an impression within the major centres of power. As power slips away from the nation-state, influence will shift increasingly into the hands of non-state actors, such as multinational corporations and civil-society organizations. Despite this, the state retains a great deal of power since its image can play a critical role in the international perception of its values, policies, and products. The purpose of this chapter is to draw some lessons from the practice of public diplomacy in three very different environments.

THE UPPER NORTH SIDE CAMPAIGN –
NEW YORK CITY

Why choose New York? New York is special for a number of reasons and puts into stark relief both the challenges and the opportunities for Canada's public diplomacy. It is possibly the toughest place in the world to make an impression; the lessons learned about branding in New York City can certainly be applied to Canada's branding efforts around the world.

New York is *the* city in which nearly all major organizations try to extend their brand and raise their profile. As the epicentre for many critical decisions in the fields of finance, public policy, and culture, it has the potential to do either tremendous good or tremendous harm for any organization (or country). Canadian corporations are listed on New York's stock exchanges, and major decisions about allocating foreign direct investment are made by New York–based power brokers. The concentration of think tanks in New York, such as the Council on Foreign Relations and the Carnegie Council for Ethics in International Affairs, constantly generates policy ideas that could influence the course of Canada's policy-making vis-à-vis the United States and the world. New York is also the centre of the news media universe, able to amplify the latest news, arts, and culture, not only to a New York audience but globally.[1]

In 1995, the Canadian brand in New York City was considered weak, engendering either neutral or negative reactions. What stung the Canadian government in particular was the charge by an editorial in the *Wall Street Journal* of 12 January 1995 headlined "Bankrupt Canada?" which stated that Canada had become an honorary member of the Third World because of its debt burden.[2] Conditions could not have been less auspicious for launching a public affairs campaign to market Canada's economic lustre.

Canada's economic state must be considered in the context of its bilateral economic and trade relationship with the United States. The Canada-US Free Trade Agreement (CUFTA) and its successor, the North American Free Trade Agreement (NAFTA), had ensured that the Canadian and American economies would become increasingly integrated and mutually dependent. The bilateral economic relationship is particularly important for Canada, as its exports to the United States in the early and mid-1990s represented more than thirty percent of Canada's gross domestic product, whereas US exports to Canada represented approximately 2 percent of the US gross domestic product. However, the relationship was also very important to the United States, although most Americans – including key media and financial opinion leaders – were unaware of just how important it was. Canada was their country's primary trading partner, the leading export destination of thirty-seven US states, and the number one supplier of energy(including crude oil) to the United States. And more than four million American jobs depended directly on Canada-US trade.

This low level of knowledge among influential Americans is what George Haynal, Canada's former consul general to New York, was referring to when he recalled that "Canada had a benign and unforceful brand."[3] One problem was that Canada was so close geographically that it tended to be overlooked. Another was that Canada itself lacked a sense of its own brand image, with the spectre of separation by Quebec looming and the country's economic decline creating a mutually reinforcing picture of high risk.[4] By the mid-1990s, the bilateral relationship, which continued to be good, given that the Canadian Liberal government and Bill Clinton's Democratic administration remained ideologically close on many concerns, nevertheless exhibited signs that each country took the other largely for granted. This situation posed a significant challenge: how to reinvigorate American interest in Canada as a major trading partner after it had become a more anonymous presence in the United States?

The Challenges

Haynal's task upon arriving in New York in 1995 was to sharpen Canada's fuzzy brand, provide more context for it, and create a more balanced image. There were three major challenges to address. First, how was the mission going to target New York's politically, financially, and culturally influential people? The premier Canadian associations in New York were the Canadian Club of New York and the largely business-oriented Canadian Society of New York. In 1963, the Canadian Club boasted 1,650 members and a clubhouse occupying two floors of the Waldorf-Astoria Hotel. By the mid-1990s, despite the estimated 200,000-plus Canadians in the New York area, the club's membership had dropped precipitously.[5] A major challenge for the Canadian consulate officials was to "out" the innumerable "closeted Canadians" in the upper echelons of New York's financial and cultural communities whom they encountered during their routine consultations and activities. The idea was to integrate these expatriate Canadians into the mission's public diplomacy activities and have them express pride in Canada. Journalist Richard Siklos highlights the paradox of the situation, for, as the influence and presence of Canadians in New York continued to grow, "their need to bond together as an old-school club dwindle[d]."[6] The fact that Canadians are the "ultimate assimilators" in the United States has been both an advantage and a drawback for Canada: an advantage in that it provides Canadians with access not afforded to other foreign nationalities and a drawback in that it is hard to present a distinct Canadian identity when Canadians integrate themselves so successfully into the American identity.[7]

The second challenge was that Haynal's public diplomacy budget of Can$25,000 was miniscule by G8 standards. The high cost of advertising in New York compounded this difficulty. As Canadian official Kevin O'Shea wrote, "[h]ow do you project a dynamic image of Canada in one of the busiest, toughest but [most] influential marketplaces in the world? And how do you do this on a budget that wouldn't rent the beach house for a Hampton wedding?"[8] The irony was that while Canada's brand was struggling, the New York financial community loved its northern neighbour because it borrowed so heavily.

Third, Haynal realized that 57th Street was the temple of style and culture, and thus a potent place to affect public opinion. With no new
resources at its disposal, the consulate had to repackage what already
existed – instead of selling policy, culture, and investment separately, it
needed to create an all-encompassing vision of Canada.

The Campaign

Canada's pilot branding campaign, which ran from September 1998 to
February 1999, was called Upper North Side: Canada in New York. It was a
way of strengthening Canada's image through public diplomacy programs
in order to advance Canadian policy objectives, such as highlighting Canada's innovation and creativity, and ultimately, in order to attract investment and expand trade. The overarching goal was to develop a "brand
image" through public diplomacy as a way of getting key Canadian messages across and repositioning Canada in the minds of business, media, and
cultural decision makers. Thrust into the Mecca of global branding, Canadian diplomacy had to "compete for the attention of the financial, corporate, media and culture elites in fierce competition with others."[9] As
O'Shea and Bernard Etzinger, another New York–based Canadian official,
describe it in their recollection of the campaign, the problem was that Canada had "enormous interests at play but little visibility or leverage."[10]

The Strategy

The consulate defined Canada's brand image around four themes: Canada:
Stable and Evolving (great diversity, model world citizen); Canada: Friend
and Partner (e.g., neighbour by geography, ally by history and shared interest, partner in the largest trading relationship on earth, complementary
approaches to common social challenges); A Canada on the Move (the
Maple Leaf Miracle, great economic fundamentals, world competitor, technological innovator, free trader, and best quality of life on earth); and Canada: Hot and Cool (hot culture, cool place to visit). The overall purpose was
to project an image of Canada as modern, confident, and vibrant, and to
stimulate economic ties by increasing awareness of the business opportunities associated with investing in and trading with Canada.

The consulate's primary branding tools were its distinctive logo (a green
apple with a red maple leaf attached to the stem) and slogan, used on the
requisite posters, pins, magazine ads, and banners. The Upper North Side
name was inspired by the attachment of New Yorkers to their neighbour-

hoods, and by similar logic, it was an obvious take on the well-known Upper West Side and Upper East Side of Manhattan. However, according to O'Shea and Etzinger, the most important promotional tool was a twenty- four-page brochure about Canada sent to seventy thousand local addresses.[11] The consulate hired a firm to distribute the brochures to more than one hundred major New York multinational corporations. A website was created (uppernorthside.org) to serve as the consulate's virtual-events newsletter and to reinforce its other two websites.

Given the small budget, Canada's strategy was to use wisely the existing planned activities for Canada's cultural institutions in New York as leverage for future gains. The goal was to be aware of every possible Canadian-related event taking place in New York in a given period, and to package these events together as a "season," so that even the event listing would bring notice to Canada. Fortuitously, five major Canadian cultural institutions had scheduled events in New York for the fall and winter of 1998: the Canadian Museum of Civilization, the National Ballet of Canada, the Canadian Centre of Architecture, the Stratford Festival, and the National Gallery of Canada. These events were strategically packaged and presented as part of a marketing program showcasing "Canada" to a wide range of stakeholders.[12] To achieve the "megaphone effect without megabucks," the consulate linked additional events with New York partners to these five major events to highlight, for example, Canadian public policy leadership such as the promotion of the human security agenda under then-foreign minister Lloyd Axworthy. At the same time, trade liberalization was an ongoing policy objective, so to support the economic message, the consulate "pushed" the Canadian Society of New York to start a Canadian Chief Executive Officer series profiling Canadian business success stories.

To highlight Canada's cutting-edge high-technology prowess, the consulate organized a conference on the Canadian animation industry involving Toronto-based Sheridan College.[13] To provide an up-to-date snapshot of Canadian society, it developed a monthly contemporary music series (*North of the Border Series*), had the Inniskillin Winery sponsor the consulate's monthly classical music recitals, and devised a *Canadian Conversation Series* with famous Canadians. The strategy was to connect these activities with other Canadian performers or institutions coming to New York, a definite challenge given the constant flow of performers (e.g., the Cowboy Junkies, Le Théâtre des Deux Mondes, Ben Heppner, Robert Lepage, and Diana Krall).

The consulate also leveraged its efforts by working with the Quebec government office in New York. Such cooperation with provincial offices, in addition to local partners, proved critical to developing the necessary public diplomacy synergies. The consulate was able to tap into a special public diplomacy fund that the Liberal government had created to promote national unity and that increased the consulate's public affairs budget. The consulate's value added was to package and promote the activities within a campaign framework, while the actual organization of events was left to partner organizations.

On any given day during the initial phase of the campaign, from September 1998 to the end of February 1999, there was at least one Canadian event in New York that had some consulate support. As O'Shea and Etzinger observed, the problematic fact was that Canada was competing with approximately five hundred other events on any day.[14] However, Canada positioned itself by promoting policy-oriented conferences: on human rights, at New York University; on the protection of children in armed conflict, at Columbia University; and a reflection on CUFTA, at the Americas Society. Highlighting Canada's perspective through conferences promoted the Canadian foreign policy agenda.[14] The consulate was thus able to leverage its role, since a number of events involved major corporate partners, often in primary sponsorship roles.

Achievements and Lessons Learned

What kind of payoff did the campaign produce? O'Shea and Etzinger concluded that the Canadian presence was amplified through strategic direct marketing (the pamphlets), some advertising, and the cooperation of many New York institutions, all in concert with the coverage of the New York media.[15] Canada became an active player with New York cultural, business, and policy institutions and was seen as a "viable partner for events, conferences and lectures."[16] O'Shea observed that the campaign also played back well in Canada through extensive media coverage in the *Toronto Star*, the *Globe and Mail*, the *National Post*, Radio-Canada, and the CBC. O'Shea and Etzinger concluded that the season did achieve its objectives of targeting Canadian messages at New York's policy and financial leaders.

So, did Canada go from an "honorary member of the Third World" to the "Maple Leaf Miracle" in the eyes of New York's opinion leaders? It would be hard to identify a direct cause-and-effect relationship between the consulate's campaign and the impressions of New Yorkers. Perhaps the single most important event was Ottawa's decision to eliminate the federal deficit over the course of the 1990s through belt-tightening at home, which gained the respect of New York's financial community. The consulate's contribution ensured that the financial community understood what the Canadian government was doing.

The more events that the consulate generated, the more local organizations wanted to work with it. The Canadian consulate was being identified as an important cultural conduit in New York. People started to think about Canada, rather than systematically overlooking it. As the expatriate Canadian community was identified and integrated, the consulate was able to leverage the "good offices" of Canadians to enhance Canada's visibility. The better the consulate was able to portray the image of Canada, the better the reception and effort it enjoyed from the Canadian expatriate community.

The primary lesson from the Upper North Side campaign is apparent – a clear, sustained image is necessary to brand successfully. One must consider what the ultimate goal is, clearly identify the target audience, synchronize efforts with the local population, and be a willing risk taker. As one senior consulate official quipped, "if you fail, you do it with style."[17] Contrary to the traditional emphasis on "quiet diplomacy," as practised at Canada's Permanent Mission to the United Nations, this version of Canada in New York had to be brazen. It had to adopt a New York state of mind.

THE THINK CANADA FESTIVAL – JAPAN

Japan is Canada's principal ally in Asia, its third-largest export market after the United States and the European Union, one of the top five sources of foreign direct investment, and an important G8 partner. As Japan has been positioning itself to play a larger role in regional and international affairs, commensurate with its economic status, it has been in Canada's interest to look for more ways to engage Japan in its foreign policy priorities. At the same time, Canada and Japan have both acknowledged that for a number of reasons, including the domestic stagnation of the Japanese economy through the 1990s, the bilateral trade and investment relationship has not been reaching its potential. Moreover, the export mix from Canada – including key products such as coal, uranium, canola, pulp, lumber, and pre-fabricated housing – has not reflected the sophistication of the Canadian market. A report commissioned by Foreign Affairs and International Trade Canada, referring to the state of economic relations in 1999 and 2000, summarized Canada's relative economic stature in Japan rather sharply: "Despite Canada's openness, proximity and similarity to the United States markets, Canada remains a distant eleventh on the list of

Japanese trading partners, after smaller markets such as Australia and regional partners such as China and Taiwan."[18]

Canadian diplomats in Japan watched with a mixture of surprise and envy as Finland, a country of some five million, made great inroads into Japan's collective consciousness through one of its multinationals, Nokia. Canadian companies, seduced by the easier opportunities emanating from the United States and encouraged by the North American Free Trade Agreement, were simply not very active in Japan. For this reason, over the decades Canada had had little success in changing its image in Japan from that of a supplier of basic foodstuffs and raw materials and a nice place to visit to one of a source of sophisticated technology.[19]

While Canada realized that it had a staid image in Japan, it was the ongoing loss of Canadian market share to other countries that were promoting themselves through large and sustained campaigns that was the catalyst for an attempt by Canada to rebrand itself to the Japanese through the Think Canada Festival campaign in 2001. Conceived and organized by the Canadian embassy in Tokyo, the goals of this five-month branding campaign were to increase awareness and knowledge of Canada in the short term and increase trade and investment ties in the long term. The campaign was unique in the practice of Canadian public diplomacy because of its large budget (relative to other public diplomacy projects) and because it was one of the few large public diplomacy campaigns that underwent an extensive evaluation. The examination of the campaign that follows here is based on the evaluation that was conducted on behalf of the Canadian embassy in Tokyo by UPSIDE Corporation and managed by the Evaluation Division of DFAIT.[20] The purpose is to place the findings in the broader context of Canada's advocacy campaigns, with a view to drawing out some lessons from the Think Canada Festival that could be applied to other public diplomacy campaigns.

The Pre-Campaign

In 1998, the Canadian embassy in Japan began a program of research and consultation to explore the reasons behind the existing state of Canada-Japan bilateral economic relations.[21] A number of interesting findings emerged from an embassy-commissioned survey of 150 members of the Japanese public. According to this survey, the single most important determinant of Japanese interest in another country was its *culture*.[22] More specifically, the Japanese, considering themselves to be a highly cultured country, were attracted to other cultured countries, and Canada, associated as it was with its vast geography and Anne of Green Gables, did not earn many marks for its high culture. That being said, although the overall level of knowledge about Canada was low, Canadian officials were surprised at the high levels of knowledge of some aspects of Canadian history and society, including an awareness and appreciation of Canada's francophone and Aboriginal heritage. However, when asked to identify a country that conveyed an image of being progressive, innovative, modern, and attractive, the Japanese respondents invariably picked the United States and not Canada. Based on the research, Canadian officials concluded that to better project the Canadian image in Japan, Canada needed to develop the "hot button" of arts and culture, emphasize its environmental leadership, stress its active role in promoting world peace, and build on the existing knowledge of Canada's history.

With a "branding committee" struck at the embassy under the leadership of Ambassador Leonard Edwards, Canadian officials proceeded to apply the findings from the survey to the development of a more focused strategy for an incoming Team Canada Trade Mission in 1999, the first such mission to a large industrialized country (see chapter 7). The programs prepared by the embassy for this mission, whether cultural activities or banquets, all emphasized Canada as a high-technology exporter. According to a DFAIT report, "The Team Canada mission emphasized the strengths of Canada's high-technology sector in an effort to 'rebrand' Canada in Japanese minds as a technologically sophisticated society, and sought to encourage a diversification of our traditional commodities-based trade relationship."[23] The Japanese media picked up the message. With few extra resources available to the embassy to devote to a more comprehensive branding exercise, sponsorship from major Canadian and Japanese corporations – which exceeded all expectations – was destined to become a key source of support for the Think Canada campaign. Adding to this momentum was a recommendation by the Canada-Japan Business Conference in 2000 to explore the possibility of a bilateral free trade agreement.[24]

The Campaign

With research on Japanese attitudes towards Canada in hand and with the experience of the Team Canada Mission, a decision was then made to organize a festival in 2001 by building around the modest and already planned New Creators Series program of cultural events. Canadian officials had observed that this was how other countries had successfully promoted themselves in Japan. However, an unprecedented level of private sector

sponsorship of Can$1 million, which represented almost one-third of the
total Can$3.2 million budget, allowed organizers to mount a different
and much larger festival than was traditionally the case for Canadian public diplomacy efforts. The campaign theme, Think Canada, was chosen
because Industry Canada and some other government departments had
already been using this catch phrase on promotional material.[25] By building the Think Canada Festival around this same simple theme, the organizers hoped to create a synergy with an already existing promotional
campaign by reinforcing strategic objectives and messages and by using
existing Japanese language materials. The Think Canada phrase also lent
support for a proposed multi-sector, common-theme approach (e.g.,
Think Investment, Think Science and Technology, Think Culture, Think
Education).

The overarching goal of the Think Canada Festival was to fill out the positive but incomplete image of Canada as a supplier of commodities and a
vacation destination held by most Japanese, by creating greater brand
awareness of Canada as a creative, industrialized country with world-class
technologies. Canadian officials were careful not to negate the positive
attributes of the traditional Canadian brand; rather, the challenge was to
use these traditional associations to help Japan see Canada as a sophisticated country as well. The objectives of the Think Canada campaign in support of this goal were clear. In order of priority they were

• To bring new vitality to trade and economic relations, particularly in the
  underdeveloped high-technology areas, while continuing to promote
  Canada's valuable traditional business in commodities;
• To undertake a vigorous pursuit of the regional program priority
  through expanded activity and an increased presence in Japan's regions;
• To further develop the "peace and security" dimension of Canada-Japan
  relations;
• To promote cooperation in culture (to contribute to the perception by
  Japanese of Canada as a sophisticated and innovative society);
• To promote cooperation in science and technology; and
• To promote cooperation in education and induce more Japanese to pur-
  sue their education in Canada, particularly at the post-secondary level.[26]

The Think Canada Festival took place over a five-month period, from
March to July 2001, in four cities (Tokyo, Nagoya, Fukuoka, and Osaka),
and consisted of over two hundred events, including concerts, dinners,
demonstrations, a Canadian naval display, exhibits, a film festival, a food

fair, a high-tech caravan, an embassy open house, and symposiums. Together, these events attracted tens of thousands of Japanese. The open house at the Canadian embassy alone attracted twenty thousand people, probably a record number of visits to any single Canadian mission abroad by the public.

The campaign allocated Can$730,000 to advertising and promotion, and approximately Can$1 million each to cultural programming (exhibits, performances, and the film festival) and commercial events (seminars and exhibitions promoting science and technology, trade, and investment). Campaign planners knew that the Japanese business community placed a high value on personal relationships and that this interpersonal contact would be lost if the campaign's sole focus was on advertising. For both reasons, a greater emphasis was placed on generating earned media – newspaper articles, local coverage of events – and on using the cultural events to maximize interpersonal contacts between Canadians and Japanese.

Two specific characteristics of the campaign are noteworthy, since both enhanced Canada's profile in a very competitive marketplace. First, the establishment of an Ambassador's Council comprising thirty-five high-profile Japanese individuals, including Their Imperial Highnesses Prince and Princess Takamado and senior members of the Japanese business community, lent high levels of prestige and credibility to the campaign in the eyes of the Japanese media and helped to enlist participants and resources for individual events.[27] Second, with over fifty Canadian and Japanese companies underwriting almost one-third of the cost of the festival, the campaign organizers were able to use the additional funding from corporate support to increase the number of major events.

Evaluation

From a logistical and financial standpoint, the Think Canada Festival represented a complex Canadian public diplomacy campaign. The organizers took risks by holding the majority of events outside Tokyo and broke new ground in soliciting the support of private sponsors. While public communication campaigns are notorious for their lack of evaluations (usually owing to a lack of money) and while research on foreign perceptions of Canada is virtually non-existent, the Think Canada campaign stands out because of the embassy's pre-campaign research, which sought to establish a baseline for Japanese perceptions of Canada and the post-campaign evaluation by UPSIDE Corporation.[28] The post-campaign evaluation offers students of public diplomacy rich detail on the challenges and opportunities facing countries striving to brand themselves in a highly competitive, media-saturated market such as Japan.

DFAIT's evaluation of the campaign was notable for the fact that it allowed for the use of as many data sources as possible to gain valuable knowledge from different audiences on the objectives, strategies, and implementation of the campaign. The evaluation included on-site field-work in Tokyo, Nagoya, and Osaka, mail and telephone surveys with event attendees, four focus groups, a mail survey of sponsors and partners, an Internet survey of DFAIT personnel, media analysis, and an administrative file review. The description of the methodology in the evaluation report indicates that there were high response rates for the attendee mail survey and that twenty-one of the fifty-seven Think Canada sponsors completed their mail survey – a high response rate considering that mail surveys are not optimal means of reaching high-profile individuals. The use of quanti-tative and qualitative forms of evaluation techniques should also increase confidence in the report's findings.

With over two hundred events bundled in Tokyo and the regions over a few months, Think Canada was an intensive and expensive campaign. Start-ing from the proposition that creating awareness is the first step in forging a new brand or seeking to expand an existing brand, it can be said that, based on the evaluation, the festival was successful in reaching Japanese audiences and in raising awareness about Canada. According to the evalua-tion report, respondents to the telephone survey "consistently stated that after attending specific Think Canada events, they had a much improved image of Canada or learned that Canada was more advanced and sophisti-cated than they previously thought."[29] On this basis, then, the campaign can be judged a success.

Charles Salmon and Lisa Murray-Johnson's conceptualization of pro-grammatic effectiveness, cost-effectiveness, and political effectiveness is helpful in providing a more systematic and nuanced evaluation of the Think Canada campaign.[30] According to these authors, "every information campaign is, or at least should be, driven by goals and objectives that spec-ify the nature and degree of the impact sought. When campaign perfor-mance is measured against these goals and objectives, an assessment of programmatic effectiveness can be made through a direct comparison between objectives and outcomes."[31]

So, did the Think Canada campaign help Canada achieve its program-matic objectives? At the level of outputs, Canada was able, through the gen-erosity of the campaign's private sector sponsors, to launch more events and therefore increase awareness through more earned media. However, the evaluation report did note that Canadian staff could have used more media training, that some events reinforced the traditional Canadian brand, and that there were too many messages. The campaign's conscious decision to favour the regions also paid dividends. The main reason for this, according to a senior DFAIT official, is that there are many media markets in Japan. While Tokyo is the most important, the regional economies are so big that even a minor public affairs event can have a huge impact in a city such as Osaka. As there are few foreign influences in these regional areas, it becomes easier to receive extensive regional media coverage with something novel.

Certainly, in terms of short-term outcomes, the campaign generated new contacts and reinforced the momentum from the earlier Team Canada Mission. It could also be argued, based on the high level of Japanese involvement in the campaign, that Japanese opinion formers and the tens of thousands who attended the events gained a more accurate sense of Canada and that some attitudes were changed. What is more difficult – indeed, almost impossible – to determine six years after the campaign is whether the intermediate outcome of increased business and partnership agreements envisioned from this campaign have in fact occurred.[32] The underlying question is whether it is indeed possible to rebrand a country in only five months. No one responsible for the campaign actually believed that this goal was realistic; indeed, the idea of rebranding an entire country in several months defies both logic and the conventional theory of marketing and branding. Rather, the hope was that Think Canada would be the first step in a longer-term process of repositioning the Canadian brand.

With regard to cost-effectiveness, while 20,000 people attended the Canadian embassy's Open House weekend and Think Canada had an unprecedented level of earned media coverage with over 600 newspaper articles and radio spots, this level of coverage in a nation of over 120 million people would have reached only a fraction of Japan's attentive public. Nevertheless, the only way Canada can really get national coverage in a sophisticated, high-cost mass market such as Japan is through free media. Even if it was short-term, Canada managed to secure substantive national coverage at minimal cost. This is no small feat in Japan, where advertising fees are significant. Indeed, the UPSIDE report cites the Canadian embassy's own calculation that the dollar value of one full-page article in a major Japanese newspaper such as the *Asahi Shimbun* (daily circulation 8.3 million) is over Can$350,000.[33] At these prices, no government, not even a rich one, has a large enough public diplomacy budget to fund a sustained advertising campaign through the conventional media in Japan. And even if it did, at those prices the net outcome of results to cost would probably be minimal.

As noted, one of the biggest surprises was the level of corporate support. Both the embassy and the private sector sponsors saw their partnership in support of a high-profile festival as a win-win opportunity. Corporate partners and sponsors cited their ability to raise the profile of their organization in Japan, support their colleagues at DFAIT upon request, and increase business for their organization in Japan. A full 81 percent of respondents stated that they thought the Think Canada Festival had been either "successful" or "very successful" in helping them meet their corporate objectives.[34]

Perhaps less noticeable in the organization and implementation of the campaign was the cost with respect to human resources. The evaluation report notes the high levels of overtime and the collective exhaustion of the Canadian embassy staff, after having organized the Team Canada trade mission the previous year. The campaign's operational costs for embassy staff exceeded Can$700,000. Since this figure would not normally include overtime payments, the final cost of the Think Canada campaign would have been higher and likely unsustainable beyond the short duration of the campaign.

From a political standpoint, the campaign was undoubtedly effective. For a moment in time, Canada's political image in Japan soared, indicating that the country valued its bilateral relationship with Japan. The question is whether Think Canada or any single campaign could elevate a political relationship permanently to a new level in the absence of other motivating factors. The Think Canada Festival, on its own, did not create a permanent change in Canada's political stature in the eyes of the Japanese government, although it certainly served as a catalyst, motivating both governments to re-examine their mutual expectations for the bilateral relationship.

Lessons Learned

The "Bundling" Effect and the National Impact. The campaign organizers focused their marketing on compressing or "bundling" public affairs events over a shorter period to create greater visibility. According to a senior DFAIT official, these events would garner much more media coverage if presented as a package[35] and, therefore, would be more effective than the traditional approach of holding a series of promotional events throughout the year. For example, a dance troupe in Osaka or a sport group visiting Hokkaido might make a local impact by themselves, but grouped together, they would create a *national* impact. While this is undoubtedly true, having a festival also means that there are no other public events in the remainder of the year, thus making it difficult to sustain Canada's image in Japan.

Reaching the Right Audience. The primary objective of the Think Canada campaign was raising awareness among the principal audience – Japanese business elites. Cultural programming and earned media were the means of reaching them. The evaluation report indicated that there was insufficient audience segmentation to identify key target groups. The main reasons for this, according to a senior DFAIT official, were time and financial constraints. Embassies, he explained, are faced with a slew of constraints and need to work with the finite resources that are available to them. To guarantee that key messages are being heard by the target audience, future campaigns will need to clarify the audience segments and target activities accordingly. Reaching the right audience also reinforces the programmatic effectiveness and the cost-effectiveness of the campaign.

The Utility of Local Platforms. In many cases, local dignitaries and patrons are essential to the success of a public diplomacy campaign, and local institutions (e.g., museums, galleries, centres for the performing arts) are often eager to be involved and to help facilitate the organization and presentation of a Canadian campaign. In general, the audience draw is larger for a Canadian exhibition that is part of a well-received local exhibition than one that is presented as a stand-alone Canadian event. While most officials with experience in public affairs and cultural programming try to give their official "bricks and mortar" a wide berth, the case of Canada's embassy in Tokyo is different. In the words of one senior DFAIT official, "[o]ur embassy in Tokyo is actually one of our flagship missions. From an architectural point of view and its location in the city ... it is one of the few embassies that actually has its own art gallery and its own auditorium."[36] In other words, the physical space of the embassy is itself an attraction and, therefore, a draw. Three other missions also fit in this category: Washington, Berlin, and London. For example, as mentioned earlier, Canada House in London is located in Trafalgar Square, one of the most desirable and visible locations in the city. So, while it is certainly true that diplomatic missions, because of security requirements and a lack of adequate presentation space, may not be ideal locations for public events, in some particular cases the mission architecture and/or location can be adopted as part of the campaign strategy because of its positive impact on Canada's image.

Reducing Key Communication Messages. The evaluation report suggested that
the Think Canada campaign tried to convey too many messages. As with
most effective communication campaigns, there should be no more than
three main messages. An overabundance of messages stems from the
nature of bureaucratic organizations and is not unique to government public relations campaigns. Consequently, the role of the campaign planners
should be to reduce the number of key messages, which may involve some
deft internal politics and negotiation. Missions should be relied upon to
apply their valuable knowledge about local political culture and the media
environment in developing campaign messages. This is the comparative
advantage provided by public affairs officials at missions.

Sponsorships. Private sponsorship was an integral component of the Think
Canada Festival. As stated, the level of campaign sponsorship succeeded in
changing the entire scale of the campaign. Nevertheless, a senior DFAIT
official cautions other missions against systematically resorting to this strategy in order to achieve branding goals. According to him, the effectiveness
of sponsorship as a tool depends on the size of the mission and the type of
relationship that the Canadian business community has with the country.
Sponsorship is appropriate in a host country with a strong Canadian business presence and established economic links with Canada. The presence
of large local business interests that may find Canada an attractive investment location is also an important factor. Sponsorship is less effective in
smaller or medium-sized missions with only one or two big Canadian companies active in that country. Before considering sponsorship, therefore,
planners must evaluate the type of bilateral relationship.

There is also the ongoing ethical question about whether it is appropriate to ask Canadian companies to underwrite government events, either
partially or wholly. Some Canadian companies actually receive little benefit
from being sponsors, since they may already have an established presence
in the local market. In these cases, receiving a telephone call from the
Canadian ambassador or a visit from embassy officials could be perceived
as subtle – or not-so-subtle – arm-twisting. The mission staff, as noted in the
evaluation report, may also not necessarily feel comfortable (from an ethical and training standpoint) going out and soliciting donations. Most
Canadian government officials are not professional fundraisers, and fund-
raising is increasingly becoming a specialized part of the public relations
business. Finally, the impact of the federal "sponsorship scandal" that
embroiled the final year of the Chrétien government and spilled over into
the new government of Paul Martin, arguably leading to his government's

defeat, is destined to have a lasting – and negative – effect on the psyches of federal officials considering the idea of sponsorships (although in the case of the so-called scandal, they were government sponsorships).

The Importance of Sustainability. One of the main concerns of the Think Canada evaluation report was the sustainability of the campaign. As the evaluation report noted, given the often high and hidden human costs of the campaign (such as staff overtime), it is clearly not feasible to sustain this level of activity as part of a long-term branding strategy. This should not serve as an excuse for avoiding high-impact, compressed campaigns, however. Japan is, after all, one of the most expensive markets in the world in which to do business. Not every Canadian mission will face such seemingly insurmountable financial obstacles to maintaining Canada's image in the public eye throughout the year, especially if campaign planners have leveraged the assets of their local networks (including Canadian companies and Canadian expatriates).

Another point to consider, in the words of the senior DFAIT official, "is the 'disconnect' between what we spend our money on and results."[37] In large missions (e.g., those in the G8 countries), the fixed overhead costs (rent, office supplies, salaries) are enormous compared to the budget spent on public diplomacy initiatives. Yet the financial resources set aside for public diplomacy objectives are likely to garner the highest return for a diplomatic mission: "It's the last, often few hundred dollars, that causes the most bang for the buck."[38] Consequently, for Canada to create a lasting impression, the argument will constantly have to be made, in the face of edicts from headquarters in Ottawa to demonstrate value for money, that public diplomacy programs are, in fact, not soft costs at all and that they will make the difference between Canada being an effective player on the world stage or not.

Leadership. Finally, the Think Canada campaign highlights the critical role played by the head of the mission in a branding or rebranding effort. The conditions, budget, tools, and tactics may change over time, but the ultimate outcome depends on the motivation and support of the chief public diplomacy officer – the head of mission. It is incumbent upon this individual and his or her public affairs managers to hold regular introspective sessions and *constantly* question their work: "Are we having the maximum impact? How can we draw linkages together? Are we going in the right direction? How can we project Canada better?"[39] There is an assumption – not unfounded – that each embassy section works independently on its own projects: a trade visit here, a political delegation there, a cultural event elsewhere. The Think Canada Festival in Japan represented a successful effort to connect the outreach activities of the mission's trade, political, and cultural affairs sections to create a critical mass and thus raise Canada's overall profile. The public "bundling" of events, which were the essence of the campaign, could not have taken place without a consensus within the embassy that there needed to be cooperation across the functional areas of operations.

In retrospect, for all its success the Think Canada campaign was not part of a common, government-wide branding strategy. Rather, it was organized through the efforts and vision of Ambassador Leonard Edwards, who saw an opportunity to extend Canada's brand. The campaign was expensive and drew significantly on the Canadian embassy's resources, a reminder that effective public diplomacy requires substantial investment and commitment. To be sure, successful national branding cannot be based on a series of one-off Canadian campaigns in selected countries around the world – no matter how useful each is in modifying and updating the national image. It is not clear how long the Think Canada campaign's messages will last without constant reinforcement. It appears that a follow up strategy (and budget) is a necessary component of any major public diplomacy campaign.[40]

CALLING 9/11: CANADA'S ADVOCACY CAMPAIGN IN THE UNITED STATES

The attacks of 11 September 2001 clearly redefined Canada's security and economic relationship with the United States. This, in turn, forced Canada to redefine how it communicates with its most important partner. As described in chapter 8, following the attacks, Canada's profile was raised, but often in a negative context, making Canada vulnerable to a panoply of inaccurate allegations on border security, law enforcement, and drug policy that fast became the conventional wisdom of a growing number of influential Americans. Michael Kergin, former Canadian ambassador to the United States, wrote: "On Sept. 13, 2001, the *Boston Herald* ran an erroneous report alleging that three of the terrorists who brought down the World Trade [Center] Towers entered the United States from Halifax. The perception that the 5500 mile Canada-US border was not secure changed the reality of Canadian-US business ... twenty-mile backup[s] of trucks and trains became the norm, $1 billion of daily trade was placed at risk, and the cliché that security trumps economy became currency."[41]

Ottawa's communications strategy in the weeks and months following the attacks demonstrated some difficulty in countering misinformation, resulting in ongoing damage to the Canadian "brand." It was through the sure-footed leadership of Canadian foreign affairs minister John Manley that Canada was able to recover some ground and negotiate the thirty-point Smart Border Declaration, to guarantee ongoing access to an open but increasingly secure border. The tragedy of 9/11 heightened the United States' focus on its borders and put into high relief how Canada manages its image in the United States.

Canada's advocacy campaign in the fall of 2001 was explicitly directed at convincing the Bush administration, and all Americans, that Canada understood their feelings of vulnerability and wanted to work with them to create a secure, efficient border. Canada's goal was to show that it "got it" when it came to North American security. In the aftermath of an attack that exceeded the death toll at Pearl Harbor, Canadian officials knew that if the United States lacked confidence in Canadian security measures, it would increasingly adopt a Fortress America approach, which could have had devastating consequences for Canada, such as border delays that would severely imperil trade and potentially incapacitate the "just-in-time" automobile industry that operated across the border. Finding the appropriate response became the Canadian government's top priority as 2001 drew to a close.

Canada's primary message, detailing Can$7 billion in new security spending, new anti-terrorism legislation, and the proposal for a Smart Border Declaration, did not seem to gain traction in US public discourse. Similarly, some twenty years of well-intentioned efforts at building longer-term understanding of Canadian values and interests in the United States through Ottawa's cultural and academic-relations programming (e.g., Canadian Studies programs across the United States) did not bear immediate fruit during a critical period in bilateral relations. Consequently, when the American media (especially the cable news networks) went on the offensive and Canadian immigration policies and border security came under scrutiny, there were few pundits or experts prepared to dispel the myriad damaging myths being perpetuated. Nor did the Canadian government execute significant leverage on the expatriate community of Canadians in the United States, an often underutilized resource. The difficulties encountered by Canada were surprising given the vital role that the United States plays in Canada's foreign and domestic policy.

The Challenge: Protecting Vital Economic and Security Ties

That the United States is important to Canada is an understatement: it anchors Canada's economic prosperity, it integrally influences culture, it dramatically affects the environment, and it serves as a de facto security blanket "whether we like it or not," according to an unnamed Canadian member of Parliament in the 1960s.

Economically, by 2001 the unprecedented deepening of economic integration, set in motion by the signing of the CUFTA and later NAFTA, resulted in an average growth rate of 7.5 percent annually for bilateral goods and services trade. With almost Can$2 billion in goods and services crossing the border daily, it is not surprising that Canada was the largest export market for a majority of American states. Almost 80 percent of Canadian exports of goods and services went to the United States (mostly by truck and passing through fewer than a dozen border crossings), accounting for roughly one-third of Canada's gross domestic product. In addition, three hundred thousand people crossed the border every day for work or pleasure. The value of two-way cumulative foreign direct investment rose from Can$68 billion in the early 1980s to more than Can$380 billion almost two decades later. The United States was by far the largest source of foreign direct investment for Canada.

Geography also dictates close interactivity in other public policy realms. Canada's close bilateral defence relationship with the United States was reflected in the establishment of the Permanent Joint Board on Defence in 1940, the North American Air (later Aerospace) Defence Command (NORAD) in 1958, and myriad other agreements (formal and informal) that have yielded highly interoperable military services and underpinned a strong defence partnership. Environmental and foreign policy partnerships bilaterally, and multilaterally through NATO, were equally intense, reflecting years of cooperation.

Canada's public diplomacy challenges were put into stark relief with the 9/11 attacks, but they can also be seen in the context of the arrival of the George W. Bush administration in 2001, after eight years of the Clinton presidency.

A Businesslike Relationship

By the late 1990s, the tone of the Canada-US relationship had been in steady evolution. The "special relationship" – despite the outward appearances of Bill Clinton and Jean Chrétien on the golf course – was businesslike. Reminiscences and histories of Canada-US relations are replete with anecdotes about the personal relationships between presidents and prime ministers. The question here is the extent to which these relationships are able to affect policy and its communication. The Canadian media certainly expends an inordinate amount of time deconstructing every statement, murmur, and gesture made by American presidents regarding Canada. But how much did this really matter, as Jean Chrétien often observed, given the sheer complexity of having innumerable daily cross-border interactions? Was the "tone" really just an insider's game?

Regardless, many Washington-based observers of Canada-US relations see the tone between presidents and prime ministers as absolutely indispensable to the effective management of the relationship. While catastrophe will not ensue if a Canadian prime minister is not invited to the country home of a US president for an informal "chat," it is certainly important for there to be evidence of regular and open communication between the two leaders, for the relationship to be recognized in Cabinet circles by heads of departments and their officials, and for the White House to hold a genuinely favourable disposition toward the Canadian leadership. Essentially, Canadians need to be seen as reliable allies – people you can do business with and whose word you can honour, people who would come to your assistance if you were in trouble. On that front, the Chrétien government appeared to send out a mixed message even before George W. Bush became president. In the run-up to the 2000 US election, Raymond Chrétien, the Canadian ambassador to Washington and nephew of the prime minister, appeared to have endorsed Al Gore as the next American president, something that, if leaks to the media were to be believed, was not forgotten once George W. Bush entered the White House.

The capture of Algerian-born Ahmed Ressam by alert American Customs agents in December 1999, as he was trying to enter the United States from British Columbia to carry out a terrorist attack at Los Angeles International Airport during the millennium celebrations, certainly marred perceptions of Canada and its contribution to the security relationship with the United States. It was reported that when Ressam was intercepted, the Canadian government was on Christmas break, and it did not provide a rapid response to these events. In the absence of an official statement from Ottawa, the story grew many legs. Self-styled American security experts were soon popping up on paper and onscreen opining about the porous northern border and Canada's weak approach to security. Their spin prevailed in the absence of any other information. The Ressam incident complicated Canadian advocacy efforts to affect provisions of US immigration policy (section 110) that threatened gridlock at the Canada-US border. After 9/11, the story of America's border vulnerability was immediately framed by the Ressam incident and the "dangerous" northern border.

Even American popular culture (most of it eagerly consumed in Canada) got into the act, feeding the "urban myth" of terrorists using Canada as a springboard when an October 2001 episode of the hit NBC series *The West Wing* featured a plot in which a terrorist snuck into the United States across the "Vermont-Ontario" border. Not only was the show's grasp of geography embarrassingly wrong, but this episode perpetuated false assumptions and potentially shaped millions of American viewers' perceptions, given that most of them have only a superficial knowledge of Canada. It was Canada's responsibility to supply America with clear messages as part of a planned and effective communications strategy.

The Canadian Government's Response to the 9/11 Attacks

As the planes slammed into the World Trade Center and the Pentagon while the world looked on in horror, governments scrambled to respond. The Canadian government's response to the attacks was a short-term, primarily media-driven strategy to counter Canadians' concerns at home and to address American expectations. Unlike the Blair government in the United Kingdom, Ottawa took some weeks to define a clear message (beyond that of sympathy) in response to the attacks. Indeed, embassy officials had difficulty defining a straightforward Canadian message, because there was no clear national consensus on key questions. Was Canada's relationship not such that in times of difficulty, it would be by America's side "shoulder to shoulder"? Did Canadians understand that a secure northern border, the vaunted undefended frontier between two neighbours, was now essential to Americans' perceptions of their safety? The awkwardness in answering these questions was manifested in a hesitant performance by Prime Minister Chrétien, who felt that he reflected the national zeitgeist by adopting a more sober and reflective reaction to the horrors of the attacks, including a televised interview in which he ruminated about the root causes of terrorism (factually correct, but seemingly ill-timed under the circumstances.)

It would take until November 2001 before the government could report that legislation was in place to heighten security measures. Part of the challenge was trying to respond to the myriad requests from journalists, many of whom were covering a foreign story for the first time. As well, it became clear that Canada's consulates were not adequately prepared to deal with a crisis of this magnitude. The first strong message and symbolic act was a remembrance ceremony on Parliament Hill in Ottawa. However, in organizing the event, Canadian officials failed to grasp that what they needed to do was communicate with Americans. The ceremony was not seen on American television. In contrast, a similar ceremony by the British government was given priority coverage by CNN, Fox, CNBC, and other major American broadcast networks.[42]

In terms of media relations at the Canadian Embassy in Washington, the crisis highlighted the importance of having up-to-date databases of opinion leaders to ensure a readily available structure for tracking and responding to commentary in order to counter inaccurate reporting or provide supplementary information to journalists. The embassy had to keep a particular lookout for expatriate Canadians writing editorials lambasting Canada's efforts.

Within Ottawa's bureaucracy, the Privy Council Office's role was to coordinate information from the various government departments and to ensure that a coherent message was provided on these difficult issues. Typically, this process involved the establishment of a coordinating committee to gather input and views from affected government departments and agencies. Initially, it was quite difficult to confirm or deny a series of initial rumours reported as fact by some American networks that three of the hijackers had crossed the border into Maine from New Brunswick. In the absence of any other information, the Ressam incident was simply recalled again and again.

Canadian officials responded to the Americans' consuming concern about border security by pushing their long-standing desire for a more efficient border to the top of the bilateral agenda. The tragic circumstances provided a "policy window" by creating a powerful incentive for the Americans to negotiate what would become the Smart Border Declaration. Signed in December 2001, the accord's principles of enhancing border security while recognizing the importance of the economic relationship to all three North American countries provided an instant platform from which to "sell" Canada's actions on the US-led war on terror.

The Primary Actors

The story of Canada's advocacy campaign cannot be told without reviewing the personal diplomacy of a pair of American and Canadian politicians: Governor Tom Ridge, the first director of the Office of Homeland Security in the United States, and Canadian foreign affairs minister John Manley, the linchpins in the communications strategy of each country. This relationship was essential to the effective communication of policy in a highly charged atmosphere, where the United States could only assume that it would be the target of future terrorist attacks. Ridge and Manley established an excellent rapport, as they liked and trusted each other. As a consequence, Manley was able to persuade and encourage Ridge to adopt an approach to border management contrary to what Ridge's own officials were advising him to follow. Manley, who as chairman of the ad hoc Cabinet committee on security and anti-terrorism was the Chrétien government's point person on Canada-US relations, would emerge as the Liberal Cabinet's star performer at a time of uncertainty in Ottawa on how to respond to this crisis.[43] It was not just good personal chemistry that made a difference at a critical time in bilateral relations. As often happens, luck played a role. Ridge, as the former governor of Pennsylvania, a state reliant on trade, understood that keeping the border open was essential to maintaining a healthy state and national economy. He grasped the belief that an open and secure border was not necessarily contradictory and did not hesitate to make his views known publicly.

Although security still trumped trade in the American consciousness, the challenge for the Canadian government, with Manley spearheading both the strategy and public communications, was to reduce the threat to a manageable risk. The personal rapport between the two Cabinet ministers made it possible to present the northern border as an exercise in risk management. The Americans, perpetually suspicious of Canada's soft approach to security and defence, were willing to give Ottawa the benefit of the doubt. There were apparently factions within the Department of Homeland Security that wanted to inspect every inch of every vehicle – railroad car, bus, truck – crossing the Canada-US border, even if it meant fully re-inspecting the same trucks crossing at the same border point sixteen times in a day (as was the case at some border crossings frequented by trucks providing materials for automobile manufacturers). With thirty thousand trucks crossing the border each day, such an approach would have had immediate and deleterious economic consequences on both sides of the border.[44] Those most affected on the front lines would have been Canada's provinces and territories, entities that would not often receive a great deal of attention in Washington. As a result, the provinces realized relatively quickly that what they could do, and do successfully, was to reassure their border counterparts – the state governments – of their concern for security. While American importers were firm allies, the state administrations were "very skittish" allies, because nobody in the initial phase after 9/11 was going to publicly stand up and say that trade with Canada was a top priority.[45]

To help sustain its public profile in the United States, Canada needed to rely on other entities to promote its image as a strong ally and as a result, turned to the government-financed Canadian Studies program. As a form of long-term public diplomacy, the significant foreign policy dividends of the program are ideally paid out when there is a bilateral crisis. The logic is that the Canadianists will act as high-credibility local sources who would be able to contextualize Canadian policy. Since the largest Canadian Studies network was in the United States (see discussion in chapter 5), there was an expectation that Canadianists across the United States would provide a balanced and informed perspective on Canada and its response to the terrorist attacks. However, there was not enough time to mobilize the network in any systematic way, nor was there any guarantee that the American members of the Canadian Studies community would have wanted to be mobilized on behalf of the government at this time.

Rather than rely only on the formal Canadian Studies network, the Washington embassy began to quickly inundate think tank members and scholars with an interest and background in security, immigration, or intelligence with information on Canadian policies and actions.[46] It was hoped that sympathetic Canadianists and sympathetic Canada-watchers inside the Washington Beltway would refute some of the more outlandish claims that Canada's border was an open corridor for terrorists. However, the performance of these third-party "validators" of the Canadian perspective as a bulwark against the spread of misinformation, which was moving like wildfire through the US media, was decidedly mixed. There were simply not enough commentators with credibility and visibility to explain Canada's position. As a result, the myth of the "Canadian connection" to the nineteen hijackers of 9/11 could not be extinguished.

Lessons for Canadian Public Diplomacy from the Advocacy Campaign

The attacks of 9/11 fundamentally changed Canada's public diplomacy efforts in the United States. Before 9/11, depending on the issue, American reaction to Canada, to use Christopher Sands' formulation, could either be indifferent, purely reactive, or neighbourly.[47] After 9/11, the United States became somewhat less indifferent to events north of the forty-ninth parallel, and the word "border" was no longer exclusively associated in American minds with the problem-plagued frontier with Mexico. A substantial number of American opinion leaders' views of Canada became clouded with uncertainty about Canada's reliability as a friend and ally. It is worth underscoring that Canada's commitment of combat troops and aid to Afghanistan, while acknowledged by the Bush administration, remains largely unknown among the general American policy-making community.

What are some lessons from Canada's communications response in the immediate aftermath of 9/11 for future Canadian public diplomacy efforts in the United States?

- *Know thine audience.* In this case, there was a clear imperative to understand the American psyche, given the different perceptions of threat among Canadians and Americans. In the years since the 9/11 attacks, Canada and the United States continue to have different perceptions of the terrorist threat, even though they share a stake in preventing terrorism. Americans clearly feel that they are targets, while polling indicates that Canadians' primary foreign policy concerns include global threats such as infectious diseases and environmental degradation. Terrorism has been a minimal concern to Canadians when stipulating their foreign policy priorities.

  Canada needed to understand that Americans face a complex world in which they are the only superpower. They have a multitude of responsibilities. Canada is seldom part of their problem – more often, it is part of the solution as a great ally and friend. Unfortunately, policymakers rarely focus their attention on pre-existing positive elements in any relationship; rather, they focus on worries and concerns. This makes advocacy critical to an effective public diplomacy strategy. Canada must take the key message to Americans: "Did you know this is what Canada contributes to your well-being?" Americans are very clear that they understand and will respond to issues of immediate (and American) concern. This insight was eventually translated in 2005 into the "boots on the ground" communication campaign that included showing Canadian solders in Afghanistan in the advertisements that appeared in the Washington, DC, transit system.

  In the same vein, Canadians talk frequently (and in the past, proudly) about Canada-US bilateral relations not requiring extensive institutionalization because of the innate understanding between the two countries and their many similar values. In the post-9/11 and NAFTA-plus environment,[48] there is once again talk of the benefits of greater institutionalization of North American relations. This desire for greater institutionalization shows a fundamental misreading of American history. The United States has never indicated any willingness to be tied down in its own hemisphere; it will act in its own interest, not in Canada's and not in Mexico's. The challenge for Canadian policy-makers, through their public diplomacy campaigns, is to become more adept at making Washington realize that what Canada wants is also in the interest of

America, thereby moving the US administration and/or Congress to act accordingly.

- *Relationship-building.* The federal government cannot be expected to go it alone. It must work with provincial partners, since the most effective way for the provinces to contribute to the overall national public diplomacy strategy is to engage with their state counterparts and to stay on message. This also applies to the Canadian business community as it engages its American counterparts.

  Successful public diplomacy is about creating networks. Just as special interest groups are creating online networks to communicate and mobilize to persuade politicians and bureaucrats to take action and help their causes, Canada must also strengthen its network of expatriate Canadians (e.g., Connect2Canada), who are embedded in all layers of American society, and stimulate it in times of need to counter falsehoods and half-truths. It is simple, practical, and effective diplomacy. More of this will be necessary if special interest groups in the United States continue to reference Canada in their domestic debates (on subjects such as health care and cross-border pharmacies).

  Congress continues to expand its role in determining US foreign policy. Therefore, Canadian advocacy efforts and public diplomacy resources will have to be increased and strategically employed to maintain and improve upon Canada's profile and relevance on Capitol Hill.

- *Developing a clear, consistent message and selling it.* While Canada is important to the United States, as its major trading partner, it is not prominent in American minds, making it almost impossible for Canada to attract attention south of the border.[49] When the American media does beam its searchlight on Canada, there is little evidence of a deeper understanding of the bilateral relationship, which allows negative and inaccurate messages to stick. This drawback is evident during periodic crises in the relationship. The initial Canadian reaction to 9/11 showed once more that Canada's key messages must be consistent and established much earlier in the communications cycle. Key spokespeople and target audiences must be identified to ensure that there are sufficient third-party "friends of Canada" who are informed and willing to jump into the fray to explain Canada's positions should a crisis emerge. If the databases are not up to date, precious time will be wasted trying to figure out who is doing what. Up-to-date websites and marketing the message in the language of the target population are critical.

  Political messages can be sold, but it will take greater all-party cooperation and greater reliance on legislators on both sides of the border.

Canadian and American politicians will listen to each other. If you show
a congressperson the thousands of jobs in his or her district that depend
on trade with Canada, that person will take notice. If you tell state governors that Canada is their largest market, they will remember. The trouble is that often someone needs to tell them, because otherwise they may
not be aware of Canada's prominence in their states.

• *Is diplomacy advocacy?* In recent years, it has been fashionable to portray the
  new diplomacy practitioners as adept at engaging in advocacy, in order to
  be effective in a media-rich international environment characterized by
  complex, overlapping networks. Allan Gotlieb challenged this notion by
  questioning whether advocacy is really an ambassador's job, since it is an
  adversarial undertaking. In his view, advocacy is not an element of public
  diplomacy because it does not contribute to confidence building through
  "better understanding of our different and sometimes conflicting interests." According to Gotlieb, the comparative advantage of diplomats
  derives from their ability to engage in quiet diplomacy and to understand
  and influence the diffuse, complex American policy process (i.e., to "read
  Washington") – not to compete publicly with the thousands of other advocates and special interest groups in the American capital.[50]

Some of the misunderstandings and miscommunications in bilateral Canada-US relations in the immediate aftermath of 9/11, particularly the
American perception that Canada was lax on security, could have been
averted if Canada had been more institutionally prepared to respond to a
crisis communications environment. In retrospect, more centralized and
coordinated public diplomacy machinery could have helped to improve
the tone of bilateral relations. As the case of Canada's response shows, the
perception within some quarters that the northern border was vulnerable
(stemming from the Ressam incident) combined with the perception that
Canada's support of the United States was somehow less complete than
that of the United Kingdom, served to blunt the effectiveness of the very
positive messages about what Canada had actually done for the United
States during the crisis, not to mention the billions of dollars that Ottawa
immediately committed to strengthening public safety in North America.
The lack of a critical mass of available, knowledgeable, and credible third-
party "explainers" of Canada's significant contribution to creating a more
secure continent meant that misinformation about Canada's role for a
time went unchallenged in the echo chamber of the cable news networks.
At the same time, Canada did not have a network of provincial officials at
the ready on the front line to help the government to manage perceptions

of state-level decision makers. Canada for a time appeared to be on the out-side looking in at decisions being made by the Bush Administration that had fundamental consequences for Canada's national interests. The lessons of this period of crisis communications in the weeks and months after 9/11 have been learned. As discussed in chapter 8 and in this chapter, Canada has adopted a much more proactive approach to its public diplomacy in the United States through the creation of the Washington Advocacy Secretariat (including the co-location of provincial representatives), more points of diplomatic contact across the United States through the Enhanced Representation Initiative, a more focused use of the Canadian Studies community, and the increased mobilization of the expatriate community of Canadians.

CONCLUSION

For most of its history, dialogic communication has not played a prominent part of Canada's public diplomacy, though this began to change with the significant expansion of cultural diplomacy under the Trudeau-led governments. Today, there is a consensus that the practice of public diplomacy is shifting from a reliance on one-way communication associated with international broadcasting and information programs to what public relations scholars Larissa A. Grunig and James E. Grunig have labeled the "two-way symmetrical" model, which, when applied to public diplomacy, means that governments will depend less on persuasion techniques and more on negotiating meaning and building mutual understanding with foreign publics. The three campaigns discussed in this chapter, each launched for different reasons and in different contexts, shared a common goal: to re-brand or reposition Canada in the minds of key foreign audiences, whether American or Japanese business leaders or American political leaders. There was a clear purpose and, in two of the three cases, a crisis. In such circumstances a more traditional, "two-way asymmetrical" public relations model most closely reflected Canada's approach, since it sought to shift foreign public opinion in specific directions, using all the tools of strategic communication or advocacy – proactive media relations, public opinion research, and cultural and academic programs to establish a positive environment in which to influence the target audiences – to advance specific national interests.

10

A New Architecture for Canada's Public Diplomacy

Eventually all diplomacy is public diplomacy. This is the end state of modern diplomacy.

Canadian foreign service officer

Truth is the best propaganda and lies are the worst. To be persuasive we must be believable; to be believable we must be credible; to be credible we must be truthful. It is as simple as that.

Edward R. Murrow

The examination of Canadian public diplomacy in this book has raised a fundamental question: what is so new about public diplomacy? It is not so much the instruments of public diplomacy that have changed as it is the environment in which they are deployed. Issues of global concern now require broad-based public consent at home and abroad. The processes pursued to achieve this consent are often as important as the final outcomes. If governments do not first prepare the publics of the states they wish to target, it will become that much more difficult to sway the governments of those states. And if there is initial resistance from the targeted government, it will be through public diplomacy that new alliances will be forged with local groups to attempt to change policy. At the same time, the more that a government can draw on the resources and support of its own citizens – at home and abroad – for its international activities, the greater will be the credibility of its public diplomacy. After all, for most countries a central government's public diplomacy resources (e.g., embassies, cultural centres such as Germany's Goethe-Institut, the United Kingdom's British Council or the Swedish Institute, France's overseas *lycées*, international broadcasters) can make – even in the most ideal circumstances – only a small difference in reinforcing or changing a nation's international image. Increasingly, central governments will have to leverage other governmental and non-governmental resources (e.g., sub-federal governments, including regions, provinces/states and municipalities, and the private and not-for-profit sectors) in support of national-image promotion.

In an age of instantaneous information, power is becoming distributed more widely, which has altered the context in which public diplomacy is pursued. As British scholars Brian Hocking and Donna Lee have asserted, "[o]n one level, the argument that the diminution of distance has demoted the significance of resident missions is countered by the enhanced complexity of information flows, the closer texture of political arenas and the engagement of a growing diversity of actors (both governmental and non-governmental) in diplomatic processes."[1] In addition to the Great Powers that have always had a stake in managing international opinion, new players are emerging, such as China, India, and Brazil, not to mention all the other countries actively engaged in "destination branding" for tourism or investment. Countries of all ideological stripes and sizes – ranging from liberal democratic to theocratic to communist regimes – understand that managing global public opinion is a necessity rather than a choice if they are to achieve their political, economic, and security goals. For example, since 2003, China has embarked on a full-blown soft-power offensive to explain its "peaceful rise," in order to dampen global concerns about its growing economic and military power, and while the administration of George W. Bush has labelled Iran a member of the Axis of Evil, it has not prevented that country from mounting an international public diplomacy counter-offensive against the United States.[2] Not to be overlooked in this multi-level global struggle for favourable public opinion are non-state organizations, whether terrorist groups sending their videos to satellite broadcasters or large non-governmental organizations appealing for donor support to address natural disasters.

As British scholar Lawrence Freedman has insightfully noted, in tandem with a revolution in military affairs, we have been witnessing a revolution in political affairs – the move away from a clash between the major powers to asymmetric and irregular conflicts – that is at least as important as the revolution in military affairs. According to Freedman, this interplay between military and political affairs constitutes a revolution in strategic affairs.[3] For example, since 1992 the number of armed conflicts has declined by more than 40 percent, and there are actually fewer international crises and coups; it is only international terrorism that is increasing.[4] With this rise in irregular warfare – mass-casualty terrorism, gangsterism, guerrilla warfare (e.g., the Maoist insurgency in Nepal), intercommunal conflict (e.g., between Tamils and Sinhalese in Sri Lanka), and warlordism (e.g., in

Somalia) – the conventional military role of members of the international community is quite limited. The only way for coalitions within the international community (whether UN- or NATO-led, or simply coalitions of like-minded states, as in the coalition in the US-led invasion of Iraq) to resolve these conflicts is to embark on complex information campaigns at home to gain support from their domestic publics, who may not see a compelling reason for their sons and daughters to die in foreign lands to stop criminal gangs or religious zealots. States must embark on complex enforcement and reconstruction campaigns that will involve a massive public communication dimension; for instance, rebuilding societies by creating democratic institutions where none have existed or have not been seen in a generation, or creating functioning societies through the establishment of accountable police forces, law courts, health services, and so on. In this new strategic universe, warfare has moved from the battlefield to the airwaves and the Internet. In the words of Freedman, "Success in such warfare depends on an understanding of behaviour and attitudes, and so science and engineering may provide fewer clues about its future than sociological and anthropological assessments of questions of identity and social cohesion."[5] Public diplomacy is thus moving to the centre of international relations management.

As outlined in the introduction (chapter 1), it is paradoxical that as the management of global public opinion has become more important, the amount invested by Canada in nurturing relationships with foreign publics and the expanding array of global non-state actors has decreased. Since at least 2003, the intellectual case has been accepted for a greater emphasis on public diplomacy within the Canadian federal government, and while there is recognition that many individual programs (e.g., arts promotion, Canadian Studies, scholarships, youth internships) are well-run and effective, this has not yet translated into a sufficient commitment of resources or a strategic whole-of-government focus.[6] Hidden resources such as Canadian expatriates living and working abroad (many of whom would no doubt view themselves as "citizen diplomats") now go largely untapped, but they could be harnessed as Canada seeks to develop closer ties with countries identified as priorities, such as Brazil and India. To be fair, however, there has been a substantial rethinking – led by Foreign Affairs and International Trade Canada – of the framework in which all the players and partners can work.

The history of Canada's public diplomacy (chapter 3), shows that few Canadian governments have articulated a clear philosophy for the role of information abroad. The preoccupation has been with the mechanics and either securing new money or protecting existing budgets. The issue of what role information plays in creating a democratic space, or how Canadians could be attracted to participating in such programs, has been largely a secondary consideration. As noted, policy-makers have been more concerned with the "how" of Canada's public diplomacy and less with the "why."

This chapter explores the lessons that can be drawn from the examination of Canada's public diplomacy process and offers some observations on how to improve its effectiveness.

TRANSFORMING PUBLIC DIPLOMACY

This book has argued that we need to think about public diplomacy in a number of dimensions: (1) temporally, in three time frames; (2) as an essentially contested concept that has many labels, such as cultural diplomacy, political communication, international public relations, democracy-building, propaganda, branding, and military information operations; (3) as an endeavour whose effectiveness is linked to the level of societal support and understanding at home; and (4) as a form of statecraft that is not exclusive to foreign ministries but that, according to Bruce Gregory, "cuts across all political, economic, and military instruments and is essential to their implementation and success."[7] Public diplomacy is not a single instrument or the exclusive preserve of a country's foreign ministry; rather, it is a process, and as Gregory writes, it has "multiple components, each with their own organizations, budgets, tribal cultures, and rules for applying principles to behavior."[8]

The primacy of the military as a public diplomacy actor is often overlooked, but the military is in fact the biggest public diplomacy player during conventional wars (after diplomacy has failed), or in other forms of conflict. The military is the first group in a theatre of operations, and because it is responsible for maintaining security as a necessary precondition for economic development and political negotiation, it must reconcile the interests of all government and non-government players (aid workers, media, NGOs) to achieve the mission's military and non-military objectives.[9] Increasingly, military intervention to stabilize failed and failing states requires a sophisticated understanding of local information space in both the lead-up to the intervention, when psychological operations aimed at both civilian and opposing forces will be necessary, and during the peace-building phase (e.g., as in the case of joint military-civilian Provincial Reconstruction Teams in Afghanistan).

Public diplomacy in the developing world is most visible through the activities of outside aid workers and aid agencies (even if some national aid

agencies have sought to hide any evidence of their affiliations), not diplomats.[10] Indeed, for French policy-makers, the act of providing assistance
to less-developed countries is part and parcel of France's *diplomatie
ouverte*, or "open diplomacy"; aid is considered a necessary precursor in
order for France to be able to influence external attitudes and policies.[11]
Not to be overlooked as well are the international public diplomacy activities of foundations linked to political parties such as Germany's Konrad
Adenauer Foundation or the United States' National Democratic Institute for International Affairs.

   Each of these examples describes public diplomacy activity, because governmental actors (diplomats, soldiers, aid workers) or organizations affiliated with national political parties seek to understand, inform, and
influence foreign and domestic audiences on matters relating to a nation's
international interests, whether narrowly or more broadly defined. This is
not to say that there is necessarily a dichotomy between values and interests
in the conduct of foreign policy. As David Wright, former Canadian Ambassador to NATO, has written, "[i]nterests can be pursued in ways that reflect a
country's values."[12] Canada's foreign policy interests are seen by the world
through the prism of its values. This book has shown how these values – this
soft power – is projected through an array of government-sponsored programs and instruments.

   Finally, a strong effort to build consensus at home on a country's international vocation, implemented through the domestic public affairs activities
of foreign ministries, will contribute to building a stronger international
brand. A country's citizens are the key building blocks of its brand.

   How can Canada's public diplomacy be transformed in the years ahead?
Government will need to make certain changes in outlook and approach in
order to improve Canada's public diplomacy. Some of these changes are
identified below. The first area concerns the need to have a much better
understanding of the societies that are being targeted, which entails a
much greater investment in public opinion research, including surveys,
focus groups, media analysis and the use of social science methodologies
such as the Delphi method (a systematic process of expert consultation), to
obtain a deeper understanding of local conditions and local populations.
Foreign ministries in the Anglo-American world (in the United States, the
United Kingdom, Australia, Canada, and New Zealand), when they do consult civil society, tend to seek the views of political scientists (area studies
experts or strategic-studies scholars); however, more attention needs to be
paid to the views of sociologists and cultural-studies specialists, who may
have a better sense of the fault lines of future conflicts. And while most

diplomats will have a fair understanding of the views of Western-educated elites in Islamabad, they may be unaware of the currents roiling in the provinces and the seventy-six million Pakistanis under the age of twenty, who will determine the country's future. As Gregory opines, "[g]overnments invest disproportionately less in [the] tools they need to understand cultures than in the tools they use to engage and influence cultures."[13] In other words, governments have been more comfortable spending billions on the tools of public diplomacy, such as expensive international broadcasting operations, attractive publications, and even websites, than they have in going out and discovering what foreign populations actually think and feel.

There is little public opinion research or penetrating cultural analysis that would pick up signals for what is going to happen tomorrow. A number of public diplomacy studies that were published after the attacks of 9/11 pointed out, for example, that the US government had spent in the range of Can$6 million per year on public opinion research abroad, a pittance compared with the hundreds of millions of dollars that American multinationals spend every year to understand foreign cultures in advance of their international advertising campaigns. Canada spends virtually no money on public opinion research abroad. Arguably, a primary role for the Canadian head of mission is to present a coherent perspective on the host nation based on consultations with his or her Canada-based staff representing the following functions: political/economic reporting, public affairs, immigration, the military, development assistance, and security/intelligence liaison. Penetrating analysis should, in theory, arise from the confluence of different perspectives within a given society. However, if the individual functions at missions do not share knowledge but operate in silos, there is much less likelihood that such understanding will take place.

"Knowing thine audience" is indeed the *sine qua non* of effective public relations and should be the mantra of every Canadian public affairs officer abroad. For instance, thirty-five million South Koreans, many of them youth, interact with each other through massive multiple-player online games. Canada must reach out to young people worldwide on their own terms (e.g., through social networking Internet sites such as YouTube and Facebook). If youth in the countries that Canada considers to be a priority are engaged in the virtual world, then Canada's messages must be delivered in this world as well. As an example, Sweden, through its CA$35 million Swedish Institute, a government-funded agency that seeks to build long-term relations between Sweden and other countries through "active communication and cultural, educational and scientific exchanges," has plunged into the virtual world by establishing a Swedish embassy – the Second House of Sweden – in the three-dimensional Internet-based virtual world of Second Life.[14]

Second, while interpersonal communication and audience research are important, Canada must nevertheless do much more to marshal its presence in global information networks, particularly television and the Internet.[15] With the growth of the terrestrial and satellite television industry, a significant percentage of the developed world's citizens and a growing proportion of the developing world's citizens receive their information from these media sources. Yet as discussed in chapter 6, Canada is unique among G8 member states in not having a visual presence on the global airwaves. The only international outlet for news on Canada is through TV5, which carries French-language Canadian content. The irony is that although Canada is one of the world's largest exporters of television programming, much of it is not identified as Canadian. Radio Canada International is not irrelevant in this visually based public diplomacy environment, but it must continue to embrace the convergence philosophy to ensure that it is an integral and effective part of an overall Canadian international broadcasting strategy. Indeed, as argued in chapter 6, Canada is missing an international information strategy that would develop a critical mass of new media (CanadaInternational.gc.ca portal) and old (TV5, RCI). Consideration could be given to marshalling the CBC's resources to create an international Canadian broadcaster that would broadcast in both English and French, and also to creating a governance structure (perhaps modelled on that of the US Broadcasting Board of Governors) to give Canada's government-supported international broadcasting a much-needed strategic direction. As a result of decades of inattention to information-based programming, Canada lags behind its G8 competitors not only in the scope of its international broadcasting efforts but also in the emphasis it places on relationship-building in foreign countries using audience-research measurement tools.

Third, Canada needs to align its public diplomacy efforts more closely with its international priorities. This seems obvious, but too often in the past, public diplomacy programs at embassies ran on automatic from year to year, with little reflection on how local public diplomacy strategies needed to change to reflect shifting foreign policy priorities. As outlined in chapter 8, following the publication of *Canada's International Policy Statement* in 2005, DFAIT embarked on a major effort to align public diplomacy strategies for missions abroad with departmental business planning. This strategic approach to public diplomacy meant hard choices. In the future, it will mean taking resources away from some regions and transferring them to higher-priority regions or to countries such as Brazil, China, and India. Simply put, public diplomacy programs should support Canada's foreign policy priorities (both generally and specifically). The assumption is that the foreign policy priorities will directly support government-wide priorities. If public diplomacy is to be taken seriously, it must be given strategic direction, which means there must be an authority to direct, task, and assign operational responsibilities to departments and diplomatic missions. This is explained below, in the discussion on governance.

A fourth proposal for transforming Canada's public diplomacy concerns the role of the private sector. A common recommendation on the future of public diplomacy found in American and British reports since 9/11 is for the need to leverage the creativity and the resources of the private sector.[16] The guiding premise is that the government alone cannot be responsible for coordinating and promoting the national brand internationally. Indeed, in any advanced industrial country with a free market, free citizens, and multiple levels of government, it is not realistic to assume that one level of government, let alone a single government department such as a foreign ministry, could single-handedly change the national brand. At most, a national government in a liberal democratic state can encourage greater coordination of efforts, align its public diplomacy activities with national priorities, and, as required, contribute the "surge capacity" in terms of personnel and resources to refute inaccuracies and prevent misinformation from damaging a country's international reputation. In a converged media environment, such misinformation can exist in the domestic media or on websites that are managed by citizens in one country but targeted at an international audience. For example, websites hosted in Canada may convey misleading information in a variety of languages (and not necessarily English) about Canada's role in Afghanistan and be accessed by audiences around the world.

As the history of Canada's public diplomacy demonstrates, some efforts – ultimately stillborn – have been made to coordinate public diplomacy by establishing a whole-of-government governance structure. However, less attention has been paid to devising a whole-of-country approach (including the private sector) to the management of Canada's international brand. Since more than 80 percent of Canada's exports and 44 percent of its foreign direct investment go to the United States, Canada's private sector does have substantial experience in marketing itself to different foreign audiences.[17] As Gregory points out, much of what public diplomacy needs to be successful actually lies outside government. He notes, for example,

that the private sector has a competitive advantage in multimedia production, opinion and media surveys, and program evaluation, as well as in measuring the impact of communication campaigns.[18]

This is not to say that the Canadian business community has not been
involved in promoting Canada abroad. As the Upper North Side and Think
Canada campaigns have shown, the business community can play an important role in helping to showcase Canada abroad through sponsoring particular events. Indeed, an effective public diplomacy mission strategy will
explicitly seek to incorporate trade and investment objectives. What should
always be remembered, however, is that Canadian companies, with the possible exception of Crown corporations, will promote Canada abroad in
concert with government when it serves their corporate interests commercially. The summary paper from the Wilton Park Conference of March
2006, entitled *Public Diplomacy: Key Challenges and Priorities*, stressed that
"[t]here are difficulties in harnessing non-governmental actors ... because
non-governmental organizations and businesses do not share the same
objectives, or limitations, as national governments."[19] It is understandable
that corporate interests may not always be best served if these "Canadian"
companies cooperate with Canadian missions in countries where they have
business interests; as a result, they may wish to disassociate themselves from
the mission. Such self-serving "business" decisions may, at first glance,
appear to smack of corporate "disloyalty," given that many of these firms –
whether they are subsidiaries of multinational corporations or not – benefit from Canadian tax breaks and other incentives (e.g., subsidized export
credits) to maintain operations in Canada. On the other hand, there will
be occasions when it will not be in the interest of a company whose headquarters is located in Canada to "flag" itself as Canadian, especially if the
Canadian government is embroiled in high-profile diplomatic disagree-
ment with the country in which this company wishes to do business.[20] The
private sector will thus make decisions about cooperating with government
on branding campaigns on a case-by-case basis. But accepting this fact
should not prevent the federal government from establishing some general
guidelines for how the private sector's presence can be leveraged on a
more systematic basis in support of image building, just as it does when
it invites Canadian firms to participate in the Canadian pavilion at
world fairs.

Finally, under certain circumstances, it makes eminent sense for countries to work together to project themselves to each other. In essence, this
would mean engaging in *mutual public diplomacy*. Assuming the inherent
benefits of such mutual public diplomacy, Canada has worked in coopera-

tion with Afghanistan to explain the purpose of Canada's substantial contribution of Can$3.5 billion (2004–9) in aid and security assistance to this country.[21] When Afghanistan's ambassador to Canada travels across Canada to explain to the Canadian public the efforts that Canada and the international community are making to bring stability to his country, the Afghan government is indirectly supporting Canada's own public diplomacy efforts in Afghanistan. It is doing so by increasing the Canadian public's awareness of the range of Canadian interests in this fragile state. The Afghan ambassador thus plays an important, though independent, role in the Canadian government's domestic public affairs strategy to explain to Canadians why Afghanistan became Canada's top foreign policy priority. With the convergence of Canadian and Afghan interests, a small, poor country will also be able to leverage its very limited public affairs resources in Canada by virtue of the fact that it is the Canadian government's responsibility to maintain public information programs on Canada's mission. Such mutual public diplomacy is not limited to relations between Canada and developing countries but can be extended to any foreign campaign in which Canada's foreign policy interests intersect strongly with the national interests of the host country. For instance, in 2008 Canada and France jointly celebrated the four hundredth anniversary of Quebec City.

A variation on this mutual public diplomacy is the need for more cooperative public diplomacy by two (or more) like-minded countries in a third country. For example, it does not make sense for donor countries in a failed state to engage in competitive public diplomacy, since this suggests a duplication of efforts and contradictory messages. The international media regularly reports the lack of coordination of donor efforts in response to natural disasters and the rebuilding of failed states. Some of this is inevitable as national bureaucracies mobilize to send aid as quickly as possible. However, there would be a distinct whiff of national politics being played out in these international reconstruction efforts if donor countries sought to plant national flags on their donations and their aid projects, and thus their national public diplomacies, in order to prove that taxpayers' money was being well-spent. This is not to say that the international division of labour whereby one country, for example, trains local NGOs on how to monitor human rights violations and another country helps to build an independent media system is counterproductive. However, there are cases where the fragile host government, beset by insurgencies and instability, must wonder why the need for visibility by donor countries sometimes seems to trump a coordinated effort at communicating with and distributing aid to its citizens. The need for more cooperative public diplomacy in third countries is certain to expand as identity conflicts become the predominant source of international conflict.

GOVERNANCE OF PUBLIC DIPLOMACY

What public diplomacy architecture should be adopted to manage a new approach? There is a range of models for achieving greater coherence. It is instructive to look at the approaches of the United States and the United Kingdom. As scholar Robin Brown has observed, in the United States, with its history of decentralized government, there is no natural inclination for single-window approaches to American public diplomacy. This started to change in 1999 with the amalgamation of the United States Information Agency within the State Department and the creation of Coalition Information Centres during the Kosovo intervention, and it gained momentum after the 9/11 attacks and the start of the Bush administration's global war on terrorism. After the public relations disaster that was the Pentagon's short-lived Office of Strategic Influence,[22] described as a body with a "huge budget and bizarre ideas," the US Department of Defense, with its simultaneous "hearts and minds" campaigns in Iraq and Afghanistan, became the front line of American public diplomacy. The overall American approach has become increasingly centralized. Following six months of quietly establishing itself, the White House's short-lived Office of Global Communications received its Executive Order in January 2003. Section 3 of that order made it very clear that, in addition to its central coordination function, the office would have the surge capacity ("information teams"), should the need have arisen, to engage in open information warfare to counter misinformation about US policies and positions. By 2005 the office would no longer be the sharp end of American strategic communication planning because of, to use the words of one analyst, the "sheer weight of the monumental undertaking."[23]

While perhaps not as radical as the American restructuring, the United Kingdom's efforts have been no less significant, starting in 1997 with the creation of Panel 2000, which brought together public and private sector partners (the British Council, British Trade International, the Department for International Development, the British Tourist Authority, BBC World Service, and NGOs). The panel identified a series of key themes, including Britain's "creativity and innovation," which were used to project the United Kingdom abroad. In order to move the branding agenda forward, the panel was followed by a cross-departmental Britain Abroad Task Force. The attacks of 9/11 created a new urgency, not only in how Britain projected itself abroad but also in how it presented its foreign policy positions at home. This concern led to the creation of an Islamic Media Unit, a Communication and Information Centre to coordinate briefings in times of crisis, and a Community Relations Unit for broader Foreign and Commonwealth Office (FCO) outreach. In 2003, a Public Diplomacy Strategy Board, chaired by the permanent secretary of the FCO, was established to create greater synergies across government and provide strategic direction for the government's public diplomacy.[24]

In 2005, Lord Carter of Coles released his review of the United Kingdom's approach to public diplomacy (hereafter referred to as the Lord Carter Review) and made far-reaching recommendations to ensure a more effective and measurable British public diplomacy effort, including

- a comprehensive medium-term public diplomacy strategy (three to five years) with core themes based on the FCO's strategic priorities;
- the creation of a Public Diplomacy Strategy and Performance Management Board (to be known as the Public Diplomacy Board), chaired by an FCO minister and having representation from the BBC World Service and the British Council (and that would be supported by an executive unit within the FCO and be responsible for measuring performance and managing projects); and
- a Public Diplomacy Advisory Board that would meet at least once each year with the Public Diplomacy Board and that could be called upon for advice or input on specific issues or areas of activity.[25]

The Lord Carter Review was careful to maintain the editorial independence of the BBC World Service as an instrument of the United Kingdom's public diplomacy by noting that it would be "inappropriate" to make its programming support "core themes." Nonetheless, the government's public diplomacy strategy did expect the BBC World Service to take into account issues such as geographic priorities and the use of new technologies. The review acknowledged the "ambiguity" in the relationship between the FCO and the British Council and called for a "whole UK agenda" that would exploit the synergies between the British Council and other government departments such as the Department for International Development and the Department for Culture, Media, and Sport. Significantly, the review conceived public diplomacy very broadly to include sport: "[i]n particular the use of sport in public diplomacy should continue to be explored, and sport should be seen as an intrinsic part of the UK's cultural diplomacy effort."

The Lord Carter Review recognized tourism, going so far as to stipulate that VisitBritain's marketing and research needed to be shared across government. It also highlighted the public diplomacy benefits of the Department for International Development's (DFID) work around the world, encouraging the FCO and the DFID to work together so that "each can support the other's agenda," and it recommended that there should be continued close cooperation between the FCO and UK Trade and Investment. With regard to the military's role, the review stated that the FCO and the Ministry of Defence should "attempt to clarify" ways in which its public diplomacy efforts could be mutually beneficial. The private sector's role was not overlooked, with the review calling for the government to find "supportive" companies and include these in the overall public diplomacy strategy.[26]

The British House of Commons agreed broadly with the recommendations of the Lord Carter Review on the instruments for creating a more strategic diplomacy. It is to be noted that its Foreign Affairs Committee recommended that the government not reduce the BBC World Service's radio services in foreign languages in order to have the budgetary room to create a new Arabic television service. Rather, the committee recognized the importance of maintaining the existing range of languages heard on the BBC World Service and called for the government to increase the World Service's budget to accommodate new services. The committee clearly believed that the imperative of winning the "hearts and minds" in the Middle East did not mean sacrificing services to other regions of the world.[27]

The lesson from the Lord Carter Review and the British parliamentary response is that an effective Canadian public diplomacy for the twenty-first century will necessarily involve maintaining the traditional public diplomacy instruments and adding new services (e.g., international Canadian television) and even new languages. Reducing investment in public diplomacy instruments can no longer be seen as part of the Cold War peace dividend.

Consistent with the recommendations of the Lord Carter Review, a Canadian Public Diplomacy Strategy Committee could be created to provide oversight and direction to a whole-of-government strategy for promoting Canada's image abroad. As noted in chapter 3, on the history of Canada's public diplomacy, expectations will have to be realistic given Canada's record of creating government-wide governance mechanisms for public diplomacy. This committee could include deputy ministers from the departments of Foreign Affairs and International Trade Canada, Agriculture and Agri-Food Canada, Canadian Heritage, National Defence, and the

Canadian International Development Agency. It could also have representatives from the Canada Council for the Arts, the CBC, and the Canadian
Tourism Commission. Given that public diplomacy cuts across most major
Canadian governmental portfolios, the committee could make regular
reports on the management and measurement of Canada's public diplomacy to the foreign affairs, international trade, and heritage ministers. Similar to the Public Diplomacy and Performance Management Board
recommended by the Lord Carter Review, a secretariat could be established
to support both a Canadian Public Diplomacy Board and the Canadian Public Diplomacy Strategy Committee. The secretariat, drawing on an interdepartmental committee of senior officials, would seek to ensure that the
synergies of the federal government's many public diplomacy activities are
exploited, that the activities are evaluated on a regular basis, that the domestic public affairs activities of key departments such as CIDA, DFAIT, and
National Defence are connected to the government's information activities
abroad, and that Canada's public diplomacy activities are consistent with and
reinforce the government's international priorities. Such an approach is critical, given that areas such as culture and education have historically lacked a
foreign policy context; since 2000 there has been more effort to embed such
a context into Canada's international cultural programs.

Given the danger of politicization, a centralized US-style Office of Global
Communications is less desirable. However, this does not mean that coherent messaging is not needed. It can be achieved by drawing on the experience of Australia's Department of Foreign Affairs and Trade, which in 2003
had a practice of sending out key messages to all of its ambassadors on a
weekly basis. Although the problem of internally competing voices is to be
expected in view of Canada's federal structure, a committee would be able to
address situations in which there are sustained contradictory messages.
Unlike the British and American experiences, where huge investments in
development assistance have been largely de-linked from public diplomacy,
Canada can leverage its investment in its aid programs by ensuring that foreign recipients are aware of Canada's contributions.[28] For example, it could
do so by sending development information officers into the field.

As is evident from an examination of the possible future architecture of a
strategic public diplomacy approach by Canada, public diplomacy campaigns will be led by the federal government's international departments,
starting with those previously mentioned. This is not to negate the vital
roles played by other federal departments or other levels of government,
or, indeed, the Canadian private sector. What this book has shown is that
the military and aid organizations are becoming more and more involved

The Process

in public diplomacy by virtue of the fact that only a coordinated whole-of-government and whole-of-country approach can respond adequately to the wide range of security challenges in the coming decades.

Seven goals for effective Canadian public diplomacy can be distilled from the experience of the Enhanced Representation Initiative, an effort aimed at increasing Canada's presence in the United States. Several changes to the practice of public diplomacy have been implemented, with varying degrees of success, to achieve the following goals:

1 Public diplomacy should amplify the Canadian message and showcase Canadian values, ideas, and achievements.
2 It should work in tandem with Canada's traditional diplomacy.
3 It should provide honest feedback to Ottawa on the international impact of Canada's foreign policy.
4 Public affairs programs at home could help Canadians to become global citizens and put them in a position to both understand and support Canada's international policy.
5 The management of complex social and economic issues could be facilitated through the exchange of ideas, research (policy or scientific), and innovations.
6 Informal networks and formal coalitions could be formed on social, environmental, economic, or political issues of concern to Canadians, thereby promoting Canadian interests through partnerships with like-minded groups and lobbies outside Canada.
7 All members of the mission should see themselves as public diplomats.[29]

The Canadian commitment to stabilizing Afghanistan serves as a perfect illustration of the need for a strategic approach in order to maintain control of both local information space in Afghanistan and domestic support at home. Afghanistan presents an ideal laboratory to test a more strategic approach to Canada's public diplomacy that combines both international and domestic public relations. Public diplomacy of the future is going to encompass much more than cultural diplomacy. The development of military-civilian units in fragile states, such as the Provincial Reconstruction Teams in Afghanistan, means that public diplomacy will be at the sharp end of the international community's interventions.

Coordination through cooperation, teamwork, and information sharing among departments is integral to a successful public diplomacy campaign. However, a strategic public diplomacy must go beyond coordination. A public diplomacy strategy, as Bruce Gregory writes, means having someone to assign (and change) operational responsibilities to departments and embassies, to approve senior public diplomacy officials, to set priorities, and to move resources.[30] In other words, a strategic public diplomacy, as opposed to one that is only coordinated, means that political direction, possibly from the Prime Minister's Office itself, will have to come into the equation in order to ensure that public diplomacy resources are aligned in support of national priorities.

SHIFTING THE BRAND BALANCE AND INSTRUMENTS: ONE-WAY TO TWO-WAY COMMUNICATION

Public diplomacy will continue to be double-tracked. However, the balance has shifted from the Cold War's reliance on "information out" programs (e.g., from international broadcasting in which governments maintain editorial control and from government publications) to attempts to develop more sophisticated forms of communication programs that emphasize mutual understanding and dialogue – academic and scientific exchanges, to be sure, but also communications efforts of joint military-civilian reconstruction teams in zones of conflict and government presence in virtual Internet worlds. As John Ralston Saul noted in his 2004 Glendon College address: "[i]t was not then, nor is it now, a simple matter of getting people to pay attention to a visiting writer or a visiting corporation. It's about getting them to pay attention to the way we think about the world, and the way we think about international policy. Understanding doesn't mean agreeing, but it means entering into a realistic understanding of our point of view."[31] There is a growing acceptance that developing this depth of understanding cannot be solely the domain of increasingly sophisticated advocacy communication, what Grunig and Grunig have described as "two-way asymmetrical" campaigns whose goal it is to understand the public, but ultimately to get the public to act as the sender wants. Advocacy should be complemented by (and sometimes counter-balanced by) a "two-way symmetrical" model of public relations that creates a "win-win zone" in which the campaign does not maximize the desired outcome for either party, but the outcome "satisfies both."[32] In other words, public diplomacy becomes a form of genuine negotiation between the sender and the receiver, leading in some cases to the sender and the receiver both modifying their original positions.

As the following discussion will show, the shift from one-way to two-way modes of public diplomacy, along with the growing utility of many-to-many forms of communication ushered in by the Internet, will have a profound effect on how the instruments of public diplomacy are used in the decades ahead. Within the array of public diplomacy instruments, we can expect a shift away from a reliance on those associated with classical cultural diplomacy, such as touring groups, to more innovative campaigns (many in conjunction with NGOs) that reach beyond elites to the mainstream public and young people. This is not to say that the opinion leaders in target countries are not important – clearly they are. It is just that practitioners will have to reach both audiences simultaneously with tailored messages to ensure a more comprehensive public diplomacy.

Branding Canada's Diversity

Canada would be well advised to leverage its reputation for diversity, tolerance, and inclusion, and to promote it as a global asset. If properly communicated and branded, this hallmark of Canadian society will go a long way towards defining Canada to the world in the twenty-first century. The Canadian "model," to use Jennifer Welsh's formulation, which "privileges pluralism ... [and] prizes mixed government ... but is also confident in its ability to sustain a unique national identity," is highly relevant internationally as countries seek to reconcile multiple identities within their borders.[33] As senior Canadian official Daryl Copeland has professed, Canada is the "globalization nation ... if you hold up a mirror to Canada, you will see your face reflected."[34] This attribute is one that few other G8 members, much less other countries can claim as their own. And if the world sees Canada as the model nation, then so too will Canadians, who will thereby shift their focus away from their differences to what they have in common. Canada's international success thus begets greater domestic social cohesion.

Canada has an opportunity to capitalize on its "northernness" to promote its unique identity abroad. This northernness is probably the most understated and underutilized part of Canada's diversity brand. It is a fact that since at least the end of the World War II, Canada, from a public diplomacy perspective, has been in active denial of its geographic reality. More than 60 percent of Canada's land mass is defined as northern, yet Canadian governments of all persuasions, in their desire to advance the notion that Canada is a modern nation, have sought to downplay this fact. There has been a perception that northernness will be equated with underdevelopment in the eyes of international investors. This is the so-called "unhelpful" stereotype of Canada as a drawer of water and hewer of wood. What is forgotten is that natural resources continue to represent 34 percent of Canadian exports.[35] For example, 99 percent of Canada's crude oil exports and 100 percent of its natural gas exports go to the United States. Yet, for many observers outside Canada, the North defines Canada in a positive way. For Americans, Canada is certainly a northern nation, as it is for Russians, Scandinavians, and many other Europeans. In fact, anyone who associates Canada with snow and ice hockey certainly thinks of Canada as a northern nation and is surprised, when visiting, to find out how hot it can actually be. No public opinion survey has ever indicated that Canada has suffered in the eyes of external observers by being identified as a northern nation. In fact, as Governor General Adrienne Clarkson's 2003 tour of northern nations demonstrated, Canada's northernness was a distinct advantage, helping to advance broader Canadian foreign policy interests.

In light of the economic and political implications of global climate change and the importance of sustainable development, it can be said that the northern agenda is now very much aligned with Canada's broader foreign policy agenda.[36] This alignment has raised the profile of circumpolar international relations and with it, the importance of growing transnational links among northern indigenous communities. The growing internationalization of Canada's northern indigenous communities, through their representation in the Arctic Council and in the creation of growing intercultural and educational links through the University of the Arctic, points to a powerful potential source of Canadian soft power in the years ahead.

Part and parcel of a discussion of the projection of Canada's unique identity abroad must be the issue of whether a "bricks and mortar" model along the lines of the British Council or the Goethe-Institut would enhance a brand of public diplomacy that is oriented to expanding cross-cultural dialogue. One has to be realistic about whether such an investment would be cost-effective. The consensus in 2005 among those working abroad as cultural affairs officers for Canada was that new resources that could go into innovative programming would be sucked up by creating new administrative structures in Ottawa and infrastructure abroad. In their view, Canada simply did not have the critical mass to create a separate institution to cover the world. For Canada, a new network of new cultural institutions abroad would be unaffordable, and if they were to be co-located with Canadian missions, there would always be security concerns.[37]

However, this book does not argue that the existing "bricks and mortar" in the form of Canada House in London and the Canadian Cultural Centre in Paris should be closed. Quite the contrary, these institutions have long histories and are the symbols of Canada's presence in two global cultural capitals. What may be more feasible is creating "Canada hotspots" that would be Internet cafés run by Canadians all over the world. Each café could offer free Internet access and information on Canada. A network of Canada hotspots would provide an informal and non-official way of connecting with the "street," particularly in countries with authoritarian regimes and with which Canada may have only limited diplomatic relations, such as Belarus.

Canada hotspots could also feature "free" direct connections to the website of the local Canadian diplomatic mission. Mission sites would need to do more than just publish the regional touring schedule of a classical ballet company, which may serve to raise Canada's profile with the local elites but would not necessarily reach out to a younger generation. Canada's mission websites should not only tell people where and when Canadian culture will be available, but they should also showcase the art itself through video-streaming. Much can be learned from the branding techniques of the private sector. For instance, BMW generated significant buzz when it invited a global audience to visit its website to view five-minute videos.[38] This is not to suggest that governments should attempt to mimic corporate marketing or engage in electronic pamphleteering to promote their policies, but they should at least keep their websites current and in touch with the multimedia expectations of today's savvy web users.

Branding through Sports

Like Canada's north, Canadian sport or participation by Canadians in international sporting activities is an undervalued and underappreciated form of Canadian public diplomacy. For most countries in the world, international sporting events are an expression of national achievement, whether it is a world championship in wrestling or participation at the World Cup of soccer, and they are thus an important means of putting countries that may never obtain much positive international attention "on the map." The Olympics is the best expression of this form of sports diplomacy, but so too are the Commonwealth Games or the Jeux de la francophonie.

However, participation in sports is not enough. The branding takes place when, as Ralston Saul points out in his 1994 report *Culture and Canadian Foreign Policy*, the international sport reflects Canada's characteristics.[39] He notes that Canada is the architect and leading proponent of the Arctic Games (started in 1970) and the North American Indigenous Games (started in 1990). If properly promoted to foreign journalists and publics, these games could focus international attention on Canada as the leading northern nation. The benefits in terms of public attention and tourism can be well imagined. As Ralston Saul suggests, "an interesting image is not necessarily created by simply doing well against other countries in world sports. [Canada] may accomplish as much by embracing what is original and proper to [its] own experience. And in the long run this is more likely to interest outsiders."[40]

Play for Peace offers an example of how Canada can better brand itself through sports. The highlight of the International Year of Sports and Physical Education, celebrated in 2005, Play for Peace was a youth camp designed for teenagers around the world. Held in Trogen, Switzerland, and organized in partnership with the Toronto-based NGO Right to Play, the event provides a blueprint for the way forward in non-traditional public diplomacy. Teenagers from twenty different countries participated in Play for Peace – an example of cooperative public diplomacy between the governments of Canada and Switzerland. Significantly, the event also leveraged partnership opportunities with Right to Play, an organization that operates in eighteen different countries with the support of the international branch of Sport Canada and CIDA. Events such as this lay the foundation for cross-cultural understanding at an early age and provide an opportunity for youngsters from war-torn homelands, such as Sierra Leone, to come into contact with the values of tolerance and respect that countries like Canada and Switzerland want to promote worldwide.

Branding International Education

Chapter 5 described international education as a critical instrument of public diplomacy because, like cultural programming, it is also a valuable but underused commodity. The tens of thousands of students who travel to Canada every year represent a significant benefit to Canada's economy and will constitute a pool of prospective skilled immigrants. These students can be powerful "ambassadors" for Canada, although until recently, Canada had not developed a tracking system to ensure that exchange students and scholarship winners could be contacted once they returned to their countries.

The relatively low levels of factual knowledge about the world displayed by Canadians will handicap Canada's public diplomacy in the years ahead. Post-secondary institutions in Canada should, therefore, be encouraged to offer more cross-cultural communication in their programs (e.g., by teaching courses in languages other than English or French) and to provide more incentives for students to study abroad and more opportunities to learn difficult foreign languages. In sum, expansion of overseas study and work experience programs should be encouraged. It may also be worthwhile for Canada to consider building its own academic research centres abroad, such as the Canadian Universities Centre in Berlin (the purpose of which is to expand and strengthen academic ties between Canadian and German scholars), taking inspiration from the American universities in Beirut and Cairo.

Branding International Broadcasting

Public diplomacy has traditionally seen communications technology in terms of broadcasting – a one-to-many form of communication. The new public diplomacy of the twenty-first century must recognize the convergence of communication technologies and the opportunities for interactivity that they will bring. This does not mean that every ambassador should have his or her own blog (although humanizing the role should be encouraged). Governments have not kept up with the rapid changes. Until recently, the Canadian foreign and trade ministry had 120 different websites, several of which ran at cross-purposes. This is not the best way to convey key messages to the world. Regulations and reputations are evolving because of technology. This is not to suggest that technology determines the environment, but it does change the nature of social relationships.

As this book has described, one of the largest gaps in Canada's public diplomacy is the lack of an effective presence in international broadcasting to support broader foreign policy aims – this despite the fact that few media outlets have more international bureaus than CBC/Radio-Canada. (CNN and the BBC are the notable exceptions.) This is a serious failure on Canada's part. International television has become the primary means of conveying a national presence, and with over a billion people with access to the Internet, there is also an urgent need to understand what the convergence of print, television, and radio means for a national presence in the international news media. Certainly, as suggested by chapter 6, there is an urgent need for greater coordination between what capacity exists at RCI, TV5, and the international portal of the federal government's Government On-Line website and the particular objectives identified by DFAIT for country-specific public diplomacy strategies. While France has created a French equivalent of CNN, Canada is still without an international English-language broadcaster. Content-driven "connectivity," whether in the traditional forms of public diplomacy (e.g., online access to Canadian artists and educational institutions) or on new and dedicated websites designed for particular policy advocacy, is of fundamental importance for credibility. This connectivity would enable Canada to build electronic communities of interest around its foreign policy priorities.

If Canada were to create an international television model, it should be modelled on the BBC World Service and not the Cold War–era state-broadcasting model, which was premised on tight editorial control (as in the example of the Voice of America).[41] In this author's view, an international television service would have to retain full editorial independence while sharing the broader values of Canada with the rest of the world. Such editorial independence would be non-negotiable and essential to maintaining global credibility for Canada.

A compelling national online presence and online services are not a choice but a necessity. It should be understood that the unlimited space of the web creates both opportunities and challenges. As noted in chapter 6, the Internet allows governments to push out information instantly to a global audience. However, the need to keep abreast of new technologies and to renew content while maintaining a parallel system of publications can be very costly. For this reason, there should be more sharing of platforms, best practices, and content among government departments. There has also been a tendency to overemphasize the benefits of communication and information technologies (CITs). Few CITs, including the Internet – whether in the form of e-mail or the web – are naturally effective communication media: they are distributive but not necessarily ideal for communication. For a country that is seeking to move its public diplomacy from an approach in which information is mostly pushed out to one that seeks to initiate greater understanding through more face-to-face contact, CITs are best used to amplify existing connections and communication between people, rather than to replace traditional means of communication.

COUNTRY BRANDING FOR ECONOMIC GAIN

It was observed in chapter 7 that international business promotion and tourism promotion represent the economic face of the public diplomacy process. These two instruments of a government's public diplomacy – for example, Team Canada Missions to raise Canada's international business profile and advertising campaigns to attract more foreign visitors – can contribute to a country's national brand in all its dimensions: diplomacy, education, culture, and immigration. For instance, tourists may become future immigrants or consumers of education or both. Foreign students may return to Canada as tourists. Promoting Canada as having an avant-garde culture or a diverse society can lead to economic gain in the form of increased trade and investment. Likewise, promoting Canada's economic advantages to international audiences also raises Canada's diplomatic advantage as a country whose views need to be heard on the world stage (e.g., in the G8 context).

It should be obvious that a country's image is much more than what Ralston Saul calls "formal representations of culture." As he notes, "the challenge for medium-sized countries that wish to have an impact on the world today is to establish a solid image of themselves abroad. That image is the platform on which a foreign policy, trade policy, cultural policy can be built at the international level."[42] For a geographically very large and highly trade-dependent country such as Canada, with a small population base, the economic components of the national brand – the degree of attractiveness for business and tourism – should be a focus of interest for all levels of government. As the case of Canada's advocacy campaign in the United States following the 9/11 attacks showed (chapter 9), the elements of the national brand are inextricably intertwined and cannot be seen in separate silos. A perception in the United States that the northern border was vulnerable was a direct threat to Canada's economic prosperity. Not only would American measures to review border security have an impact on bilateral trade and investment, but they would also affect cross-border tourism and education. This book has argued that the federal government through its public diplomacy instruments has an important role in maximizing the synergies that exist between and among the different elements of the national brand so that opportunities to achieve Canada's international economic and security goals can be maximized and vulnerabilities reduced.

The above discussion has called for a shift in how the Canada brand is to be seen and how the instruments of public diplomacy are to be used. With Canada spending approximately one-tenth of what its G8 counterparts spend on public diplomacy, most of Canada's public diplomacy programs could be enhanced with more resources. The obvious examples are the bare-bones budgets for cultural diplomacy, Canadian studies, mobility, and scholarships. But as a former director in DFAIT's International Cultural Relations Bureau has pointed out, there are many other things that are essential to the projection of the Canadian identity but that are not now being done at all, or minimally so. In this official's view, new programs need to be created, including Internet-based youth travel and exchange programs to connect young people, language teaching, and cultural education abroad, in order to introduce foreigners to Canada. (These initiatives have all been successfully implemented by the British, the French, the Germans, and the Australians.) It goes without saying that projecting Canadian identity abroad will require a close partnership among the departments and agencies now delivering the programs involved. In the view of the DFAIT official, "creating synergies and common strategies will strengthen all programs, maximize opportunities, and leverage resources, and will build toward the critical mass necessary to consider whether new programs and new resources will be required for further progress" in promoting Canada's image.[43]

THE ADMINISTRATION OF PUBLIC DIPLOMACY

The Making of "Public Diplomats"

As is evident from this book's discussion of the ascendance of public forms of diplomacy, today's diplomats should spend at least as much time listening to and understanding others as they do learning what to say. Practitioners must know the language of their target countries before they begin their assignments. At the same time, one must be cautious not to overestimate the role of diplomats. It is not the diplomats who will make or break a country's image. That being said, and as argued in chapter 2, the only way to answer the slow-pulse questions that lie beneath the rush of daily events is for diplomats to consult a wide range of non-governmental actors. As Copeland states, the new diplomat, the "guerilla diplomat," is the embodiment of the public diplomacy practitioner.[44] This diplomat will have to be not only an effective communicator, cross-culturally equipped, but also an advocate. Diplomats will have to function in an information environment permeated by rumour and conspiracies and fuelled by advances in communication technologies.[45]

As noted in chapter 8, one of the challenges of managing Canada's public diplomacy is the lack of a specialized career track for this function. The US Department of State, for example, offers public diplomacy as one of five career tracks. For Ralston Saul, the ideal profile for a cultural affairs attaché is someone who is a combination of agent and producer ("beyond the act of creation, all jobs in culture are entrepreneurial"), who has a facility for language, and who displays sophisticated levels of political, social, and cultural understanding to penetrate local societies.[46] In his eyes, if a cultural attaché neither creates, produces nor sells, he or she is "dead-weight."[47] He advocates that one-third of their careers should be spent in the cultural community in Canada, including in publishing companies, theatre companies, and cultural organizations, and that

cultural postings should not be for less than five years, given the need to
build long-term relationships.[48]

Finally, as discussed in chapter 2, in addition to the work of diplomats,
ordinary citizens, both at home in Canada and as part of an expanding
expatriate network abroad, can contribute a great deal to the outside perception of Canada, both positively and negatively. In the words of John
Sorrell, "[p]eople represent countries," and the Canadian people "are all
ambassadors now."[49] Indeed, travellers will tell you that when they meet
someone from a foreign land, especially a country that they are unfamiliar
with, the initial contact becomes the impression of (and prejudice toward)
that country, and it is carried with them. All Canadian citizens should be
aware that they are the face of Canada abroad: the symbolic act of having a
Canadian flag visible when in a different country means something to the
Canadian who is wearing it *and* to the non-Canadian who encounters it.

Evaluation

It is not easy to evaluate public diplomacy programs. While measuring the
outputs can be a straightforward and uncontroversial exercise, the results
are often ignored by government agencies that could ideally use the information. Outcome measurements, conversely, are more challenging to
obtain, given the difficulties with attributing and justifying causality, and they
can force bureaucratically and politically unpopular decisions to be made.

So, how are we to determine whether the investment in the 2001 Think
Canada Festival in Japan had any direct impact in changing Japanese attitudes towards Canada? That is, did it "move the needle"? To have a sense of
whether it did, Canada would have had to have put in place a sophisticated
and expensive evaluation system before and after the initiative. And even if
the initiative changed attitudes in the short term among those Japanese
elites who had been targeted by the embassy, how long would it last? The
truth is that single public diplomacy events – with the exception of world
fairs or major international sporting events such as the Olympics that focus
international attention on one country for a sustained period – have very
little long-term impact. However, the cumulative effect of a public diplomacy program (e.g., the Upper North Side campaign) that makes full use
of the synergies that exist among the various public diplomacy tools (e.g.,
Canadian Studies programs, a web presence, speakers programs, cultural
tours, tapping expatriate networks) can make a lasting impression. This
suggests that one-off, "big bang" public diplomacy projects or routine Canada Week events may not be the most effective approach.[50] Projects will

need to be monitored and outputs measured. For longer-term public diplomacy projects, however, such as the creation of greater goodwill towards Canada by a chosen country, it makes little sense to attempt to constantly measure impact, since this would be akin, in the words of Nicholas Cull, a professor of public diplomacy at the University of Southern California, to "constantly running out into the forest to see if the trees have grown."[51]

CONCLUSION

The fact is that the global community will never think that a country is as exciting as its population or government thinks it is. For this reason, to succeed at nation branding, countries must design and project ever more creative and exciting national images. Constantly heralding past achievements is a quick route to international irrelevance, especially when these past achievements are not relevant to the present or future challenges. The key to successful public diplomacy or nation branding is to give people an exciting story about Canada that they are interested in and to prove it over and over again in a variety of ways, thus creating accumulated recognition.

Canada has a high positive rating in the world and does very well within its limitations, the biggest of which is that it is in the shadow of the United States. Moreover, it is competing for attention with other G8 members, a growing number of emerging powers (Brazil, Russia, India, and China), and the so-called "pathfinder" nations, such as Spain, Poland, and Norway. The problem for Canada is that it has not generated a critical mass of programs. Its public diplomacy machinery and capacity has been fragmented for too long.

The attacks of 9/11 spawned the most intense public debate on public diplomacy since the start of the Cold War. Indeed, public diplomacy is most closely associated with periods of war, when the imperatives to convey a nation's point of view and to mobilize audiences at home and abroad have been most acute. This book has endeavoured to show that political support for public diplomacy only in periods of crisis is short-sighted and counterproductive, as the United States has discovered to its chagrin as it now seeks to rebuild the public diplomacy apparatus that was allowed to erode after the end of the Cold War.

Each country's approach to public diplomacy is based on widely different needs and goals. For the United States, public diplomacy efforts are essential to smooth the way for and to justify what can often be seen as unpopular policy decisions by a world that at once respects and fears the

United States' capacity to shape the international system. The French use their public diplomacy (although they eschew the use of the term), especially the teaching of the French language, as a means to present France's world view as a viable alternative to that of the United States. The Germans have used public diplomacy, including their acknowledgement of their collective national responsibility for the Nazi regime's war crimes, to help rehabilitate their international image.[52]

For Canada, a country whose relative power has been in decline since the end of World War II, public diplomacy is a means of slowing the loss of power. Samuel Huntington demonstrated in "The Clash of Civilizations," in which he conceptualized power as a three-dimensional chessboard (with military, economic, and soft-power planes), that a nation can be vulnerable on one plane and make up this power deficit with gains on another plane[53] – what Nye has referred to as the fungibility of power.[54] Applying this idea to Canada, one could conclude that while Canada's international power capacity at the political and security levels was degraded in the 1990s as a result of budget cuts implemented mostly by the Liberal government under Prime Minister Jean Chrétien, there was at the same time an effort to redress this loss of power through Canadian involvement in soft-power initiatives such as the Rio Summit (1992), the Ottawa Convention on land-mines (1997), the Kimberly Process to ban conflict diamonds, and the creation of the International Criminal Court. However, some academic observers and media commentators harshly criticized the government for engaging in foreign policy on the cheap ("penny-pinching diplomacy"), as it was becoming all too apparent that the rhetoric of Canada's global engagement was straining credulity at home and abroad. But by 2003, with Canada's deployment of troops to Afghanistan (the largest Canadian deployment since Korea), Canada was once more raising its profile on the international military stage.

The paradox of Canada's image is that its non-threatening and "non-imperial" nation-brand is both a strength and a curse. International surveys repeatedly show that the Canada brand – "warm but fuzzy" – is among the most popular and well-liked in the world.[55] The curse is that unless Canada's brand is broadened to include being seen as an "innovation nation," it risks becoming the Argentina of the twenty-first century.[56] This book has shown that trying to *re-brand* Canada as a high-tech nation (a goal of all industrialized nations), as opposed to *stretching the brand*, would be akin to throwing the baby out with the bathwater. Nor would it be a successful enterprise, given that it would be impossible to "hide" the fact that Canada is a large, sparsely inhabited country with abundant natural resources. The challenge will be to leverage the benefits of the existing brand – prosperous, open, diverse, trustworthy, law-abiding, and free of corruption – to promote Canada as an innovative nation. As a senior Canadian official has argued, the fundamental challenge is to decide what is most critical: "[y]ou can't be all over the map. You want to have two or three messages to come forward ... [and] be a little bit prudent about that, a little bit focused."[57]

Stretching the national brand means that rather than just promoting the fact that Canada has the world's second-largest oil reserves after Saudi Arabia, it should also be pointed out that Canada has also developed new technology to extract oil from the tar sands in Alberta. The international labour market of the twenty-first century will favour those countries that invest in creating new knowledge bases, making the research and development sectors increasingly critical to national success. Canada's universities, with their expanding industrial sites, are thus destined to play a much larger role in projecting Canada's international comparative advantage as a nation on the leading edge of science and technology.

The Inherent Limits of Public Diplomacy

We must also be realistic about the limitations of public diplomacy. As Josef Joffe reminds us about America's ubiquitous and overwhelming global cultural power, "soft power does not necessarily increase the world's love for America. It is still power, and it can still make enemies."[58] As the profiles of the 9/11 hijackers and other religious zealots show, soft power and exposure to Western values and ideas does not always bend hearts; it can create rage and resentment just like hard power. And, indeed, there may be no causal relationship between a country's ubiquity and its actual influence. The American presence in a country, despite the good work of its diplomats and the substantial investment of aid, may be viewed as more threatening than a more limited presence by a smaller, less powerful country. It may sometimes be impossible for a great power to achieve high returns on public diplomacy because of its colonial or military "baggage."

Communications alone cannot resolve the underlying challenges, for instance, of global poverty and disease. Public diplomacy, as we have learned, is not a panacea for bad policy. As American congressman Adam Schiff has asked, "How much of the problem that we face [in the world] is a result of our policies and how much is a result of our communication?"[59] While this question is important, it may be more relevant to American approaches. For Canada, the issue is not necessarily how the country communicates its policies but how it can communicate them at all. A critical mass of information is needed before the international community takes notice, and for a country such as Canada, that critical mass is difficult to achieve.

Policy splits at home over a country's international relations or fundamental policy disagreements between or among states cannot be reconciled by slick public relations campaigns either. Such campaigns may in fact end up further eroding a nation's credibility rather than enhancing it as the gap between rhetoric and reality widens. Sometimes a straightforward message in clear and unambiguous terms is more effective. At other times, if the differences are irreconcilable, it may be better not to say anything at all and wait for a more propitious time to resume discussions or negotiations. A country can garner more respect by stating its specific agenda and national interest, rather than trying to spin the message to its intended targets.

The branding problem is more acute for brands that are "thinner." For example, Denmark has a much shallower brand than the United States, and as a result, it will sustain longer-term damage from the controversy in 2005, when one of its newspapers printed cartoons that were deemed blasphemous by the global Islamic community. Canada also has a shallower brand, and as the Upper North Side campaign demonstrated, what little coverage appeared in the American financial media in the 1990s portrayed Canada as a poor economic brand. Since Canada has fewer opportunities to get onto the global radar screen (e.g., Canadian content in film and television is often not obvious), it must worry about real and potential public relations black eyes, such as the perennial protests in Europe against the Canadian seal hunt.

Resources also have the ability to trip up any initiatives envisioned in the name of public diplomacy. While a measured expansion of Canada's current public diplomacy capability through more realistic budgets and clearer government-wide public diplomacy objectives would be welcomed with open arms, as chapter 3 showed, it is unlikely that this will occur in the absence of a major domestic crisis on national unity or a major international conflict. It is also not realistic to assume an expansion of public diplomacy resources, given that modern governments are inherently oriented to shorter-term, results-based calculations that are often anathema to long-term, resource-intensive public diplomacy, whose true outcomes may not be evident for years, if not decades. Effective public diplomacy is contingent not only on the traditional resources of time and money but also on the situation facing Canadians from the other end of the dialogue: how can Canada convince other societies to embrace the values of democracy and to pursue social justice if the basic needs of people are not being met? In short, if the French model were adopted, then cultural resources would be bundled with adequate development assistance to achieve an optimal effect – a "good" public diplomacy.[60]

Final Word: Where is Public Diplomacy Going?

Public diplomacy is at a crossroads. It will be either sidelined or embraced as the key foundation of all future diplomacy. The challenge is not about finding distribution channels (there are plenty), and it is not even about brand management (most governments, after all, have only a limited ability to change a brand representing an entire country). The fundamental challenge for a government today is to use the techniques of public diplomacy in direct service of its international policy goals, such as ensuring, say, that new generations of Muslims do not subscribe to militant ideologies. Public diplomacy will either remain in the shadows and continue to be synonymous with routine cultural diplomacy, or it will begin to "go retail" and connect with new audiences and influence countries to deal with each other in new ways.

At the centre of the new public diplomacy is the human element, which may seem anachronistic in the Information Age. What is old is new again. The attacks of 11 September 2001 spawned the Bush administration's "war on terror" and its ancillary global campaign for the hearts and minds of the Muslim world. There are, in fact, parallels between the East-West propaganda campaigns during the Cold War, which included significant people-to-people exchanges in education to reinforce the respective values of liberal capitalism and communism, and the post-9/11 campaigns to reach out to the Muslim world in order to reinforce "universal" values. The key difference between the two eras is the fragmentation in today's global communication environment. Governments can no longer rely on the broadcast mode of public diplomacy to persuade foreign populations, as they did during the Cold War. On the other hand, they can also not assume that putting information on the Internet will suffice. Instead, with the abundance of conflicting information, there must be more person-to-person contact to allow for the interpretation of this information. In retrospect, the reduction in budgets for exchange programs that developed people-to-people links (particularly in the us State Department) after the end of the Cold War was premature. It is the cumulative impact of hundreds of thousands of person-to-person connections by diplomats travelling outside capital cities into the hinterlands, of young people on government-supported working holidays who have developed a command of local languages, and of students who have decided to participate in exchange programs that will take them outside the Anglo-American and European worlds that will be the true measure of public diplomacy's ascendancy in the decades ahead.

There will be perpetual challenges, of course. How will countries balance their short-term advocacy goals with longer-term dialogue goals? These will have to be deftly managed. The new public diplomacy will see a further shift away from a reliance on government to drive public diplomacy activities, to government indirectly supporting private and third-sector organizations to develop long-term links. But this shift will not be the privatization of public diplomacy, which would be a contradiction in terms. As long as government provides guidance in support of national interests, the activities should be considered public diplomacy.

So, is boring beautiful? The consensus seems to be that Canada's stolid international image of modesty hurts more than it helps the national brand. Certainly, the argument in this book is that a country must create a buzz about itself to remain relevant. It must seize the imagination and create willing followers. Consider the similarities between Canada and California – their economies are of comparable size, their political cultures both progressive. But unlike California, there is no hype surrounding Canada, as it is modest about itself to a point of disappearing from the global eye.[61] On the other hand, a country's very boringness may engender confidence, because it is unthreatening. The question is, therefore, How can one turn Canada's "boring" quality into a soft-power capability? As this book has shown, Canada needs some help – mediation – from the government as it attempts to create a meaningful and compelling nation brand.

Projecting one's country abroad is not superfluous. It is of fundamental importance to national survival. In the end, Canada needs to adopt a more strategic, whole-of-government and whole-of-Canada approach to its public diplomacy, one that will take into account a multitude of interests such as tourism, culture, sports, export promotion, immigration, investment attraction, and the promotion of international peace and security. This approach must anticipate controversial issues, develop clear policies that are in line with Canadian interests, and ensure that certain images (e.g., the image of an environmentally friendly country) do not negate others (e.g., the image of a country that is open to foreign investment). Canada needs public diplomacy strategies that combine, in an optimum fashion, traditional and new public affairs tools and techniques.

Moreover, they need to be implemented by staff with the appropriate training, and they need to be consistent with a commonly accepted framework, one agreed to by both Ottawa and the provinces, for promoting Canada's image abroad.

Notes

PREFACE

1 Nye first developed the concept of "soft power" in *Bound to Lead: The Changing Nature of American Power* (1991). He examined the idea with co-author Robert O. Keohane in Keohane and Nye, "Power and Interdependence in the Information Age" (1998). The third edition of Keohane and Nye, *Power and Independence* (2001), provides a valuable update to their 1998 article. Nye returned again to the concept of soft power in his 2001 book, *The Paradox of American Power*. However, it was with his 2004 book, *Soft Power*, that Nye sought to answer his critics and to place the concept into a fuller context.

2 Nye, "The Challenge of Soft Power." Nye likely has a particular appreciation of Canada's soft power because he spent a sabbatical term in Ottawa at Carleton University in the 1970s.

3 For Axworthy's early views on soft power, see his "Canada and Human Security" and "A Ban for All Seasons." In a newspaper article, "Why Soft Power is the Right Policy for Canada," Axworthy responded aggressively to his critics who averred that the concept of soft power was, at best, a naïve way of thinking about how Canada could best make a contribution to the world and, at worst, a cynical means of covering up the persistent underfunding of Canada's hard assets, particularly its military. Axworthy adopts a more reflective tone on Canada's comparative advantage in the exercise of soft power in *Navigating a New World*, 74–5.

4 Department of Foreign Affairs and International Trade, *A Dialogue on Foreign Policy*, 19–20.

CHAPTER ONE

1 Castells, *The Information Age*, 21.

2 I am indebted to my colleague Alan Bowker for this observation.

3 Nye andOwen, "America's Information Edge," 20–36.

4 Ralston Saul, "Position Paper on Culture and Foreign Policy," 3.

5 Ibid.

6 Franklyn Griffiths makes this argument memorably in his treatise on culture, sovereignty, and international security: *Strong and Free*.

7 For an in-depth overview of the revolution in diplomatic affairs, see Arquilla and Ronfeldt, "What If There Is a Revolution in Diplomatic Affairs?"

8 See Arquilla and Ronfeldt, *The Emergence of Noopolitik*. The authors explain that "noosphere" is derived from the ancient Greek word *noo*, which translates into English as "knowledge."

9 A contemporary example is the impact of the United States' defeat in Vietnam on national identity, sapping Americans' sense of self-assurance, a feeling that re-asserted itself only with the overwhelming victory of Desert Storm against Saddam Hussein's Iraq in 1991.

10 A perfect illustration of this national self-identification with peaceful settlement of disputes is an episode in the *Heritage Minutes* series of educational advertisements on Canadian history that was produced with the support of the Charles R. Bronfman Foundation and of the Canadian government. In this particular spot, Superintendent Sam Steele, of the Canadian Northwest Mounted Police, the fore-runner of the Royal Canadian Mounted Police, seizes, apparently by the force of his authority in a red tunic, the firearms of an American who has wandered into Canadian territory. This ad is intended to illustrate that the Canada of the late-nineteenth century was a bastion of peace, order, and good government and that Canadians did not subscribe to the frontier mentality of the United States. The ad is startling in its simplicity, but it carries a powerful message that reinforces national self-perceptions of who Canadians are at home and, in turn, in the world.

11 The solid public support for Canada as a peacekeeper, as reported in all public opinion surveys examining attitudes toward Canada's international role, is a testa-ment, at least in part, to four decades of government-supported information cam-paigns highlighting Canada's leadership as the "inventor" of peacekeeping. Liberal prime minister Lester B. Pearson was awarded the Nobel Peace Prize in 1957 for his instrumental role in helping to defuse the 1956 Suez Crisis through the interpositioning of UN peacekeepers between the antagonists. Thereafter, Canada became strongly associated with international peacekeeping both at home and abroad. In Ottawa, a monument is dedicated to Canada's peacekeepers. Located across from the National Gallery of Canada, it is seen by millions of visitors – Canadian and non-Canadian.

12 Surveys undertaken by Pollara between 1999 and 2005 indicate that a very strong majority of Canadians support peacekeeping as a primary role for Canada's mili-

tary. Support for peacekeeping is highest in Quebec, as the province has historically been opposed to armed interventions by Canadian Forces personnel.

13 I am indebted to Alan Bowker for this observation.

14 Welsh, *At Home in the World.*

15 What other G8 nation has subjected itself to a referendum on its future as a nation
   twice in fifteen years?

16 Bowker, internal memorandum.

17 See Anholt Nation Brand Index, *How the World Sees the World.*

18 Ralston Saul, "Projecting a Middle Power Into an Imperial World."

19 Ibid.

20 Bowker, internal memorandum.

21 Ibid.

22 Ralston Saul, "Position Paper on Culture and Foreign Policy," 2–3.

23 As McComb and Shaw showed with regard to the agenda-setting role of the mass
   media, the mass media does not tell us what to think, but rather, what to think
   about. Applying this dictum to Canada, it is clear that Canada's cultural presence
   provides content for global audiences and allows them to "think about" Canada.
   Such awareness about Canada thus frames non-Canadians' perceptions when they
   "encounter" Canada for any purpose, whether for business, tourism, immigration,
   or diplomacy. See McComb and Shaw, "The Agenda-Setting Function of Mass
   Media."

24 Canada, *Royal Commission on National Development in the Arts, Letters, and Sciences,* 253.

25 The 1994 foreign policy review led to a redefinition of Canadian foreign policy on
   the basis of a three-pillar approach, i.e., security, trade, and culture. Culture as the
   third pillar meant the projection of the idea of Canada. See Canada, Department
   of Foreign Affairs and International Trade, *Canada in the World.*

26 Canada, Department of Foreign Affairs and International Trade, *Canada's International Policy Statement,* 40.

27 Greenhill, "Making a Difference?" 22.

28 See Fukuyama, *The End of History.* Fukuyama's landmark book posited the thesis
   that with the disintegration of the Soviet empire, the world was heading for a liberal democratic endpoint. Given the many vicious "little wars" since the book's
   first publication and the current global war on terror, the thesis has been challenged as being highly premature (see Huntington's "Clash of Civilizations"),
   though it is true that by 2005 there had been a substantial increase in the number
   of nation-states that could be credibly defined as liberal democratic.

29 I am indebted to Colin Robertson and Daryl Copeland who have both contributed
   substantially to this section on branding. After so many discussions, e-mails, conversations, briefing notes, and PowerPoint presentations, I cannot claim owner-
   ship of any of the ideas.

30 Cernetig, "Canada Isn't Working."

31 Cohen, *While Canada Slept.*

32 *Time* (Canadian edition), 26 May 2003.

33 "Canada's New Spirit."

34 The scholarly analysis of Canada's international decline is ably chronicled in the annual review *Canada among Nations*, published by The Norman Paterson School of International Affairs, Carleton University (Ottawa).

35 The *Economist* is influential in Canadian policy-making circles not because of its circulation in the United Kingdom, but because of its considerable influence among policy-makers in the United States. Indeed, nearly half of its 1,096,154 weekly circulation (47 percent) comes from the United States. Regional breakdowns for the circulation are available on the *Economist* website: "ABC Region Breakdowns."

36 The focus groups were conducted in San Diego, Denver, Houston, and Raleigh by MB Goldfarb Consultants for the federal government's Enhanced Representation Initiative (launched in 2003). The author received a copy of a presentation that contained findings of the focus groups.

37 The Chicago Council on Foreign Relations' regular surveys of America's attitudes towards the world have, since 1978, tested other countries' favourability ratings by asking Americans about the degree of warmth they feel toward them. These surveys show that Americans have had the warmest feelings towards Canada and Britain. Before the Iraq war, the last council survey in 2002 showed that Americans' warmth towards Britain had increased by seven percent since a similar question was asked in 1998, giving the United Kingdom the same favourability rating as Canada. See the survey *WorldViews 2002 Survey of American and European Attitudes and Public Opinion*, at www.worldviews.org/intermediate/questionnaire.html. Much to the consternation of Canadian officials, the Canadian media highlighted the reverential praise heaped on British prime minister Tony Blair by both the White House and Congress each time he made an official visit to the United States. This was in contrast to the much cooler reception accorded to Prime Minister Chrétien.

38 Leger Marketing, "Canada-US Relations." The specific question posed to Americans was, "Among the following countries (Canada, England, France, Japan, Mexico, China), which one in your opinion is USA's best friend?" Sixty-two percent of Americans felt that England was their country's best friend, compared with 20 percent who felt that this was Canada's role. The full survey is posted at www.legermarketing.com.

39 The turbot, a fish found in the deep waters off Newfoundland, was at the centre of a conflict dubbed the Turbot Wars, in which the Canadian government, out to protect its fishing zone, confronted foreign vessels that were overfishing along the

boundary of Canada's territorial waters. The crisis came to a head on 9 March 1995, when Canada fisheries officers seized the *Estai*, a ship flying the Spanish flag, after firing across its bow to make it stop. The move, which was authorized by Brian Tobin, then Canada's minister of fisheries, enraged the Spanish government and angered several European Union governments but elevated Tobin to stardom at home (he became known as Captain Canada) and had British fishermen, who had also been angered by Spanish overfishing, flying Canadian flags in support of the Canadian action. This episode was not only a diplomatic stand-off between Canada and its NATO partner, but, as revealed in James Bartleman's book *Rollercoaster*, the crisis nearly precipitated military retaliation by the Spanish government: "We were within hours of a high seas conflict." Bartleman, *Rollercoaster*, as quoted in Blizzard, "Fish Flight Left a Stench." The robust Canadian response has now entered the lore of Canada's foreign policy, because it shows an uncharacteristically self-interested side of Canada to the international community or, as Blizzard put it, "Canada, the world's No. 1 Boy Scout, became the unlikely armed aggressor in a game of gunboat diplomacy." It revealed the tough, uncompromising side of Canada to the world. See also Cooper, "Snapshot of an Emergent Cyber-Diplomacy."

40 For a greater exploration of this topic, see Nossal, "Pinchpenny Diplomacy." Denis Stairs, a long-time scholar of Canadian foreign policy and Canada-US relations, probably expressed the dissenting view in Canada the best when he stated: "I do think it likely that most Canadians would be surprised if they knew how little their country is actually doing – and is capable of doing – in real terms, relatively to how much noise it makes about its efforts in rhetorical terms." This excerpt from a speech was cited in "No Respect for Canada: The Nice-Guy Approach to Foreign Relations Makes Us Look Weak," *Ottawa Citizen*, 29 July 2003, A14.

41 In response to the outdated foreign images of Canada, Daryl Copeland, then in DFAIT's Communications Bureau, developed a proposal for an international communications framework that sought to begin the process of re-positioning Canada's "brand" abroad. The proposal advocated an overarching message, or mantra – "Canada. Cool. Connected" – that could be adapted for all regions.

42 The study, commissioned by Daryl Copeland as the DFAIT official responsible for re-thinking how Canada projected its image abroad, represented the first comprehensive examination of how Canada's image was received internationally. It validated the anecdotal evidence that suggested that the Canada brand was in need of updating.

43 York, "Canada: Nice Place.

44 In 2001, on behalf of Investment Partnerships Canada, Earnscliffe Research & Communications, working with Wirthlin Research in the United States, was asked

to conduct a qualitative assessment of American executives in Boston and Dallas to explore their attitudes towards investment in Canada. Although the executives tended to hold Canada in high regard, it was clearly not "top-of-mind" as a potential investment destination. Virtually half the executives indicated that Canada received either no consideration or only initial consideration as an investment destination. The Brand Canada Report can be accessed at www.ic.gc.ca/cmb/welcomeic.nsf/VRTF/PublicationSpecialSpeciaux/$file/March2001Wirthlin.pdf.

45 Angus Reid Group, *Canada and the World.* The Angus Reid Group is now known as Ipsos Canada, and its public affairs research branch is known as Ipsos-Reid. The survey sample consisted of 5,700 adults in twenty countries.

46 Daryl Copeland, DFAIT, personal communication.

47 I am indebted to Gaston Barban, a DFAIT official, for this observation.

48 The reference to Canada being the second-largest exporter appears on the website of Canadian Heritage and seems to be based on statistics from the mid-1990s, though there are no sources listed for this statistic. The reference appears in official government documents and is frequently cited by regulators and members of the television production community. For example, the reference was cited by a Julia Keatley, representing the Canadian Film and Television Production Association when she appeared in front of a Commons Standing Committee on Canadian Heritage in 2005. See Canada, Standing Committee on Canadian Heritage, Evidence, Thursday, 9 June 2005, 8. See also Government of Canada, Public Works and Government Services, *Canadian Heritage 2000–1 Estimates,* 4.

49 Potter, "Information Technology and Canada's Public Diplomacy," 184.

50 Canada, Treasury Board, *The Government Expenditure Plan, 2005–2006,* 17.

51 Bowker, internal memorandum (2003).

52 The most important offices for Quebec abroad are the general delegations, which offer services in the areas of economy, immigration, culture, and education. Quebec has general delegations in Brussels, London, Mexico City, New York, Paris, and Tokyo. For more details on Quebec's offices abroad, please consult the province's international relations website: Quebec, Ministère des relations internationales, *Québec in the World.*

53 For a comprehensive treatment of Quebec's international relations, see Paquin, *Histoire des relations internationales du Québec.* A major thesis of this volume is that Quebec's presence on the international stage did not start with the Quiet Revolution of the 1960s. Of particular relevance to the study of Quebec's public diplomacy are the contributions by Samy Mesli ("La coopération franco-québécoise en éducation 1965–1982"), Louise Beaudoin ("Le Québec et le combat pour la diversité culturelle"), and Nelson Michaud ("La doctrine Gérin-Lajoie").

54 Bernier, "Mulroney's International 'Beau Risque,'" 131–2.

55 Ibid., 129.

56 Simpson, "Who Speaks for Canada?"

57 Quebec, Secrétariat aux affaires intergouvernementales Canadiennes, "Open letter from Mr Benoît Pelletier."

58 Perreaux, "Quebec Move Undermines Canada.

59 According to Quebec's 2006 International Policy statement, "In 2005, the Quebec government made public its position vis-à-vis international organizations and identified five mechanisms likely to strengthen Quebec's role with regard to them: Access to all information and participation during the initial stages of negotiations toward establishing Canada's position; full member status in Canadian delegations and exclusive responsibility for designating its representative; the right to speak for itself at international forums on matters related to its responsibilities; recognition of Quebec's right to give its approval before Canada signs or declares itself bound by a treaty or agreement; the right to express its position when Canada appears before supervisory bodies of international organizations for matters involving Quebec or affecting its interests." Quebec, Ministère des relations internationales, *Québec's International Policy*, 28.

60 Ibid., chap. 5.

61 See Quebec, Ministère des relations internationales, *Rapport annuel de gestion 2004–2005*, 82.

62 Personal communication from Troy Machan, director of international marketing, NAFTA and EU regions, Marketing, Investment and Trade Division, British Columbia Ministry of Economic Development, 27 August 2007.

63 Kunczik, *Images of Nations and Intenational Public Relations*, 107. Kunczik refers to research by Donsbach, *Medienwirkung trotz Selektion*.

64 Before it joined the European Union and started to benefit from regional development funds, Ireland was portrayed in the international media as poor and underdeveloped in comparison to the rest of Western Europe. The Ireland that emerged in the 1980s and 1990s received considerable and mostly positive (and sometimes fawning) international media coverage as the "Irish Miracle," in reference to the overwhelmingly predominant role played by the Catholic Church in Irish history.

65 Ralston Saul, *Projecting a Middle Power into an Imperial World*.

66 Ibid.

67 I am indebted to Tim Martin from DFAIT for this observation.

CHAPTER TWO

1 For a useful summary of the history of American public diplomacy, see Nelles, "American Public Diplomacy as Pseudo-Education."

2 Tuch offers an excellent survey of slightly different definitions of public diplomacy,
   although all agree that for public diplomacy to exist it must be projected outside a
   country's borders by an official body. Tuch, *Communicating with the World*, 3.
3 Kunczik, *Images of Nations and International Public Relations*, 12.
4 Malone, *Political Advocacy and Cultural Communications*, 12.
5 Sorrell, "Branding, Relevance, Diplomacy."
6 This is the definition used by the US Advisory Commission on Public Diplomacy,
   United States Information Agency Alumni Association, "Public Diplomacy
   Defined."
7 Wilcox et al., *Essentials of Public Relations*, 283.
8 Gotlieb, "*I'll Be With You in a Minute, Mr. Ambassador.*"
9 Gregory, "Not Your Grandparents' Public Diplomacy."
10 Australian Government, Department of Foreign Affairs and Trade, *Public Diplomacy Handbook.*
11 Ralston Saul, *Culture and Canadian Foreign Policy*, 3–4.
12 Fulton, *Diplomacy in the Information Age*; Carlucci et al., *Equipped for the Future.*
13 Council on Foreign Relations, *Public Diplomacy.*
14 See US Department of State, *Cultural Diplomacy.* See also Kaniss, "Public Diplomacy in a Changing World." These two volumes contain the most complete bibli-
   ography of American sources on public diplomacy. For a British perspective, see
   Leonard, Small, and Rose, *British Public Diplomacy.*
15 Nye, *Bound to Lead.* For references to "prestige," see chapter 6 on "The Struggle
   for Power: Policy of Prestige," and part 5, on world public opinion, in
   Morgenthau, *Politics Among Nations*, and Holsti, *International Politics.*
16 Keohane and Nye identify three characteristics of "complex interdependence":
   multiple channels of contact among society, lack of clear hierarchies of issues, and
   irrelevance of military force. See their *Power and Interdependence* (1977) and *Power
   and Interdependence* (2000).
17 For a selection of readings, see Cull, *American Propaganda and Public Diplomacy*;
   Melissen, *New Public Diplomacy*; Leonard, *Public Diplomacy*; Leonard, "Diplomacy by
   Other Means"; Leonard, *Going Public* and Arquilla and Ronfeldt, "What If There Is
   a Revolution in Diplomatic Affairs?"
18 For a broad overview of the topic of international communications, see Professor
   Phil Taylor's website at the Institute of Communications Studies, University of
   Leeds. UK Available at http://ics.leeds.ac.uk/papers/index.cfm?outfit=pmt
   [August 2006].
19 For a selection of readings, see Cull, *Selling War*; Snow, *Information War.*
20 For a selection of readings, see Kamalipour and Snow, *War, Media, and Propaganda*; Payne, "The Media as an Instrument of War"; Thussu and Freedman, *War
   and the Media.*

21 For a selection of readings, see Arquilla and Ronfeldt, *The Emergence of Noopolitik*; Molander, Riddile, and Wilson, *Strategic Information Warfare.*

22 For a selection of readings, see Deibert, *Parchment, Printing and Hypermedia*; Rawnsley, *Radio Diplomacy and Propaganda*; Mowlama, *Global Information and World Communication.*

23 For a selection of readings, see Dizard, *Digital Diplomacy*; Thussu, *International Communication*; Kamalipour, *Global Communication*; Rosenau and Singh, *Information Technologies and Global Politics.*

24 For a selection of readings, see Rampal, "Global News and Information Flow in an Internet Age"; Emtman, *Projections of Power.*

25 For a selection of readings, see Arndt, *The First Resort of Kings*; Ninkovich, "US Information Policy and Cultural Diplomacy"; Finn, "The Case for Cultural Diplomacy.

26 Gilboa, "The CNN Effect"; Gilboa, "Media and International Conflict"; Gilboa, "Effects of Global Television News on US Policy in International Conflict"; Gilboa, "Diplomacy in the Media Age."

27 Taylor, *Global Communications, International Affairs and the Media since 1945.* See also Cowan and Cull, *Public Diplomacy in a Changing World.*

28 Consult the *Journal of Brand Management* (9, no. 4/5, April 2002) for a wide range of nation branding discussions. These include Morgan, Pritchard, and Piggott, "New Zealand, 100% Pure"; and Lodge, "Success and Failure."

29 See M. Laroche, et al., "The Influence of Country Image Structure on Consumer Evaluations of Foreign Products."

30 Anholt, *Competitive Identity.*

31 L'Etang and Pieczka, *Critical Perspectives in Public Relations.*

32 Signitzer and Coombs, "Public Relations and Public Diplomacy."

33 Grunig and Hunt, *Managing Public Relations.*

34 Peisert, *Die auswärtige Kulturpolitik der Bundesrepublik Deutschland.*

35 Signitzer and Coombs, "Public Relations and Public Diplomacy," 140.

36 Geert Hofstede, *Cultures Consequences.*

37 Leonard, *Going Public.*

38 Signitzer and Coombs, "Public Relations and Public Diplomacy."

39 For a selection of scholarly work on Canadian public diplomacy, see Hubert, "The Landmine Ban"; Cameron, Lawson, and Tomlin, *To Walk without Fear*; Hay, "International Summits and Civil Society"; Price, "Reversing the Gun Sights"; Potter, "Information Technology and Canada's Public Diplomacy."

40 Graham, "Third Pillar or Fifth Wheel?"; Bélanger, "Redefining Cultural Diplomacy"; Bélanger, "Globalization, Culture, and Foreign Policy"; Jackson and Lemieux, "The Arts and Canada's Cultural Policy."

41 I am indebted to Colin Robertson, consul general of Canada (Los Angeles), for this observation.

42 Castells, *The Rise of the Network Society.*

43 Green, "Present and Future Public Diplomacy."

44 Bollier, "The Rise of Netpolitik."

45 Bollier citing Shanthi Kalthil, in "The Rise of Netpolitik" 21.

46 For an in-depth study of this phenomenon, see Florida, *The Rise of the Creative Class.*

47 The above paragraph draws from internal DFAIT documentation. I am indebted to colleagues from the International Cultural Relations Bureau for making this available to me.

48 Nye, *Soft Power*, 3

49 Anholt, "Introduction to Special Issue on Nation Branding."

50 Hocking, conference lecture.

51 Nye, *Soft Power*, 32.

52 Ibid., 106.

53 Gregory, "Not Your Grandparents' Public Diplomacy."

54 Ibid.

55 Leonard, *Public Diplomacy*; and Leonard, "Diplomacy by Other Means."

56 Gregory, "Not Your Grandparents' Public Diplomacy."

57 Gotlieb, "Martin's Bush-League Diplomacy."

58 Department of Foreign Affairs and International Trade Canada, "Formative Evaluation of the US Enhanced Representation Initiative."

59 Gotlieb, "Martin's Bush-League Diplomacy."

60 Gregory, "Not Your Grandparents' Public Diplomacy."

61 Ibid.

62 Louis Bélanger argues with some merit that the international movement to promote cultural diversity, of which Canada and France are the leaders, is rendering obsolete the notion that cultural diplomacy is simply about a foreign ministry or a national cultural agency projecting or legitimating its national culture (as opposed to encouraging reciprocal access). For this reason, he believes that it is no longer appropriate to conceptualize cultural diplomacy as being the exclusive purview of foreign ministries and, therefore, that it is by definition a subset of broader public diplomacy. Bélanger, "Cultural Diplomacy and Public Diplomacy as Dialogical Statecraft."

63 I am grateful to my colleague Robin Higham for this observation.

64 See Rose and Wadham-Smith, *Mutuality, Trust and Cultural Relations.*

65 Stephens, "Public Diplomacy in the 21st Century," 7.

66 Nye, *Soft Power.*

67 Ibid., 16.

68 Gregory, "Not Your Grandparents' Public Diplomacy."

69 See Hawes, *Sport and Canadian Diplomacy.*

70 Higham, "Canada, Super Star."

71 Hocking, "Public Diplomacy in the New International Security Environment."

72 These sentiments are outlined by Jozef Bátora in the only scholarly work on the domestic roots of public diplomacy. See Bátora, "Public Diplomacy between Home and Abroad." 78–9.

73 Nossal, "The Democratization of Canadian Foreign Policy."

74 I am indebted to Roman Waschuk of DFAIT's Policy Planning Division for this point.

75 Bensimon-Byrne, "Canadian Pride: Lessons from Molson Canadian Advertising."

76 Canada, Speech from the Throne, 1991.

77 The Canadian group Nickelback achieved a milestone in October 2005 when it reached the number one position on Billboard's ranking of the top two hundred albums. This was only the second time a Canadian rock band had achieved this distinction in over thirty years.

78 I am indebted to Dr Biljana Scott for making this observation at a panel, "Calling '9/11': The New Diplomacy in the War on Terror," at the Annual Meeting of the 46th International Studies Association, Hawaii, 2005.

79 For an excellent overview of propaganda and its effects, see Jowett and O'Donnell, *Propaganda and Persuasion.*

80 Copeland, "Public Diplomacy and Branding."

81 Gerth, "Military's Information War Is Vast."

82 On applying Grunig's four models of public relations to public diplomacy, see Signitzer and Coombs, "Public Relations and Public Diplomacy."

83 See Kotler and Gertner, "Country as Brand, Product, and Beyond."

84 Anholt, "Introduction to Special Issue on Nation Branding."

85 Ibid.

86 The Team Canada trips were high-visibility missions, with the Canadian prime minister, as *primus inter pares*, leading a Canadian delegation consisting of the minister for international trade, provincial premiers and territorial government leaders, and hundreds of Canadian business people to different priority markets.

87 Stephens, "Public Diplomacy in the 21st Century."

88 Gilboa, "The CNN Effect," 37.

89 The *Convention on the Protection of the Diversity of Cultural Expressions* is a UNESCO document adopted at the group's October 2004 conference. Canada was the first state to ratify the convention in 2005. Diversity provides credibility to Canada that other states lack, marking it as a key feature of Canada's international image.

90 See Friedman, *The World Is Flat.*

91 Lampert, "London, Sydney Exciting ."

92 Hocking, conference lecture, "Public Diplomacy in the New International Security Environment."

93 Braudel, *On History*, 25–55.
94 Hennessey, "The Role of the Foreign Ministry."
95 Leonard, *Public Diplomacy* .
96 I am indebted to Daryl Copeland, a senior official at DFAIT, for his synthesis of the prevailing criticisms of public diplomacy as practised in the Anglo-American countries.
97 Djerejian, *Changing Minds, Winning Peace*, 65.
98 Daryl Copeland, DFAIT, personal communication, 14 February 2006.
99 Van Ham, "The Rise of the Brand State," 3.
100 Ibid.
101 Ibid.
102 Ibid.

CHAPTER THREE

1 Chandler, "Selling the Prairie Good Life," 26.
2 Ibid., 30.
3 Evans, *John Grierson and the National Film Board.* 16.
4 Ibid., 17.
5 Ibid.
6 Ibid., 18.
7 Ibid., 19.
8 Ibid., 51–4.
9 Ibid., 56.
10 Ibid., 58. See also Cull, "Reluctant Persuaders."
11 Ibid.
12 Ibid., 61.
13 Ibid., 83.
14 Ibid., 88, 89.
15 Ibid., 113.
16 Ibid., 89.
17 Stephens, *Study of Canadian Government Information Abroad*, chap. 1, 8.
18 Evans, *John Grierson and the National Film Board*, 84.
19 Ibid., 104–5.
20 Ibid., 167.
21 Ibid., 167–8.
22 Ibid., 223.
23 Stephens, *Study of Canadian Government Information Abroad*, chap. 1, 10.
24 Evans, *John Grierson and the National Film Board*, 224–5.
25 Ibid., 261.

26 Siegel, *Radio Canada International*, 1, 3.

27 Ibid., 81.

28 Ibid., 5.

29 Ibid., 91, 96.

30 Stephens, S*tudy of Canadian Government Information Abroad*, chap. 2, 9.

31 Hilliker and Barry, *Canada's Department of External Affairs*, Vol. 2, 11.

32 For a history of the department, see Hill, *Canada's Salesman to the World*, 44–5, 72–3.

33 Siegel, *Radio Canada International*, 9–35.

34 Stephens, *Study of Canadian Government Information Abroad*, chap. 3, 13.

35 Ibid., chap. 9, 2–5.

36 See Joyal, *Refocussing Canada's International Cultural Policy.*

37 Ibid., chap, 4, 27.

38 Ibid., chap. 5, 17.

39 Ibid., chap. 5, 25.

40 Ibid., chap. 5, 26.

41 Halloran, "Cultural Diplomacy in the Trudeau Era," 3.

42 In 1954, the Canadian Institute was opened in Rome. Joyal, *Refocussing Canada's International Cultural Policy*, annex 3, 1.

43 Stephens, *Study of Canadian Government Information Abroad*, chap. 7, 50.

44 Ibid., chap. 7, 3.

45 Ibid., chap. 7, 23.

46 Ibid., chap. 7, 42.

47 Ibid., chap. 8, 1–2.

48 Halloran, *Cultural Diplomacy in the Trudeau Era*, 4.

49 Ibid.

50 Stephens, *Study of Canadian Government Information Abroad*, chap. 9, 12.

51 Ibid.

52 Ibid., chap. 9, 12–14.

53 Ibid., chap. 9, 21.

54 Halloran, *Cultural Diplomacy in the Trudeau Era*, 2–5.

55 Stephens, *Study of Canadian Government Information*, chap. 10, 6–7.

56 Ibid., chap. 10, 36.

57 Ibid., chap. 11, 2.

58 Ibid., chap. 11, 3.

59 Ibid., chap. 11, 10.

60 Sharp, "Canada-US Relations."

61 Halloran, *Cultural Diplomacy in the Trudeau Era*, 6.

62 Ibid.

63 Ibid., 22.

64 Macintosh and Hawes, *Sport and Canadian Diplomacy*, 3.
65 Ibid., 4.
66 Ibid., 5.
67 Ibid., 12.
68 Ibid., 16. It cannot be said that all the Canadian hockey players contributed to this "peacekeeper" image, as several Canadian players, including Bobby Clarke, were known more for their aggressive style of play than their gentlemanly conduct on the ice.

CHAPTER FOUR

1 US Department of State, *Cultural Diplomacy*, 4.
2 Ralston Saul, *Culture and Canadian Foreign Policy*, 2–3. For an excellent overview of Canada's cultural face to the world, see Andrew Holman and Robert Thacker, "Literary and Popular Culture," in Patrick James and Mark Kasoff, eds., *Canadian Studies in the New Millenium* (Toronto: University of Toronto Press 2007).
3 US Department of State, *Cultural Diplomacy*, 1.
4 I distinguish between the mass public, which may be only intermittently engaged in public policy debate; the attentive public, the members of which are regular consumers of news; and opinion-formers, who are recognized as experts or are representatives of industry, the public sector, or civil society or who are journalists themselves (particularly columnists or editorial writers).
5 See Canada, Treasury Board of Canada Secretariat, The Communications Policy of the Government of Canada. The report notes that "the government has a duty to explain is policies and decisions, and to inform the public of its priorities for the country." The policy took effect 29 November 2004.
6 Australia has also received the same fate in the global media, although the animals are usually different – sharks and crocodiles.
7 Ralston Saul, "Culture and Canadian Foreign Policy," 43–4.
8 Ibid., 44.
9 Governments can exercise a higher degree of indirect control because of their subsidization of the arts domestically, which in effect determines their influence abroad.
10 I am indebted to Robin Higham for this observation.
11 Joyal, *Refocussing Canada's International Cultural Policy*, 21.
12 Hillmer, "A Border People."
13 The decision to adopt cultural practices as the third pillar within the 1995 foreign policy review is likely the result of the Chartrand Study, in which a comparative analysis of the international cultural policies of fourteen states was conducted – with Canada ranking significantly below the others in terms of spending. See Chartrand, "International Cultural Affairs."

14 A senior Canadian official has suggested that one reason the budget cuts have affected cultural (and academic) programs is that they fall under the "Vote 10," allotment as set out in the government's principal estimates. Vote 10 money is given to the grant programs where the recipient organizations are clearly identified. Essentially, it becomes easier for officials to cut Vote 10 money than operations money (such as salaries and pensions).

15 Cultural Human Resources Council, *Export Marketing Competency Profile 2003*, 5.

16 Curtis Barlow, personal interview with Evan Potter, 11 July 2006, Ottawa.

17 It is important to distinguish the different roles played by Canadian Heritage, through Trade Routes, and by the Canada Council for the Arts. Canadian Heritage is mandated to create markets for the Canadian arts and culture sector abroad, whereas the Canada Council's role is focused on supporting the creation and production of "works of merit" across the range of the arts.

18 Ralston Saul, "Culture and Canadian Foreign Policy," 38.

19 Ibid.

20 Ibid.

21 Renetta Siemens, personal interview with Evan Potter, 11 July 2006, Ottawa.

22 Ralston Saul, "Culture and Canadian Foreign Policy," 39.

23 Both were slated to be closed as a result of 1993 budget cuts (coincidentally, major renovations were needed on Canada House in London at the time), but the decision to close the centres was reversed by the Canadian Senate.

24 Tuch, *Communicating with the World*, 69.

25 Ralston Saul, "Projecting a Middle Power into an Imperial World."

26 See Canada, Office of the Governor General, *Role and Responsibilities of the Governor General.*

27 Ralston Saul, "Projecting a Middle Power into an Imperial World."

28 Curtis Barlow, personal interview with Evan Potter, 11 July 2006, Ottawa. It was the governor general's role in the early twentieth century to negotiate land treaties. While that power was subsequently divested from the governor general to the Canadian government, the Office of the Governor General continues to vigorously promote the achievements of Canada's Aboriginal peoples at home and abroad.

29 Editorial, *Ottawa Citizen* (5 February 2001), as quoted in Ralston Saul, "Projecting a Middle Power into an Imperial World."

30 Ralston Saul, "Projecting a Middle Power Into an Imperial World."

31 Mills, "Well Done Madame," *National Post* (26 October 2001), A15, as quoted in Ralston Saul, "Projecting a Middle Power into an Imperial World."

32 Confidential interview with senior Canadian official (July 2006), Ottawa.

33 Ralston Saul, "Projecting a Middle Power into an Imperial World."

34 In 2000, this author was witness to a telling example of this stereotype of Canadian diffidence as seen through foreign eyes when he viewed a focus group of
Americans in San Diego talking about Canada's image in the United States. When
the moderator from Toronto's Goldfarb Associates described Canada's
well-respected system of public universities, a number of the focus group members
expressed their surprise at not being more aware of these educational opportunities. They concluded that Canada had to be more aggressive in marketing itself.
Of course, the very same cultural trait – perceived Canadian modesty – that is seen
as a weakness can also be seen by non-Americans around the world as a strength,
since it is the antithesis of the "hard-sell American" stereotype.

35 As part of the effort to prevent existing Russian military hardware from posing an
environmental threat after the Cold War, many of the NATO-bloc states have contributed large amounts of money to safely dismantle decommissioned nuclear
submarines, missile warheads, and the like. This Can$100 million contribution is
solely for the purpose of dismantling submarines from Russia's Barents Sea fleet.
See Canada, Foreign Affairs and International Trade, "Dismantlement of Nuclear
Submarines."

36 Ralston Saul, "Projecting a Middle Power into an Imperial World."

37 Confidential interview with senior Canadian official (July 2006), Ottawa.

38 Ralston Saul, "Projecting a Middle Power into an Imperial World."

39 Ibid.

40 Ibid.

41 An example of the intangible benefits of such trips was given by Madame Clarkson
when she was quoted by Michael Posner as saying: "The circumpolar trip was
extremely valuable to us. I just had a farewell note from President [Vladimir]
Putin – that's not name-dropping – and he said, 'I hope you understand that your
visit was the turning point in Russia-Canada relations.'" Posner, "Adrienne Clarkson: Take 65."

42 Ralston Saul, "Projecting a Middle Power into an Imperial World."

43 Cordoba Serrano, "Transferts culturels Espagne-Canada." 33–4.

44 Ibid., 34.

45 Von Flotow, "Telling Canada's Story in German."

46 Ibid.

47 Leonard Cohen reads the English translation of his foreword in the 2005 documentary, *Leonard Cohen: I'm Your Man.*

48 Von Flotow, "Telling Canada's Story in German," 24–5.

49 Ralston Saul, "Culture and Canadian Foreign Policy," 61.

50 Canadian Heritage, "Canadians Are Invited to Join Their Country's Participation
in Expo 2005."

51 Mason, "The Year the World Discovered BC."

52 Ibid.

53 This money came from Canadian Heritage's International Expositions Program budget.

54 Senior Canadian official, personal interview with Evan Potter, 4 August 2006, Ottawa.

55 Curtis, "Cirque du Soleil."

56 Ibid.

57 Ralston Saul, "Culture and Canadian Foreign Policy," 72–3.

58 Ibid., 73.

59 Senior Canadian official, personal interview with Evan Potter, 11 July 2006, Ottawa.

60 Ibid.

61 The May 2006 federal budget under the Conservative government of Prime Minister Stephen Harper included a two-year increase of $50 million in the council's funding beyond its regular Parliamentary appropriation. The total council support for international activities, including an array of programs such as travel grants for writers, artists, musicians, and production grants totalled Can$12.4 million.

62 Making a worthwhile investment with DFAIT funding is not restricted to touring groups, as it can also play an influential role in assisting Canadian visual artists domestically. Funding allows Canadian conferences and festivals to invite international buyers to come to Canada to view Canadian art, creating potentially huge business transactions.

63 Senior Canadian official, personal interview with Evan Potter, 11 July 2006, Ottawa.

64 Ibid.

65 Canadian official, personal interview with Evan Potter, 18 July 2006, Ottawa.

66 Ibid.

67 Communication by Senior Canadian official made available to Evan Potter (December 2005).

68 Communication by Senior Canadian official made available to Evan Potter (December 2005).

69 Communication by senior Canadian official made available to Evan Potter (December 2005).

70 Ebert, "Why Is Festival So Big?"

71 Australian Tourism Commission, "Australian Tourism Commission Olympic Games Strategy."

72 "Net Wealth: The Global Economic Impact of the World Cup."

73 Bellos, Futebol.

74 Ibid.

75 When Salé and Pelletier appeared as guests on *The Tonight Show with Jay Leno* on
    18 February 2002, after receiving the gold medal, Leno described their deport-
    ment in the midst of the worldwide media hoopla as "classy."
76 Loat, "Canada Is Where Canadians Are," 38.
77 Senior Canadian official, personal interview with Evan Potter, 11 July 2006,
    Ottawa.
78 Ralston Saul, "Culture and Canadian Foreign Policy," 45.
79 Brock, "The Possibilities of and Limits to Public Diplomacy."
80 Ralston Saul, "Culture and Canadian Foreign Policy," 94.
81 Ibid., 95.
82 Bélanger, "Cultural Diplomacy and Public Diplomacy as Dialogical Statecraft."
83 Senior Canadian official, personal interview with Evan Potter, 11 July 2006,
    Ottawa.
84 Barlow, personal interview with Evan Potter, 11 July 2006, Ottawa.

CHAPTER FIVE

1 Association of Universities and Colleges of Canada, *Canadian Excellence in and for
   the World*.
2 International Council for Canadian Studies, "A Brief Overview."
3 International Council for Canadian Studies, "Scholarly Journals."
4 Previously, any academic research on Canada was conducted by individual scholars with an interest in Canada, and any institutional interest was housed in Commonwealth Studies programs, such as that at Duke University, which opened in
   1955.
5 Nossal, "Painting the Map with Maple Leaves."
6 Duncan Edmonds reports that the purpose of the National Resource Centre and
   Foreign Language and Areas Studies Fellowships Program is to train specialists in
   foreign languages and area studies. The total funding for Canadian studies from
   the Department of Education is just over US$400,000 (Can$420,320). Edmonds,
   Creating Vital Linkages, 16.
7 Building understanding is a two-way street. Not only do Americans need greater
   exposure to Canada, but Canadians also need a deeper understanding of American society – beyond what they receive on a daily basis through the mass media.
   Given the United States' role as Canada's most important diplomatic partner, it is
   paradoxical that so little attention is paid to that country on Canadian campuses.
   Even accounting for the relative size differential, there are far fewer courses on
   the United States offered by Canadian universities than there are courses on Canada offered by American colleges and universities. The imbalance can also be
   illustrated by noting that only a handful of Canada Research Chairs are devoted to

the study of the United States, while many more are devoted to the study of China.

8 Edmonds, *Creating Vital Linkages*, 15.

9 See Adams, *Fire and Ice*.

10 Edmonds, *Creating Vital Linkages*, 10.

11 As quoted in Nossal, "Painting the Map with Maple Leaves."

12 A description of the Enhanced Representation Initiative can be found at www.tbs-sct.gc.ca/rma/eppi-ibdrp/hrdb-rhbd/eri-ireu/description_e.asp [April 2006].

13 Edmonds, *Creating Vital Linkages*, 34.

14 Ibid., 4.

15 Ibid., 5.

16 Archibald, "Canadian Studies Programs."

17 Edmonds, *Creating Vital Linkages*, 19.

18 Ibid., 24.

19 Ibid., 22.

20 Archibald, "Canadian Studies Programs."

21 Jean Labrie, personal interview with Evan Potter, July 2006, Ottawa.

22 Each time there is an international forum and people are speaking about the common programs, they often thank Canada for the academic freedom. They tell diplomats that this gives them credibility with their own governments, and their own institutions; people can honestly say that, yes, they receive grants from the Canadian government, but that there are no strings attached.

23 Dion's book was published in French as *Le pari de la franchise: Discours et écrits sur l'unité canadienne*, and in English as *Straight Talk: Speeches and Writings on Canadian Unity*. (Montreal: McGill-Queen's University Press 1999). It was published in Spanish (translated by Maria Dolores Torres Paris) as *La Politica de la claridad: discursos y escritos sobre la unidad canadiense*. (Madrid: Alanza Editorial, S.A. 2005).

24 Nossal, "Painting the Map with Maple Leaves."

25 Commonwealth Scholarship and Fellowship Plan, *Directory of Commonwealth Scholars and Fellows 1960–2002*, ix. Award holders are typically expected to return to their home countries as part of the terms of the scholarship.

26 Ibid.

27 For a comprehensive list of award programs – federal, provincial, and non-governmental – for international students and young scholars to study in Canada, see Canadian Bureau for International Education, *Awards for Study in Canada*. It should be noted that a small number of private foundations, such as the Pierre Elliott Trudeau Foundation, the Rotary Foundation, and the J. Armand Bombardier Foundation, also provide scholarships for non-Canadians to study in Canada.

28 Canada's research councils include the Natural Sciences and Engineering Research Council of Canada, the National Research Council of Canada, and the Canadian Institutes of Health Research.

29 Canada-US Fulbright Program, *Mission Statement.*

30 Ibid.

31 Interview with Michael Hawes, the executive director of the Canada-US Fulbright Program.

32 Edmonds, *Creating Vital Linkages,* 33. More recently, since 2005 the Canada-US Fulbright program has focused its attention on expanding American Studies programs at Canadian universities. In May 2005, the Canada-US Fulbright Program held the conference The Current State and Future Prospects for US Studies in Canada, in Montreal, with the purpose of establishing a National Strategy to build capacity in this area. Over 140 representatives from research institutes, Canadian universities, the private sector, NGOs, and the governments of the United States and Canada were invited to reflect on "the current state and future prospects for US studies in Canada." As of 2005, there was only one dedicated American Studies centre in Canada, although Canadian universities had many individual courses that focused on the United States. Canada, US Fulbright Program, *News & Events.*

33 Canada-US Fulbright Program, *Canada-US Fulbright Research Chairs Program.*

34 Edmonds, *Creating Vital Linkages,* 32.

35 The Canada Institute, founded in 2001, holds events, issues publications, and hosts a variety of scholars on policy issues related to Canada. The Institute also co-sponsors an annual visiting chair for Canada-US relations, in collaboration with the Fulbright Program, bringing a top academic to the center for a four-month research term. Edmonds, *Creating Vital Linkages,* 18.

36 The historical background information on the Commonwealth scholarships, as well as the number of total and annual recipients are found in the Commonwealth Scholarship and Fellowship Plan, *Directory of Commonwealth Scholars and Fellows,* vii.

37 Ibid.

38 Ibid.

39 The information on the program was obtained from Canada, Canadian International Development Agency, *Programme canadien des bourses de la Francophonie.*

40 I am indebted to a senior DFAIT official for this point, Confidential interview, July 2006.

41 For a complete program description, see http://www.hrsdc.gc.ca/en/gateways/nav/top_nav/program/iam.shtml [accessed July 2006].

42 The maximum HRSDC project support for each project is up to $160,000 under the North American Program and up to $200,000 under the Canada-EU Program, which is shared among the Canadian partner institutions. In 2005, projects under

the Canada-EU program had titles such as Developing International Competence in Health Care, which allowed participating students (29) from Canada (Dalhousie University and the Community College of New Brunswick), INHOLLAND University, London South Bank University, and the Europese Hogeschool Brussel to acquire an understanding of the impact of culture on the provision of health care.

43 Joyal, *Refocussing Canada's International Cultural Policy*, 37.

44 Huikang, "Let's Witness a Bright Future of China-Canada Relations."

45 Ralston Saul, "Culture and Canadian Foreign Policy," 54.

46 The programs include the Working Holiday Program, the swap Working Holiday program, the Young Workers' Exchange Program, and the Co-Op Education program. The Working Holiday and the swap Working Holiday (run by the Canadian Federation of Students) are the most popular, probably because they do not require Canadians to have a guarantee of a job in advance of travelling to the participating foreign countries.

47 Johne, "Doors Open for Young Workers."

48 Some exchanges are based on bilateral memoranda of understanding; others happen without any formal documents. The Australia-Canada exchange is done on an informal basis without any negotiated agreements.

49 Canadian officials report that by promoting the programs once a year, they have increased participation by 9 percent annually.

50 See the YPI website: Canada, Department of Foreign Affairs and International Trade, *Young Professionals International.*

51 Ibid.

52 Canada, Department of Foreign Affairs and International Trade, *Young Professionals International: Connect and Contribute.*

53 See IYIP website: Canada, Canadian International Development Agency, *International Youth Internship Program.*

54 Canada, Privy Council Office, "Prime Minister Announces Co-chairs."

55 The Australians have pledged $1.4 billion Australian dollars to this endeavour; in Canadian dollars (as of 9 August 2006), this was equal to Can $1.2 billion. Australian Government, "Australian Scholarships: Frequently Asked Questions."

56 It is estimated that on average, each foreign undergraduate student spends Can$30,000 in Canada per year. This estimate is based on an undergraduate student in a general arts program. Given the higher tuition fees for professional programs such as law, business, or medicine, foreign students pursuing postgraduate studies in Canada would contribute more than $30,000 per year. The number of foreign students – secondary or less, trade, university, other post-secondary – doubled between 1996 and 2005. As of December 2005, according to Statistics Canada, there were 154,000 foreign students in Canada (of whom 82,000 were at

university). Recruitment of foreign students has been on the upswing since the early 1990s; some three hundred offices in Canada's publicly funded universities, colleges, and CEGEPs target students from abroad. This does not include the burgeoning market of private language schools and private career colleges.

57 McGregor, "Student Visa Program ."

58 Joyal, *Refocussing Canada's International Cultural Policy*, 34.

59 Knight, *Progress and Promise*, 62.

60 In 2006, Australian Education International's network of dedicated posts consisted of five posts in the Americas, two posts in Europe (Brussels and Paris) and, significantly, nineteen posts in Asia. For a good articulation of the Australian model of gaining advantage from the internationalization of education, see Nelson, "Australian Government, Engaging the World through Education."

61 Joyal, *Refocussing Canada's International Cultural Policy*, 36.

62 Historically, Quebec has been the most active province in pursuing international academic relations. Education is a major component of its international policy objectives. Indeed, a key priority in Quebec's 2005 International Policy is to "Make knowledge, innovation and education core elements of international initiatives." There are five initiatives cited under this priority: "1) Increase funding allotted to international research partnership development and to attract foreign researchers; 2) Intensify and better coordinate the international promotion of Quebec's educational opportunities; 3) Restructure tuition exemption scholarship programs for foreign students to attract more candidates to university postgraduate programs and a greater number of students to college-level technical training programs; 4) Develop an integrated public sector offer with regard to educational services in order to support reforms and the development of education systems, with special emphasis on emerging economies; 5) Expand international internship opportunities for young people and increase support for youth entrepreneurship projects abroad." Quebec, Ministère des relations internationales, Quebec's International Policy, 63. The Quebec government actively pursues greater academic mobility, international research partnerships, and student exchanges, including increasing the number of foreign students who study in Quebec (21,000 foreign students in Quebec in 2004). Quebec, Ministère des relations internationales, Rapport annuel de gestion 2004–2005, 26; and Quebec, Ministère des relations internationales, Quebec's International Policy , 57.

63 Personal interview with DFAIT official in International Academic Relations division, 22 March 2002.

64 The figures for foreign students are approximations, since not all students identify themselves. For instance, foreigners may state the official purpose of a visit to Canada as being a vacation and then use their stays to take courses. For this

reason, the total number of foreign students identified by Statistics Canada (tabulated from E311 forms – the Customs Declarations Card – completed by persons entering Canada at border points) does not match the total number of foreign students holding study permits as calculated by Citizenship and Immigration Canada.

65 The total cost to the government of Canada in the first five years of operation was estimated to be $16 million, with CIDA absorbing the bulk of the government's cash contribution and DFAIT providing mostly an in-kind contribution by having the CEC's co-located in certain Canadian embassies. The contribution agreement with the federal government was based on the partial recovery of the centres' operating costs using subscription and service fees collected from educational institutions. See Canada, Foreign Affairs and International Trade, *Evaluation of the Canadian Education Centres Network*. According to the CECN's annual financial statements, CIDA and DFAIT contributed $7,956,380 between 2000 and 2005.

66 Curiously, at the time of writing (2006), there was only one CEC office in Europe, located in Norway.

67 In 2008, the Canadian government introduced open and longer work permits to make Canada a destination of choice for international students.

68 Commonwealth Scholarship and Fellowship Plan, *Directory of Commonwealth Scholars and Fellows*. This directory is the first formal attempt to track some 22,000 individuals who have received awards under the plan. DFAIT made a valuable financial contribution to the directory, as did the Foreign and Commonwealth Office and the Commonwealth Scholarship Commission in the United Kingdom.

69 See website for scholarship alumni at www.scholarships.gc.ca/alumni-en.html. Alumni of the Canadian Commonwealth Scholarship Program, the Government of Canada Awards Program, and the Canada-China Scholars' Exchange Program are encouraged to complete an online questionnaire that is designed as an evaluation tool for the scholarships program. This website does not offer an opportunity for alumni to get in touch with each other, however.

70 Ralston Saul, "Projecting a Middle Power into an Imperial World."

71 Ibid.

72 Based on the Can$1.8 billion annual budget. See Canada, Treasury Board of Canada, *Part I – The Governmental Expenditure Plan, 2005–2006 Estimates*, 17.

CHAPTER SIX

1 Price, *Media and Sovereignty*. See especially chapter 8, "Public Diplomacy and the Transformation of International Broadcasting."

2 Potter, "Information Technology and Canada's Public Diplomacy"; Siegel, *Radio Canada International*.

3 This section on Canada's international broadcasting is adapted from a more detailed description and analysis in Potter, "Information Technology and Canada's Public Diplomacy."

4 After the attacks of 11 September 2001, in stark contrast to American and British discussions of their respective international broadcasting strategies and institutions, Canada made only a vague reference to radio in *Canada's International Policy Statement*, but did not refer directly to Radio Canada International.

5 Price, *Media and Sovereignty*, 200.

6 The daily editorials on the Voice of America are edited and approved, although the remainder of its entertainment and public affairs programming is not.

7 Al-Jazeera was developed with a sizeable financial grant from the Emir of Qatar. It was openly acknowledged by Al-Jazeera journalists that despite their significant room to maneuver journalistically (significantly more so than other media outlets in the Arab world), there were still topics that were off limits for public discussion.

8 Price, *Media and Sovereignty*, 201.

9 Ibid.

10 The International Broadcasting Bureau in Washington is an independent, federally funded agency providing support for broadcasters such as the Voice of America, Radio Sawa, Radio and TV Martí (Cuba), and Radio Free Europe. It had originally been part of the USIA.

11 Exchange between Conniff and Renner, "Public Diplomacy in the New International Security Environment."

12 Comment by senior BBC World Service official, "Public Diplomacy in the New International Security Environment."

13 That is why the broadcasting agreement setting out the framework for the BBC World Service's relationship with the Foreign and Commonwealth Office begins by clearly recognizing that the World Service is a constituent part of the BBC and has full editorial freedom.

14 The Foreign and Commonwealth Office is the British government department responsible for promoting the interests of the United Kingdom abroad. The head of the FCO is the secretary of state for foreign and commonwealth affairs.

15 Price, *Media and Sovereignty*, 201.

16 The debate has not completely disappeared, even in the wake of the 11 September 2001 attacks.

17 Bush, "Address to a Joint Session of Congress and the American People."

18 Lasswell, *Propaganda Technique in the World War*, as cited in Price, *Media and Sovereignty*, 201.

19 Price, *Media and Sovereignty*, 203. On the transformation of international broadcasting in the wake of the Cold War, see 203–10.

20 Ibid., 204–5.

21 Ibid., 206.

22 Ibid., 206–7.

23 Gowing, conference lecture.

24 "The Revolution in Military Affairs" refers to the increasing use and applicability of new technology on the battlefield. This is not a new concept, though in its current form, the Revolution in Military Affairs has highlighted the importance of communications technology, and with it, improved c4isr (Command, Control, Communications, Computers, Intelligence, Surveillance, and Reconnaissance).

25 Murray, conference lecture.

26 Personal interview with DFAIT official in International Academic Relations division, 22 March 2002.

27 Radio Canada International, *La radiodiffusion internationale.*

28 As quoted in Siegel, *Radio Canada International,* 175.

29 Radio Canada International, "Radio Canada International on Sirius Satellite Radio."

30 Harold Redekopp, executive vice-president of CBC television, personal communication, 16 March 2004.

31 Radio Canada International, "Radio Canada International Takes a New Turn."

32 Murray, conference lecture.

33 Ibid.

34 Private communication by senior Canadian official made available to Evan Potter, December 2005.

35 CBC-Radio-Canada, *Power Broadcasting Inc. and CBC.*

36 Ibid.

37 Personal communication with DFAIT official responsible for developing the CanadaInternational portal, 15 March 2004.

38 Soderlund, Lee, and Gecelovsky, "Trends in Canadian Newspaper Coverage."

39 Murray, conference lecture.

40 A senior Canadian government official stated in his 10 August 2006 retirement address, after thirty-eight years of service, that Canada is "still deprived of the communications tools to sustain [its] voice promotionally … In the absence of significant news outlets from Canada, the communications activity the Canadian Government brings to bear through representation abroad provides the vital value-added."

41 In an attempt to crack down on the influence of Western culture, the Iranian government has begun to enforce a law (originally created in the 1990s) forbidding the use of satellite dishes, by removing them from homes in Tehran. See Iran Focus, "Iran Police Hunt Banned Satellite Dishes."

CHAPTER SEVEN

1 Kunczik, *Images of Nations and International Public Relations*, 25.

2 See the section on investment in Hart, *A Trading Nation*.

3 Van Ham, "The Rise of the Brand State," 2.

4 Anholt, *Brand New Justice*.

5 Ibid., 167.

6 Ibid., 134.

7 Greg Klassen, personal interview with Jason Bouzanis, 8 February 2006, Ottawa.

8 Potter, "Branding Canada."

9 Ibid., 55.

10 Ibid.

11 Hill, Canada's Salesman to the World, 9.

12 For a detailed history, see Hart, *A Trading Nation*.

13 A wide range of perspectives on this issue can be found in Wolfe, *Diplomatic Missions*.

14 This was an increase from 110 missions in 79 countries in 1981, and 38 missions in 1945. Potter, "Branding Canada," 56.

15 Ibid.

16 In 2004, with the separation of DFAIT into Foreign Affairs Canada and International Trade Canada, a similar organization, the Investment Partnership Branch, was created.

17 Potter, "Branding Canada," 57.

18 Canada, DFAIT, *Canada in the World*.

19 International Trade Canada, *State of Trade 2005*.

20 Potter, "Branding Canada," 58.

21 Ibid., 57.

22 Director, The Ditchley Foundation, "A Note by the Director."

23 Potter, "Branding Canada," 59.

24 Burney, "(Re)Gaining Global Ground," 6.

25 Canada, Department of Foreign Affairs, *A Role of Pride and Placement in the World – Commerce*, 6.

26 Ibid., 18.

27 Papadopolous and Heslop, *Country Equity and the Image of Canada*.

28 Stassen, "Beefing Up Brand Canada."

29 Ibid.

30 Klassen, personal interview, 2006.

31 World Tourism Organization, *The World's Top Tourism Destinations*.

32 Canadian Tourism Commission, *Annual Report 2004*.

33 Global Market Insite, *How the World Sees the World*, 4.

34 Klassen, personal interview, 2006.

35 Blain, Levy and Ritchie, "Destination Branding," 328.

36 Klassen, personal interview, 2006.

37 cbc News, "China Hands Canada Potential Tourism Windfall," 21 January 2005.

38 Wilson, "More than a Maple Leaf."

39 "Tactical advertising" refers to a targeted advertising campaign, as opposed to strategic, broad-based advertising efforts – representing differences, not just diversity.

40 Klassen, personal interview, 2006.

41 Ibid.

42 Ibid.

43 Ibid.

CHAPTER EIGHT

1 Tuch, *Communicating with the World*, 39.

2 Ibid., 43.

3 Approximately six thousand people write the examination for the Canadian Foreign Service each year. The eventual in-take is approximately 1 percent. The successful candidates are unlikely to be thinking about a career in public affairs or cultural relations: they will be focused on promoting either Canada's trade or its security interests.

4 The PERPA program is complemented by the trade, consular, and immigration programs at a typical diplomatic mission.

5 As minister counsellors, they would be members of the senior ranks of the federal public service.

6 At the time of writing there were approximately 115 DFAIT employees classified as Information Services officers out of some 3,400 government communicators.

7 Non-rotational officers in the department can expect a one-time assignment abroad, usually for a position that is not being sought by the rotational officers.

8 I am indebted to Daryl Copeland, a senior DFAIT official, for this comment.

9 Australia's permanent secretary for the Department of Foreign Affairs and Trade, in a foreword to a departmental booklet on public diplomacy, stated that all embassy staff should consider themselves as public diplomacy practitioners.

10 Michael Kunczik agrees, stating that "[t]he credibility of the communicator," in this case the head of mission, "is of decisive importance to successful propaganda." Kunczik, *Images of Nations and International Public Relations*, 110.

11 Less than 50 percent are Canada-based DFAIT staff.

12 Interviews with Canadian ambassadors indicate that the nature of the reporting relationship between a head of mission, who will most likely be a career foreign

service officer, and subordinates, who are from other Canadian government departments, really depends very much on the interpersonal relationships that develop. Some subordinates who are on a single assignment abroad from another federal department may not view the head of mission as having much sway over their public service careers and therefore maintain a more distant relationship. Others will view the head of mission as their *de facto* boss and act accordingly. In the end, it will depend on the personalities of the individuals involved, creating either a benefit or a cost to the projection of Canada's image abroad.

13   Humphreys, "How Ottawa Wooed Oscar," RB1. As a testament to the Canadian government's involvement, when accepting the award, Arcand's wife, Denise Robert, also the film's producer, was the only Oscar recipient who publicly thanked a government agency for its support.

14   Ibid. Within the Canadian Consulate General, Robertson was able to rely on a very experienced locally engaged staff member, Rosalind H. Wolfe, the senior officer, political/economic & public affairs. The Consulate General was also able to coordinate its efforts with the Délégation du Québec à Los Angeles/Québec Government Office in Los Angeles, under the leadership of Marc Boucher as the Quebec government representative to thirteen states. The delegation office in Los Angeles represents the second most important type of Quebec government office outside of Quebec, after the Délégation Générale.

15   Ibid.

16   Haynal's thesis about diplomacy adapting to intermesticity is explicated in George Haynal, "DOA: Diplomacy on the Ascendant," 29, a paper he wrote while he was a fellow at Harvard's Weatherhead Center for International Affairs in 2001–2.

17   Ibid.

18   Ibid., 33.

19   On Mobilizing Citizens, see Canada25, *From Middle Power to Model Power*.

20   Mank, "Retooling the Political Officer," 20.

21   Tuch, *Communicating with the World*, 47.

22   Ibid., 44.

23   "Envoy Enters 'Virgin Territory.'"

24   Graves, presentation on American and Canadian attitudes towards North America.

25   The Chicago Council on Foreign Relations has, since the early 1970s, measured American "warmth" towards different countries in the world. Canada consistently garnered the "warmest" temperature and thus America's "best friend" rating until 2002.

26   Graves, presentation on American and Canadian attitudes towards North America.

27   According to Transport Canada, the number may have been as high as forty-five thousand stranded passengers. Transport Canada, *Chronology*.

28 For a description of American disappointment with Canada's decision making, see Paul Cellucci, *Unquiet Diplomacy*.

29 John Kneale, personal interview with Evan Potter, 18 July 2006, Ottawa.

30 They are Industry Canada, the National Research Council, Western Development, Canada Economic Development (Quebec), the Atlantic Canada Opportunities Agency, and Agriculture and Agri-Food Canada.

31 Colin Robertson, notes used for an address to the Council of the Federation, Banff: 11 August 2005.

32 Ibid.

33 Ibid.

34 "Envoy Enters 'Virgin Territory'," 32.

35 Holmes, *Life with Uncle*, 94.

36 On this case, see Vincent, *See No Evil*.

37 For a detailed history of the dispute between Bombardier and Embraer, including an excellent analysis of why the dispute has been so contentious, see Daudelin, "Trapped: Brazil, Canada, and the Aircraft Dispute."

38 It is worth noting that during this time, Canadian visitors to Brazil had to obtain a visa for entry into the country, a practice not required previously.

39 Jean Daudelin to Evan Potter, 3 August 2006, personal electronic-mail communication.

40 Under "Key Initiatives," the Government of Canada stated its intention to "[u]se our developing economic relationship with India, Brazil and China to build stronger political ties." Canada, Department of Foreign Affairs and International Trade, *A Role of Pride and Influence in the World*, 27.

41 Daudelin to Evan Potter, 3 August 2006, personal electronic-mail communication.

42 Ibid.

43 Annette Hester has noted that while it is important for Canada to seize the opportunity and re-engage with Brazil, and thus create this ideal public diplomacy mission, it is unlikely to occur. See Hester, "Canada and Brazil."

44 Following a decision by the Liberal government of Paul Martin, in December 2003 the former DFAIT was separated into two organizations: Foreign Affairs Canada (FAC) and International Trade Canada. This decision was reversed in 2006 under the Conservative government of Stephen Harper, and the two departments again became one organization called DFAIT. The internal emphasis on public diplomacy within FAC during these three years of significant organizational change was part of an effort to carve out a clearer mandate for the foreign ministry.

45 Peter Harder, "Speaking Notes" (Ottawa: Public Diplomacy Practitioners' Retreat, 1 December 2005, presentation).

46 Copeland, "New Rabbits, Old Hats," 755. For a more developed perspective on this new-style diplomat, see Copeland, "Guerrilla Diplomacy."
47 Harder, "Speaking Notes."
48 Ralston Saul, *Culture and Canadian Foreign Policy*, 33.
49 Ibid., 31.
50 DFAIT employees who are being posted abroad are encouraged to take public diplomacy courses at the Canadian Foreign Service Institute, which provide overviews of public diplomacy activities at Canada's missions, including public affairs work, communication (understanding media), and cultural and educational promotion. Participants focus on the application of advocacy methods for the systematic promotion of specific Canadian interests and have an opportunity to meet and discuss public affairs/public diplomacy activities with DFAIT's clientele and potential partners.
51 These comments by Stéphane Gompertz and Christopher Ross were made at a public diplomacy conference organized by Evan Potter in London, England, in October 2002. Ross's thoughts are also well-articulated in a separate academic article: see Ross, "Public Diplomacy Comes of Age."
52 Personal communication to the author on Canada's public diplomacy from a senior DFAIT Official, June 2007.

CHAPTER NINE

1 Kevin O'Shea, interview with Evan Potter, February 2005, Ottawa.
2 Fund, "Bankrupt Canada?"
3 George Haynal, conference remarks.
4 The second referendum on Quebec independence had taken place in October 1995, with only 50,000 votes separating the Yes and No campaigns, making many Canadians and non-Canadians nervous about the state of the country.
5 Siklos, "Any Club That Would Have You...," 23. Note that the Canadian Club and the Canadian Society merged in 2004.
6 Ibid.
7 Simpson, *Star-Spangled Canadians*.
8 O'Shea and Etzinger, "The Upper North Side," 29.
9 Ibid., 30.
10 Ibid.
11 O'Shea writes that the consulate had bought a mailing list of 45,000 names from a company that specialized in mixing and matching mailing lists from New York cultural organizations. O'Shea and Etzinger, "The Upper North Side," 33.
12 Ibid., 30.
13 Ibid., 33.

14 Ibid.

15 Ibid., 34.

16 Ibid.

17 Anonymous senior Canadian government official, personal interview with Evan Potter, 2006, Ottawa.

18 Canada, Department of Foreign Affairs and International Trade, Office of the Inspector General, "Evaluation of the Think Canada Festival in Japan." The reference to Canada's relative stature as an economic partner was made in appendix A of this report and drew from a report prepared in 2000 for the Canada-Japan Business Committee.

19 Ibid. Favourite destinations for Japanese tourists have apparently been Banff, Alberta, and Prince Edward Island, the setting of the Anne of Green Gables stories, which are tremendously popular in Japan.

20 Ibid.

21 The details of the pre-campaign research were outlined to the author in an interview with a mid-level Canadian official who worked at the Canadian embassy in Tokyo during the initial phases of what would eventually become a formal campaign. The in-person interview was conducted in Ottawa at DFAIT on 22 March 2002.

22 JMRB Research International, *The Image of Canada*. The market research involved administering a structured questionnaire to a general sample of 150 members of the Japanese public. Fieldwork was conducted from 12 to 14 March 1999, in Tokyo.

23 Department of Foreign Affairs and International Trade Canada, *Opening Doors to the World*.

24 "Co-chairmen's summary of the 23rd Japan-Canada Business Conference."

25 Canada, Department of Foreign Affairs and International Trade, *Evaluation of the Think Canada Festival in Japan*, appendix A.

26 Ibid., appendix A, exhibit 1.

27 Ibid., 11.

28 The JMRB Research International report, *The Image of Canada*, based as it was on a sample of 150 Japanese, would have had a considerable margin of error even in a homogeneous society such as Japan. For instance, firm conclusions about the Japanese business community's view of Canada could hardly be based on the responses of the five executives who were interviewed for this survey. Rather, the survey raised interesting questions and was suggestive of a Japanese person's awareness and knowledge of Canada.

29 Department of Foreign Affairs and International Trade Canada, *Evaluation of the Think Canada Festival in Japan*, iii.

30 Salmon and Murray-Johnson, "Communication Campaign Effectiveness."

31 Ibid., 175.
32 Canada, Department of Foreign Affairs and International Trade, *Evaluation of the Think Canada Festival in Japan*, 8. Since little has come of the Canada-Japan free trade initiative, a possibility that spawned the festival, the intermediate impact of the campaign remains in doubt.
33 Ibid., 21.
34 Ibid., iii.
35 Confidential interview with Evan Potter, 13 July 2006.
36 Ibid.
37 Ibid.
38 Ibid.
39 Ibid.
40 Canada, Department of Foreign Affairs and International Trade, *Evaluation of the Think Canada Festival in Japan*, 25.
41 Kergin, "A Case for Postmodern Diplomacy."
42 Much of the Canadian government's investment in communicating to the world – that is, its public diplomacy – is actually spent on communicating to domestic audiences about what Canada is doing abroad.
43 Manley was voted *Time Canada*'s Man of the Year in December 2001.
44 A typical North American assembly plant generates approximately US $1.5 million in revenue per hour, and one lost hour of assembly output owing to a parts shortage can cost approximately US $60,000 per hour in lost profits. See Kergin, "Notes for a Statement."
45 Senior Canadian official, confidential interview with Evan Potter, 25 February 2005.
46 Ibid.
47 On the different reactions of the United States to Canada, see Sands, "How Canada Policy Is Made in the United States." On foreign elites' views of Canada, see the excellent report by Greenhill, *Making a Difference?*
48 NAFTA-plus refers to the environment in which ongoing discussion regarding free trade arrangements between Canada, the US, and other current and future partners occurs.
49 Gorman, "Canada Largely Ignored by US." The outgoing envoy being referred to is Canadian ambassador Michael Kergin.
50 Gotlieb, "When Mr McKenna goes to Washington."

CHAPTER TEN

1 Hocking and Lee, "The Diplomacy of Proximity and Specialness," 36.
2 An excellent example of Iran's public diplomacy counter-offensive is the letter sent by Iranian president Mahmoud Ahmadinejad on 8 May 2006, to US presi-

dent George W. Bush, proposing "new solutions for getting out of international problems and the current fragile situation of the world." This letter, made public by Iran in support of its own global public diplomacy campaign, was the first direct communication between the head of government of Iran and an American president since the Iranian revolution in 1979.

3 Freedman, "The Transformation of Strategic Affairs," 10. So important is the new political dimension to managing international conflict that Freedman devotes a full chapter of his study (chapter 5) to strategic communications, including the role of the media, public diplomacy, and networks, in this new environment.

4 Ibid., 92.

5 Ibid., 93.

6 See Canada, Department of Foreign Affairs and International Trade, *A Dialogue on Foreign Policy*. This was the first time since the government of Canada's 1995 white paper, *Canada in the World*, that the government acknowledged explicitly the important role played by Canada's image on the world stage.

7 Gregory, "Not Your Grandparents' Public Diplomacy," 6.

8 Ibid.

9 See Mackenzie, *Peacekeeper: Road to Sarajevo.*

10 The United Kingdom's Department for International Development was criticized in the media when its staff apparently painted over the Union Jack insignia on their vehicles.

11 This point appeared quite obvious to the head of France's aid program when he attended a conference in fall 2002 on public diplomacy at which this author was a participant. He noted that someone who does not have clean water or food will not be a good candidate for a public relations campaign. He was thus fairly bemused by the Anglo-American conception of public diplomacy as being distinct from development assistance. He remarked that as head of France's public diplomacy program, managed by the French foreign ministry (Quai D'Orsay), he was responsible for thousands of aid workers around the world, including agronomists and teachers.

12 Wright, *Managing Global Crises*," 2.

13 Gregory, "Not Your Grandparents' Public Diplomacy," 7–8.

14 It is significant that the description of the Institute's mandate on its homepage (www.si.se/templates/CommonPage____471.aspx) uses words such as "active communication" and "strategic communication" to establish that its transparent purpose is to cultivate a positive interest in Sweden around the world through the instruments of culture and education. The virtual embassy was inaugurated in Second Life in May 2007. The rationale for creating this virtual embassy was quite simply that as the media landscapes change, so too will the means of gathering information. With about nine million registered accounts (though it is impossible to say how many are inactive or how many single users with multiple accounts

exist), real life corporations and organizations are now creating a presence in Second Life as one more platform through which to engage in public relations. This author used his Second Life avatar (an on-line representation of a user created for the purpose of interacting with others) to take a guided tour of the Second House of Sweden in September 2007 and was impressed by the ability to interact in real time with an employee of the Swedish Institute whose job it was to guide visitors through the virtual embassy's exhibitions. The employee, acting like a tour guide, answered any questions this author had about Sweden while his avatar guided the author's avatar through a series of virtual rooms. The institute employed eight virtual tour guides who could interact in several languages. The first exhibit in the Second House was a re-creation of the last day of Raoul Wallenberg, the Swedish diplomat who has been credited with saving thousands of Hungarian Jews from the Nazis during World War II. This virtual exhibit was synchronized with a real-world exhibition entitled Raoul Wallenberg: One Man Can Make a Difference, which the institute organized in Moscow in September 2007.

15 For a definition of the model of communication excellence, see Dozier, Grunig, and Grunig, "Public Relations as Communication Campaign."

16 See Leonard, *Public Diplomacy.*

17 Canada, Statistics Canada, Imports, Exports and Trade Balance of Goods on a Balance of Payments Basis.

18 Gregory, "Not Your Grandparents' Public Diplomacy," 11.

19 United Kingdom, Foreign and Commonwealth Office, *Report on Wilton Park Conference,* 10.

20 In the years following the 1995 fisheries dispute between Canada and Spain, Canadian companies complained that they were being shut out of competitions for contracts not only in Spain but also in the wider European Union (when Spain had the presidency).

21 Canada's contribution of Can$3.5 billion to the reconstruction of Afghanistan, one of the most underdeveloped countries in the world, makes it the single largest recipient of Canadian aid.

22 In February 2002, the Pentagon shut down the office following a public outcry that it was going to be used to spread false information.

23 Josten, "Strategic Communication," in *Iosphere* (2006). This periodical is published through the Cyberspace and Information Operations Security Centre at the Air War College of the United States Airforce.

24 Sweeney, "UK Public Diplomacy."

25 Lord Carter of Coles, *Public Diplomacy Review,* 72–3.

26 Ibid., 74, 76, 77.

27 United Kingdom House of Commons, Foreign Affairs Committee, Proceedings, 29 March 2006.

28 With regard to the creation of development information officers to publicize American aid projects in host countries, see the recommendation in United States, Report Submitted to the Committee on Appropriations, US House of Representatives, *Changing Minds, Winning Peace*, 67.

29 These points are derived from a presentation delivered at Canada's Department of Foreign Affairs in December 2005.

30 Gregory, "Not Your Grandparents' Public Diplomacy," 9.

31 Ralston Saul, "Projecting a Middle Power Into an Imperial World."

32 Dozier, Grunig, and Grunig, "Public Relations as Communication Campaign," 235. See also, Grunig and Grunig, "Models in Public Relations and Communication."

33 Welsh, "Canada as a Model Citizen."

34 Daryl Copeland, personal interview with Evan Potter, 3 August 2006, Ottawa.

35 This percentage is composed of 6.7 percent from agricultural and fishing products, 19.2 percent from energy products, and 8.1 percent from forestry products. See Canada, Statistics Canada, *Exports of Goods on a Balance-of-Payments Basis*.

36 See Canada, Department of Foreign Affairs and International Trade, *The Northern Dimension of Canada's Foreign Policy*.

37 The effectiveness of such cultural endeavors can be debated as well. See Graham Carr, "Diplomatic Notes."

38 I am grateful to my colleague Daryl Copeland, from the Department of Foreign Affairs and International Trade Canada, for providing me with this example.

39 Ralston Saul, *Culture and Canadian Foreign Policy*, 77.

40 Ibid., 79.

41 The editorials on Voice of America broadcasts must be approved by the State Department. All other programming is free from external control.

42 Ralston Saul, "Projecting a Middle Power into an Imperial World."

43 Senior Canadian government official, confidential interview with Evan Potter, 2006, Ottawa.

44 Copeland, "New Rabbits, Old Hats.".

45 Comments by Nancy Snow at a conference on public diplomacy attended by the author at Wilton Park, United Kingdom, 9–10 March 2006.

46 Ralston Saul, *Culture and Canadian Foreign Policy*, 37.

47 Ibid.

48 Ibid., 35–7.

49 Sorrell, "Branding, Relevance, Diplomacy."

50 Senior Canadian official, confidential personal interview with Evan Potter, 3 August 2006, Ottawa.

51 Nicholas Cull, personal communication with Evan Potter, March 2006. In response, Michael Brock, a former director general for DFAIT's Cultural Relations Program, has said that one should never lose sight of the fact that the purpose of

the trees is to provide shade, and ultimately, one has to determine whether they are actually providing that shade. This is an apt metaphor for the evaluation of public diplomacy programs, because they will have to be measured to determine whether they are supporting Canada's foreign policy interests. It goes without saying that you cannot improve your efforts without measuring your successes or failures.

52 The Germans have self-consciously and openly invited discussions in foreign countries of the Nazi period. Japan and Austria have not featured their periods of fascism to the same degree in their public diplomacies.

53 For an in-depth perspective, see Huntington, "A Clash of Civilizations."

54 Nye, *Soft Power*, 3.

55 This is the conclusion arrived at by Daryl Copeland at Canada's Department of Foreign Affairs and International Trade, after having surveyed foreign attitudes towards Canada in 2000.

56 This statement refers to the disappointing performance of Argentina, a country that held great promise early in the twentieth century and then faded into deliquescence.

57 Curtis Barlow, personal interview with Evan Potter, 11 July 2006, Ottawa.

58 Joffe, "The Perils of Soft Power," *New York Times Magazine*, 15.

59 Schiff, *Hearing of the House International Relations Committee Subject.*

60 Delaye, "Possibilities and Limits of Public Diplomacy."

61 I am indebted to my colleague Lesley Strutt for making this observation about Canada and California.

Bibliography

"ABC (July–Dec. 2005) Region Breakdowns." *Economist* (2005). Available at http://printmediakit.economist.com/fileadmin/pdfs/ABC_certificates/ World_Circ_Breakdowns.pdf [June 2006].

Adams, Michael. *Fire and Ice.* Toronto: Penguin Books 2004.

Alberts, Sheldon. "Envoy Enters 'Virgin Territory': Canadian Diplomat Has Spent a Year Begging U.S. Officials Not to Implement Border Restrictions." *Kingston Whig-Standard,* 14 February 2006.

Angus Reid Group. *Canada and the World.* 1997.

Anholt Nation Brand Index. *How the World Sees the World* (third quarter, 2005). Available at http://www.nationbrandindex.com/report.phtml [June 2006].

Anholt, Simon. "Introduction to Special Issue on Nation Branding." *Journal of Brand Management* 9, nos. 4/5 (April 2002): 229–39.

– *Brand New Justice: The Upside of Global Branding.* Oxford: Butterworth Heinemann 2003.

– *Competitive Identity: The New Brand Management for Nations, Cities, and Regions.* New York: Palgrame Macmillan 2007.

Archibald, David. "Canadian Studies Programs Foster Understanding between Canada and the United States." *Embassy,* 28 September 2005. Available at http://embassymag.ca/ html /index.php?display=story&full_path=/2005/ september/28/understanding/ [April 2006].

Arndt, R. *The First Resort of Kings: American Cultural Diplomacy in the Twentieth Century.* Dulles, VA: Potomac Books 2005.

Arquilla, John, and David Ronfeldt. *The Emergence of Noopolitik: Towards an American Information Strategy.* Santa Monica, CA: Rand Corporation 1999.

– "What If There Is a Revolution in Diplomatic Affairs?" *Virtual Diplomacy* (September 1999). Available at http://www.usip.org/virtualdiplomacy/ publications/reports /ronarqISA99.html [June 2006].

Association of Universities and Colleges of Canada. *Canadian Excellence in and for the World: How the Globalization of Higher Education and Research Contributes to Canada's Foreign Policy* (1 May 2003). Available at http://www.aucc.ca/_pdf/english/reports/2003 /foreign_policy_dialogue_e.pdf [July 2006].

Australian Government. "Australian Scholarships: Frequently asked questions." Available at http://www.australianscholarships.gov.au/FAQs.htm [August 2006].

Australian Government. Department of Foreign Affairs and Trade. *Public Diplomacy Handbook: A Practical Guide to Public Advocacy.* Canberra: Commonwealth of Australia 2003.

Australian Tourism Commission. "Australian Tourism Commission Olympic Games Strategy. Summary." February 2001, 27. Accessed at www.ausport.gov.au/full text/2001/atc/olympicreview.pdf [September 2007].

Axworthy, Lloyd. "Canada and Human Security: The Need for Leadership." *International Journal* 52, no. 2 (spring 1997): 183–96.

– "A Ban for All Seasons." *International Journal* 53, no. 2 (spring 1998): 189–203.

– "Why Soft Power is the Right Policy for Canada." *Ottawa Citizen*, 25 April 1998.

– *Navigating a New World: Canada's Global Future.* Toronto: Alfred A. Knopf Canada 2003.

Bartleman, John. *Rollercoaster.* Toronto: McClelland & Stewart 2005.

Bátora, Jozef. "Public Diplomacy between Home and Abroad: Norway and Canada." *The Hague Journal of Diplomacy* 1, no. 1 (2006): 53–80.

BBC World Service Official. Commentary during presentation at "Public Diplomacy in the New International Security Environment." London, 24–25 October 2002.

Bélanger, Louis. "Redefining Cultural Diplomacy: Cultural Security and Foreign Policy in Canada," *Political Psychology* 20, no. 4 (December 1999): 677–99.

– "Globalization, Culture, and Foreign Policy: The Failure of 'Third Pillarization' in Canada." *International Journal of Canadian Studies (Canada and the World in the Twentieth Century)* 22 (fall 2000): 163–95.

– "Cultural Diplomacy and Public Diplomacy as Dialogical Statecraft." Presentation at "Public Diplomacy in the New International Security Environment," London, 24–25 October 2002.

Bellos, Alex. *Futebol: The Brazilian Way of Life.* New York: Bloomsbury 2005.

Bensimon-Byrne. "Canadian Pride: Lessons from Molson Canadian Advertising." Powerpoint presentation, Ottawa, 20 March 2002.

Bernier, Luc. "Mulroney's International 'Beau Risque.'" In Nelson Michaud and Kim Richard Nossal, eds., *Diplomatic Departures: The Conservative Era in Canadian Foreign Policy; 1984–1993.* Vancouver: UBC Press.

Blain, Carmen, Stuart Levy, and J.R. Brent Ritchie. "Destination Branding: Insights and Practices from Destination Management Organizations." *Journal of Travel Research* 43, no. 4 (May 2005): 328–38.

Blizzard, Christina. "Fish Fight Left Stench." *Toronto Sun,* 27 March 2005.

Bollier, David. "The Rise of Netpolitik: How the Internet is Changing International Politics and Diplomacy." *A Report of the Eleventh Annual Aspen Institute Roundtable on Information Technology,* 2003.

Bowker, Alan. Internal memorandum. Ottawa: Department of Foreign Affairs and International Trade Canada, 2003.

Braudel, Fernand. *On History.* London: Weidenfeld 1980, 25–55.

British Council. *Through Other Eyes 2: How the World Sees the United Kingdom.* 2000. Available at www.britishcouncil.org/work/survey/index.htm.

Brock, Michael. "The Possibilities of and Limits to Public Diplomacy." Presentation at "Public Diplomacy in the New International Security Environment," London, 24–25 October 2002.

Burney, Derek. "(Re)Gaining Global Ground: Canada in the World." Presentation at the National Club, Toronto, 9 December 2005.

Bush, George W. "Address to a Joint Session of Congress and the American People." Washington, DC United States Capitol, 20 September 2001. Available at http://www.whitehouse.gov/news/releases/2001/09/20010920–8.html [July 2006].

Cameron, Maxwell A., Robert J. Lawson, and Brian W. Tomlin, eds. *To Walk without Fear: The Global Movement to Ban Landmines.* New York: Oxford University Press 1998.

Canada. Atlantic Canada Opportunities Agency. *2005 Performance Report: Horizontal Initiatives.* Ottawa: March 2005. Available at http://www.acoa.ca/e/library/reports/ performance2005/horizontal.pdf [July 2006].

Canada. Canadian Heritage. *Canadians are Invited to Join Their Country's Participation in Expo 2005.* Ottawa, 23 February 2004. Available at www.canadianheritage.gc.ca/newsroom/ news_e.cfm?Action=Display&code= 3N0473E [January 2006].

Canada. Canadian International Development Agency. *International Youth Internship Program.* Ottawa: Queen's Printer 2006. Available at http:// www.acdi-cida.gc.ca/internships [July 2006].

– *Programme canadien des bourses de la Francophonie.* Available at http:// www.pcbf.qc.ca/ [July 2006].

Canada. Department of Foreign Affairs. *Canada's International Policy Statement, A Role of Pride and Influence in the World – Commerce.* Ottawa: Queen's Printer 2005. Available at http://www.dfait-maeci.gc.ca/cip-pic/IPS/IPS-Overview.pdf [June 2006].

Canada. Department of Foreign Affairs and International Trade Canada. *Canada in the World: Canadian Foreign Policy Review.* Ottawa: Queen's Printer 1995. Available at http://www.dfait-maeci.gc.ca/foreign_policy/cnd-world/chap2-en.asp [June 2006].

– *Evaluation of the Canadian Education Centres Network.* Ottawa: December 1999. Available at www.dfait-maeci.gc.ca/department/auditreports/evaluation/evalCECN99-en.asp [July 2006].

– *Opening Doors to the World: Canada's International Market Access Priorities 2000.* Ottawa: 2000. Available at http://dsp-psd.pwgsc.gc.ca/Collection/E74-88-2000E.pdf [12 July 2006].

– *A Dialogue on Foreign Policy.* Ottawa: Queen's Printer 2003. Available at http://www.foreign-policy-dialogue.ca/pdf/DialogueEng.pdf [June 2006].

– *The Northern Dimension of Canada's Foreign Policy.* Ottawa 2004. Available at http://www.dfait-maeci.gc.ca/circumpolar/pdf/ndcfp-en.pdf [August 2006].

– *Young Professionals International.* Ottawa: Queen's Printer 2004. Available at http://www.dfait-meaci.gc.ca/ypi-jpi/brochure2004-en.asp [July 2006].

– *Young Professionals International: Connect and Contribute.* Ottawa: Queen's Printer 2004. Available at http://www.dfait-meaci.gc.ca/ypi-jpi/connect_and_contribute-en.asp [July 2006].

– "Formative Evaluation of the U.S. Enhanced Representation Initiative." Presentation at the Department of Foreign Affairs and International Trade Canada, Ottawa, 2005.

– "What Is a Canada Trade Mission." *Canada Trade Missions.* Ottawa 2005. Available at http://www.tcm-mec.gc.ca/ctm-en.asp [June 2006].

– "Dismantlement of Nuclear Submarines." *Global Partnership Program.* Ottawa 2006. Available at http://www.dfait-maeci.gc.ca/foreign_policy/global_partnership/submarine-en.asp [July 2006].

Canada. Department of Foreign Affairs and International Trade Canada, Office of the Inspector General. *Evaluation of the Think Canada Festival in Japan: Final Report.* Ottawa, June 2002. Available at www.dfait-maeci.gc.ca/department/auditreports/evaluation /evalThinkCanada02-en.pdf [July 2006].

Canada. Department of International Trade. *State of Trade 2005.* Ottawa 2005. Available at http://www.dfait-maeci.gc.ca/eet/trade/sot_2005/sot_2005-en.asp [June 2006].

Canada. Industry Canada. *Brand Canada Report.* Wirthlin Worldwide presentation. March 2001. Available at www.ic.gc.ca/cmb/welcomeic.nsf/VRTF/PublicationSpecialSpeciaux/$file/March2001Wirthlin.pdf [August 2006].

Canada. Office of the Governor General. *Role and Responsibilities of the Governor General.* Ottawa 2005. Available at http://www.gg.ca/gg/rr/index_e.asp [June 2006].

Canada. Privy Council Office. "Prime Minister Announces Co-chairs of Canada
Corps and Major Contribution towards Initiative to Fight AIDS." News release.
Ottawa, 10 May 2004. Available at http://www.pco-bcp.gc.ca/default.asp?
Language=E&Page=archivemartin&Sub =newscommuniques&Doc=news_
release_20040510_202_e.htm [August 2006].

Canada. Public Works and Government Services. *Canadian Heritage 2000–2001
Estimates, Part III, Report on Plans and Priorities.*

Canada. *Royal Commission on National Development in the Arts, Letters, and Sciences.*
Report. Ottawa: King's Printer 1951. Canada.
Speech from the Throne. 1991

Canada. Standing Committee on Canadian Heritage. Number 046, 1st Session,
38th Parliament. Evidence, Thursday, 9 June 2005.

Canada. Statistics Canada. *Exports of Goods on a Balance-of-Payments Basis, by Product.*
Ottawa 2006. Available at http://www40.statcan.ca/l01/cst01/gbleco4.htm
[August 2006].

– *Imports, Exports and Trade Balance of Goods on a Balance-of-Payments Basis, by
Country or Country Grouping.* Ottawa 2006. Available at http://
www40.statcan.ca/l01 /cst01/gbleco2a.htm [July 2006].

Canada. Transport Canada. *Chronology – Transport Canada Responds to September 11
Attacks.* Backgrounder. Available at http://www.tc.gc.ca/majorissues /
transportationsecurity/Chrono.htm [June 2006].

Canada. Treasury Board of Canada Secretariat. *The Communications Policy of the
Government of Canada.* Ottawa. Available at www.tbs-sct.gc.ca/Pubs_pol/
sipubs/comm/comm1_e.asp [June 2006].

– *Part I – The Governmental Expenditure Plan, 2005–2006, Estimates.* Ottawa 2006.
Available at http://www.tbs-sct.gc.ca/est-pre/20052006/001_e.pdf [June
2006].

"Canada's New Spirit," *Economist,* 25 September 2003.

Canada25. *From Middle Power to Model Power: Recharging Canada's Role in the World.*
Toronto: Canada25, 2004. Available at http://www.canada25.com/
collateral/canada25 _from_middle_to_model_power_en.pdf [July 2006].

Canada-U.S. Fulbright Program. *Canada-U.S. Fulbright Research Chairs Program.*
Available at http://www.fulbright.ca/en/award.asp [July 2006].

– *Mission Statement.* Available at http://www.fulbright.ca/en/blank1.htm [July
2006].

– *News & Events.* Available at http://www.fulbright.ca/en/news.asp [July 2006].

Canadian Bureau for International Education. *Awards for Study in Canada.* CBIE
2004.

Canadian Heritage. "Canadians Are Invited to join their Country's Participation in
Expo 2005." (online). 23 February 2004. Available at www.canadianheritage.
gc.ca/newsroom/ news_e.cfm?Action=Display&code=3N0473E [January 2006].

"Canadian Pride: Lessons from Molson Canadian Advertising." Presentation by Bensimon-Byrne D'Arcy at the Department of Foreign Affairs and International Trade Canada, Ottawa, 20 March 2002.

Canadian Tourism Commission. *Annual Report 2004: The Power of Attraction* 2004. Available at http://www.canadatourism.com/ctx/files/publication/ data/en_ca/general _publications/annual_report_2004/ AR%202004%20EN.pdf [May 2006].

Carlucci, Frank, et al. *Equipped for the Future: Managing U.S. Foreign Affairs in the 21st Century*. Washington, DC: Henry L. Stimson Center, October 1998. Available at http://www.stimson.org/pubs/ausia/ausr1.pdf [June 2006].

Carr, Graham. "Diplomatic Notes: American Musicians and Cold War Politics in the Near and Middle East, 1954–60." *Popular Music History* 1, no. 1 (2004): 37–63.

Castells, Manuel. *The Rise of the Network Society*. Oxford: Blackwell 1996.

– *The Information Age: Economy, Society and Culture*. 2d ed. Oxford: Blackwell, 2001.

CBC News. "China Hands Canada Potential Tourism Windfall," 21 January 2005. Available at http://www.cbc.ca/story/business/national/ 2005/01/21/chinatourism-050121.html [June 2006].

CBC-Radio Canada. "Power Broadcasting Inc. and cbc Sell Trio and Newsworld International to USA Cable". News Release, 19 May 2000.

Cellucci, Paul. *Unquiet Diplomacy*. Toronto: Key Porter Books 2005.

Cernetig, Miro. "Canada Isn't Working." *Report on Business Magazine* (*Globe and Mail*). Toronto, May 2001, 38–49.

Chandler, Graham. "Selling the Prairie Good Life." *The Beaver* (August-September 2006): 24–30.

Chartrand, Harry Hillman. "International Cultural Affairs: A 14 Country Survey." 1992. Available at http://www.culturaleconomics.atfreeweb.com/ 2.%20HHC%20articles.htm [July 2006].

Chicago Council on Foreign Relations. *WorldViews 2002 Survey of American and European Attitudes and Public Opinion*. Available at www.worldviews.org/ intermediate/ questionnaire.html [June 2006].

"Co-chairman's Summary of the 23rd Japan-Canada Business Conference." Tokyo: Canada-Japan Business Conference, 15 May 2000. Available at http:// www.keidanren.or. jp/english/policy/2000/021.html [July 2006]

Cohen, Andrew. *While Canada Slept: How We Lost Our Place in the World*. Toronto: McClelland & Stewart, 2003.

Commonwealth Scholarship and Fellowship Plan. *Directory of Commonwealth Scholars and Fellows 1960–2002*. London: Association of Commonwealth Universities 2003.

Conniff, Brian T., and John Renner. Personal exchange during presentation. "Public Diplomacy in the New International Security Environment," London, 24–25 October 2002.

Cooper, Andrew F. "Snapshot of an Emergent Cyber-Diplomacy: The Greenpeace Campaign against French Nuclear Testing and the Spain-Canada 'Fish War.'" In Evan H. Potter, ed., *Cyber-Diplomacy: Managing Foreign Policy in the Twenty-first Century*. Montreal: McGill-Queen's University Press 2002.

Copeland, Daryl. "Guerrilla Diplomacy: Delivering International Policy in a Digital World." *Canadian Foreign Policy* 11 (winter 2004): 165–75.

– "New Rabbits, Old Hats: International Policy and Canada's Foreign Service in an Era of Reduced Diplomatic Resources." *International Journal* 60, no. 3 (summer 2005): 743–64.

– "Public Diplomacy and Branding." *Public Diplomacy Blog – USC Center on Public Diplomacy* (3 April 2006). Available at http://uscpublicdiplomacy.com/index/php/newsroom/pdblog_detail/060403_public_diplomacy_and_branding/ [August 2006].

Cordoba Serrano, Maria Sierra. *Transferts culturels Espagne-Canada, à travers la traduction des œuvres littéraires canadiennes en Espagne*. PHD dissertation, University of Ottawa, 2006.

Council on Foreign Relations. *Public Diplomacy: A Strategy for Reform* (30 July 2002). Available at http://www.cfr.org/publication/4697/public_diplomacy.html [June 2006].

Cowan, G., and N.J. Cull. "Public Diplomacy in a Changing World." *The Annals of the American Academy of Political and Social Science.* 616 (March 2008).

Cull, Nicholas J. *Selling War: The British Propaganda Campaign against American "Neutrality" in World War II*. New York: Oxford University Press 1995.

– "Reluctant Persuaders: Canadian Propaganda in the United States, 1939–1945." *British Journal of Canadian Studies* 14, no. 2 (1999): 207–22.

– *American Propaganda and Public Diplomacy*. Cambridge: Cambridge University Press 2006.

Cultural Human Resources Council. *Export Marketing Competency Profile 2003*. Ottawa 2003. Available at http://www.culturalhrc.ca/competencies/Export%20Marketing/ExpMkt-e.pdf [July 2006].

Cummings, Dale. "Global Community Flicks Finger at Canadian Influence." *Winnipeg Free Press*, 4 February 2005. Available at http://zone.artizans.com/product.htm?pid294886 [July 2006].

Curtis, Bryan. "Cirque du Soleil: Canada's Insane Clown Posse." *Slate* (online), 20 July 2005. Available at http://www.slate.com/id/2123103/ [June 2006].

Daudelin, Jean. "Trapped: Brazil, Canada, and the Aircraft Dispute." In Norman
    Hillmer and M.A. Molot, eds., *Canada among Nations 2002: A Fading Power.*
    Toronto: Oxford University Press 2002, 256–79.
de Adder, Michael. "Jean Chrétien Flexes Canada's Soft Power at the UN." *Halifax
    Daily News*, 27 February 2003. Available at http://zone.artisans.com/
    product.htm?pid=271525 [July 2006].
Deibert, Ronald J. *Parchment, Printing and Hypermedia: Communication in World
    Order Transformation.* New York: Columbia University Press 1997.
Delaye, Bruno. "Possibilities and Limits of Public Diplomacy." Presentation at
    "Public Diplomacy in the New International Security Environment," London,
    24–25 October 2002.
Director, the Ditchley Foundation. "A Note by the Director." *World Opinion and
    Public Diplomacy: How Should Policy Makers Influence and Be Influenced?* Cantigny,
    IL, 4–6 May 2005. Available at http://www.ditchley.co.uk/page/101/
    public-diplomacy.htm [August 2006].
Dizard Jr, Wilson. *Digital Diplomacy: U.S. Foreign Policy in the Information Age.*
    Washington, DC: CSIS Publications 2001.
Djerejian, Edward P. *Changing Minds, Winning Peace: A New Strategic Direction for US
    Public Diplomacy in the Arab and Muslim World.* Report of the Advisory Group on
    Public Diplomacy for the Arab and Muslim World, 2003.
Doern, Bruce. "Science, Technology and Institutional Policy." In Bruce Doern,
    Les Pal, and Brian Tomlin, eds., *The Internationalization of Canadian Public Policy.*
    Toronto: Oxford University Press Canada 1995.
Donsbach, W. *Medienwirkung trotz Selektion: Einfluss faktoren auf dem Zuwendung zu
    Zeitungsinhalten.* Cologne: Bohlau 1991.
Dozier, David M., Larissa A. Grunig, and James E. Grunig. "Public Relations as
    Communication Campaign." In Ronald E. Rice and Charles T. Atkin, eds.,
    Public Communication Campaigns. Thousand Oaks, CA: Sage Publications 2001.
    231–48.
Ebert, Roger. "Why Is Festival So Big? It Works: More Useful, More Important
    than Cannes." *National Post*, 9 September 1999.
"Envoy Enters 'Virgin Territory': Canadian Diplomat Has Spent a Year Begging
    US Officials Not to Implement Border Restrictions." *Kingston Whig-Standard*, 14
    February 2006, 32.
Edmonds, Duncan. *Creating Vital Linkages: The Future of Canadian Studies in the
    United States.* Report prepared for the Department of Foreign Affairs and
    International Trade, 2003.
Entman, R. *Projections of Power: Framing News, Public Opinion, and U.S. Foreign Policy.*
    Chicago: University of Chicago Press 2004.

Evans, Gary. *John Grierson and the National Film Board: The Politics of Wartime Propaganda*. Toronto: University of Toronto Press 1984.

Finn, Helena K. "The Case for Cultural Diplomacy: Engaging Foreign Audiences." *Foreign Affairs* 82, no. 6 (November/December 2003): 15–20.

Florida, Richard. *The Rise of the Creative Class: And How It's Transforming Work, Leisure, Community and Everyday Life*. New York: Basic Books 2002.

Freedman, Lawrence. "The Transformation of Strategic Affairs." *Adelphi Paper* 379. London: International Institute for Strategic Studies, March 2006.

Friedman, Thomas. *The World Is Flat: A Brief History of the Twenty-first Century*. New York: Farrar, Straus and Giroux 2005.

Fukuyama, Francis. *The End of History and the Last Man*. New York: Freepress 1992.

Fulton, Barry, ed.. "Diplomacy in the Information Age." *Information Impacts Magazine*. July 2001.

Fund, John. "Bankrupt Canada?" *Wall Street Journal*, 12 January 1995, A14.

Gerth, Jeff. "Military's Information War Is Vast and Often Secretive." *New York Times*, 11 December 2005. Available at http://www.nytimes.com/2005/12/11/politics/11propaganda.html?ex=1291957200&en=3b2903137c652493&ei=5088&partner=rssnyt&emc=rss.

Gilboa, Eytan. "Diplomacy in the Media Age: Three Models of Uses and Effects." In C. Jonsson and R. Langhorne, eds., *Diplomacy*, 3d ed. London: SAGE Publications 2004, 96–199.

– "The CNN Effect: The Search for a Communication Theory of International Relations." *Political Communication* 22, no. 1 (2005): 27–44.

– "Effects of Global Television News on U.S. Policy in International Conflict." In P. Selb, ed., *Media and Conflict in the Twenty-first Century*. Palgrave Macmillan 2005: 1–31.

– "Media and International Conflict." In J. Oetzel and S. Ting-Toomey, eds, *The SAGE Handbook of Conflict Communication: Integrating Theory, Research and Practice*. Thousand Oaks, CA: SAGE Publications 2006, 595–626.

Global Market Insite. *How the World Sees the World: The Anholt Nation Brands Index* (Fourth quarter 2005), 4. Available at http://www.nationbrandindex.com/docs/NBI_Q4_2005.pdf [July 2006].

Gorman, Beth. "Canada Largely Ignored by U.S., Outgoing Envoy Says." *Kingston Whig-Standard*, 28 February 2005.

Gotlieb, Allan. *"I'll Be with You in a Minute, Mr. Ambassador": The Education of a Canadian Diplomat in Washington*. Toronto: University of Toronto Press 1991.

– "When Mr. McKenna Goes to Washington." *Globe and Mail,*. 21 February 2005, A15

– "Martin's Bush-League Diplomacy." *Globe and Mail*, 26 January 2006.

Gowing, Nik. "Conference Lecture." Presentation at "Public Diplomacy in the New International Security Environment," London, 24–25 October 2002.

Graham, John. "Third Pillar or Fifth Wheel? International Cultural Education and Cultural Foreign Policy." In Fen Osler Hampson, Martin Rudner, and Michael Hart, eds., *Canada among Nations 1999: A Big League Player?* Toronto: Oxford University Press 1998: 139–54.

Graves, Frank. (Ekos Research Associates). Presentation on American and Canadian Attitudes towards North America at Foreign Affairs Canada, Ottawa, September 2005.

Green, Sir David. "Present and Future Public Diplomacy: A View from the British Council." Presentation at the Department of Foreign Affairs and International Trade, Ottawa, 19 June 2006.

Greenhill, Robert. "Making a Difference? External Views on Canada's International Impact." *The Interim Report of the External Voices Project.* Canadian Institute of International Affairs: 27 January 2005.

Gregory, Bruce. "Not Your Grandparents' Public Diplomacy." Presentation at the Department of Foreign Affairs and International Trade, Ottawa, 30 November 2005. Transcript.

Griffiths, Franklyn. *Strong and Free: Canada and the New Sovereignty.* Toronto: Stoddart Publishing 1996.

Grunig, J.E., and L.A. Grunig, "Models in Public Relations and Communications." In J.E. Grunig, ed., *Excellence in Public Relations and Communication Management.* Hillsdale, NJ: Lawrence Erlbaum 1992, 285–325.

Grunig, James, and Todd Hunt. *Managing Public Relations.* New York: Holt, Rinehart & Winston 1984.

Halloran, Mary. "Cultural Diplomacy in the Trudeau Era: 1968–1984." Ottawa: Department of Foreign Affairs and International Trade, Canada. Conference paper, 1996.

Harder, Peter. Untitled Address. Presentation at conference, "Internal Public Diplomacy," Department of Foreign Affairs and International Trade Canada, Ottawa, 1 December 2005.

Hart, Michael. *A Trading Nation.* Vancouver: University of British Columbia Press 2002.

Hay, John. "International Summits and Civil Society." *Canadian Foreign Policy* 6, no. 1 (fall 1998): 97–104.

Haynal, George. "Conference Remarks." Presentation at the Eric Sprott School of Business, Carleton University, Ottawa, 2002.

– "DOA: Diplomacy on the Ascendant in the Age of Disintermediation." Harvard's Weatherhead Center for International Affairs, 2001–2. Available at www.wcfia.harvard .edu/fellows/papers/2001–02/haynal.pdf [July 2006].

Hennessey, Peter. "The Role of the Foreign Ministry in the 21st Century."
    Presentation at the Department of Foreign Affairs, Ottawa, 27 January 2004.

Hester, Annette. "Canada and Brazil: Confrontation or Cooperation?" In Andrew
    F. Cooper and Dane Rowlands, eds., *Canada among Nations 2005: Split Images.*
    Montreal: McGill-Queen's University Press 2005: 203–24.

Higham, Robin. "Canada, Super Star." Presentation at the International Studies
    Association annual conference "Dynamics of World Politics: Capacity,
    Preference and Leadership," Hawaii 2005.

Hill, O. Mary. *Canada's Salesman to the World: The Department of Trade and Commerce,
    1892–1939.* Montreal: McGill-Queen's University Press 1977.

Hilliker, John, and Donald Barry. *Canada's Department of External Affairs:* Vol. 2,
    Coming of Age, 1946–1968. Montreal: McGill-Queen's University Press 1995.

Hillmer, Norman. "A Border People." *Canada World View* 24 (winter 2005).
    Available at http://www.dfait-maeci.gc.ca/canada-magazine/issue24/
    01-title-en.asp [July 2006].

Hocking, Brian. "Conference Lecture." Presentation at "Public Diplomacy in the
    New International Security Environment," London, 24–25 October 2002.

Hocking, Brian, and Donna Lee. "The Diplomacy of Proximity and Specialness:
    Enhancing Canada's Representation in the United States." *The Hague Journal of
    Diplomacy* 1, no. 1 (2006): 29–52.

Hofstede, Geert. *Cultures Consequences: International Differences in Work-Related
    Values.* Thousand Oaks, CA: Sage Publications 1984.

Holmes, John. *Life with Uncle: The Canadian-American Relationship.* Toronto:
    University of Toronto Press 1981.

Holsti, K.J. *International Politics: A Framework for Analysis.* Englewood Cliffs, NJ:
    Prentice Hall 1995.

Hubert, Don. "The Landmine Ban: A Case Study in Humanitarian Advocacy."
    Occasional Paper No. 42. Providence, RI: Watson Institute for International
    Studies 2000.

Huikang, Huang. "Let's Witness a Bright Future of China-Canada Relations."
    Presentation at the International Conference "One Country, Two Systems,"
    Waterloo, ON, 24 March 2006.

Humphreys, Adrian. "How Ottawa Wooed Oscar: Diplomatic Corps Lobbied Hard
    for Barbarian Invasions." *National Post,* 18 September 2004.

Huntington, Samuel. "A Clash of Civilizations," *Foreign Affairs* 72, no. 3 (summer
    1993): 22–49.

International Commission on State Sovereignty. *The Responsibility to Protect.*
    Ottawa: International Development Research Centre 2001.

International Council for Canadian Studies. "A Brief Overview." Available
    at http:// www.iccs-ciec.ca/pages/1_theICCS/a_overview.html [August 2006].

– "Scholarly Journals." Available at http://www.iccs-ciec.ca/pages/a _pdfs/ reader_guide/15_journ.pdf [August 2006].

International Trade Canada. *State of Trade 2005*. Ottawa 2005. Available at http://www.dfait-maeci.gc.ca/eet/trade/sot_2005/sot_2005-en.asp [June 2006].

Iran Focus. "Iran Police Hunt Banned Satellite Dishes." (20 August 2005). Available at http://www.iranfocus.com/modules/news/ article.php?storyid=3400 (accessed August 2006).

Jackson, Joseph, and René Lemieux. "The Arts and Canada's Cultural Policy." *Current Issue Review* 93–3E (revised 15 October 1999).

JMRB Research International. *The Image of Canada: Research Report*. Tokyo: March 1999.

Joffe, Josef. "The Perils of Soft Power." *New York Times Magazine*, 14 May 2006.

Johne, Marjo. "Doors Open for Young Workers." *Globe and Mail*, 22 February 2006, C 10.

Josten, Richard J. "Strategic Communication: Key Enabler for Elements of National Power." *Iosphere* (summer 2006).

Jowett, Garth S., and Victoria O'Donnell. *Propaganda and Persuasion*. 3d ed. Thousand Oaks, CA: SAGE Publications 1999.

Joyal, Serge. *Refocussing Canada's International Cultural Policy in the Nineties: Issues and Solutions*. Report to the Minister of Foreign Affairs. Ottawa: September 1994.

Kamalipour, Yahya R., ed. *Global Communication*. 2d ed. Belmont, CA: Thomson Wadsworth 2007.

Kamalipour, Yahya R, and Nancy Snow, eds. *War, Media, and Propaganda: A Global Perspective*. Lanham, MD: Rowman & Littlefield 2004.

Kaniss, Phylliss, ed. "Public Diplomacy in a Changing World." *The Annals of the American Academy of Political and Social Science* 16 (March 2008).

Keohane, Robert O., and Joseph S. Nye Jr. *Power and Interdependence: World Politics in Transition*. Boston: Little, Brown 1977.

"Power and Interdependence in the Information Age." *Foreign Affairs* 77, no. 5 (September/October 1998): 81–4.

– *Power and Interdependence*. 3d ed. Boston: Longman Publishing 2000.

Kergin, Michael. "A Case for Postmodern Diplomacy." *Globe and Mail*, 1 March 2005.

– "Notes for a Statement by Michael Kergin, Ambassador of Canada to the United States to the Joint Industry Group, 2002 Annual Meeting." 5 March 2002. Available at www. canadianembassy .org/ambassador/020305-en.asp [July 2006].

Knight, Jane. *Progress and Promise: The 2000 AUCC Report on Internationalization at Canadian Universities*. Ottawa: Association of Universities and Colleges of Canada 2000.

Kotler, Philip, and David Gertner. "Country as Brand, Product, and Beyond: A
    Place Marketing and Brand Management Perspective." *Journal of Brand
    Management* 9, nos 4/5 (April 2002): 249–61.
Kunczik, Michael. *Images of Nations and International Public Relations.* Mahwah, NJ:
    Lawrence Eribaum Associates 1997.
Lampert, Allison. "London, Sydney Exciting but Canada 'Perceived as Bland' by
    Foreign Students." *Ottawa Citizen.* 23 May 2006, A 3.
Laroche, M., N. Papadopolus, L. Heslop, and M. Moural. "The Influence of
    Country Image Structure on Consumer Evaluations of Foreign Products."
    International Marketing Review 22, no. 1 (2005): 96–115.
Lasswell, Harold D. *Propaganda Technique in the World War.* New York: Knopf
    1927.
Leger Marketing. "Canada-U.S. Relations." 15 March 2004. Available at
    www.legermarketing.com [July 2006].
Leonard, Mark. *Going Public: Diplomacy in the Information Age.* London: The
    Foreign Policy Centre 2000.
– "Diplomacy by Other Means." *Foreign Policy* 132 (September/October 2002):
    48–56.
– *Public Diplomacy.* London: The Foreign Policy Centre 2002.
Leonard, Mark, Andrew Small, and Martin Rose. *British Public Diplomacy "in the Age
    of Schisms."* London: The Foreign Policy Centre 2005.
L'Etang, Jacquie, and Magda Pieczka. *Critical Perspectives in Public Relations.* Boston:
    International Thomson Business Press 1996.
Loat, Alison. "Canada Is Where Canadians Are: The Canadian Expatriate as an
    Element of International Policy." Kennedy School of Government, Masters
    thesis, 2004.
Lodge, Creenagh. "Success and Failure: The Brand Stories of Two Countries."
    Journal of Brand Management 9, no. 4/5 (April 2002): 372–84.
Lord Carter of Coles. *Public Diplomacy Review.* December 2005. Available at
    http://www. britishcouncil.org/home-carter-report [May 2006].
Macintosh, D., and M. Hawes. *Sport and Canadian Diplomacy.* Montreal:
    McGill-Queen's University Press 1994.
Mackenzie, Major General Lewis. *Peacekeeper: Road to Sarajevo.* Vancouver: Douglas
    and McIntyre 1993.
Malone, Gifford D. *Political Advocacy and Cultural Communications: Organising the
    Nation's Public Diplomacy.* Lanham, MD: University of America 1988.
Mank, Randolph. "Retooling the Political Officer," *Bout de papier* 13, no. 2
    (summer 1996): 18–20.
Mannheim, J.B., and R.B. Albritton, *Changing National Images: International Public
    Relations and Media Agenda Setting.*

Mason, Gary. "The Year the World Discovered BC" *Globe and Mail,* 29 April 2006, A9.

McComb, M., and P. Shaw. "The Agenda-Setting Function of Mass Media." *Public Opinion Quarterly* 36, no. 2 (summer 1972): 176–87.

McGregor, Sarah. "Student Visa Program Will Boost Economy, Population." *Embassy.* 3 May 2006. Available at http://www.embassymag.ca/html/index.php?display=story& full_path =/ 2006/may/3/student/ [July 2006].

Melissen, J., ed. *New Public Diplomacy: Soft Power in International Relations.* New York: Palgrave Macmillan 2006.

Molander, Roger C., Andrew S. Riddile, and Peter A. Wilson. *Strategic Information Warfare: A New Face of War.* Santa Monica, CA: RAND Corporation 1996.

Morgan, Nigel, Annette Pritchard, and Rachel Piggott. "New Zealand, 100% Pure: The Creation of a Powerful Niche Destination Brand." *Journal of Brand Management* 9, no. 4/5 (April 2002): 335–54.

Morgenthau, Hans J. *Politics among Nations: The Struggle for Power and Peace.* New York: Alfred A. Knopf 1948.

Mowlama, Hamid. *Global Information and World Communication: New Frontiers in International Relations.* 2d ed. Thousand Oaks, CA: SAGE Publications 1997.

Murray, Don. "Conference Lecture." Presentation at "Public Diplomacy in the New International Security Environment," London, 24–25 October 2002.

National Post (editorial). "Well Done Madam." *National Post,* 26 October 2001, A15.

Nelles, Wayne. "American Public Diplomacy as Pseudo-Education: A Problematic National Security and Counter-Terrorism Instrument." *International Politics: A Journal of Transnational Issues and Global Problems* 41, no. 1 (March 2004): 65–93.

Nelson, Brendan. "Australian Government, Engaging the World through Education: Statement on the Internationalization of Australian Education and Training." Hon. Dr Brendan Nelson, Minister for Education, Science and Training, October 2003. Available at http://aei.dest.gov.au/AEI/AboutAEI/PoliciesAndPriorities/Ministerial Statement/Minstatement_pdf.pdf [accessed September 2007].

"Net Wealth: The Global Economic Impact of the World Cup." *Sunday Times,* 11 June 2006. Available at http://www.timesonline.co.uk/article/02087–2220280,oo.html [June 2006].

Ninkovich, F. "U.S. Information Policy and Cultural Diplomacy." *Headline Series No. 308.* New York: Foreign Policy Association 1996.

Nippon Keidanren (Japan Business Federation). "Co-chairmen's Summary of the 23rd Japan-Canada Business Conference." Tokyo: Canada-Japan Business Conference, 15 May 2000. Available at http://www.keidanren.or.jp/english/policy/2000/021.html [July 2006].

Nossal, Kim Richard. "The Democratization of Canadian Foreign Policy: The Elusive Deal." In M. Cameron and Maureen A. Molot, eds., *Canada among Nations 1995*. Ottawa: Carleton University Press 1995: 29–43.

– "Pinchpenny Diplomacy: The Decline of 'Good International Citizenship' in Canadian Foreign Policy." *International Journal* 54 (winter 1998–9): 88–105.

– "Painting the Map with Maple Leaves: The 'Canadian Studies Enterprise' Reconsidered." *Crossings* 10, no. 2 (2005).

Nye, Joseph S. Jr. *Bound to Lead: The Changing Nature of American Power*. New York: Basic Books 1991.

– "The Challenge of Soft Power." *Time* (Canadian edition), 8 March 1999.

– *The Paradox of American Power*. New York: Oxford University Press 2001.

– *Soft Power: The Means to Success in World Politics*. Cambridge, MA: Perseus Book Group, Public Affairs 2004.

Nye, Joseph S. Jr, and Williams A. Owen. "America's Information Edge." *Foreign Affairs* 75, no. 2 (1996): 20–36.

O'Shea, Kevin, and Bernard Etzinger. "The Upper North Side: Canada in New York." *Bout de papier* 16, no. 2 (summer 1999): 29–34.

Papadopolous, N., and L.A. Heslop. *Country Equity and the Image of Canada and Canadian Products*. Ottawa: International Markets Bureau, Agriculture and Agri-Food Canada, 2003

Paquin, Stéphane, ed. *Histoire des relations internationales du Québec*. Montreal: VLB Editeur 2006.

Payne, Kenneth. "The Media as an Instrument of War." *Parameters* 35, no. 1 (2005): 81–93.

Peisert, H. *Die auswärtige Kulturpolitik der Bundesrepublik Deutschland*. Stuttgart: Klett-Cotta 1978.

Perreaux, Les. "Quebec Move Undermines Canada, Critics Say." *Globe and Mail*, 15 November 2004.

Posner, Michael. "Adrienne Clarkson: Take 65." *Globe and Mail*, 24 September 2005, F8.

Potter, Evan H. "Information Technology and Canada's Public Diplomacy." In Evan H. Potter, ed., *Cyber-Diplomacy: Managing Foreign Policy in the Twenty-First Century*. Montreal: McGill-Queen's University Press 2002, 177–200.

– "Canada and the New Public Diplomacy," *International Journal* 58, no. 1 (winter 2002–3): 43–64.

– "Branding Canada: The Renaissance of Canada's Commercial Diplomacy." *International Studies Perspectives* 5, no. 1 (February 2004): 55–60.

Powell, Chris. "Marketing the State in a New Environment." Presentation at "Public Diplomacy in the New International Security Environment," London, 24–25 October 2002.

Price, Monroe E. *Media and Sovereignty: The Global Information Revolution and Its Challenge to State Power.* Cambridge, MA: The MIT Press 2002.

Price, Richard. "Reversing the Gun Sights: Transnational Civil Society Targets Land Mines." *International Organization* 52, no. 3 (summer 1998): 613–44.

Quebec. Ministère des relations internationales. *Quebec's International Policy.* Quebec City 2005.

– *Rapport annuel de gestion 2004–2005.* Quebec City 2005.

– *Québec in the World.* Quebec City. Available at http://www.mri.gouv.qc.ca/en/action _internationale/representations_etranger/representations_etranger.asp [July 2006].

– *Québec's International Policy: Working in Concert.* Quebec City 2006. Available at http://www.mri.gouv.qc.ca/en/pdf/Politique_en.pdf [July 2006].

Québec. "Secrétariat aux affairs intergouvernmentales Canadiennes. "Open Letter from Mr. Benoît Pelletier." *Globe and Mail,* 12 October 2005. Available at www.saic.gouv.qc.ca/centre_de_presse/lettres_ouvertes/2005/saic_lettre20051012_2.htm. [Accessed on 26 August 2007.]

Radio Canada International. *La radiodiffusion internationale.* Ottawa, RCI Powerpoint presentation at the Department of Foreign Affairs and International Trade, 2003.

– "Radio Canada International Takes a New Turn." News release. 2 February 2004. Available at http://www.rcinet.ca/rci/en/communiques_7.shtml [July 2006].

– "Canadians Will Now Be Able to Hear Radio Canada International on Sirius Satellite Radio." News release. 22 November 2005. Available at http://www.rcinet.ca /rci/en / communiques_12.shtml [July 2006].

Ralston Saul, John. "Position Paper on Culture and Foreign Policy." Prepared for the Special Joint Committee of the House of Commons and the Senate Reviewing Canadian Foreign Policy. Ottawa, August 1994, typescript.

– "Projecting a Middle Power into an Imperial World." The John W. Holmes Memorial Lecture, Glendon College, Toronto, 25 February 2004.

Rampal, Kuldip R. "Global News and Information Flow in an Internet Age." In Yahya R. Kamalipour, ed., *Global Communication.* 2d ed. Belmont, CA: Thomson Wadsworth 2007, 105–32.

Rawnsley, Gary D. *Radio Diplomacy and Propaganda: The BBC and VOA in International Politics, 1956–64.* New York: St Martin's Press 1996.

Rose, Andrew K. "The Foreign Service and Foreign Trade: Embassies as Export Promotion." *National Bureau of Economic Research Working Paper No. 11111,* February 2005. Available at http://www.nber.org/papers/w11111 [June 2005].

Rose, Martin, and Nick Wadham-Smith. *Mutuality, Trust, and Cultural Relations.* London: Counterpoint, British Council 2004. Available at http://www.counterpointonline.org/download/156/Mutualit_Report.pdf.

Rosenau, James N., and J.P. Singh, eds. *Information Technologies and Global Politics: The Changing Scope of Power and Governance.* Albany, NY: State University of New York Press 2002.

Ross, Christopher. "Public Diplomacy Comes of Age." *Washington Quarterly* 25, no. 2 (spring 2002): 75–83.

Salmon, Charles T., and Lisa Murray-Johnson. "Communication Campaign Effectiveness: Critical Distinctions." In Ronald E. Rice and Charles K. Atkin, eds., *Public Communication Campaign*, 3d ed. Sage Publications 2001, 168–80.

Sands, Christopher. "How Canada Policy Is Made in the United States." In Maureen Appel Molot and Fen Osler Hampson, eds., *Vanishing Borders: Canada among Nations 2000.* Toronto: Oxford University Press 2000, 51–55.

Schiff, Adam. "Hearing of the House International Relations Committee Subject: An Around-the-World Review of Public Diplomacy." Washington: Rayburn House Office Building, 10 November 2005. Transcript.

Scott, Bijana. "Calling '9/11': The New Diplomacy in the War on Terror." Presentation at International Studies Association annual conference "Dynamics of World Politics: Capacity, Preference and Leadership," Hawaii, 2005.

Sharp, Mitchell. "Canada-U.S. Relations: Options for the Future." *International Perspectives*, Special Issue, Autumn 1972.

Siegel, Arthur. *Radio Canada International: History and Development.* Oakville: Mosaic Press 1996.

Signitzer, B.H., and T. Coombs. "Public Relations and Public Diplomacy: Conceptual Convergences." *Public Relations Review* 18 (1992): 137–47.

Siklos, Richard. "Any Club That Would Have You ...," *Report on Business Magazine* (*Globe and Mail*), January 2005.

Simpson, Jeffrey. *Star-Spangled Canadians.* Toronto: HarperCollins Publishers 2000.

– "Who Speaks For Canada? Take a Number." *Globe and Mail*, 21 September 2005.

Snow, Nancy. *Information War: American Propaganda, Free Speech and Opinion Control since 9/11.* New York: Seven Stories Press 2004.

Soderlund, W., M. Lee, and P. Gecelovsky. "Trends in Canadian Newspaper Coverage of International News, 1988–2000: Editors' Assessments." *Canadian Journal of Communication* 27, no. 1 (2002). Available at http://www.cjc-online.ca/viewarticle. php?id=696 [August 2006].

Sorrell, John. "Branding, Relevance, Diplomacy." Presentation at "Public Diplomacy in the New International Security Environment," London, 24–25 October 2002.

Sriramesh, K., and Pauline Leong. "Romancing Singapore: Anatomy of a Communication Campaign Aimed at Reversing Population Control."

Presentation at "Annual Conference of the International Communication
Association," New York, May 2005. Transcript.

Stassen, Joanne. "Beefing Up Brand Canada." 2002. Available at http:// temagami.
carleton.ca/jmc/cnews/18102002/connections/c1.html [June 2006].

Stephens, Hugh. "Public Diplomacy in the 21st Century." *Bout de papier* 16, no. 2
(summer 1999): 7–8.

Stephens, L.A.D. *Study of Canadian Government Information Abroad 1942–1972: The
Development of the Information, Cultural and Academic Divisions and their Policies.*
Unpublished mimeograph. Ottawa: Department of Foreign Affairs and
International Trade Canada Library 1977.

Sutter, Robert. "Why Does China Matter?" *Washington Quarterly* 27, no. 1 (winter
2003–4): 86–7.

Sweeney, Carole. "U.K. Public Diplomacy." Presentation at "Public Diplomacy in
the New International Security Environment," London, 24–25 October 2002.

Taylor, Philip M. *Global Communications, International Affairs and the Media since
1945.* London: Routledge 1997.

– "Phil Taylor's Web Site," The Institute of Communications Studies, University
of Leeds, England. Available at http://ics.leeds.ac.uk/papers/
index.cfm?outfit=pmt [August 2006].

Thussu, Daya. *International Communication: Continuity and Change.* New York:
Oxford University Press 2000.

Thussu, Daya K., and Des Freedman, eds. *War and the Media: Reporting Conflict
24/7.* Thousand Oaks, CA: SAGE Publications 2003.

Time (Canadian edition). 26 May 2003.

Transport Canada. *Chronology – Transport Canada Responds to September 11 Attacks*
(backgrounder). Available at http://www.tc.gc.ca/majorissues/
transportationsecurity/Chrono.htm [June 2006].

Tuch, Hans. *Communicating with the World: U.S. Public Diplomacy Overseas.* Washington,
DC: Institute for the Study of Diplomacy, Georgetown University, 1990.

United Kingdom. British Council's Report. *Through Others' Eyes: How the World Sees
the United Kingdom.* British Council 1999.

United Kingdom. House of Commons, Foreign Affairs Committee, Proceedings,
29 March 2006. Available at www.publications.parliament.uk/pa/
cm200506/cmselect /cmfaff /903 /90302.htm [May 2006].

United Kingdom. Foreign and Commonwealth Office. *Report on Wilton Park
Conference, WPS 06/21: Public Diplomacy: Key Challenges and Priorities.* 10–12 March
2006.

United States. US Advisory Commission on Public Diplomacy. *Building America's
Public Diplomacy through a Reformed Structure and Additional Resources.* Washington,
DC: US Department of State 2002.

– United States Information Agency Alumni Association. "Public Diplomacy
  Defined." In *What Is Public Diplomacy?* June 2006. Available at
  http://www.publicdiplomacy.org/1.htm [June 2006].
United States. US Department of State. *Cultural Diplomacy: The Linchpin of Public
  Diplomacy – Report of the Advisory Committee on Cultural Diplomacy.* Washington, DC:
  Government Printing Office 2005.
United States. US House of Representatives. Report submitted to the Committee
  on Appropriations by the Advisory Group on Public Diplomacy for the Arab
  and Muslim World. *Changing Minds, Winning Peace: A New Strategic Direction for
  US Public Diplomacy in the Arab and Muslim World.* Washington, DC, 1 October
  2003. Available at www.state.gov/r/pa/prs/ps/2003/21239.htm [July 2006].
Van Ham, Peter. "The Rise of the Brand State." *Foreign Affairs* 80, no. 5
  (September/October 2001): 2–6.
Vincent, Isabel. *See No Evil: The Strange Case of Christine Lamont and David Spencer.*
  Toronto: Reed Books Canada 1995.
Von Flotow, Luise. "Telling Canada's 'Story' in German: Using Cultural
  Diplomacy to Achieve Soft Power." In Luise von Flotow and Reingard Nischik,
  eds., *Translating Canada.* Ottawa: University of Ottawa Press, 2007.
Welsh, Jennifer. *At Home in the World: Canada's Global Vision for the 21st Century.*
  Toronto: HarperCollins Publishers 2004.
– "Canada as a Model Citizen." *Canada World View* 23 (autumn 2004). Available at
  http://www.international.gc.ca/canada-magazine/issue23/01-title-en.asp [June
  2006].
Wilcox, D.L., P.H. Ault, W.K. Agee, and G.T. Cameron. *Essentials of Public Relations.*
  New York: Longman 2001.
Wilson, Nathan. "More than a Maple Leaf: Selling Canada to Tourists," *Made in
  Canada: The Branding of a Nation.* 2002. Available at http://temagami.carleton.
  ca/jmc/cnews/18102002/connections/c3.html [May 2006].
Wolfe, Robert, ed. *Diplomatic Missions: The Ambassador in Canadian Foreign Policy.*
  Montreal: McGill-Queen's University Press 1999.
World Tourism Organization. *The World's Top Tourism Destinations.* 2006. Available
  at http://www.infoplease.com//ipa/A0198352.html [May 2006].
Wright, David. *Managing Global Crises – and the U.S. Colossus.* Commentary 207. C.D.
  Howe Institute, December 2004.
York, Geoffrey. "Canada: Nice Place, but a Tad Too Boring." *Globe and Mail,* 29
  October 2005.

Index

Italicized page numbers refer to tables and figures.

Krall, Diana, 97, 229
Kunczik, Michael, 25, 32, 313n10

Labrador, 53
Labrie, Jean, 136
lacrosse teams, 91
Lafrance, Sylvain, 162
Laliberté, Guy, 116
Lamont, Christine, 213
land mines convention. *See* Ottawa
  Convention
Lasswell, Harold, 156
Latin America, 40, 79–80, 108, 121,
  164, 181
LeBlanc, Romeo, 108–9
Lee, Donna, 255
Léger, Jules, 108
Leno, Jay, 304n75
Leonard, Mark, 37-8, 44–6, 70-1
Leonard Cohen: I'm Your Man (documen-
  tary), 302n47
Lepage, Robert, 229
L'Etang, Jacquie, 36–7
Levy, Stuart, 187
Lewis, Stephen, 98
liberal democracies, 67, 73, 98, 155,
  255, 261, 289n28
Life with Uncle (Holmes), 212
"likeability" factor (as brand), 14, 186
Lincoln Group (Pentagon contractor),
  61
Living Canada (film shorts), 76–7, 91
lobbying, 45, *50*, 51, 64, 176, 202, 210
locally engaged staff, 130, 178,
  199–200, 214, 216, 277, 314n14,
  316n50
London South Bank University,
  306–7n42
long-term public diplomacy, 31, 44, *44*,
  46–53, *50*; and cultural relations, 98,
  111–12, 115, 122; and debates about
  public diplomacy, 59–60, 63–5, 67;
  and economic programs, 176, 184–6,
  189, 192; and education programs,
  128–30, 133, 149; and international
  broadcasting, 155, 158, 168, 170;
  and nation branding, 232, 241, 243,

249; and new architecture of public
  diplomacy, 72–3, 259-60; and new
  media, 166; practice of, 198, 214,
  217, 222; and tourism promotion,
  186-7, 189, 192
Lord Carter Review, 16, 265–7

Macintosh, D., 91–2
"mad cow disease," 51, 63, 136, 210,
  213
mainstreaming public diplomacy, 34,
  216–18, 125
Malaysia, 181
Malone, Gifford, 32
mandate letters (for Canadian ambassadors), 206
Manhattan campaign. *See* Upper North
  Side campaign
Manitoba, 210-11
Mank, Randolph, 203-4
Manley, Elizabeth, 122
Manley, John, 243, 247-8, 318n43
Mannheim, J. B., 23–4, *24*
many-to-many forms of communication, 269-70
Maoist insurgency in Nepal, 255
"Maple Leaf Miracle," 228, 230
marijuana, decriminalization of, 11
marketing campaigns, 33, 35–6, 42, 62;
  and conceptualization of public
  diplomacy, 45–6, 175–6; and economic programs, 175–6, 187–91; for
  education programs, 135, 145–9,
  147, *148*, 151, 307–8nn56,62,
  308–9nn64,65; and tourism promotion, 187–91; and Upper North Side
  campaign, 229
Marlboro brand, 53, 59
Martel, Yann, 97
Martin, Paul, 10, 101, 143–4, 183, 213,
  240-1, 315n44
Martin, Tim, 293n67
Mason, Gary, 115
Massey Commission, 8, 10, 84–5, 103
mass publics, 32, 48–9, *48*, 98, 174,
  270, 300n4
McGill University, 146

McLaren, Norman, 97
McLuhan, Marshall, 97–8
measuring impacts, 37, 47, 64, 71–2; of
cultural relations, 98, 104–5, 115; of
economic aspects of public diplomacy, 185; of education programs,
135, 136–7, 149–50; of international
broadcasting, 155, 168–9, 311n40;
and nation branding, 232, 235–41,
250–3; and new architecture of public diplomacy, 278–9; and practice of
public diplomacy, 198, 219–22, 221,
223–4
media relations, 7, 10–12, *11*, *13*, 21,
289n23, 290n38; and changing context of public diplomacy, 39–41; and
conceptualization of public diplomacy, 44–5, 48–53, *50*, 58; and cultural relations, 92-3, 98–102, 111–12,
115, 118, 122–5, 300n6; and debates
about public diplomacy, 32, 60–1,
65–8; development of, 76, 79-80,
82–4; and economic programs,
175–6, 187–8; and education programs, 130, 134, 136-7, 304–5n7;
and multidisciplinary perspectives on
public diplomacy, 35–6; and new
architecture of public diplomacy, 73,
256–8, 260-1, 263, 274–5; and new
media, 13, 39, 52, 60, 69, 93, 153–4,
157, 165–9, 172, 260; positioning
national images in, 23–5, *24*; and
post-9/11 advocacy campaign, 243,
245, 247, 249, 251–3; and practice of
public diplomacy, 198–9, 202,
203–4, 211–15, 220–1, 316n50; and
Think Canada Festival, 233, 235–8,
240; and tourism promotion, 187–8;
and Upper North Side campaign,
226, 228, 230. *See also* broadcasting,
international
media relations officers, 99–101, 124-5,
199
medium-term public diplomacy, 31,
44–9, *44*, 50–2, *50*, 63, 65; and economic programs, 176; and new architecture of public diplomacy, 265; and

new media, 166; and Think Canada
Festival, 237
Mexico, 21, 23–5, *24*, 59; and economic programs, 179, 181, 184–5,
187; and education programs, 135–6,
141–2; and international broadcasting, 160; and post-9/11 advocacy
campaign, 250–1; and practice of
public diplomacy, 199, 207-8; and
tourism promotion, 187; during Trudeau years, 90
Middle East, 38, 135, 156–8, 266. *See
also names of Middle East countries*
middle-ranking countries, 37–8, 92,
150, 213, 216
military affairs, ix, 6, 25, 266, 287n3,
294n16; and changing context of
public diplomacy, 42–3; and con
ceptualization of public diplomacy,
44, *50*, 51–2; and debates about
public diplomacy, 60–1, 65–7; and
international broadcasting, 155–6,
159, 311n24; and media relations,
36; and new architecture of public
diplomacy, 70–1, 73, 255–8, 266,
268–9, 280; and post-9/11 advocacy
campaign, 244, 248, 250; and
practice of public diplomacy, 206,
210, 212
Ministry of Defence (UK), 266
Ministry of Information (UK), 78-9
misinformation, 39–40, 48, 60, 70, 82,
102; and new architecture of public
diplomacy, 261, 264, 320n22; and
post-9/11 advocacy campaign,
242–3, 245–7, 249, 251-2
Mistry, Rohinton, 60, 97
MITnet (DFAIT communication system),
165
"model nation," Canada as, 5, 228,
270, 289n15
Morrisseau, Norval, 97
motion pictures. *See* films
Mulroney, Brian, 178
multiculturalism, 5, 14, 68
multilateralism, 4, 7–8, 22, 92, 167,
203, 214, 244

new architecture of public diplo-
macy, 256, 261, 266, 268, 284; and
practice of public diplomacy, 202,
209–11, 221, 222
WIB (Wartime Information Board),
79–82
Wilcox, D. L., 33
Willingdon, Lord, 108
Wilson, Nathan, 189
Wilson, Woodrow, 77
Wilton Park Conference (2006), 262
Wolfe, Rosalind H., 314n14
women, treatment of, 46, 68, 158
Woodrow Wilson Center for Scholars
(Washington, DC), 139, 306n35
Working Holiday Program, 19, 307n46
working holiday programs, 18, 283-4,
307n46
World Anti-Doping Agency, 122
world fairs, 17, 112, 114–16, 262, 278,
303n53
World Health Organization, 22
World Tourism Organization, 186
World Trade Organization, 213
World War I, 77–8, 177

World War II, 77–83, 91–2, 153, 270
World Wide Web, 165–8. *See also*
websites
Wright, David, 258

Yellowknife, 189
York, Geoffrey, 14
York University, 108, 150, 269
Young, Neil, 97
Young Professionals International
(YPI), *16*, *19*, 143
Young Workers Exchange Program,
307n46
youth camps, 273
Youth Employment Strategy (YES), 143
youth exchanges, international, 7, 9,
16, 18, *19*; and changing context of
public diplomacy, 41; and conceptualization of public diplomacy, 46, *50*,
52, 56; and economic programs, 182;
and education programs, 142–5,
307nn46,48,49; and "new diplomacy," 70. *See also* student exchange
programs
YouTube, 259